A New People in Christ

A New People in Christ

Adam, Israel, and Union with Christ in Romans

WENDEL SUN

☙PICKWICK *Publications* · Eugene, Oregon

A NEW PEOPLE IN CHRIST
Adam, Israel, and Union with Christ in Romans

Copyright © 2018 Wendel Sun. All rights reserved. Except for brief quotations in critical publications or reviews, no part of this book may be reproduced in any manner without prior written permission from the publisher. Write: Permissions, Wipf and Stock Publishers, 199 W. 8th Ave., Suite 3, Eugene, OR 97401.

Pickwick Publications
An Imprint of Wipf and Stock Publishers
199 W. 8th Ave., Suite 3
Eugene, OR 97401

www.wipfandstock.com

PAPERBACK ISBN: 978-1-5326-3535-9
HARDCOVER ISBN: 978-1-5326-3537-3
EBOOK ISBN: 978-1-5326-3536-6

Cataloging-in-Publication data:

Names: Sun, Wendel

Title: A new people in Christ : Adam, Israel, and union with Christ in Romans / by Wendel Sun.

Description: Eugene, OR : Pickwick Publications, 2018 | Includes bibliographical references and index.

Identifiers: ISBN 978-1-5326-3535-9 (paperback) | ISBN 978-1-5326-3537-3 (hardcover) | ISBN 978-1-5326-3536-6 (ebook)

Subjects: LCSH: Bible. Romans—Criticism, interpretation, etc. | Jesus Christ—Person and offices. | Bible. Romans—Theology.

Classification: LCC BS2665.52 S88 2018 (print) | LCC BS2665.52 (ebook)

Manufactured in the U.S.A. 03/21/23

Some material from Wendel Sun, "Biblical Theology and Cross-Cultural Theological Education: The Epistle to the Romans as a Model." *Global Missiology* 4.12 (July 2015) 1–14, is included in chapter 2. Used with permission.

Some material from Wendel Sun, "Seeking (Exchanged) Glory: The Gentiles of Romans 2." *Journal of Asian Evangelical Theology* 20.2 (Sept 2016) 45–54, is used in chapter 4. Used with permission.

Some material from Wendel Sun, "Difficult Texts: Romans 6.14." *Theology* 120.3 (May-June 2017) 208–210, is used in chapter 5. Used with permission.

To my wife and children

εὐχαριστῶ τῷ θεῷ μου διὰ Ἰησοῦ Χριστοῦ περὶ πάντων ὑμῶν

Contents

List of Tables | viii
Acknowledgments | ix
List of Abbreviations | x

1 Introduction | 1
2 The Story of Adam (and Israel) in Romans 1–4 | 40
3 The Story of Adam (and Israel) in Romans 5–8 | 77
4 Adam, Israel, and Union with Christ in Romans 1–4 | 106
5 Adam, Israel, and Union with Christ in Romans 5–8 | 152
6 Union with Christ in Romans 9–16 | 204
7 Conclusion | 229

Bibliography | 237
Index of Ancient Documents | 255
Index of Names and Subjects | 261

Tables

Table 2.1: Allusions to Genesis in Romans 1:18–32 | 44

Table 2.2: Textual Links between Romans 1:23 and Psalm 106:20 | 46

Table 4.1: Adam (and Israel) and Union with Christ in Near Context | 107

Table 4.2: Jeremiah 31:33 and Romans 2:15 | 119

Table 4.3: Isaiah 52:5 in Romans 2:24 | 125

Table 5.1: Union with Adam and Union with Christ in Rom 5:12–21 | 163

Acknowledgments

MANY HAVE CONTRIBUTED TO the publication of this book. Above all, I thank God for the opportunity to study the topic of union with Christ. It has been a rich and rewarding experience and I pray the final product will prove beneficial to the kingdom.

It would not be possible to adequately express my thanks to my wife. Her unceasing love, support, and encouragement sustained me through the writing process. I could not have completed this book without her. Thanks also to our four children who have loved their daddy well. It is to my wife and children that I gratefully dedicate this book.

The material in this book is a lightly revised version of my PhD thesis submitted to the University of Chester and Spurgeon's College, London. Many thanks go to my doctoral supervisor, Dr. Stephen I. Wright. He skillfully brings both academic rigor and pastoral care to the supervisory role. It was an honor and blessing to work with Stephen during my time as a student. In addition, I thank the faculty and staff of Spurgeon's College who welcomed me to campus, encouraged me along the way, and engaged the ideas of this book in research seminars. I also thank my examiners, Rev. Dr. Robert Evans (University of Chester) and Prof. Grant Macaskill (University of Aberdeen). It is a privilege to have such scholars critically engage my work. This book is much improved as a result.

Many others listened to ideas and offered suggestions along the way. The initial idea for this book grew out of a conversation with Da Wei, who also read and critiqued the manuscript. Dr. Jackson Wu and Dr. Terry Griffth read an initial draft of this book and offered valuable feedback. My fellow PhD students at Spurgeon's interacted with the ideas during our campus gatherings. My students at ICTS heard many of these ideas in class and responded with good questions.

Finally, I'm grateful to Pickwick Publications for publishing this work.

Abbreviations

AB	Anchor Bible
ACCSNT	Ancient Christian Commentary on Scripture New Testament
ANTC	Abingdon New Testament Commentaries
BBR	*Bulletin for Biblical Research*
BDAG	Walter Bauer, Frederick W. Danker, William Arndt, and F. Wilbur Gingrich, *A Greek-English Lexicon of the New Testament and Other Early Christian Literature.* 3rd edn. (Chicago: University of Chicago Press, 2000)
BECNT	Baker Exegetical Commentary on the New Testament
BI	*Biblical Interpretation*
BR	*Biblical Research*
BTB	*Biblical Theology Bulletin*
BibSac	*Bibliotheca Sacra*
BZNW	Beihefte zur Zeitschrift für die neutestamentliche Wissenschaft Und Die Kunde Der Älteren Kirche
CBQ	*Catholic Biblical Quarterly*
COQG	Christian Origins and the Question of God
CTJ	*Calvin Theological Journal*
CTR	*Criswell Theological Review*
DSD	*Dead Sea Discoveries*
EC	*Early Christianity*

EKKNT	Evangelisch-Katholischer Kommentar Zum Neuen Testament
ESV	English Standard Version
ExpT	*The Expository Times*
HBT	*Horizons in Biblical Theology*
HTR	*Harvard Theological Review*
ICC	International Critical Commentary
JBL	*Journal of Biblical Literature*
JETS	*Journal of the Evangelical Theological Society*
JPS	The JPS Torah Commentary
JQR	*Jewish Quarterly Review*
JSNT	*Journal for the Study of the New Testament*
JSNTSup	Journal for the Study of the New Testament Supplement
JSOT	*Journal for the Study of the Old Testament*
JSOTSup	Journal for the Study of the Old Testament Supplement
JSPSup	Journal for the Study of the Pseudepigrapha Supplement
JSPL	*Journal for the Study of Paul and His Letters*
JTI	*Journal of Theological Interpretation*
JTS	*Journal of Theological Studies*
LNTS	Library of New Testament Studies
LXX	Septuagint
MT	*Modern Theology*
NAC	New American Commentary
NCC	New Covenant Commentary
NICOT	New International Commentary on the Old Testament
NICNT	New International Commentary on the New Testament
NIVAC	The NIV Application Commentary
NovT	*Novum Testamentum*
NovTSup	Supplements to Novum Testamentum
NSBT	New Studies in Biblical Theology

NT	New Testament	
NTS	*New Testament Studies*	
OT	Old Testament	
PNTC	Pillar New Testament Commentary	
PRS	*Perspectives in Religious Studies*	
ResQ	*Restoration Quarterly*	
RevExp	*Review & Expositor*	
SBJT	*The Southern Baptist Journal of Theology*	
SBLDS	Society of Biblical Literature Dissertation Series	
SBLSS	Society of Biblical Literature Symposium Series	
SJT	*Scottish Journal of Theology*	
TynB	*Tyndale Bulletin*	
TJ	*Trinity Journal*	
WBC	Word Biblical Commentary	
WTJ	*Westminster Theological Journal*	
WUNT	Wissenschaftliche Untersuchungen Zum Neuen Testament	
ZNW	*Zeitschrift für die neutestamentliche Wissenschaft und die Kunde der älteren Kirche*	

1

Introduction

INTRODUCTION AND THESIS

What is the Old Testament background of union with Christ in Romans? This is the primary question asked and answered in this book. Perhaps some would argue that the more fundamental question is whether or not there is an OT background for union with Christ that can be reasonably discerned from the text of Romans. Yet two important preliminary observations would seem to give weight to the assumption that there is an OT background for this important concept. First, Romans, more than any other Pauline epistle, is filled with OT quotations and other references.[1] It is clear from the opening of the letter that Paul is seeking to set his entire argument as the outworking of the gospel, which was "promised beforehand through his prophets in the holy writings" (Rom 1:2).[2] Further, the repetition of "as it is written" (καθὼς γέγραπται) indicates that the OT forms the most important source and authority for Paul's theology.[3] Second, while scholars debate the exact role of union with Christ, it is undeniable that this doctrine is important not only in Romans, but in Pauline theology more generally. Though other

---

1. According to Longenecker, "Prolegomena," 146, Romans contains at least 45 citations of the OT, not including allusions and echoes.

2. Unless otherwise noted, all NT quotations are my own translations.

3. Rom 1:17; 2:24; 3:4, 10; 4:17; 8:36; 9:13, 33; 10:15; 11:8, 26; 15:3, 9, 21.

theological themes have typically dominated scholarly discussion (particularly justification), proper study of Romans demands that one give careful attention to the prominence of union with Christ. This, then, leads back to the original question. Given the importance of both the use of the OT in Romans and the concept of union with Christ, how are these two marks of the great epistle related?

Having undertaken this study with the above question in mind, the following thesis will be argued: a study of Romans with careful attention given to Paul's use of the OT shows that the Adam and Israel stories together form the background of union with Christ within the epistle. When reading Romans with adequate consideration of Paul's use of the OT stories, it becomes clear that he saw them as organically related as one continuous story, which provides the OT background for union with Christ. In short, Paul argues that unbelievers (those outside of Christ) are united to Adam. This union is basic to all humanity, Jew and Gentile alike. Conversely, believers (those in Christ) are united to Christ and to one another and this provides the basis for church unity. Indeed, union with Christ is Paul's primary theological tool for encouraging church unity and his use of the OT is an essential aspect of this tool. Within the broader argument of the letter, union with Christ as understood with this OT background in mind demonstrates that God has been faithful to his covenant promises to Abraham in giving him a worldwide family: a new people in Christ. Such an argument will draw on the narrative approach to Paul's theology, particularly in the work of N. T. Wright, and seek to bring clarity to the function and meaning of union with Christ.[4] Though other approaches are possible, I will argue that the narrative approach is a fruitful means of understanding union with Christ in Romans.

LITERATURE REVIEW

While this book is an attempt at a fresh reading of Romans to discover OT backgrounds for union with Christ, the investigation does not take place in a vacuum. Union with Christ in Paul's letters has been an area of intense interest in contemporary scholarship. Before embarking on a study of this topic, it will be helpful to survey the scholarly discussion in order to set the present work within contemporary scholarship. It will not be possible to attempt an exhaustive analysis of all contributions to the

---

4. See the methodological discussion below.

study of union with Christ in Paul.[5] Rather, a few key works drawn primarily from recent scholarship will be mentioned to set the stage for the present work. The purpose will be to briefly summarize the main argument of the key works and the way in which these writers have discussed (or not discussed) Paul's use of the OT in relation to union with Christ.

Recent Literature

While a few earlier works gave attention to the topic,[6] Schweitzer's *The Mysticism of Paul the Apostle*, first published in 1931, has been a very influential work on the importance of union with Christ in Pauline theology. Schweitzer argued that Paul's basic understanding of salvation was mystical in nature. Contra traditional Protestant thinking since the Reformation, Schweitzer believed that union with Christ was far more important in Paul's theological program than forensic justification. He writes, "The doctrine of righteousness by faith is therefore a subsidiary crater, which has formed within the rim of the main crater—the mystical doctrine of redemption through being-in-Christ."[7] Thus, for Schweitzer, union with Christ is the "prime enigma of Pauline teaching," which is the key to understanding the whole of Paul's theology.[8] While various features of Christ-mysticism have clear OT connections, Schweitzer gives little attention to this, especially in relation to potential OT backgrounds for the doctrine.

Sanders's *Paul and Palestinian Judaism* is often credited with being a primary catalyst for the New Perspective on Paul through his reassessment of early Judaism.[9] However, much of the second half of the book is focused on a participatory understanding of Paul's soteriology. He writes, "the main theme of Paul's gospel was the saving action of God in Jesus Christ and how his hearers could participate in that action."[10] Sanders

---

5. For recent surveys, see Campbell, *Paul and Union*, 31–64; Macaskill, *Union with Christ*, 17–41; and Vanhoozer, "From 'Blessed in Christ' to 'Being in Christ,'" 5–11.

6. See especially Deissmann, *Die Neutestamentliche Formel*; Deissmann, *St. Paul*; Bousset, *Kyrios Christos*.

7. Schweitzer, *Mysticism*, 225.

8. Ibid., 3.

9. Sanders, *Paul and Palestinian Judaism*. Sanders recognized that Schweitzer, *Mysticism*, and Davies, *Paul and Rabbinic Judaism*, argued similar points. Davies's influence particularly is seen in Sanders.

10. Sanders, *Paul and Palestinian Judaism*, 447.

holds that participation in Christ was so central for Paul that it served as the foundation for other teaching, particularly issues of unity and morality.[11] Thus, participatory categories of thought subsume forensic themes since participation in Christ is the "real bite" of Paul's theology.[12] Interestingly, though Sanders's investigation is a comparative analysis of the "pattern of religion" in Palestinian Judaism and the Pauline literature, he devotes little attention to possible backgrounds for Paul's participatory soteriology.

In his monumental work on Pauline theology, Dunn echoes Sanders in arguing that participation in Christ, as opposed to justification by faith, is "the more natural extension of Paul's Christology."[13] That is, Paul's soteriology is built upon his Christology. Since one of the most important aspects of Pauline Christology is Adam Christology, it follows that participation in Christ, in contrast to participation in Adam, is central to Paul's soteriological formulations. Dunn's study of the participation motif in Paul proceeds along exegetical lines, focusing on the related Pauline phrases ("in Christ"; "with Christ"; etc.), noting that the prevalence of the phrases demands that the motif be taken seriously. Paul uses "in Christ" and related phrases in at least three ways—objectively, indicating God's salvific work in Christ; subjectively, indicating the believer's connection to Christ; and to express a particular activity or disposition for believers.[14] In relation to OT backgrounds, Dunn makes no direct claims.

Gorman has written widely on Pauline soteriology, specifically emphasizing the relationship between justification and participation. For Gorman, the key term is *theosis*, which in Paul's writings should be defined as "transformative participation in the kenotic, cruciform character of God through Spirit-enabled conformity to the incarnate, crucified, and resurrected/glorified Christ."[15] According to Gorman, this concept most accurately describes Pauline soteriology. Having established *theosis* as foundational, Gorman seeks to show that rather than two separate models of salvation (judicial and participatory), "for Paul there is *one* soteriological model: justification is by crucifixion, specifically co-crucifixion, understood as participation in Christ's act of covenant fulfillment."

---

11. Ibid., 456.
12. Ibid., 502.
13. Dunn, *Theology of Paul*, 390.
14. For example, "speaking the truth in Christ" (Rom 9:1).
15. Gorman, *Inhabiting*, 18.

Thus, Gorman links together justification and participation resulting in a model that emphasizes both declaration and transformation.

Campbell's recent work, *Paul and Union with Christ*, offers a comprehensive study by providing a broad exegetical analysis of the phrases and metaphors within the Pauline corpus related to union with Christ as well as theological reflection on the exegetical findings. Thus, he has produced a more detailed and far-reaching study than some other works included in this literature review. The bulk of the book is concerned with interpreting every Pauline passage that relates to union with Christ via specific prepositional phrases and metaphors. Campbell studies every occurrence of ἐν Χριστῷ, εἰς Χριστὸν, σὺν Χριστῷ, and διὰ Χριστοῦ, as well as related phrases and metaphors.

Campbell then turns to theological study, seeking to apply the exegetical results to theological questions. One significant advance in Campbell's work is his attempt to define union with Christ. Drawing from his exegetical work, Campbell concludes that no one term exists to adequately define Paul's theological meaning. Instead, he opts for four terms, which together "function as 'umbrella' concepts, covering the full spectrum of Pauline language, ideas, and themes."[16] He elucidates these terms as follows:

> *Union* gathers up faith, union with Christ, mutual indwelling, Trinitarian, and nuptial notions. *Participation* conveys partaking in the events of Christ's narrative. *Identification* refers to the believers' location in the realm of Christ and their allegiance to his lordship. *Incorporation* encapsulates the corporate dimensions of membership into Christ's body.

These particular terms are intended to draw together the various theological threads Campbell deems most common in his study of union with Christ in the Pauline corpus.

Regarding possible OT backgrounds, Campbell believes that while there may be some thematic OT antecedents, union with Christ is "boldly innovative."[17] That is, while there are some connections to the OT in regard to Paul's usage of metaphors, there is no clear OT background that provides the language and theology of union with Christ. Campbell omits interaction with OT quotations and allusions in the analyzed texts and contexts.

---

16. Campbell, *Paul and Union*, 413.
17. Ibid., 417.

Macaskill's wide-ranging *Union with Christ in the New Testament* is unique in this survey in that he explores varying conceptions of union with Christ in the entire NT, in biblical scholarship, and in historical theology. Further, he devotes space to investigation into possible backgrounds for the doctrine. Macaskill considers various proposals for antecedents, concluding that covenant "provides the framework within which the bond between God and his people can be conceived."[18] Further, much of the messianic content of the OT, particularly the servant songs in Isaiah, incorporate ideas of covenant representation that could lay groundwork for union with Christ.[19] Additionally, the concept of glory in the OT and in the Jewish literature includes the theme of shared glory, which is probably related to concepts of Christ's glory shared with those united to him.[20]

Most pertinent for the discussion of this book is Macaskill's discussion of possible adamic backgrounds for union with Christ. He devotes a chapter to possible connections between the understanding of Adam as a glorious being in Judaism and the NT doctrine of union with Christ. After surveying both NT Adam-Christology and Jewish literature, Macaskill concludes that the glorious-Adam motif had little influence on NT writers in general and that adamic glory plays an insignificant role in Paul's conception of union.[21] According to Macaskill, the restoration taking place in believers through union with Christ is not the restoration of Adam's lost glory, but is "a different substance altogether."[22]

Like Campbell, one of the important contributions of Macaskill's work is his attempt to clarify the meaning of union with Christ. He writes,

> To be united to Jesus, to be in him, is to be in the covenant through his representative headship. Thus, it is to be in a condition of covenantal communion with God, with the covenant-fulfillment of Jesus serving as the grounds for our own communion. In Christ, we keep the covenant.[23]

Thus, covenantal relationship is central for the NT picture of union with Christ. This covenant relationship, along with temple themes, constitutes

---

18. Macaskill, *Union with Christ*, 127.
19. Ibid.
20. Ibid., 117–21.
21. Ibid., 136.
22. Ibid., 143.
23. Ibid., 298.

stronger possibilities for OT backgrounds than adamic themes in Macaskill's interpretation of the texts.

Union with Christ features prominently in Wright's many publications on Pauline theology. In his recent *Paul and the Faithfulness of God*, he draws attention to union with Christ in numerous places.[24] For Wright, the concept of "incorporation" into Jesus is important and fits into his overall narrative conception of Paul's theology. Wright believes the gospel story of Jesus to be the climax of Israel's story.[25] Moreover, believers in Jesus enter his story in union with him. Thus, participatory themes are very significant in Wright's conception of Paul's soteriology. Nevertheless, a narrative analysis leads Wright to argue that forensic and participatory models of salvation in Paul are complimentary rather than conflicting. That is, those who are justified are those who are "incorporated into the Messiah."[26]

For Wright, incorporation into Christ is ecclesiological in nature: the people of God are those who are incorporated into the Messiah.[27] Christians find unity "in the Messiah" and this unity transcends ethnic and social identity.[28] At the heart of this conception is Wright's view of Jesus as Israel's "incorporative Messiah."[29] As such, Jesus is the hoped for Jewish Messiah who restores the people of God, Jew and Gentile together, in himself. He is Israel's representative, "Israel in person."[30] In other words, Wright's conception of union with Christ is largely an outworking of his Christology.

Regarding OT backgrounds for union with Christ, Wright makes very few direct arguments. He argues that Paul reread OT narratives through the lens of the resurrection of Jesus. Such a rereading caused Paul to recognize corporate notions in the stories of Adam and Abraham.[31] Further, Wright argues for the presence of corporate personality themes in the OT stories of Israel's king, but offers little exegetical evidence of

24. Union themes can be found in his other writings, particularly *The Climax of the Covenant* and *The Resurrection of the Son of God*. For conciseness, the summary here will focus on *Paul and the Faithfulness of God*.

25. See the discussion below.

26. Wright, *Paul and the Faithfulness of God*, 950.

27. Ibid., 405.

28. Ibid., 397.

29. Ibid., 825.

30. Ibid., 828.

31. Ibid.

Paul's use of this notion.[32] Finally, and most importantly for Wright, the concept of union with Christ somehow fits into Paul's understanding of the grand narrative of Scripture.[33] This is natural in Wright's work as all theological concepts fit within the broad narrative framework of Paul's theology.

Evaluation

While there have been many valuable contributions to the study of union with Christ, especially in recent years, there are some gaps within the body of literature which this book seeks to address.[34] First, scholars have given little attention to the role of union with Christ within the arguments of particular NT books. For example, Campbell examines union with Christ language within the Pauline canon as a whole as opposed to the role of the doctrine within each Pauline letter. Likewise, Macaskill offers a broad study of the theme across the entire NT. The present work builds on these studies by focusing more narrowly on Romans and the particular function of union with Christ themes within the letter.

Second, while some have studied OT antecedents to union with Christ, few have given serious attention to OT backgrounds as presented by the NT authors. Most studies of union with Christ omit examination of OT backgrounds. Those who do explore possible OT connections usually begin with the OT and hypothesize about potentially overlapping themes and theological concepts. I build on the broad surveys of potential OT backgrounds, but work from the NT into the OT via quotations, allusions, and echoes. That is, there is a need for a study that focuses both on Paul's use of the OT and his theology of union with Christ. This book seeks to fill this gap.

Third, in this book I will draw on observations by Macaskill with regard to the covenantal nature of union with Christ, but will utilize the narrative approach of Wright.[35] As such, I will seek to extend the work of Wright by giving focused attention to union with Christ in Romans.

32. Ibid., 829–30.
33. Ibid., 832–33.
34. Several contributions from systematic theologians have been recently published. See especially Horton, *Covenant and Salvation*; Letham, *Union with Christ*; Johnson, *One with Christ*; and Peterson, *Salvation Applied by the Spirit*.
35. See the methodological discussion below.

While union with Christ is prominent in Wright's work, it remains somewhat nebulous and is always treated in relation to some other theological topic, whether Christology, justification, or ecclesiology. I will seek to bring some clarity to the discussion through a narrative analysis that gives sustained attention to union with Christ as the main topic. That is, this book will attempt to clarify the particular function of union with Christ in Romans, which may have implications for Paul's theology more broadly. Further, I will seek to show that a narrative analysis helps understand not only the covenantal aspects of union with Christ, but Paul's use of Adam's story in Romans for a more complete picture of this central concept.

KEY ISSUES IN INTERPRETING ROMANS

This book is focused narrowly on the concept of union with Christ in Romans. Therefore, it is important to first examine a few important issues related to interpreting the epistle, though it is not possible or necessary to discuss every issue normally labelled "introductory."[36] Instead, the following discussion is limited to a few matters that directly affect the argument presented in the chapters to come. These matters will be treated only briefly with references to supporting publications.

Audience

Scholars continue to debate the intended audience of Romans, with seemingly no resolution in sight.[37] Though most have understood the composition of the Roman church to include both Jewish and Gentile believers in Jesus to varying degrees, some scholars continue to maintain a more exclusive view of the audience. In multiple publications, Nanos has vigorously argued for a Jewish context for the recipients of Romans.[38] Nanos holds that while Romans may have been written primarily to Gentile believers in Christ, the audience was embedded within Roman Jewish life, especially the synagogue.[39] This argument is based largely on

---

36. For more in-depth discussion on introductory issues, in addition to the introductions in the major commentaries, see Bryan, *Preface*; and Longenecker, *Introducing*.
37. See Donfried, *Romans Debate* and Sumney, *Reading Paul's Letter*.
38. Nanos, *Mystery*; "To the Churches."
39. Nanos, *Mystery*, 41–84.

his understanding of the historical evidence. Though this is a creative approach, few have followed Nanos's views.

Others contend that the audience was entirely, or almost entirely, Gentile. This view was championed by Stowers,[40] followed by Das,[41] and has been taken up recently by Rodriguez.[42] Stowers claims that this is the only conclusion to be drawn from a close reading of the text of Romans and that other opinions concerning the audience are only formed from outside sources.[43] Das builds on this argument, adding that the Gentile audience was familiar with Jewish tradition and belief as a result of past association with the synagogue, but at the time of writing were separated from any synagogue affiliation.[44] In addition, Das avers that external evidence upholds his thesis.[45]

However, most scholars hold that the church in Rome was a mixed congregation.[46] In order to ascertain the ethnic identity of the believers in Rome, one must take into consideration both the textual evidence (often called "mirror reading") and the extra-textual historical background. The order in which such an investigation takes place is a matter of dispute. Longenecker argues that beginning with the textual data has resulted in an impasse in scholarship.[47] Thus, he moves from historical background to textual examination. Longenecker concludes:

> (1) as for their ethnic identity, the Christians at Rome constituted both Gentile and Jewish believers in Jesus, but (2) as for their religious character and concerns, they considered themselves closely tied to the Jerusalem church and they thought and expressed themselves in ways congenial to Jewish Christianity.[48]

According to Longenecker, and in keeping with a majority view, the Roman church was mixed ethnically, but theologically closely related to

40. Stowers, *Rereading*.
41. Das, *Solving*.
42. Rodriguez, *If You Call*.
43. Stowers, *Rereading*, 29–33.
44. Das, *Solving*, 53–70.
45. Ibid., 149–202.
46. While differing on the exact composition of the Roman congregation, the following commentators hold to an ethnically mixed group: Cranfield, *Romans*, 17–22; Fitzmyer, *Romans*, 33–34; Byrne, *Romans*, 10–13; Schreiner, *Romans*, 12–14; Keener, *Romans*, 11–14; Matera, *Romans*, 6–8. Hultgren, *Romans*, 9–10; Kruse, *Romans*, 2–3.
47. Longenecker, *Introducing*, 55, 79.
48. Ibid., 83. See also Campbell, *Paul and the Creation*.

Jewish Christianity. Dunn likewise avers that Roman Christianity probably was birthed out of the synagogue and included both converted Jews and Gentiles who had formerly been associated with Judaism, perhaps as proselytes.[49] However, by the time Romans was written the church(es) most likely included numerous Gentile converts who had no previous contact with the synagogues.[50]

In this book, I will work from the assumption, based on the work of the aforementioned scholars, that the church in Rome included both Jewish and Gentile Christians. The Jewish background believers in Christ as well as those Gentiles formerly connected to the synagogues would have had foundational knowledge of the OT and Jewish traditions, thus making it feasible that they would have heard Paul's more subtle echoes of the OT.[51] Indeed, this understanding is fundamental to the purpose of the letter and the function of union with Christ within the argument.

Purpose

For much of the history of interpretation, the purpose of Romans has been one of the most debated issues. The debate continues as recent scholarship has produced a plethora of options.[52] Yet, as Longenecker notes, the various proposals can be broadly categorized into two groups: pastoral and missionary.[53] Those arguing for a pastoral purpose tend to focus on the situation with the Roman church, at least as Paul seems to have understood it. Thus, for these scholars, Paul wrote in order to address particular issue(s) within the church. On the other hand, those arguing for missionary purposes believe that Paul's fundamental aim in writing was related more to his own ministry and missionary aspirations than the local situation in Rome.

---

49. Dunn, *Romans*, 1:l.

50. Ibid., 1:liv.

51. Contra Stanley, *Arguing*, who argues that Paul's audience would have understood only the most obvious allusions to the OT.

52. For a comprehensive assessment of proposals, see Longenecker, *Introducing*, 92–128. See also the discussion in Das, *Solving*, 26–52. Though slightly dated, Donfired, *Romans Debate*, includes defences of various proposals. See also Wedderburn, *Reasons*. In the history of interpretation, some, following Philip Melancthon, have held that Romans is to be read as a theological treatise or a summary of Paul's theology. Few (if any) biblical scholars hold to this today. Thus, discussion of this position is omitted.

53. Longenecker, *Introducing*, 93.

A detailed examination of the proposals for the purpose(s) of Romans is unnecessary for the argument of this book. Instead, the purpose of Romans that will be assumed throughout the argument is that Paul wrote in order to encourage unity among the believers in Rome for the purpose of mission. Thus, Romans was written with pastoral, missionary, and theological purposes. This understanding builds on the work of several recent scholars and needs only to be summarized here.

First, Paul wrote Romans as an extension of his apostolic ministry. Specifically, the letter was written as an act of missionary service and as a request for support for further missionary service. That Paul's own ministry as apostle to the Gentiles was central to his purposes in writing Romans is clear from the content of letter's opening and closing remarks. In Rom 1:1–6, Paul refers to himself as "an apostle" (ἀπόστολος) and says that his "apostleship" (ἀποστολή) is received through Jesus Christ. Further, this apostleship was for the purpose of the gospel (Rom 1:1), which he announces "to bring about the obedience of faith among all the Gentiles for the sake of his name" (εἰς ὑπακοὴν πίστεως ἐν πᾶσιν τοῖς ἔθνεσιν ὑπὲρ τοῦ ὀνόματος αὐτοῦ).[54] Scholars have long noted the importance of Paul's salutations, particularly related to the purposes and content of the letter.[55] Thus, the self-identification as an apostle to the Gentiles points to the missionary concerns of the letter.

Paul notes his desire to preach the gospel in Rome in order "to impart some spiritual gift" to the believers (Rom 1:11). The reason for this is the obligation to all Gentiles Paul feels through the calling he has received (Rom 1:14). It follows that at least part of Paul's reason for writing is to fulfill his missionary calling to the Gentiles, including those within the church in Rome. Jervis holds that the purpose of writing is discerned through a comparative analysis of Romans with other contemporary Greek letters, concluding that Paul's primary purpose was to assert his apostolic authority over the church in Rome.[56] Jervis's point is apt; Paul certainly believed that writing to the Roman believers was well within his apostolic calling. Kruse has similarly argued that the "primary purpose in writing Romans was to minister to the believers in Rome for whom he had an apostolic responsibility."[57] Yet, there seems to be more to the story

---

54. Rom 1:5.
55. See Longenecker, *Introducing*, 380–82.
56. Jervis, *Purpose*.
57. Kruse, *Romans*, 10.

than a simple claiming of authority over the church, especially considering the scholarly consensus that the church in Rome was composed of both Gentiles and Jews.

In addition to his work among the Roman believers themselves, Paul also wrote in order to elicit support for and participation in his further missionary activity. This is clear from Paul's words in Rom 15:14–33, where he again reminds his readers of his calling to missionary service among the Gentiles and announces his plans to travel to Spain after visiting Rome. It would seem that these verses are more than the mere imparting of information. Indeed, Kruse identifies this as "secondary" purpose.[58] Whether or not this purpose should be relegated to secondary status is debatable, but it is clear that Paul sought to persuade the Roman believers to participate in his mission.[59]

Despite the importance of these purposes, there is a second, and perhaps more important, reason for writing Romans. The ministry and missionary purposes also spurred Paul to write in order to encourage unity among the believers in Rome. Schreiner identifies this as one of the primary purposes of Romans, stating that the text of Romans reveals the existence of conflict between Jewish and Gentile believers.[60] Primary among the supporting passages is the discussion of the "strong" and the "weak" in Rom 14:1—15:13. The exact identity of these two groups need not detain the discussion here.[61] For the present purposes, it is enough to simply affirm that Paul's discussion in this passage probably reveals his felt need to push for unity among the believers. The importance of this purpose, particularly in relation to union with Christ as Paul's chief tool for combating disunity, will feature prominently throughout the argument of this book.

Watson argues that the unity of the church in common Christian identity is the primary purpose behind the composition of Romans. Watson avers that Paul sought to encourage Jewish Christians to separate themselves from the synagogues in order to fully identify with Gentile believers.[62] Though his thesis is problematic at points,[63] Watson draws

58. Kruse, *Romans*, 11.
59. Wright, "Romans and the Theology of Paul," 35. So also Dunn, *Romans*, 1:lv.
60. Schreiner, *Romans*, 19–22.
61. See the discussion in Longenecker, *Introducing*, 142–45.
62. Watson, *Paul, Judaism, and the Gentiles*, 260.
63. See Dunn's critique of Watson's first edition in Dunn, *Romans*, 1:lvii.

attention to the key issue at hand: the unity of Jew and Gentile in Christ. It seems beyond doubt that the unity of the church was in Paul's mind when writing Romans. Indeed, much of the exegetical work of this book will demonstrate that throughout the letter, this issue crops up time and again.

Third, the two above purposes are closely related and are deeply theological in nature. Bird holds to an eclectic purpose for Romans, involving both missional and pastoral issues. He argues that Paul was seeking to gain both spiritual and financial support from the Roman church for his planned mission to Spain. In addition, he wrote pastorally to overcome any possible divisions among the believers in Rome. To accomplish this purpose, Paul explained in great detail his understanding of the gospel and, "in effect, 'gospelizes' them, by which I mean that he endeavors to conform them to the evangelical character of his vision for Christian communities."[64]

The unity of the church in the gospel is clearly identified as important in the opening verses of Romans. Having described himself as an apostle, Paul immediately moves into a summary of the gospel message, which is the announcement of Jesus as Israel's Messiah, the risen Davidic king. Paul opens the letter with this announcement to set the stage for the argument that follows. The gospel is the source of unity among the believers, as well as the content and motivation for Paul's apostolic mission. The kingship motif will be important throughout, especially in Rom 6, which contains some of the most explicit union with Christ language in the letter. The point is that the gospel proclaims Jesus as the risen Messiah-King and therefore his people should find their unified identity in him.

Many have noted that the Christians in Rome had probably heard of Paul, his ministry, and his gospel. It is also possible that they either had some doubts about him and his message or that they had some misinformation concerning him.[65] While this is possible, the important point to note here is that the content of Romans reflects Paul's desire to give a detailed exposition of his gospel. If this exposition was for the purpose of defending his gospel against detractors, it was secondary to the primary reasons for writing. In any case, it is clear that Paul makes a deeply theological argument in order to encourage unity among the believers within the church, to explicate his message for their benefit, and to therefore

---

64. Bird, "Letter to the Romans," 191.
65. Longenecker, *Introducing*, 150–54.

elicit support for his continuing ministry in Spain. Jewett holds that it was necessary for Paul to clarify his understanding of the gospel in order to unite the Roman believers in Christ, which would result in the establishment of Rome as a center for future missionary service.[66] Thus, Paul wrote theologically for the purpose of mission.

The proposal offered here for the purposes of Romans are not novel. However, what is often neglected among scholarly accounts is the central importance of union with Christ within the letter, particularly as it relates to the purpose of writing. The investigation into the OT background for union with Christ in Romans may also shed some light on the function of union themes in the letter.

THE USE OF THE OLD TESTAMENT IN PAUL

As stated above, this book focuses on the relationship between Paul's use of the OT in Romans and the concept of union with Christ. My approach to the use of the OT in Paul is similar to that of Wright, but also draws on insights from other scholars, such as Hays and Tooman. In this section, I will briefly summarize and evaluate some recent approaches to the use of the OT in Paul and describe my chosen methodology.[67] In short, I argue that the narrative approach is a plausible approach to the study of Paul's use of the OT, is consistent with interpretive practices of the Second Temple period, and potentially explicates Paul's theology of union with Christ in Romans. The detailed exegesis in the following chapters will serve to test this chosen methodology, at least as it relates to explaining Paul's concept of union with Christ.

Richard Hays: Retrospective Reading

Hays has established himself as one of the most important and influential scholars in regard to the use of the OT in the NT, particularly related to the Pauline corpus. The importance of Hays's work lies in two primary features of his approach. First, Hays believes that the use of the OT in

---

66. Jewett, *Romans*, 1.

67. For a recent survey of approaches to Paul's use of the OT, see Moyise, *Paul and Scripture*. The rapid growth of publications makes the following survey necessarily selective. I have chosen approaches that relate most closely to my immediate concerns in this book.

the NT extends beyond quotations to allusions/echoes.[68] He identifies an echo as a subtle intertextual reference embedded within a NT text.[69]

Hays lists seven criteria for the identification of echoes in the letters of Paul.[70] These criteria include the following: (1) Availability: was the proposed source of the echo available to the author and/or original readers?; (2) Volume: how distinctive or prominent is the precursor text within Scripture, and how much rhetorical stress does the echo receive in Paul's discourse?; (3) Recurrence: how often does Paul elsewhere cite or allude to the same scriptural passage?; (4) Thematic Coherence: How well does the alleged echo fit into the line of argument that Paul is developing?; (5) Historical Plausibility: could Paul have intended the alleged meaning effect? Could his readers have understood it?; (6) History of Interpretation: have other readers heard the same echoes?; (7) Satisfaction: does the proposed reading make sense?

Second, Hays believes that when NT authors quote or allude to an OT text, they are making reference to the wider context of the OT text. He refers to this understanding of the use of the OT in the NT as "metalepsis," which "is a rhetorical and poetic device in which one text alludes to an earlier text in a way that evokes resonances of the earlier text beyond those explicitly cited. The result is that the interpretation of a metalepsis requires the reader to recover unstated or suppressed correspondences between the two texts."[71] Thus, in studying a particular use of the OT in Paul, "we must go back and examine the wider contexts in the scriptural precursors to understand the figurative effects produced by the intertextual connections."[72] When Paul cites, alludes to, or echoes the OT, his reference goes beyond the cited passage to the wider context of the OT text. Therefore, when one studies Paul's use of the OT, one must study the context of the OT passage and draw conclusions as to how Paul uses that context to communicate his message.

Though Hays's approach has been widely influential, he is not without critics. Much of the criticism has focused on the criteria for identifying echoes, the subjective nature of his approach, or his presuppositions.

---

68. Though he makes a distinction between allusion and echo, Hays uses these two terms nearly interchangeably.

69. Hays, *Echoes*, 29.

70. Ibid., 29–32. These criteria are repeated and expanded upon in Hays, *Conversion*, 34–44.

71. Hays, *Conversion*, 2.

72. Ibid., 3.

Porter, for example, takes aim at the seven criteria, arguing that the first three could be helpful but that the others are related more to interpretive issues rather than identification and verification.[73] For Porter, though Hays's criteria have been influential, they are too subjective to provide a reliable way forward. Despite his disagreement with Hays, Porter admits to the usefulness of the category "echo" and offers no alternative criteria for identification. Stanley complains that Hays gives too little attention to the original audience.[74] He believes the original recipients would not have "heard" the subtle echoes Hays claims to be in the text. However, Stanley's audience-centered approach is problematic itself.[75] Scholars widely agree that Paul's use of the OT goes beyond quotations to allusions and echoes. While there is some merit to the objections of Porter and Stanley, they offer little in regard alternative methods for identifying and interpreting echoes.

William Tooman: The Reuse of Scripture

Tooman, like Hays, believes that later authors use (or reuse) Scripture in more subtle and implicit ways rather than only via quotations. Unlike Hays, Tooman focuses on later OT texts and Second Temple literature.[76] Fishbane provides the stimulus for Tooman and others connected with the "inner-biblical interpretation" movement.[77] Fishbane's ground-breaking study mined the reinterpretation of earlier OT texts in later ones, showing that (re)interpretation and application of texts is not merely a post-biblical phenomenon but took place within the canonical OT itself.[78] Further, Tooman notes that Fishbane's insistence on proper methods, especially related to the identification and confirmation of scriptural reuse, has highly influenced subsequent studies.[79]

---

73. Porter, "Allusions and Echoes," 38–39.
74. Stanley, "Paul's 'Use' of Scripture," 133.
75. See below.
76. Tooman, *Gog of Magog*.
77. Zakovitch, "Inner-Biblical Interpretation," 27, defines inner-biblical interpretation as "the light that one biblical text shines onto another—whether to solve some problem that has emerged in close or distant proximity or to adapt a verse to the beliefs and ideologies of the interpreter."
78. Fishbane, *Biblical Interpretation in Ancient Israel*.
79. Tooman, *Gog of Magog*, 18.

For Tooman, much of the study of the reuse of Scripture, particularly studies on the NT use of the OT, is methodologically suspect.[80] In particular, Tooman complains that few consider the uses of Scripture in the Second Temple period and, following Hays, many opt for modern literary methods. Accordingly, more precisely defined controls are needed with adequate consideration of Jewish reuse of Scripture. Implicit reuse of Scripture includes "a demonstrable repetition of some element, or elements, of an antecedent text. An 'element' can be a word, phrase, clause, paragraph, *topos*, or form."[81] In order to identify implicit allusions to the OT, Tooman lists five principles: (1) Uniqueness: the element in question is unique to a particular source; (2) Distinctiveness: the element, while used in other texts, is particularly associated with a certain text; (3) Multiplicity: multiple elements from the source text appear in the later text; (4) Thematic correspondence: the earlier and later texts share themes and topics; and (5) Inversion: the elements in the later texts are inverted in the earlier text.[82]

Some of these principles overlap with Hays's criteria for identifying echoes, though Tooman has sought to distinguish his approach by focusing on Second Temple interpretive methods rather than literary categories. Nevertheless, the similarities should not be overlooked. For example, uniqueness, multiplicity, and thematic correspondence roughly correspond to Hays's volume, recurrence, and thematic coherence, though there are differences in the ways the two scholars detail these criteria. The benefit of Tooman's approach is that it gives attention to Second Temple interpretive methods. The first two of Tooman's principles (uniqueness and distinctiveness) seem closely related and inadequately distinguished. The final principle (inversion) applies primarily to reuse within the OT itself and does not readily apply to the study of the OT in the NT.

N. T. Wright: Storied Theology

Wright believes that human literature is inherently "the telling of stories which bring worldviews into articulation."[83] As such, interpretation must involve the analysis of the underlying worldview narratives. This applies

---

80. Ibid., 15n55.
81. Tooman, "Between Imitation and Interpretation," 58.
82. Tooman, *Gog of Magog*, 27–31.
83. Wright, *New Testament*, 65.

directly to the interpretation of the NT as there are stories being communicated through these texts, either explicitly or implicitly. With regard to Paul, Wright believes that the theological statements found in the epistles are in fact interpretations and retellings of Israel's story in the light of the coming of the Messiah. More specifically, Paul's use of the OT should be understood "not as mere proof-texting, but. . .to suggest new ways of reading well-known stories, and to suggest that they find a more natural climax in the Jesus-story than elsewhere."[84] Further, Wright believes that a fundamental conviction of the Apostle Paul was that "the covenant purposes of Israel's God had reached their climatic moment in the events of Jesus's death and resurrection."[85] Thus, for Wright, the story of Jesus and his followers is intimately connected to the story of the OT. Therefore, when Paul quotes or alludes to the OT, one purpose is to show how Jesus completes the OT narrative. Therefore, one must understand quotations and allusions in relation to their (OT) narrative context.

A key piece of Wright's argument is that his understanding of Paul's use of the OT narratively fits within the wider background of Second Temple Judaism. According to Wright, all worldviews are articulated through stories. The Jewish worldview is built upon, expressed through, and passed on by the basic story, or metanarrative, of the OT: creation by a good and wise God who chose Israel as his covenant people and would eventually restore the world.[86] The smaller stories of the OT fit within and contribute to the overarching story. In short, there was a common grand narrative within which Second Temple Jews lived, a story that they believed was the true history of the world in search of its proper ending.[87] Paul himself fits within this storied worldview and his references to the OT must be understood as evoking the broader story:

> Within all his letters, though particularly in Romans and Galatians, we discover a larger implicit narrative. . .Like his own story, this larger narrative is the Jewish story, but with a subversive twist at almost every point. Paul presupposes this story even when he does not expound it directly, and it is arguable that we can only understand the more limited narrative worlds of the different letters if we locate them at their appropriate points

---

84. Ibid., 79.
85. Wright, *Climax*, xi.
86. Wright, *New Testament*, 216–19.
87. Wright, *Paul and the Faithfulness of God*, 109.

within this overall story-world, and indeed within the symbolic universe that accompanies it.[88]

Thus, for Wright, the key to understanding Paul's use of the OT is the narrative structure of Paul's theology. Specifically, when Paul cites or echoes the OT, the scriptural reference must be understood within the OT story.

Summary and Defense of Methodology

In this book, I will make use of the insights from Hays, Tooman, and Wright. Hays and Tooman provide helpful criteria for identifying Paul's more subtle uses of the OT. Drawing on the work of these two scholars, I will use the following criteria for identifying biblical allusions and echoes: (1) distinctiveness: is the element pointing to a possible allusion unique to a particular OT text or texts?; (2) recurrence: is the text or theme used elsewhere in Paul, particularly in Romans?; (3) multiplicity: are there multiple elements from the source text used in the text of Romans?; (4) thematic coherence: are the theological themes within the two texts similar?. These four criteria for identifying allusions and echoes are emphasized by both Hays and Tooman and seem to be the most clearly identifiable marks of Paul's usage of the OT.[89]

However, moving beyond Hays and Tooman, I will follow Wright's insistence on the importance of a metanarrative in Paul's theology. I will argue exegetically that when Paul quotes from or alludes to OT narratives, he most likely has the wider stories in mind and would expect that most of his readers would be able to follow the argument based on the wider narratives. Such a narrative approach makes good sense with regard to the compositional strategy of the letters and with consideration of the audience. First, I will argue below that a narrative approach fits broadly within Second Temple interpretive approaches. Many Second Temple writings draw heavily on the OT narratives, often via retelling. These retellings were interpretive in nature and shaped by the author's purposes in writing, but were heavily dependent on the biblical narratives. These writings seem to be attempting to apply the biblical stories to their particular audiences. This sets the stage for the argument to follow: Paul in

---

88. Wright, *New Testament*, 405.

89. It should be noted that I will not necessarily work through each of these criteria in proposing possible allusions/echoes. Nevertheless, the criteria stand behind the proposed echoes in the exegetical analysis to follow.

a similar, yet distinctive, manner also draws on the OT narratives, applying them to the Roman church situation. Second, regarding the original audience, I would argue that most of the readers (or hearers) would be able to recognize allusions to the biblical narratives. Even if many in the first century churches were illiterate, they would have been taught the foundation OT stories and would probably be able to recall these stories upon hearing allusions to them. Oral learners are able to memorize and recall stories and the early Christians were probably taught the OT stories, either through their involvement with the synagogues or simply through the teaching of the early church.[90]

Though I will argue that the narrative approach provides a legitimate means of studying Romans, many scholars remain unconvinced. Though Wright and others have argued for the existence of the grand narrative within Second Temple Judaism, some have doubted these conclusions. For example, de Boer claims that Wright's grand narrative is just that—Wright's—and not Paul's.[91] He believes that Wright has constructed a narrative from his own study of the OT and Second Temple literature and then applied this narrative to Paul's letters, a process de Boer believes borders on eisegesis. For de Boer, the primary emphasis in Paul's gospel is the invasion of God into the cosmos and the defeat of the evil powers that enslave humanity. Thus, rather than a theology built upon a continuous narrative, Paul's theology is a theology of newness: the Christ event changes everything and leaves the past behind. Thus, for de Boer and others of the apocalyptic approach, Paul's theology rests not on a grand narrative, but on a singular, world-changing event.[92] Paul then rereads the OT from this new vantage point, finding texts that support various aspects of his apocalyptic message.

Further criticism of a narrative approach to Paul comes from the rhetorical approach to the use of the OT in the NT, particularly represented by Stanley.[93] He holds that investigation into Paul's use of the OT must begin with an analysis of Paul's original audiences. Stanley believes it unlikely that many of the first readers (or hearers) of Paul's letters would have been able to evaluate his use of the OT against the original context since they were largely Gentiles with little prior understanding of the OT

90. See Abasciano, "Diamonds," especially 164–73, and the cited literature therein.

91. de Boer, "N. T. Wright's Great Story," 52.

92. A brief response to de Boer and others from the apocalyptic approach will be offered in chapter 3 below.

93. Stanley, *Paul and the Language*; Stanley, *Arguing*.

and little access to written texts.[94] Moreover, Stanley argues that most church members would have been illiterate, thus rendering it impossible that they would have read the OT for themselves.[95] Therefore, for Stanley, Paul intended his quotations to give weight to his overall argument. Paul provided the necessary interpretive keys to understand quotations without reference to the OT context. Paul uses the OT authoritatively to bolster his argumentation, not as a primary source for his theology. As such, Paul uses the OT selectively, choosing relevant passages to add persuasiveness to his letters. Therefore, Paul did not intend for his audience to reflect on the original context of the quotation, but to listen to his arguments as supported by the ancient texts.[96]

In response to these objections, I offer the following points as a defense of the narrative approach.[97] The exegetical analysis in the chapters that follow also serves to argue for the appropriateness of the chosen methodology.

Narrative in the Old Testament and Second Temple Literature

The Old Testament

At the outset, it should be noted that the retelling of Israel's story is not a completely new feature of biblical interpretation in the Second Temple period. Indeed, the retelling of the biblical story is found in a number of places within the OT itself. Perhaps the clearest example of this is the Chronicles, which via genealogies retells Israel's story from Adam to the return from exile, focusing on David and his family. Of course, this is a selective retelling, but it is a retelling nonetheless. Other examples abound, such as Deuteronomy as a retelling of the exodus and wilderness wanderings, Psalms 105 and 106 as well as the numerous mentions

---

94. Stanley, *Arguing*, 60.

95. Ibid., 43–46.

96. Space does not allow for a full evaluation of Stanley's proposals. In short, the reader-centered approach rests on speculation regarding the ethnic and educational composition of the audience and thus is inadequate in evaluating the role of Scripture in Paul's letters. Further, Stanley fails to take seriously oral learning in the ancient world as well as the textual evidence in Paul's letters. See the thorough criticism of Stanley's approach in Abasciano, "Diamonds."

97. This defense will be brief with references to the appropriate literature. The exegetical analysis in this book applies the claims to the interpretation of Romans and seeks to demonstrate the veracity of the methodological claims.

of Israel's story in the prophets.[98] The list could continue, but these few examples show that as later writers penned OT Scripture, the larger story remained in mind.

Second Temple Literature

Retelling the biblical story was a common means of biblical interpretation in the Second Temple period. Kugel claims that "retelling...was actually the preferred form of biblical commentary in this period."[99] This is not to say that the retellings of Israel's story in the various writings of the period were uniform in either content or emphasis. Indeed, authors retold the biblical story in ways that fit their individual aims and compositional strategies.[100] However, this fact does not lead to the conclusion that the grand narrative of the OT was a nonfactor in Second Temple thinking and interpretation.[101] The following brief survey will show that Israel's story remained important in various texts and that this provides historical context for Paul's narrative use of the OT.

The book of *Jubilees* is one of the clearest examples of the interpretive retelling of Israel's story. The author focuses on the biblical account of creation through the giving of the Law at Sinai. The stories of the Pentateuch are retold in a selective manner, focusing heavily on the obedience to the Mosaic Law. The author presents characters from Genesis, including Adam and Abraham, as observing the Law.[102] The rewritten narrative of *Jubilees* divides the history of Israel into "jubilees" (49 year periods) and ends with the eschatological hope of restoration for Israel since, in the end, Israel will be "purified from all the sin of fornication,

---

98. For example, Jer 33:23–26; Isa 40–55.

99. Kugel, "Beginnings of Biblical Interpretation," 11. For a concise definition and description of "rewritten Bible," see Brooke, "Rewritten Bible," 777–81. Brooke holds that "rewritten Bible" refers to a technique or procedure for biblical interpretation, not a particular literary genre. On the other hand, Bernstein, "Rewritten Bible," 169–96, argues that the term more narrowly describes a particular genre of literature in the Second Temple period. I tend to favor a broader definition as biblical interpretive methods varied during period and rewritings of Scripture are found in different genres, as I note below.

100. Teeter, "On 'Exegetical Function,'" 374.

101. Neither does it mean that *all* Jews knew/retold the grand narrative. The survey below only shows that the narrative was important for at least *some* Jewish writers and communities.

102. van Ruiten, "Biblical Interpretation," 127.

and defilement, and uncleanness, and from sin and error" (50:5). The chronological shape of the narrative is probably intended to be eschatological itself. In addition, the introduction includes reflection on the exile and restoration, which alludes to Deut 26–31.[103] Thus, while the main text of *Jubilees* tells only the story of Israel from creation to Sinai, the wider story is nonetheless in view.

In Sir 44–50, Ben Sira praises many of the heroes of Israel in "a short theology of history,"[104] moving roughly chronologically beginning with Enoch, Noah, and Abraham before moving through Moses, David, and Isaiah among others. While the entire story in not told, it is clear that the OT story lies behind the content of these chapters and that there is an eschatological movement within the poem, culminating with the rebuilding of the Temple and the ministry of the high priest Simon in chapter 50. In addition to this section, Sirach contains other references to the OT narratives.[105] Thus, while Sirach's primary aim is the communication of wisdom, the OT narratives play an important role in Ben Sira's compositional strategy.

A near complete, albeit strange, recounting of Israel's story is found in the "Animal Apocalypse" in *1 Enoch* 85–90. The author uses animals to retell the history of Israel, but nevertheless tells the story from the flood through the period after the exile. Regardless of the difficulties in the exact interpretation, the Animal Apocalypse is important in that it is an early (probably second century BC)[106] retelling of the metanarrative of the OT. The main focus is on God's chosen people (pictured as cows or sheep) over against non-elect ones (pictured as donkeys or wolves) and the eventual victory of Israel. While this particular retelling is unquestionably selective and unique in style, it nevertheless covers the broad story and includes a hint of possibly messianic eschatology.[107]

Retelling of Israel's story is also present in some Qumran documents. For example, the *Damascus Document* 3 briefly recounts the stories of Noah, Abraham, Isaac, Jacob, and Israel in Egypt. The document then tells of the exodus and the wilderness wanderings, focusing on the covenant, or more specifically, Israel's breaking the covenant (3:9–11).

---

103. *Jub.* 1:7–18.

104. Skehan and Di Lella, *Wisdom of Ben Sira*, 30.

105. The mention of the Adam narratives in Sirach will be noted in chapter 2 below.

106. Isaac, "1 (Ethiopic Apocalypse of) Enoch," 6–7.

107. Scholars debate whether or not *1 Enoch* 90 refers to a future messiah. See Collins, *Scepter*.

This resulted in punishment and death for that generation. Nevertheless, in 3:12–21, hope is promised to the remnant that would be faithful to the covenant, leading to the restoration of Adam's glory, which will be given to the faithful. It seems that for the Qumran community, the goal of the biblical story is being reached within the community itself—the true heirs of the covenant promises. Thus, while brief, the retelling of Israel's story is important within the strategy of the document.[108]

Other Second Temple works could be mentioned, such as Pseudo-Philo's *Liber Antiquitatum Biblicarum*, *Psalms of Solomon*, and Josephus's *Antiquities*. Each of these recounts part or most of the OT story, particularly focusing on some aspect of Israel's history. In sum, while these retellings have their own idiosyncrasies, they have in common the retelling of either the whole or parts of the OT storyline.[109] Even when the entire story is not explicitly retold, there are often hints toward the rest of the story or eschatological flavorings, pointing forward to a continuation/completion of the narrative. The primary point is that Israel's metanarrative played a role in at least some Second Temple writings, making plausible the claim that when Paul alludes to or partially retells the OT stories, he probably had the wider stories in mind. In Romans, Paul argues that his gospel was "promised beforehand through his prophets in the holy Scriptures" (Rom 1:2) and "witnessed by the law and the prophets" (3:21). These statements link the gospel directly to the OT story and show that the gospel is not to be severed from that story. While Paul does not retell the OT stories in the same manner as the retellings found in *Jubilees* or Sirach,[110] these and other texts demonstrate that Second Temple Jews were aware of the wider narratives and that the grand narrative was significant in theological development. Paul seems to have reconsidered the narrative around the coming of the Messiah. He draws on the story, often via quotation or allusion, and shows the way in which the story of Jesus and believers fit into the story.[111] As Fisk summarizes:

> If Paul the interpreter was sometimes more radical than some
> of his peers, if he had his own unique exegetical spin, it was not

---

108. Other retellings within the Dead Sea Scrolls can be found in *Genesis Apocryphon* and 4QMMT.

109. Bernstein, "Rewritten Bible," 174.

110. Though see Fisk, "Paul Among the Storytellers," 78–84, who argues that Paul is retelling the story of Elijah in Rom 11:2–5.

111. This will be demonstrated through the exegetical analysis in chapters 2–6 below.

because he stood outside the Jewish exegetical tradition but because, standing within it, he read his text tradition by a different light: the radiance of the resurrection of a crucified messiah.[112]

The above examples show that at least some Second Temple Jewish writers held to the OT grand story and made reference to this story via retellings. Likewise, when Paul alludes to OT stories, the wider story is foundational for his use of the smaller stories. The interesting point about the retellings noted above is that while written by various authors for differing purposes, they still follow the same basic sequence, the same basic story. That is, though they diverge in detail and emphasis, they retell the OT story in virtually the same order: according to the biblical ordering of events. This seems to support the argument that a common metanarrative did indeed exist and that Paul probably drew on it.

Allusion in Second Temple Literature

While retelling was one of the most prominent ways in which Scripture was reused/interpreted in the Second Temple writings, it was not the only way. Direct quotation and allusion/echo were both used by Jewish writers, often in exegetical and interpretive ways, leading Brooke to conclude that in studying the use of Scripture in the Dead Sea Scrolls, one must consider "the multiple use[s] of the biblical books."[113] Authors utilized allusions to evoke OT stories. Tzoref identifies three types of Scripture use in the Dead Sea Scrolls (other than retelling): explicit citation, allusion, and use of biblical idiom.[114] She identifies numerous allusions to the OT in *Community Rule*, basing identification primarily on verbal correspondence with "distinctive biblical terminology."[115] Similarly, Brooke argues that *gĕzērâ šāwâ* (the linking of biblical verses on the basis of key word association) is the most common form of scriptural reuse in 4QFlorilegium.[116]

---

112. Fisk, "Paul Among the Storytellers," 57.
113. Brooke, *Exegesis at Qumran*, 37.
114. Tzoref, "Use of Scripture." See also Hughes, *Scriptural Allusions*.
115. Tzoref, "Use of Scripture," 217.
116. Brooke, *Exegesis at Qumran*, 279. See his chapter 2 for an extensive analysis of the use of Scripture in 4QFlor.

Shemesh has recently shown the influence of the Pentateuch in the *Damascus Document* and *Community Rule*.[117] Though he does not use the term, Shemesh demonstrates the influence of Leviticus, Numbers, and Deuteronomy in the list of sins and punishments in these documents via key word and thematic allusions rather than retelling or direct quotation. Specifically, Shemesh shows that certain sins and punishments within these two Qumran documents can be linked directly to three passages in the Pentateuch (Lev 19; Deut 23; Num 16–17) and that these allusions to Scripture are intended to identify the Qumran community as the true covenant people of God. In other words, by alluding to three passages from the Pentateuch, the author(s) of these documents ground the holiness of the Qumran community in its identity with the Israelites with whom Yahweh made a covenant.[118] To extend the point, the allusions make little sense if divorced from the story of Israel in the wilderness, making it probable that the author(s) intended to evoke the wider story. Similarly, VanderKam argues that *Community Rule* is saturated with allusions to Exod 19–20 and 24, which serves to further identify the community as God's covenant people.[119] VanderKam shows that the document uses Scripture via allusions to the OT text rather than retelling. Such an argument demonstrates the pervasive and varied uses of Scripture in the Qumran writings.

In her examination of the use of Scripture in Pseudo-Ezekiel (4Q383–391), Brady notes several different ways in which the manuscripts contain references to the OT.[120] In addition to the reworking, summarizing, or quoting of biblical texts, Brady argues that many subtle uses of Scripture are present in the fragments by way of "strong allusions," which occur when "biblical words and phrases are placed into larger frameworks of narrative or speech not as direct quotes by as summarized reference to a biblical theme or idea."[121] For example, the covenant with Abraham, Isaac, and Jacob is alluded to numerous times in the fragments without retelling the biblical story or quoting directly from Genesis. Though the allusions can be used in various ways, it is clear

---

117. Shemesh, "Scriptural Background."
118. Ibid., 216.
119. VanderKam, "Sinai Revisited."
120. Brady, "Biblical Interpretation."
121. Ibid., 105.

that the mention of the covenant with Abraham assumes the reader has knowledge of the OT story and is able to recall this story.

Wisdom of Solomon provides another example of allusive uses of Scripture. While the book uses Scripture in other ways, there are times in which the author alludes to a biblical story, seeking to apply the story to his contemporary situation. The author of Wisdom partially retells the exodus story in 10:15–21 and 19:1–9,[122] but he alludes to the story prior to the retelling. Chapters 10–19 are largely a retelling of Israel's history with particular attention given to the role of wisdom throughout that history. However, as Enns has pointed out, there are allusions to the exodus story in 3:2 and 7:6, where the author describes death as "ἔξοδος."[123] This usage seems to refer to life after death, with Israel's exodus from Egypt as the primary example. In any case, the use of this key term, especially considering the retelling of the exodus story later in the book, demonstrates the use of allusion in Second Temple literature that seems to have the wider biblical story in mind.

Wagner has argued that Paul's use of Isaiah in Romans must be understood within the wider OT stories. He points to Second Temple readings of Isaiah, which interpret the prophet within "the story of Israel's sin, punishment, and (future) restoration by God."[124] According to Wagner, Paul uses Isaiah with this particular story in mind, which forms the context for his interpretation and application of Isaiah.[125] Through detailed exegetical analysis, Wagner argues that Paul quotes and alludes to Isaiah in Romans, particularly chapters 9–11, to show that Paul himself is living out the fulfillment of prophecies concerning the restoration of Israel and the salvation of the Gentiles. Yet, for Wagner, such an understanding of Paul's use of Isaiah hinges on the wider OT stories, particularly the story of restoration as it was commonly understood in Second Temple writings.[126]

One example in Romans, which was mentioned above, will suffice to show the plausibility of the approach being utilized here. There is a

---

122. See Enns, *Exodus Retold*.
123. Enns, "Pseudo-Solomon," 395.
124. Wagner, *Heralds*, 29.
125. Ibid., 31.
126. This is not to say that all Second Temple Jews saw the restoration in exactly the same way, whether in terms of form (return from ongoing exile, etc.) or timing (present or future). It is to say that the hope of restoration was a commonly held belief and often expressed in stories.

clear allusion to (or rewriting) of the Elijah story in Rom 11:2–5. As Fisk points out, Paul begins with the phrase "ἢ οὐκ οἴδατε," indicating that he expected his audience to know the story to which he alludes.[127] Accordingly, Paul does not retell the entire story, but one can assume that the entire story is evoked through the retelling of one part. The story is told selectively for Paul's immediate compositional purposes, but this does not mean that the rest of the story is irrelevant. Paul, like other Second Temple Jewish writers, retold an OT story interpretively, applying the story to his contemporary situation. It is also important to notice that Paul, in contrast to other examples of rewritten Bible, alludes to the story rather than retelling the wider story. Thus, Paul seems to use the OT narratively via allusions that point to wider stories.[128]

In sum, Second Temple Jewish writers were able to reuse Scripture in a number of ways. Though retelling was a common method of interpretation and contextualized application of the OT texts, authors also made use of allusion via key word or thematic associations with prior texts. Thus, when Paul alludes to OT texts via key words or unique themes, this use of the OT fits broadly within the Second Temple patterns of interpretive methods. Given the above argument concerning the retellings of Israel's story, it is plausible to assume that wider narratives are in mind when Paul alludes to particular parts of the stories. This assumption will be tested through the exegetical analysis of Romans in the following chapters.

NARRATIVE IN PAUL

In the above section, I argued that a narrative approach to Paul's use of the OT fits broadly within the spectrum of Second Temple Jewish biblical interpretation and potentially leads to fruitful study of the epistles. However, the nature and function of narrative in Paul remains a matter of debate. Even among those arguing for the presence of such a narrative framework, there seems to be little consensus as to the way in which

---

127. Fisk, "Paul Among the Storytellers," 78.

128. This particular example is illustrative of the "grand narrative background" in that Romans' context is focusing on God's faithfulness to Israel, which is situated in the wider OT story.

narrative functions in Paul's argumentation.[129] Therefore, it will be necessary to briefly examine some important approaches to narrative in Paul.

Defining Narrative

One challenge to the study of narrative in Paul's letters is defining the term itself. Indeed, Barclay has complained that in Wright's work, "the term 'story' becomes so all-encompassing that it is hard to know what would *not* qualify for this category."[130] I will suggest below that such a criticism misses the point: it is not that everything in Paul is narrative, but that all Paul's theology is derived from and evokes the basic narrative found in the OT. Nevertheless, it remains the case that narrative needs defining.

Adams, drawing on the work of Toolan, a literary theorist, offers a concise definition: "A story/narrative is a series of events that can be perceived as sequentially and consequentially connected. Typically, stories have characters, settings, and a trajectory."[131] This definition, while concise, denotes the fundamental features of narrative. First, a story contains a related series of events. That is, the events comprising a story are interconnected rather than random and follow a particular pattern or sequence. Second, stories normally include characters to perform the action, which takes place in a certain setting. Finally, narrative usually has a trajectory: the story moves toward a certain goal or climax. While the constituent parts of the definition are far more complex than this simple explanation, the definition itself suits the needs of this book as it provides a flexible basis from which to analyze Romans.[132] Campbell warns that a detailed definition of story is not possible since the notion of story changes in various cultures and generations. Rather, "stories are recognizable as such because they share a number of overlapping features."[133] Thus, Adams's proposed definition seems helpful as it points to broad characteristics of narrative rather than a narrow definition.

---

129. As evidenced in the various assessments in Longenecker, *Narrative Dynamics*.

130. Barclay, "Paul's Story," 134. It should be noted at this point that I, like most scholars writing on the topic, use "story" and "narrative" interchangeably.

131. Adams, "Paul's Story," 23. See also Toolan, *Narrative*, 6.

132. See Adams, "Paul's Story," 19–24, for further discussion and references to secondary literature.

133. Campbell, "Story of Jesus," 99.

I will argue through exegetical analysis that these various elements of narratives can be seen in Paul's argument.[134] Paul does not tell a story with a beginning, middle, and ending sequentially as in many stories, but I suggest that the story elements found throughout the epistle fit together to tell a coherent story from Adam through Israel to Christ and the church. Further, I will argue that union with Christ as a concept is best understood within this narrative framework.

Richard Hays

Having briefly defined narrative, the following sections interact with the primary proponents of the narrative approach to Paul and respond to objections. Though not the originator of the study of narrative in Paul, Hays's published doctoral dissertation brought the issue to the forefront and set the agenda for future investigation.[135] In this seminal study, Hays argues that "a story about Jesus Christ is presupposed by Paul's argument in Galatians, and his theological reflection attempts to articulate the meaning of that story."[136] In addition to the story of Jesus, Hays believes Paul likewise assumes the basic story of Israel. For Hays, these stories are related: the story of Israel is a "prefiguration" of the story of Jesus.[137] That is, Paul's "narrative soteriology" reflects "patterns of narrative unity between Israel's story and the gospel."[138]

The concept of "narrative pattern" emphasizes a key point in Hays's approach to narrative in Paul, which sets his understanding apart from that of Wright. Hays believes Paul's gospel to be intimately related to Israel's story, but not in the same way Wright sees the metanarrative connections. For example, in his reflections on 1 Corinthians, Hays holds that Paul was encouraging the Corinthian church to see Israel's story as their own.[139] Nevertheless, Hays stops short of arguing for a controlling metanarrative shaping Paul's theology. This is perhaps a result of the role Hays believes the concept of covenant to hold. Hays argues that πίστις

---

134. It is readily admitted that some elements are more obvious and important than others as Romans is epistolary rather than narrative in genre. Thus, setting is probably less important than trajectory.

135. Hays, *Faith of Jesus Christ*.

136. Ibid., xxiv.

137. Ibid., xxxviii.

138. Hays, "Christ Died for the Ungodly," 61.

139. Hays, *Conversion*, 9.

(which he forcefully argues to be participatory in nature) is unrelated to the concept of διαθήκη. He writes, "In no case does Paul bring the concepts of πίστις and διαθήκη into explicit relation with one another."[140] The separation of πίστις and διαθήκη in Hays's account leads to the downplaying of the role of covenant themes in Paul's theology. This stands in distinction from Wright (see below), who sees "covenant" as central to Paul's narrative theological exposition. For Hays, then, while there is continuity between the OT story and the gospel, this should not be regarded as a continuous "covenantal story" in which the story of Jesus completes the covenantal promises and responsibilities of Israel.[141] Moreover, Hays describes Paul's primary story as an "apocalyptic narrative" in which Jesus delivers his people from the present evil age.[142] Thus, Hays attempts to strike a balance between continuity in the repeated narrative pattern and discontinuity in the apocalyptic nature of Paul's gospel.

For Hays, Paul is not retelling the stories. Instead, Paul further explicates the stories in retrospect from the Christ-event while assuming that his readers are familiar with the evoked stories.[143] The fundamental point for Hays is that the story of Jesus and the story of Israel form the "substructure" for Paul's theological argumentation. Allusions to these stories point to "a more comprehensive narrative pattern" that forms the framework for the gospel.[144] Hays emphasizes Paul's use of the stories in his theologizing, labelling Paul an "interpreter of stories" rather than a "storyteller."[145] In short, Hays views Paul as a reader of Israel's Scripture through the apocalyptic lens of the gospel. While continuity is present, Paul makes little use of a covenantal framework in his narrative theology.

N. T. Wright

I have already described some of the key aspects of Wright's approach to Paul's use of the OT narratives. Here, I simply expound further the way

---

140. Hays, *Faith of Jesus Christ*, 187.

141. Hays, "Adam, Israel, Christ," 81–82. Though Hays does agree that "Romans is a defense of the covenant faithfulness of the God of Israel" (84).

142. Hays, *Faith of Jesus Christ*, xxxix. Hays notes the influence of J. Louis Martyn on his thinking.

143. Ibid., 6.

144. Ibid., 8.

145. Hays, "Is Paul's Gospel Narratable?," 221.

in which Wright believes narrative to function within Paul's theology.[146] In addition to the points made above, there are a few key elements to Wright's approach. First, narratives are essential in the analysis of any text because they reveal the author's underlying worldview. For Wright, this is precisely the reason that narratives in Paul's letters function as the substructure: worldview material normally remains implicit. Wright draws on the work of Petersen, who argued that texts have both "poetic sequence" (the order in which material is presented) and a "referential sequence" (the order in which things take place in a reconstruction of the world narrated in the text).[147] Wright argues that the referential sequence points to a metanarrative, which in turn reflects the worldview of the writer.[148] This worldview is situated within the wider literature and beliefs of Second Temple Judaism.

Second, as noted above, the concept of metanarrative is central to Wright's understanding of narrative in Paul. For Wright, the smaller stories (Adam, Abraham, Israel, etc.) are parts of the larger *story*. The individual stories can be examined in their own right, but Paul's use of these stories can be rightly understood only as they fit within the metanarrative. Wright argues, "looking at Paul's worldview with the aid of this narrative analysis sheds a positive flood of light. . .on passage after passage of tricky exegesis."[149] He goes on to describe the individual stories, emphasizing the way in which these stories are intertwined and form a metanarrative. For Wright, the most fundamental story is that of "God and creation," which is presupposed throughout Paul's argumentation.[150] This story includes the purpose of creation and the problem introduced through human rebellion. In Paul's writings, the problem is resolved through Jesus who inaugurates the new age.[151] Within this major story, there are three "sub-plots": the story of humanity; the story of Israel; and the story of Jesus.[152]

---

146. Though Wright has discussed narrative in numerous publications, because of space limitations, I will limit this discussion to his most recent and most robust defense found in *Paul and the Faithfulness of God*.

147. Petersen, *Rediscovering Paul*.

148. Wright, *Paul and the Faithfulness of God*, 463–64.

149. Ibid., 474.

150. Ibid., 475.

151. Ibid., 477.

152. Ibid., 485; further explored on 485–537.

Third, the heart of Paul's metanarrative is the covenant God made with Abraham and Israel. This story is central in that it advances the main plot: God's restoration of his world. This restoration takes place through his people Israel in fulfillment of the covenant promises made to Abraham.[153] However, Israel failed in her vocation, a vocation subsequently fulfilled through Jesus as Israel's Messiah.[154] For Wright, Paul's gospel only makes sense within this (Jewish) narrative framework. Thus, references to Abraham or to Israel's story evokes the wider narrative of Israel as the covenant people God, but this narrative must be situated within the metanarrative as noted above. The centrality of Israel's story gives a covenant flavor to the entire narrative substructure.[155]

In sum, Wright believes that allusions and echoes to OT stories in Paul's letters point to wider worldview narratives, which together form a basic metanarrative. This metanarrative begins with creation, continues through the story of Israel to Jesus and the church, culminating in the new creation. As such, Paul's gospel is the climax of the story and apart from the metanarrative, Paul's gospel is easily misunderstood. Thus, for Wright, narrative is central to Paul's argument in Romans as it ties together Paul's theology within the narrative framework from the OT to Paul's gospel. In this regard, the implicit narrative running through Paul constitutes an "implied retelling" of the biblical story.[156]

The Non-Narratable Gospel: Francis Watson

In his response to the essays in *Narrative Dynamics in Paul*, Watson first argues that the primary reason for non-conformity among the contributors "is that Paul is simply not a storyteller."[157] According to Watson, Paul's gospel "is not in itself a 'story.'"[158] That is, while Paul draws on the OT stories, he does not connect his gospel to those stories in an organic manner. Instead, Watson believes that Paul simply references the OT stories in order to explain various aspects of the gospel. Paul is an interpreter of the OT stories but does not retell the stories or extend the OT stories to

---

153. Ibid., 495.
154. Ibid., 496.
155. See also Wright, "Romans and the Theology of Paul."
156. Wright, *Paul and the Faithfulness of God*, 506.
157. Watson, "Is There a Story," 232.
158. Ibid., 234.

incorporate the gospel. Thus, there is no metanarrative in Paul's writings running from Adam through Israel to the gospel message. Paul merely uses individual stories "with the sole aim of uncovering their testimony to a divine act."[159] According to Watson, there are stories, but not *one story*.

This construal of Paul's use of the OT stories raises a further issue of definition: what is the gospel? If Paul's gospel is not a story, then what is it? Watson holds back from detailed exposition, but does offer a hint in response to the narrative approach. He writes,

> The Pauline gospel announces a definitive, unsurpassable divine incursion into the world…that both establishes the new axis around which the entire world thereafter revolves and discloses the original meaning of the world as determined in the pretemporal counsel of God.[160]

Clearly this statement resonates with the apocalyptic approach as described above since those from the apocalyptic school typically see the gospel as narrative-breaking rather than narrative-completing.[161] Thus, for Watson, rather than story, the gospel is a singular event that supersedes the concept of story. It is punctillar in nature and cannot be thought of in narrative terms.

In response, a number of points can be made. First, one may ask how exactly the gospel could be articulated without the use of story. That is, even the supposed non-narrative form noted above seems to include a story: the story of Jesus. One could scarcely announce Paul's gospel apart from the story of the death and resurrection of Jesus. Indeed, Watson holds that the gospel is a "the singular divine saving action" but actions are most naturally expressed in the form of stories.[162]

Second, Watson seems at times to misunderstand the basic tenets of the narrative approach. For example, in his criticism of Campbell's essay on Rom 8, Watson complains that the incarnation and death of Christ are mentioned in Rom 8:3, but the story between these two events

---

159. Ibid., 239.

160. Ibid., 232.

161. For example, Martyn, *Theological Issues*, 221, argues, "For Paul, then, there are no through-trains from the scriptural, patriarchal traditions and the perceptive criteria to the gospel of God's Son."

162. Watson, "Is There a Story," 232.

is completely absent.¹⁶³ For Watson, this means that Paul does not intend to evoke the wider story of Jesus, but only draws attention to individual events. However, this seems to miss a fundamental aspect of the narrative approach: allusions to the stories are intended to evoke the wider narratives. That is, Paul need not (re)tell the entire story in order to evoke the story in his argument. Indeed, parts of the evoked stories make little sense apart from the wider story, especially in relation to the story of Jesus. As noted above, Wright believes the references to the OT stories (and the connection of the gospel to those stories) are indicative of Paul's worldview.¹⁶⁴ Worldviews are typically implicit, but are not therefore non-existent. Narrative in Paul functions in the same manner: beneath the surface, but importantly present.

Third, Watson seems to argue against the narrative approach while simultaneously admitting to Paul's widespread use of the OT narratives. For example, he writes, "this [Paul's] gospel does align itself with a prior 'story,' encompassing both the creation of the world and the history of Israel."¹⁶⁵ However, since these are not Paul's stories, Paul cannot be said to be a storyteller. It seems difficult to imagine the way in which the OT stories are correlated to Paul's gospel if Paul's gospel is not in some sense the completion or climax of the prior stories. Watson appears to draw conclusions that do not necessarily follow from the evidence he provides.¹⁶⁶

Conclusion

In this book, I will use a narrative approach similar to that of Wright and Hays.¹⁶⁷ With Hays, I argue that allusions and echoes point to wider

163. Ibid., 233.

164. Wright, *Paul and the Faithfulness of God*, 463.

165. Watson, "Is There a Story," 234.

166. In addition to Watson's response essay, *Narrative Dynamics* contains a number of opinions of the narrative approach, some critical, some complimentary. I have noted some of the essays in the discussion above, but it is beyond the scope of the present section to evaluate the thirteen essays individually. See Hays, "Is Paul's Gospel Narratable?" for a thorough assessment of the book.

167. Three other approaches to narrative in Paul are worthy of mention. First, Wagner, *Heralds*, was mentioned above. Broadly speaking, Wagner follows Hays's approach to narrative. Second, Gignilliat, *Paul and Isaiah's Servants*, argues that Paul reads a narrative movement in Isa 40–66. This narrative moves from Israel, to the Servant, finalizing around the servants of the Servant. According to Gignilliat, Paul identifies Jesus as the Servant and Paul, along with other followers of Jesus, as the

narrative contexts in Paul's writings and that there is a basic narrative substructure running through the epistles. With Wright, I emphasize the metanarrative that links the OT stories into one coherent story. Paul extends the story to include the story of Jesus and the story of the church and union with Christ as an important aspect of this story. Against Hays, I will seek to show exegetically that the concept of covenant is much more significant in Paul's narrative theology than he allows. This will be important in understanding Paul's narrative movement from the OT stories to union with Christ.

The above discussion, along with the discussion of Paul's use of the OT in the previous section, is intended to give a basic rationale for the narrative methodology employed in this book. That is, I have argued that the narrative approach, particularly with a metanarrative in mind, is a plausible approach to Paul's theology. The chapters that follow seek to demonstrate the fruitfulness of the narrative approach in explicating union with Christ in Romans.

THE HONOR/SHAME MOTIF

A further distinguishing feature of the approach taken in this book is the attention given to honor/shame motif in Romans. The exegetical analysis offered throughout this book will show that Paul often frames his discussion in terms of honor and shame, especially related to union with Christ. Throughout much of the history of interpretation, scholars typically emphasize justification, guilt, law, and the like and sometimes neglected themes of glory, honor, and shame. The argument here will show that when one recognizes the importance of union with Christ in Romans, it will lead to a complementary recognition of the honor/shame motif.

A few recent scholars recognize the importance of the honor/shame motif in Romans.[168] Jewett gives particular attention to the motif

---

servants of the Servant. Gignilliat's approach has affinities with Hays in that he sees a narrative movement within Paul's use of the OT, but he also draws on the canonical approach of Brevard Childs and Christopher Seitz. Finally, Beale, *New Testament Biblical Theology*, nuances Hays's intertextual approach to include a metanarrative within the OT and NT. As such, Beale explicates the theology of the NT as a narrative continuation and fulfillment of the OT storyline. Of these three approaches, Beale's has the closest affinity with my approach, but Wagner and Gignilliat do not necessary stand in opposition.

168. Moxnes, "Honor and Righteousness"; Moxnes, "Honor, Shame, and the Outside World"; Jewett, "Honor and Shame in the Argument of Romans"; Jewett, *Romans*;

throughout his commentary. However, the primary emphasis in Jewett and others is on the social aspect of honor and shame within first century Roman culture. While this is not to be denied and indeed plays a role in Paul's use of the motif, the emphasis of this book is Paul's use of honor and shame with regard to 1) one's standing before God and 2) one's status as a member of the new covenant community.[169] Further, particular to the argument offered here is the use of honor and shame in Paul's exposition of union with Christ in Romans. In short, Paul presents union with Christ as a restoration of the shared glory of God, which was lost through the sin of Adam. This will be substantiated in the exegetical argument.

INTRODUCTION TO THE ARGUMENT AND SUMMARY OF CHAPTERS

The argument of this book will be made through exegetical analysis of Romans and will proceed in two steps. First, the study will begin with an analysis of the use of Adam and Israel narratives in Romans, arguing that these OT stories are closely related and together form the background for union with Christ. I will seek to show that whenever Paul alludes to Adam, an additional allusion to Israel will be found in the near context. Methodologically, Paul's allusions to Adam will be the starting point since there are relatively few allusions to Adam as compared to allusions to Israel.[170] This allows the investigation to focus more narrowly on those passages in which both Adam and Israel are included. Next, Paul's discussion of union with Christ will be examined with particular attention given to the way in which he builds this discussion upon the allusions to Adam and Israel. I will argue that union with Christ is closely related

---

Longenecker, *Introducing*, 330–37.

169. One should not strictly dichotomize the theological and social aspects of honor and shame. The point here is that within the argument of this book, more attention will be given to the theological aspects and the way in which this applies to the social situation among the Roman Christians. That is, the concept of union with Christ will be shown to include the notion of restored honor and this restoration is equal among all those who are "in Christ." Thus, the theological (restoration of honor in Christ) affects the social (equality in Christ). See Wu, *Saving God's Face*.

170. This methodological decision also limits the discussion of Paul's use of the OT narratives to Rom 1–8 since these chapters contain all but one of the allusions to Adam. There is an additional allusion in Rom 16, but this particular use has little impact on the overall argument of the letter and, thus, to the overall argument of this book.

to the Adam and Israel narratives such that Paul's doctrine (and indeed the argument of the entire letter) cannot be adequately understood apart from his use of these OT narratives. Finally, a concluding chapter will summarize the argument and reflect on the fruitfulness of the chosen methodology.

Chapters 2 and 3 will seek to establish the foundation for the argument by showing the consistent use of the Adam and Israel narratives through Romans. Chapter 2 will examine allusions to Adam in Romans 1-4 and show the way in which Paul weaves Israel's story into the discussion. Chapter 3 will continue the investigation by examining the Adam and Israel narratives in Romans 5-8. By drawing on these OT stories, I argue that Paul believes all people to share a basic solidarity in Adam and that this union transcends ethnic identity. This then provides the OT foundation for Paul's argument for new covenant unity in Christ.

Chapters 4 and 5 will revisit previously studied texts, this time focusing on union with Christ language. Direct discussion of union with Christ, as well as allusions to the doctrine, will be studied. Chapter 4 will return to Romans 1-4 and show the way in which Paul links union with Christ to the Adam and Israel narratives in those chapters. Chapter 5 will do the same for Romans 5-8. These chapters will argue for a clear and close connection between the OT narratives and union with Christ and that Paul exploits this connection for his argument.[171]

Chapter 6 will briefly examine remaining union with Christ passages in Romans 9-16. While there are no commonly recognized allusions to Adam in these chapters,[172] the OT narratives were most likely in the background here as well. That is, Paul's references to union with Christ in Romans 9-16 are consistent with his previous references, which were all closely connected to the Adam and Israel stories. These connections will be explored in this chapter.

Chapter 7 will conclude the book by briefly reflecting on the results of the exegetical analysis.

---

171. It should be noted that the division of Romans into chapters 1-4 and 5-8 in chapters 2 and 3 and in chapters 4 and 5 is not intended to imply that Paul's argument is structured in this way as some interpreters have done. It will be shown that Paul's argument is much more fluid than to allow for a neat division. See especially the discussion on Rom 2 in chapter 4 below.

172. Except for Rom 16:18-20.

2

The Story of Adam (and Israel) in Romans 1–4

INTRODUCTION

THE ROLE OF ADAM within Paul's theology has been an issue of debate in recent scholarship, with some scholars arguing for a central role for Adam while others believe him to be of minimal importance. Nevertheless, even a minimalist approach that only sees references to Adam where he is explicitly mentioned would note the importance of Rom 5:12–21, particularly related to the Christology of the epistle.[1] Among those who acknowledge references to Adam in other places, no consensus exists as to their exact meaning and importance. In this chapter and the next, I will argue for the importance of Adam in the argument of Romans by giving particular attention to allusions and echoes to the narratives of Genesis within the text and in conversation with opposing views. Moreover, I will seek to demonstrate the importance of the story of Adam in relation to union with Christ.

On the other hand, it cannot be said that Adam is the primary OT character throughout the epistle. Indeed, most commentators recognize the importance of Israel's story in the argument. This fact raises a basic question: what is the relationship between references to Adam and references to Israel in Romans? In addition, what role do these narratives play

---

1. I will engage minimalist positions in the exegetical analysis below.

within Paul's overall argument? While it is obvious that the OT narratives play a fundamental role in the letter, the way in which these various narratives relate needs to be explored further. The purpose of this chapter and the next is to explore Paul's use of the stories of Adam and Israel in relationship to one another and as potential OT background for union with Christ.[2]

The chapter title places Israel in parenthesis to allude to the argument to be presented. Throughout Romans, Paul makes both explicit and implicit references to Adam, focusing primarily on Adam's sin. However, in the near context of each allusion, Paul also alludes to some aspect of Israel's story, usually focusing on Israel's sin. The purpose of this juxtaposition seems to be to place Israel within the realm of "in Adam," thus showing 1) that all people, regardless of ethnic identity, are sinners and 2) that there is a basic unity among those who do not believe in Jesus as the Messiah. These points are foundational for the argument of this book: the story of Adam, along with the story of Israel, is the OT background for the concept of union with Christ in the epistle. That is, these OT narratives have a forward-pointing outlook that Paul views as being fulfilled in union with Christ.

In this chapter, I will argue that taking a narrative approach to the study of Adam in Romans sheds considerable light on the importance of Gen 1–3 for Paul's argument. Specifically, I will argue that the story of Adam (and Israel) gives a clear OT background for the concept of union with Christ because the story of Adam is the essential starting-point of the story of God's people, which Paul believes climaxes in Christ. Of course, no discussion of the true people of God can disregard Israel. Paul includes Israel in the discussion through allusions to Israel's story woven into his use of the Adam narrative. Thus, the narratives of Adam and Israel cannot be read in isolation from one another, especially when one observes Paul's use of these narratives in Romans.

As will be noted below, scholars have often noticed the allusions and echoes of the Adam and Israel stories that will be studied in this chapter.

---

2. It should be noted at this juncture that it is not the purpose of this chapter (or this book) to examine every reference to Israel within Romans. Rather, methodologically, the argument below will begin with possible references to Adam, seeking to show the way in which Paul weaves Israel's story, particularly the story of Israel's failure in the wilderness, into the story of Adam to present one unified story of human failure to live in communion with God. This unified story will then be shown to point forward to Christ and, specifically, to the ultimate rectifying of humanity's failure in union with Christ.

However, none have consistently put these allusions together with a narrative approach that is being utilized in this book. In addition, while these allusions have been analyzed before, scholars have yet to see the connection between Paul's use of the OT narratives and his understanding of union with Christ, particularly as it relates to the argument of Romans. Thus, this chapter and the next seek to provide a fresh exegetical analysis of the relevant texts 1) using a narrative approach to Pauline theology; 2) using the tools of intertextual analysis of Paul's use of the OT; and 3) with an eye toward union with Christ.

Interestingly, the story of Adam (and Israel) provides a mostly negative background for Paul's understanding of union with Christ. Witherington notes that when Adam is mentioned in Paul's writings, it is almost always in the context of explaining sin or the present state of creation awaiting redemption.[3] For the purposes of this chapter, it will be important to see the sin of Adam in a representational and collective sense. That is, the sin of Adam profoundly impacts those "in Adam." As Dunn writes, "Paul's understanding of man as he now is is heavily influenced by the narratives about Adam in Gen 1–3 and especially the account of Adam's 'fall' in Gen 3."[4] Therefore, it is unsurprising that the Adam story shows up in the early chapters of Romans, even when his name does not appear.

Many interpreters realize this, but fail to give attention to the way Paul draws Israel's story into the story of Adam. Paul evidently saw a close relationship between the two sets of OT narratives and exploits this for the purposes of the letter. This chapter and the next will explore these links exegetically while later chapters will show the connection to union with Christ and the theological significance of them. Indeed, Hays, in responding to the essays in *Narrative Dynamics in Paul*, suggests that one of the primary benefits of the narrative approach is that it can "illuminate the 'participationist' aspects of Paul's soteriology: that is, those who are in Christ receive salvation precisely by being drawn into and conformed to his story, and his life."[5] This is precisely the point to be argued below: a proper understanding of the story of Adam (and Israel) illuminates union with Christ in Romans by providing OT context for the doctrine, which allows one to situate union with Christ in relation to the narrative movement of the OT.

---

3. Witherington, *Paul's Narrative Thought World*, 9.
4. Dunn, *Christology*, 101.
5. Hays, "Is Paul's Gospel Narratable?," 228.

EXEGETICAL ANALYSIS

The following exegetical analysis will proceed through the text of Romans, studying the implicit and explicit references to Adam and the way in which Paul weaves the story of Israel into these allusions. This chapter will focus on Romans 1–4 and the following chapter will continue the discussion with an analysis of Romans 5–8.

Romans 1:18–32

Scholars have detected several allusions to the Adam narrative within Romans. The first allusion often identified is found at the beginning of Paul's exposition of human sin, which occupies much of Rom 1–3. In Rom 1:18–32, there are several key terms and themes that seem to point to the story of creation and fall from Gen 1–3. These terms and themes will be analyzed and shown to indeed evoke the memory of the first stories of the Hebrew canon. At the outset, it should be admitted that the possible allusions and echoes vary in clarity and certainty. Indeed, scholars have pointed other potential backgrounds for Paul's discussion.[6] Westerholm believes Paul to be recalling any number of OT passages that deal with the human predicament without consciously recounting one particular story.[7] While other backgrounds are certainly possible, the exegesis below will argue that he cumulative evidence points to the narratives of Gen 1–3 as the most consistent background of the passage. That is, though other backgrounds are possible, there is a clustering of allusions to Adam that make his story the most likely point of reference. This, in turn, will be shown to contribute to a major part of Paul's argument: the unity of those outside of Christ in Adam.

Further, though the argumentation of Rom 1:18–32 flows, at least in the main contours, like a typical Jewish indictment of Gentile sin, there is a surprising twist embedded within that sets Paul apart from other contemporary writings: there are subtle references to Israel woven into the argument, thus including Jews in the number of those who are subject to the wrath of God. The basic point is that while Gentiles have largely rejected the revelation of God in willful rebellion, Israel is no better off since they too have rebelled against the Creator. Taken together with the

---

6. Objections to the detection of adamic allusions will be addressed below.
7. Westerholm, *Perspectives*, 386.

allusions to Adam, Paul's point becomes clear: all people, Jew and Gentile alike, are "in Adam."

The table below identifies possible allusions to Adam and the OT references.[8]

Table 2.1: Allusions to Genesis in Romans 1:18–32

Romans Reference	Genesis Reference
1:20	1:1
1:23	1:26–28 (Psalm 106:20)
1:25	3
1:26–27	1:27
1:32	2:17

Though these possible allusions vary in clarity and likelihood, the concentration of key terms and themes suggests that Paul indeed had the Adam narrative in mind when he composed these verses.[9] Each of these possible allusions will be briefly studied and summarized in order to show that there is a cohesive story within this passage. In addition, exegetical analysis will clearly demonstrate the subtle inclusion of Israel's story within the argument.

In Rom 1:18–32, Paul begins his extended discourse on the universal human predicament by announcing the coming wrath of God against human sin.[10] In this section, most scholars believe that the primary critique is against Gentile sin, reflecting injunctions similar to those found in other Jewish writings, such as Wis 13–14. However, some scholars see this entire section (1:18—3:20) as an extended dialogue in which Paul engages a hypothetical Jewish interlocutor regarding the truth of the gospel.[11] In any case, Dunn has rightly argued that echoes of the Adam narratives are "significant for the initial setting up of the argument."[12] If,

---

8. This summary of possible allusions is drawn from Adams, "Paul's Story of God," 34–35.

9. The following paragraphs are an expansion of Sun, "Biblical Theology."

10. Campbell, *Deliverance*, 519–47, argues that 1:18–32 is not Paul's own view, but that of a false teacher. According to this interpretation, Paul enumerates the view of this teacher in order to destroy it. For Campbell, this is a part of Paul's rhetorical strategy to combat false teachings in Rome. While fiercely argued, few follow this approach. The exegesis that follows offers an alternative and preferable reading.

11. Byrne, *Romans*, 62–63; Kruse, *Romans*, 82–85; Käsemann, *Romans*, 34.

12. Dunn, *Romans*, 1:53.

as Käsemann argues, this section "deals with the totality of the cosmos" and "humanity as such," an allusion to the Adam narratives fits perfectly within the argument.[13]

In Rom 1:20, Paul explicitly mentions "the creation of the world" (κτίσεως κόσμου).[14] It is difficult to imagine that a Jewish writer such as Paul could produce these words without having the Genesis account of creation in mind. The point of the passage is that all people have failed to glorify God. Verse 20 shows that people are "without excuse" (ἀναπολογήτους) because the power of God has been revealed through creation. Though Dunn believes the language used here reflects an attempt to build "an apologetic bridge to non-Jewish religious philosophy,"[15] Hooker notes that the wording used by Paul here "suggests that Paul is thinking in particular of God's creative activity."[16] Thus, at the outset of the argument, Paul has called to mind the Genesis story of creation. This serves to set the entire section within a creational (and therefore adamic) framework. Further, the preposition ἀπό implies the on-going significance of the statement.[17] That is, God's divine attributes have been plainly revealed since the creation of the world and this revelation continues into the present. This signals the continued importance of Adam's story, which Paul will show to be the story of all humanity.

Further, in 1:23, Paul, enumerating the most heinous of human sin—idolatry—uses the term "image" (εἰκόνος), which is the same term used in the LXX of Gen 1:27. Hooker points out that in every other use of the term within Paul's writings, the reference is always to the image of God, alluding to the early chapters of Genesis.[18] This would seem to indicate that apart from convincing evidence to the contrary, one should assume a similar meaning here. No such evidence exists, particularly since the term is surrounded by creational language in the context. That is, the numerous allusions to creation both before and after verse 23 sets the use of the term εἰκόνος within a creational context. Thus, the common theological use of the term (image of God) along with the creational context point to an adamic meaning.

13. Käsemann, *Romans*, 33.
14. All quotations from the Greek NT are from *NA28*.
15. Dunn, *Romans*, 1:58.
16. Hooker, "Adam in Romans 1," 299. See also Jewett, *Romans*, 155–56. Contra Kruse, *Romans*, 97.
17. Linebaugh, "Announcing," 230.
18. Hooker, "Adam in Romans 1," 298.

Commentators often point to a clear allusion to Ps 106:20 in this verse. Note the parallels:

Table 2.2: Textual Links between Romans 1:23 and Psalm 106:20

Romans 1:23	Psalm 106:20 (LXX 105:20)
καὶ ἤλλαξαν τὴν δόξαν τοῦ ἀφθάρτου θεοῦ ἐν ὁμοιώματι εἰκόνος φθαρτοῦ ἀνθρώπου καὶ πετεινῶν καὶ τετραπόδων καὶ ἑρπετῶν.	καὶ ἠλλάξαντο τὴν δόξαν αὐτῶν ἐν ὁμοιώματι μόσχου ἔσθοντος χόρτον.

Interestingly, Paul seems to have expanded the OT text and imported the term "image" from Genesis.[19] In context, Ps 106:20 reflects on the golden calf incident of Exod 32. The addition of the image language may be intended to evoke the memory of the story of Adam's sin in Gen 3.[20] If so, Paul uses OT language for Israel's idolatry and universalizes it to include all humanity. The effect would be to root the human predicament in the sin of Adam and make it clear that all people—Jew and Gentile alike—share in the problem of sin. While the section may primarily concern Gentile sin, the use of Ps 106 subtly includes Jews in the number of idol-worshipers. Thus, it could be said that Israel has been caught up in the tragic story of Adam.[21] Put otherwise, Paul is interpreting the story of the golden calf in light of the story of Adam's sin, thus demonstrating a close relationship between the two OT stories. Israel's sin is pictured as a repetition of Adam's sin.

Paul's use of Ps 106:20 in the midst of his analysis of the human condition serves to set his understanding in stark contrast to the parallel analysis found in Wis 13–15.[22] The discussion in Wisdom follows much the same pattern and contains similar allusions to the creation account. However, the author of Wisdom is clear that the idolatrous state of humanity applies only to Gentiles. In Wis 15:1–4, the author makes the distinction between Jew and Gentile clear, writing in verse 2, "For even if we sin we are yours, knowing your power; but we will not sin, because we

---

19. Ibid., 297; So also Käsemann, *Romans*, 45.

20. The mention of "reptiles" (ἑρπετῶν) may also allude to the serpent of Gen 3.

21. Käsemann, *Romans*, 46, argues that Paul saw the OT narratives as interconnected typologically, pointing both forward and backward.

22. Similar indictments can be found in Philo, *On the Decalogue*, 52–81; and *The Sibylline Oracles* 3:8–45.

know that you acknowledge us as yours." The "we" is the Jewish people, who "will not sin" as the Gentiles in their idolatry.[23] Thus, while Wisdom divides the world according to ethnicity, Paul argues that Jews are no less "in Adam" than Gentiles.[24]

The echo in Rom 1:23 may also include Jer 2:11 ("my people have changed their glory for something that does not profit"), which would confirm the point.[25] The setting of the Jeremiah passage is impending exile and would evoke the memory of judgment among Jewish hearers or those who were familiar with the OT.[26] Again, this serves to link together the stories of Adam and Israel. Emphasizing the differences between Rom 1:18–32 and Wisdom of Solomon, Linebaugh aptly summarizes the point: "Whereas Wisdom of Solomon's polemic serves to reinforce the anthropological distinction between Jew and Gentile (qua non-idolaters and idolaters), Paul reworks the aniconic tradition to establish the essential unity of humanity."[27] This serves Paul's purposes in setting the stage for his exposition of the unity of all those who are "in Christ."

Romans 1:23 also links the concepts of glory and image, which will be important to the argument below. While the language of "exchange" is clearly derived from Ps 106, the addition of the term "image" juxtaposed to "glory" may point back to the Adam narrative of Gen 3.[28] This would mean that Israel's sin in the wilderness is a recapitulation of Adam's sin. Adam exchanged the glory of being created in the image of God for idolatry when he listened to a created being (the serpent) instead of the voice of God. Likewise, Israel exchanged the glory of being the people of God for idolatry in creating the golden calf.[29]

---

23. See the analysis in Watson, *Paul and the Hermeneutics*, 406–11.

24. While Wisdom of Solomon makes this clear ethnic distinction, such a view is not uniform in Jewish literature. Barclay points out *4 Ezra* and *Liber Antiquitatum Biblicarum* as examples of Jewish writings that incorporate Israel in the general sinfulness of humanity. See Barclay, *Paul and the Gift*, 462–63.

25. Unless otherwise noted, all English quotations of the Hebrew Bible and Apocrypha are from the NRSV.

26. Keesmaat, *Paul and His Story*, 85.

27. Linebaugh, "Announcing the Human," 217.

28. I will argue below that in Rom 3:23 Paul draws on Jewish tradition that presented the result of Adam's sin as the loss of glory.

29. Postell, *Adam as Israel*, 37, notes a number of textual parallels between the account of Adam's sin in Gen 3 and the golden calf incident in Exod 32. Postell, drawing on the work of Tvi Erlich, argues that this was intentional shaping by the biblical author such that the theological significance of the covenant breach by Israel is to

Finally, the mention of "birds, four-footed animals, and reptiles" almost certainly echoes the creation account, where God gives humanity dominion over all created things (Gen 1:26). Moreover, the list of animals in Rom 1:23 fits the pattern and vocabulary of the animals listed in Gen 1:20–24 (πετεινόν—Gen 1:20; τετράποδος—Gen 1:24; ἑρπετόν—Gen 1:24).[30] This serves to confirm that Paul indeed had the Adam narratives in mind when he composed Rom 1. Jewett notes that the listing of various animals as idols serves to universalize Paul's argument, moving beyond Jewish idolatry to that of all humanity, "which reaches back to the fall of the human race."[31]

That the story of Adam's sin is in mind here is confirmed by an additional allusion to Gen 3 in Rom 1:25. There, Paul says that humans have "exchanged the truth of God for a lie and worshiped and served the creature rather than the Creator" (μετήλλαξαν τὴν ἀλήθειαν τοῦ θεοῦ ἐν τῷ ψεύδει καὶ ἐσεβάσθησαν καὶ ἐλάτρευσαν τῇ κτίσει παρὰ τὸν κτίσαντα). Clearly Gen 3 portrays the first couple as believing the words of the serpent over the words spoken by God and thereby exchanging the truth for a lie. Additionally, Adam and Eve chose to serve the serpent ("the creature") rather than the Creator.[32] The repetition of the verb "exchange" (here μετήλλαξαν) links back to verse 23 and further expands on its meaning.

The echoes of Adam continue in Rom 1:26–27. Having already alluded multiple times to the creation narratives, Paul here uses the terms "male" and "female" in close context, again echoing the creation of humanity. In these verses, Paul yet again uses the term "exchange" (here again μετήλλαξαν), which calls to mind the exchanging of glory for idols in verse 23 and the truth for a lie in verse 25. Paul's meaning seems to be that homosexual relations are distortions of the Creator's original intentions for human sexuality. The use of "male" and "female" within these verses evokes the creation account, showing the sinfulness of humanity is corporate and universal.

The final echo of the Adam narratives in Rom 1 is found in verse 32. Here Paul echoes Gen 2:17, linking disobedience of known commands with death. His argument to this point has shown that the wrath of God

---

be understood in light of the sin of Adam. For the present argument, Postell's thesis would seem to be upheld by Paul's use of Scripture in Rom 1.

30. Hyldahl, "Reminiscence," 286–87.
31. Jewett, *Romans*, 161.
32. Grieb, *Story of Romans*, 27.

is coming against all those who have rejected their created purpose: the worship of the one true God. Verse 32 closes the section with a reference to Genesis in order to show that this has been true from the beginning of time.[33] Again, this also serves to universalize the human predicament. In other words, the story of Adam is part of every person's story, both individually and corporately. The allusions to Israel's sin serve to emphasize that Gentiles are not the only people with a sin problem. Indeed, linking together the failure of Israel in the wilderness with the sin of Adam highlights the sin of the golden calf as a heightening of the problem of sin.

The allusions proposed above vary in certainty, but collectively meet the criteria of multiplicity, recurrence, and thematic coherence. In alluding to the early chapters of the Hebrew Bible, Paul is showing that all humanity is caught up in the story of Adam: one created in the image of God, yet through sinful rebellion fallen from the original status of glory. The stage is set for the rest of his argument and the crucial role of the concept of union with Christ. Wright has argued that in this section of Romans, Paul is retelling the stories of Gen 3 and Israel in the wilderness.[34] However, this is no mere retelling of the stories. Rather, Paul is using a narrative technique to show that all people, Jew and Gentile alike, are a part of the larger story of fallen humanity.[35] This point will prove important in understanding the OT background for Paul's later discussion of union with Christ.

Though the numerous verbal allusions to Gen 1–3 seem to make the echoes of Adam clear throughout Rom 1, some scholars deny the presence of such connections. Against the interpretation offered here, Fitzmyer believes that "the alleged echoes of the Adam stories in Genesis are simply non-existent."[36] He claims that the text of Rom 1:18–32 contains no allusion to Gen 1 and that supposed allusions to Gen 2–3 can only be detected in light of much later rabbinic literature. Yet Fitzmyer himself recognizes the close parallels between Rom 1 and Wis 13–15, which, as will be noted below, evokes the stories of creation and

33. Dunn, *Romans*, 1:69.

34. Wright, "Letter to the Romans," 432–33.

35. Dunn, *Paul*, 93, goes further, arguing that Paul views the exodus and Israel's sin of the golden calf are pictured as a new creation and fall of sorts. Whether or not this is true, the point remains clear: in arguing for the universality of sinfulness in Adam, Paul draws on Israel's story in order to show that the Jews are included as those who are "in Adam."

36. Fitzmyer, *Romans*, 274.

fall. Moreover, while Fitzmyer forcefully denies the presence of adamic allusions, he offers little by way of preferable alternative interpretations. Despite the numerous allusions detailed in the above argument, he argues that Paul shows no influence of the opening chapters of the Hebrew Bible.[37] He seems to ignore the mention of creation in Rom 1:20 and seeks to place Paul's argumentation within the context of first century Greco-Roman culture apart from Paul's Jewish worldview. With regard to the term εἰκόνος in Rom 1:23, Fitzmyer denies that this could possibly reference Gen 1:26 because Rom 1:23 uses a different term for "likeness" (ὁμοίωμα) than the LXX (ὁμοιόω).[38] However, the two words are clearly related and a slight adjustment does not render the echo non-existent. In addition, Fitzmyer holds that Rom 1:18–32 is strictly about "the totality of pagan society" and that the allusions to Ps 106:20 and Jer 2:11 should not be taken as Paul's inclusion of the Jews in the indictment. Instead, Paul is merely applying principles from the history of Israel to the Gentile world.[39] According to Fitzmyer, Paul only turns his attention to Jewish sin in chapter 2. Such an interpretation artificially divides the argumentation of Rom 1 and 2 and misses Paul's point: there is no distinction between Jew and Gentile since all stand equally sinful before God. In short, Fitzmyer denies the presence of Adam but fails to provide a convincing alternative while giving little attention to the actual text of the proposed allusions.

Stowers launches perhaps the most aggressive attack on adamic allusions in Rom 1, concluding that such interpretations are "profoundly unconvincing."[40] Throughout his "rereading" of Romans, Stowers places a heavy emphasis on the way in which he believes the original audience would have heard the letter. For Stowers, the audience consisted of Gentiles.[41] As such, Rom 1:18–32 must be read in light of the cultural values

---

37. Ibid.

38. Ibid., 283.

39. Fitzmyer, *Romans*, 270–71.

40. Stowers, *Rereading*, 86. Likewise, Keck, *Romans*, 63, dismisses the Adam narrative as background without adequately dealing with the verbal allusions. Esler, "Sodom Tradition," argues that the background for Rom 1 is the Sodom stories rather than the Adam narratives. However, this interpretation lacks clear textual correlations and fails to explain the numerous allusions to Gen 1–3.

41. Stowers gives much weight to the concept of encoded (discerned through the text) and empirical (discerned through historical reconstruction) audience. See Stowers, *Rereading*, 21–29.

The Story of Adam (and Israel) in Romans 1–4   51

that gave rise to such texts.[42] He argues that "the first half of 1:18—2:16 reflects not the Adamic fall but a Jewish account of human degeneration into the non-Jewish peoples."[43] For Stowers, Paul's argument draws not on the Adam narratives, but on more general degradation stories from the ancient world. The Greco-Roman world largely viewed the contemporary world as a sort of "fall" from primitivism, which was believed to be an "ideal" past age.[44] Further, Stowers argues that the supposed Jewish background for an adamic interpretation of Rom 1:18–32 simply does not exist.[45]

Stowers is correct that Rom 1 argues primarily that Gentiles are guilty of sinful rebellion and that the Jewish people as a whole have followed the way of non-Jews in sin. Yet his argument that a Jew steeped in the OT would do so without reference to Genesis fails to convince, especially considering the numerous verbal connections. Instead, Stowers prefers to interpret in light of possible Greco-Roman cultural and literary connections with far less textual support than the allusions to Adam argued for above. In particular, Stowers emphasizes the "quest for self-mastery" in the ancient world, arguing that in Romans, Paul is putting forth Christ as the one through whom self-mastery is attained.[46] Such a reading is far more speculative (and individualistic) than the case offered for adamic allusions through a close reading of the text. Though some cultural and literary overlap is possible, it remains the case that Paul quoted and alluded to the OT as authoritative throughout Romans (and other letters) while never quoting or unambiguously drawing on Greco-Roman sources. Thus, interpreters should work from the assumption that the OT normally provides the primary background for Paul's argumentation.[47] Stowers admits that "there is no evidence that Paul read or knew . . . any other Hellenistic degeneration story."[48] It is, by contrast, abundantly clear that he knew the stories of Gen 1–3. In short, Stowers

---

42. Ibid., 84.
43. Ibid., 107.
44. Ibid., 85.
45. Ibid., 87.
46. Ibid., 42.
47. This statement is not intended to claim the OT as the *only* possible background for Paul's writing. Rather, the OT is the *primary* background, especially when textual evidence points to OT stories/passages as I am arguing Rom 1:18–32 demonstrates.
48. Stowers, *Rereading*, 99.

seems to give more prominence to unreferenced Greco-Romans sources over against referenced OT sources.

Stowers mentions several Jewish texts, arguing that Paul's contemporary Jewish writers did not view Adam's sin in the way an adamic interpretation of Romans 1 would seem to demand. Though he criticizes others for their selectivity in only mentioning isolated texts that support their position, he is no less selective in his analysis. For example, he argues that *Jubilees* 8–9 shows the decline of humanity as "the division of earth into homelands," but ignores that chapter 4 of the same book presents Eden as the place where evil entered the world and describes the death of Adam because of his sin.[49] He also asserts that while texts such as *4 Ezra* and *2 Baruch* show interest in the effects of Adam's sin, this reflects a later Judaism that "would have been unimaginable to the apostle."[50] Yet this assumes that no Jew prior to the destruction of the temple thought of Adam's sin as affecting his progeny and that Paul could not have read Gen 1–3 in this manner. Stowers draws heavily on Levison's analysis,[51] but as will be seen below, Levison himself believes Paul to be alluding to Adam in Rom 1. In short, though Jewish thought on Adam was neither uniform nor a primary topic of theological discussion, it does not follow that Paul could not have drawn on the stories of Gen 1–3 in Rom 1, especially considering the textual and contextual evidence offered above.

As noted above, most interpreters recognize the similarities between Rom 1:18–32 and Wis 13–14. Interestingly, while Paul subtly rejects the assessment of Wisdom with regard to the differences between Jews and Gentiles, both Paul and the author of Wisdom hold that sin originated through Adam. In Wis 2:23–24, the author argues that though God created people for "incorruption" and "in his image," death came into the world "though the devil's envy" resulting in the death of all who "belong to his company." While Adam is not named here, creation in the image of God unquestionably refers to Adam[52] and the identification of "the devil's envy" as the vehicle of death's entry into the world probably refers

---

49. Ibid., 89.
50. Ibid., 88.
51. Stowers draws on Levison, *Portraits*.
52. Levison, *Portraits*, 50, believes Wis 2:23 to contain an allusion to Gen 1:26–27. It is not my intention to argue for a particular meaning of this passage, but only to point out that Wisdom has an adamic background in several passages. Given the thematic similarities with Rom 1:18–32, it is plausible that Paul also is reflecting on Gen 1–3.

to the story of Gen 3.⁵³ Thus, while Paul disagrees with Wisdom in regard to Israel's sin, it would seem that the human predicament is a result of Adam's sin in both accounts. Further, both texts do so through the use of allusion to Genesis account. The crucial point for Paul is that, unlike the author of Wisdom, he views Israel as no less "in Adam" than the Gentiles. Thus, while Stowers argues that Wis 10:1 describes Adam as "saved from transgression," he ignores the mention of Adam's sin earlier in the book.

In addition to Wisdom of Solomon, Levison demonstrates numerous verbal and thematic parallels between Rom 1 and the Greek *Life of Adam and Eve* (*GLAE*).⁵⁴ He argues that while the text of Gen 1–3 is the scriptural background for Rom 1:18–32, Paul's interpretation of the OT passages exists within the matrix of Jewish development of the text, which is illustrated in the *GLAE*. De Jonge and Tromp assert that the embellishments on the story of Adam and Eve's sin in Gen 3 found in *GLAE* "are probably not the invention of the authors of *GLAE*, but part and parcel of the stories about the fall of the protoplasts as they knew it."⁵⁵ Thus, while *GLAE* may not have preceded Paul and was probably not known to him in its written form, both were drawing from a shared interpretive heritage and tradition.⁵⁶ Nevertheless, Macaskill has argued that given the ambiguity of the provenance of *GLAE*, with regard to the discussion of adamic backgrounds to Paul, it "probably ought to be taken out of the equation altogether."⁵⁷ Such argumentation does not taken into account Levison's study on the many parallels between Rom 1 and *GLAE* as well as the likelihood of a shared tradition. Further, it simply assumes the argument for Christian origins of *GLAE*, which while probable, is not

---

53. Though see Levison, *Portraits*, 51–52, who sees this as an allusion to Gen 4, the story of Cain killing Abel. However, given that the author alludes to the creation of Adam in 2:23, the more likely allusion is to Gen 3.

54. Levison, "Adam and Eve."

55. de Jonge and Tromp, *Life of Adam and Eve*, 48.

56. Ibid., 65–75, surveys the evidence for Jewish and Christian origins for *GLAE*. While admitting that a definitive answer to the question of origins is difficult, they hold to a Christian provenance for the written text. However, they believe that it was composed using "traditional material available to them [the authors of *GLAE*], much of which was already of Jewish origin" (74). Therefore, one can reasonably assume a common (Jewish) tradition behind both *GLAE* and Paul. Alternatively, other scholars believe *GLAE* to be a translation of an original Hebrew text written by a Jew. See Johnson, "Life of Adam and Eve," 251–52.

57. Macaskill, *Union with Christ*, 141.

universally accepted. Indeed, even if influenced by Christians, Levison dates *GLAE* as first century to early second century.[58]

Particularly important for the argument here is that both Paul and the *GLAE* link sin to the loss of glory. In *GLAE* 20–21, both Adam and Eve describe the result of their disobedience as being "estranged" from glory. Eve refers to this as the "glory with which I was clothed" (20:2) while Adam blames Eve, saying "You have estranged me from the glory of God" (21:6). As Levison notes, this closely resembles Paul's language of exchange in Rom 1:23 and 1:25.[59] Thus, in a retelling and expansion of the story of Adam and Eve, *GLAE* views the nature and results of Adam's sin much the same as Paul in Rom 1.[60] This is not to say that Paul and the authors of *GLAE* wrote with the same purpose or read the story of Gen 3 in the exact same manner. The point is that the *GLAE* demonstrates similar themes of sin, glory, and the effects of the fall on all people.[61]

Finally, it must be asked: if Adam is important to the argument of Rom 1:18–32, why does Paul not explicitly name him? In other words, for some interpreters, the adamic shape of the passage is mere speculation since Adam is not more clearly named. In response, two points could be made. First, as noted in the methodological discussion in chapter 1, allusive argumentation is not uncommon in Paul or in other Jewish writings. The OT prophetic literature is filled with allusions to the exodus and other earlier stories.[62] That Paul would draw on the Adam narratives without explicitly naming him does not itself rule out the possibility of the allusion. Second, Paul most likely alludes to Adam rather than naming him because this manner of argumentation best fits his purposes. The indictment here is not against Adam, but all people. As Linebaugh points out, having made a distinction between the "Jew and the Greek" in 1:16, Paul refers to the recipients of wrath in 1:18 as ἄνθρωπος, thus encompassing both Jews and Gentiles.[63] Thus, the allusive nature of Paul's

---

58. Levison, "Adam and Eve, Life of," 64–66.

59. Levison, "Adam and Eve in Romans 1:18–25," 531.

60. *GLAE* 39 contains a promise from God for the restoration of glory after the death of Adam. This could provide some background for the restoration of glory in Christ, which I will argue Paul has in mind in Rom 8.

61. Indeed, de Jonge and Tromp, *The Life and Adam and Eve*, 49, identify the purpose of *GLAE* as providing an encouraging message of hope. In contrast, Paul presents an argument for universal sinfulness in Rom 1.

62. For example, many note the importance of the exodus in Isaiah.

63. Linebaugh, "Announcing the Human," 235–36.

argument allows him to put the emphasis on a particular point: all people are unified in sin (in Adam).

In sum, Rom 1:18–32 begins Paul's indictment of all humanity, arguing that all people, Jew and Gentile, are in sin and thus deserve to experience God's wrath. The numerous allusions to Gen 1–3 within the text as well as the similarities to other Jewish writings make the adamic background probable. Interpreting Rom 1:18–32 in this way reveals Paul's fundamental argument which will be developed further in the following chapters: all people are "in Adam." Paul's use of the Adam narrative shows that the sin problem is universal. Weaving Israel's idolatry into the narrative makes it clear that this includes Jewish people as a part of the problem. Indeed, though a strong can be made for adamic allusions with the text, Rom 1:23 contains a near quotation of Ps 105:20 (LXX), thereby bringing Israel into the story.[64] Within the context of the entire letter, this serves Paul's purposes of church unity by showing that 1) all are sinners, thus none can boast; 2) there is a basic unity among humanity in sin; and 3) there is to be a greater unity among the new humanity in Christ (to be argued in later chapters). Watson aptly argues that Paul draws on Israel's sin within the section in order "to legitimate separation from the Jewish community [by Jewish Christians] and identification with Gentile Christians."[65] In other words, the community of those "in Christ" is to be valued over ethnic identity.[66]

---

64. Levison, "Adam and Eve in Romans 1:18–25," 524–25, argues that interpreting Rom 1:23 as an allusion to Ps 106:20 does not in itself "adequately explain the whole of Paul's assertion." As the above exegesis shows, this is undoubtedly correct. Paul indeed draws on other OT passages, particularly the early chapters of Genesis. However, Levison leaves aside the significance of the allusion to the Psalm in his exposition, namely the subtle, yet clear, inclusion of Israel within the realm of sin in Adam.

65. Watson, *Paul, Judaism, and the Gentiles*, 196.

66. To nuance Watson's point, Paul's intention is to encourage unity in Christ, regardless of ethnic origin. Since both groups (Jews and Gentiles) are equally sinful, hope is only in the redemption in Christ. Continuing to find one's primary identification with one's ethnic group over the community of faith results in a primary identity with those outside of Christ—those "in Adam" rather those "in Christ." Thus, Jews should not identify themselves as Jews *primarily*, but as Christians. Likewise, Gentiles should not identify themselves as Gentiles *primarily*, but as Christians. Identity in Christ trumps all other allegiances. Christians should experience a closer affinity with other Christians, despite cultural differences.

Romans 3:23

Having already alluded to the Adam narratives in Rom 1, Paul again draws on these foundational Jewish stories in Rom 3. If Rom 1 was indeed written with the opening chapters of the Hebrew Bible in mind, it is reasonable to assume that Adam is again echoed in the transitional pericope of Rom 3:21–31. In 3:23, Paul writes:

> πάντες γὰρ ἥμαρτον καὶ ὑστεροῦνται τῆς δόξης τοῦ θεοῦ
> For all sinned and are lacking the glory of God

This verse lies within the context of one of the most important passages of the epistle. Indeed, Luther believed that Rom 3:21–31 was "the chief point, and the very central place of the Epistle, and of the whole Bible."[67] While this is almost certainly an overstatement, this passage is no doubt important since it mentions some of the primary themes of the letter, including righteousness, faith, sin, etc. The presence of an adamic reference here would signal the importance of the story of Adam in Romans.

While this verse does not explicitly name Adam and does not contain a quotation or direct allusion to the creation account of Genesis, many commentators have detected a reference to Adam via the term δόξης (glory). This word is possibly a link to Ps 8, which is a reflection on creation. In support of the existence of an allusion to the Psalm, it may be noted that 1) Paul has interpreted Ps 8 messianically in 1 Cor 15:24–28; 2) this understanding of glory, though not uniform, was present in other Jewish literature; and 3) this interpretation will be shown to fit in the overall context of the passage. These reasons will be substantiated in what follows.

To understand Paul's allusion, a brief analysis of Ps 8 is in order. In his praise of Yahweh as Creator, the psalmist exults him for making people "a little lower than God, and crowned them with glory and honor." The glory here is probably the glory of the original creation and therefore reflects the vocation given to humanity at creation. Being crowned with glory and honor is most likely a reference to creation in the image of God.[68] In the flow of the Psalm, the concept of glory and honor is followed immediately in verse 7 by an intertextual link to Gen 1:28 where

---

67. In the marginal note of the Luther Bible, at verse 23. Available at www.luther-bibel.net.

68. Goldingay, *Psalms*, 1:159.

humans are given dominion over the rest of creation. There are several important features that need attention.

First, the concept of glory carries regal connotations in the OT. VanGemeren notes that "glory and honor" are used in the Psalms to refer to the kingship of God.[69] Thus, humanity has a royal status, but only as derived from God at creation.[70] Alternatively, humanity could be said to share in the glory of God on account of being created in his image. Alongside this, the "dominion" of Gen 1 is almost certainly intended to communicate the kingly role of Adam in the garden.[71] In short, humanity is described as being in an honorable position, particularly in relation to God and the rest of creation. Divine glory is shared and enjoyed.

Second, the psalmist links the concepts of glory and dominion. Linking glory with the image of God confirms the interpretation of the human vocation as reflecting the glory of God to the rest of creation. In other words, man was made "a little lower than God" in order to reflect the glory of God to all creation.[72] In verse 6, the psalmist further elaborates on this idea, claiming that God has "put all things under their feet." Humanity was to rule the world under God's rule by reflecting his glory to all things. Humanity was to enjoy a special relationship with God. The imperfect verbs seem to indicate that the original intentions for humanity still stand and look forward to ultimate fulfillment.[73] Beale holds that

---

69. VanGemeren, *Psalms*, 140–41. VanGemeren notes specifically Ps 29:1 and 104:1 as reflecting the kingly themes of glory and honor.

70. Grogan, *Psalms*, 54.

71. Wenham, *Genesis*, 33, 36–37. See also Dempster, *Dominion and Dynasty*, 56–62; Beale, *Temple*, 81–87.

72. This assumes that אֱלֹהִים should be translated "God" (with the NRSV) rather than "gods" or "heavenly beings" (ESV). While the LXX translates the term as ἀγγέλους, contextually, the reference is probably to God rather than angels or other gods for the following reasons: (1) the Psalm is a poetic reflection on the creation account of Gen 1, where no mention is made of angels; (2) being made in the image of God means that humans are like God, but not equal to God, which fits with being "a little lower"; and (3) it would be difficult to explain what it means to be lower than angels. See Craigie, *Psalms 1–50*, 108; Kraut, "Birds and the Babes," 23–24. Of course, ἀγγέλους is retained in the quotation in Heb 2:7–9, but this does not conflict with the interpretation here since the author of Hebrews was using the Psalm to explain the humiliation and exaltation of Christ. See Longenecker, *Biblical Exegesis*, 147.

73. Tate, "Exposition of Psalm 8," 348. Goldingay, *Psalms*, 1:161, denies any eschatological sense within the Psalm. However, as Craigie, *Psalms 1–50*, 110, points out, the NT authors saw the Psalm as Christologically significant.

Ps 8:5–8 describes an "ideal Adam" and thus points forward to a future king who would fulfill all that God originally intended for humanity.[74]

Third, humans were created to share in the glory of God. This possibly reflects a participation in God's glory at creation, which could intimate that humanity was originally united to God. The original glory of humanity was not inherent, but was received from God. God is the one who crowned humanity with glory and honor. It was God's glory that humanity was intended to reflect. That is, humanity shared in God's glory as creatures made in his image.

Thus, there is a strong connection between Ps 8 and Gen 1. The psalmist praises the God of creation who has created humanity in his image to reflect and share in his glory. The main point in relation to the argument of this chapter is that the glory of Ps 8:5 is the glory given by God to humanity at creation. This will be crucial to Paul's point in Rom 3.

There may be a further connection between glory and creation in Dan 7. There has been much debate over the identity of the "one like a human being" (or son of man) in verse 13. However, for our purposes, it is important to point out that verse 14 ties together the concepts of glory and dominion, possibly reflecting on the creation account of Gen 1. Given the links between Daniel and Genesis, the allusion to creation is plausible.[75] In other words, Dan 7 draws together the concepts of dominion (from Gen 1) and glory (from Ps 8), most likely reflecting on the two texts. Keesmaat believes that Paul is drawing on this very connection in Rom 8.[76]

Returning to Rom 3, the allusion to Ps 8 suggests that Paul's intention is to explain the human predicament not merely as failure to keep the law, but as failing to fulfill God's original intention. When Paul says that humans lack the glory of God, he means that they no longer reflect and share in God's glory as they were intended to do. This understanding takes the glory of 3:23 as the glory given by God to Adam, which he subsequently lost through sin. It should be clear that this glory is not inherent to humanity, as if humans have a glory of their own. Rather, this is the glory of God which humanity possessed as a gift.[77] In Ps 8, this is clear as humanity is "crowned" with glory by God. Thus, the adamic

---

74. Beale, *New Testament Biblical Theology*, 262.
75. Dempster, *Dominion and Dynasty*, 215–17.
76. Keesmaat, *Paul and His Story*, 85.
77. Blackwell, "Immortal Glory," 301.

background of Rom 3:23 does not mean that Paul believed Adam to have been ontologically glorious, but that Adam enjoyed and shared in *God's* glory (τῆς δόξης τοῦ θεοῦ) before he sinned. The first humans were created to share in the glory of God, but, in sinful rebellion, lost the ability to do so.[78]

Several other points need to be made. First, the exposition here points back to Rom 1, where Paul began his explanation of the universal nature of sin.[79] Humans were created to share in the glory of God.[80] References to glory in Rom 1 and 2 have already hinted at this meaning. In 1:23, Paul writes, "and they exchanged the glory of the immortal God for an image in the likeness of a mortal human, birds, four-footed animals, and reptiles." The use of the terms "likeness" (ὁμοιώματι) and "image" (εἰκόνος) doubtlessly recall the creation account, where these terms are found together in a single verse (Gen 1:26). In Rom 1, the point is similar to 3:23—people have rebelled against the Creator and failed to reflect his glory. Here, Paul says that humanity has traded the glory of God for images. That is, they have forsaken the glory of being created in the image of God for the worship of created things. There is a possible link to the story of the fall in Gen 3, since in that story, Adam and Eve chose to listen to a created being over the command of God.[81] Thus, Rom 3:23 builds on and further explains the charge of universal sin from Rom 1.

Additional references to glory are found in Rom 2:7 and 2:10. These uses of the term "glory" seem to give considerable support to the interpretation advocated here. The support comes through the idea of derived glory. In these two verses Paul writes:

2:7
τοῖς μὲν καθ' ὑπομονὴν ἔργου ἀγαθοῦ δόξαν καὶ τιμὴν καὶ ἀφθαρσίαν ζητοῦσιν ζωὴν αἰώνιον

---

78. As noted above, the Greek *Life of Adam and Eve*, which many scholars hold to be roughly contemporary to Paul, also links the creation of humanity and glory. Beale, *New Testament Biblical Theology*, 456, believes creation in the image of God to be nearly equivalent to creation with glory in *GLAE*.

79. While differing in their particular interpretations, many scholars see Rom 3:23 and 1:21, 23 as connected. See, for example, Wilckens, *Römer*, 1:181; Byrne, *Romans*, 125; Jewett, *Romans*, 280; Schreiner, *Romans*, 187. Thus, if one holds Rom 1 to be adamic in background, 3:23 would most likely contain adamic allusions as well.

80. Seifrid, "Romans," 618. So also Käsemann, *Romans*, 95.

81. Eve chose to listen to the voice of the serpent (possibly the "reptile" of Rom 1:23), while in Gen 3:17, God charges Adam with listening to the voice of his wife.

to those who persevere in good works, seeking glory and honor and immortality, eternal life

2:10

δόξα δὲ καὶ τιμὴ καὶ εἰρήνη παντὶ τῷ ἐργαζομένῳ τὸ ἀγαθόν, Ἰουδαίῳ τε πρῶτον καὶ Ἕλληνι

but glory and honor and peace to all who do good, to the Jew first and the Greek

In these verses, eternal life comes to those who seek glory (δόξαν ... ζητοῦσιν). This is certainly a reference to God's glory, especially since in 3:11 Paul describes sinful humanity as those who fail to "seek God" (ὁ ἐκζητῶν τὸν θεόν). That is, the glory sought in verse 7 and the glory granted in verse 10 is the glory of God. Thus, those who do good are those who seek the glory of God. The most feasible explanation is that in both cases, glory refers both to God's glory and honor and to the glory and honor given to humanity by God. The glory terminology running through the first three chapters of Romans is to be understood in concert. That is, Paul consistently uses glory language in these chapters to describe the results of sin or the restoration of redemption.[82] Thus, the glory that humanity lacks in 3:23 is the same glory that was exchanged in 1:23 and the same glory that is granted in 2:10.[83] Indeed, Paul will later connect this to the glory that is renewed in Christ (8:17–30). If the above exegesis of Rom 1:18–32 holds, the adamic interpretation of 3:23 is most probable.

"Good works" and "do good" in the context should be understood in relation to Rom 1:5, the "obedience of faith." Those who by faith continue in good works will receive glory, honor, peace, and eternal life.[84] Paul here is not advocating salvation by doing good works. In the context, he is most likely describing Gentiles who are members of the new covenant. In 2:14–15, Paul says that these people have the law written on their hearts and in 2:29, he mentions the circumcision of the heart. Though contested, these are probably references to new covenant promises fulfilled in

---

82. Rom 2 will be further analyzed in chapter 4 below.

83. The terms "glory" and "honor" appear together in Ps 8:6 LXX: ἠλάττωσας αὐτὸν βραχύ τι παρ' ἀγγέλους, δόξῃ καὶ τιμῇ ἐστεφάνωσας αὐτόν.

84. Fitzmyer, *Romans*, 297; So also Kruse, *Romans*, 123–24; Schreiner, *Romans*, 116.

Gentile believers.[85] Thus, the glory, honor, immortality, eternal life, and peace are "eschatological reward[s] or blessing[s] for the godly."[86]

These verses also interestingly link glory with honor. Fitzmyer notes that in the LXX, glory (δόξα) and honor (τιμή) were linked together in Job 40:10 as God's intention for humanity.[87] Paul has already placed the terms in close context in 1:21–24 in his exposition of Gentile (and Jewish) sin. There, Paul argues that since people have failed to glorify God as God, they have lost all honor and are involved in shameful things. This helps to frame the discussion of sinfulness not only in judicial terms, but also in terms of honor and shame. God's people, because of their sin of failing to rightly reflect his glory, have now lost the glory intended for them and are full of shame. The honor of being God's people is lost through sinful rebellion.

This concept is mentioned again in 2:23 where Paul speaks directly to the Jews who "dishonor God." Blackwell notes that the terms glory (δόξα) and honor (τιμή) are used virtually synonymously throughout Romans.[88] Glory and honor come full circle in Rom 15:6, where Jews and Gentiles are exhorted to glorify God together as the true people of God. In short, the link between glory and honor lends considerable support to the interpretation given here because honor is inherently a relational term. Thus, because of sin, humanity has failed to glorify God (by not reflecting his glory and fulfilling the creational vocation) and thus lost all honor (their position as the people of God).

In addition, Jewett detects honor and shame connotations with Paul's use of the term "distinction" (διαστολή) in Rom 3:22. He notes that Paul's purpose here is to claim that God does not separate people on the basis of status or ethnicity. He writes, "disregarding the honor/shame distinctions that humans claim in competition with one another, God treats all persons fairly while holding each equally accountable."[89] The point is clear: all are equally sinners. Jews and Gentiles stand on equal (shameful) ground before God.

The reference to the fall through the allusion to Ps 8 in verse 23 clinches Paul's exposition. The problem of sin affects Jews and Gentiles

---

85. This will be explored further in chapter 4 as it relates to union with Christ.
86. Witherington, *Romans*, 82.
87. Fitzmyer, *Romans*, 302.
88. Blackwell, "Immortal Glory," 293.
89. Jewett, *Romans*, 279.

alike because all without distinction are descended from Adam and share in his sin. Humans were intended to share in the glory of God, but instead share in the sinful rebellion of Adam. Thus, Adam failed to be the true son of God and all those "in Adam" fail to be the people of God, including both Jews and Gentiles. Implicitly in 3:23, Jews are included in the "all" and there is a probable veiled reference to the golden calf incident. This will become clear in the following verses, where redemption is pictured in language related to the exodus.[90] In other words, both the wider context of Rom 1–2 and the near context of Rom 3 make it clear that Jews also lack the glory of God.

In addition to the numerous links between Rom 1–2 and 3:23, a second point relates to the translation of πάντες . . . ἥμαρτον as "all sinned" in order to make plain the connection to Rom 5:12, to be analyzed below. The common translation "all have sinned" implies individual sin as the primary point: all have individually committed sins. While this is possible, given that the same form of the verb is used in in 5:12, the phrase more readily indicates the same event: Adam's sin.[91] The same construction here (all sinned) can hardly be coincidental. "All sinned" means that all share in the sin of Adam. That is, Paul is not saying that all people have committed individual sins, though that is certainly true. Rather, he is saying that the sin problem is universal because all share in Adam's sin, for "there is no distinction."[92] Thus understood, the reference to sin here is not sin in general, but the specific sin of Adam, in which all humanity shares.[93] This sin is further explained as lacking the glory of God.

Third, ὑστεροῦνται has been translated "are lacking" to show the meaning argued for in this chapter.[94] While the term is often translated

---

90. This idea will be explored further in chapter 4 below.

91. Moo, *Romans*, 226, believes this is a "summary aorist" that draws together the sins of all people into a "single moment." This seems to take a longer route to the same destination as it still sums up the sin of all people into one. It appears probable that the reference is to the sin of Adam and its effects on all people.

92. Rom 3:22.

93. Johnston, "Which 'All' Sinned?," argues that the "all" in Rom 3:23 refers to the "all who believe" in 3:22 and therefore indications that all believers are equally lacking the glory of God. This is most likely correct and lends additional support to the argument of this book: Jews and Gentiles together equally share the shamefulness of Adam's sin and the glory of Christ's redemption.

94. BDAG lists Rom 3:23 under the fifth meaning, which is "to experience deficiency in something advantageous or desirable, lack, be lacking, go without, come short of."

as "fall short," the word normally communicates the shortage or lacking of something, especially in the Pauline corpus.[95] Thus, sinful humanity is not simply failing to reach a high standard, but lacking in the derived glory they were created to possess and reflect. In other words, people "fail to share that perfect communion with God for which humanity was created."[96] As Jewett points out, this is also an issue of honor. Humans have brought shame upon themselves by sinning and failing to live up to the honor given by God.[97] The honor and shame dimension of Paul's theology of sin and restoration should not be forgotten as it plays an important role in properly understanding union with Christ.

Enderlein argues that Paul's use of the verb ὑστερέω indicates the adamic background of the verse, particularly in light of the connection of the first half of Rom 3:23 with Rom 5:12.[98] Contra Enderlein, Porter and Cirafesi doubt the adamic background of Rom 3:23, centering their argumentation on linguistic grounds.[99] For them, the fact that the Jewish literature never uses the verb ὑστερέω to describe Adam's loss of glory means that Paul was not drawing on a similar tradition and therefore did not have Adam in mind when composing Rom 3:23. That is, while several Jewish texts do link Adam and glory, they never use the same vocabulary as Paul. Interestingly, they do not dispute the translation of ὑστεροῦνται as "lacking," but believe this term has no connection to Jewish Adam speculation.[100] However, this line of argumentation seems to assume that two authors must use the exact same vocabulary in order to describe similar themes. Paul could very well have Adam in mind without using the exact vocabulary as other writers.[101] As Enderlein points out, though the Jewish texts use different terms, they often speak of glory as being either possessed or lost, which thematically connects to Paul's

---

95. Enderlein, "To Fall Short," 213, notes that Paul uses the term seven other times and in each instance the most likely meaning is to lack something rather than to come short of an intended goal. Though he does not see an allusion to Adam in the verse, Cirafesi, "'To Fall Short," argues for the translation of "are lacking" on the basis of linguistic and semantic factors.

96. Hultgren, *Romans*, 155.

97. Jewett, *Romans*, 280.

98. Enderlein, "To Fall Short," 215–20.

99. Porter and Cirafesi, "ὑστερέω."

100. Ibid., 5.

101. To be fair, Porter and Cirafesi are arguing that the use of ὑστερέω does not demand the presence of adamic backgrounds. While true, they go further to deny the possibility of an allusion to Adam.

point in Romans.¹⁰² Moreover, Porter and Cirafesi give little attention to the textual connections between Rom 3:21–26 and Rom 5:12–21 (not to mention the other allusions to Adam in Romans), which gives considerable weight to the argument for adamic backgrounds in 3:23. Thus, while disputed, Paul's wording seems to reflect themes similar to Jewish writings on Adam and glory.

The present tense-form (imperfective aspect) of the verb shows continuing action.¹⁰³ Not only is the sinning a past event in Adam, but humans continue to lack the glory of God. This gives the exposition of the human predicament an eschatological flavor that will be filled out later in the epistle. The πάντες indicates that all, without distinction, are lacking God's glory. This would include Christians since the full redemption of God's glory in humanity awaits eschatological fulfillment.¹⁰⁴ Thus, Paul has thoroughly levelled the ground, demonstrating that none have reason for boasting or claiming ethnic or social advantage within the community of believers.

Fourth, the allusion to creation via Ps 8 is intended to evoke memory of the sin of Adam and Eve in Gen 3. Paul has alluded to Ps 8, but rather than reflecting on the glory of the original state of man, Paul has drawn attention to disastrous effects of sin. VanGemeren points out that the psalmist speaks of humanity as if the fall of man had never occurred.¹⁰⁵ Yet, Paul emphasizes the exact opposite point. He agrees with the psalmist that humanity was created with the honor and glory given by God, yet because of the sin of Adam and Eve, they now lack that original glory.

Though the adamic interpretation offered here seems to make sense of Paul's argument, some have seriously questioned the adamic backgrounds, not just in 3:23, but also for Paul's theology of participation as a whole.¹⁰⁶ In a nuanced treatment of the subject, Macaskill explores potential adamic backgrounds for Paul's theology, specifically focused on

---

102. Enderlein, "The Faithfulness," 15.

103. Campbell, *Basics of Verbal Aspect*, 40–43.

104. Moo, *Romans*, 227; Schreiner, *Romans*, 187.

105. VanGemeren, *Psalms*, 140.

106. It should be noted that while not universal, many recent commentators hold to an adamic background for Rom 3:23. See, among others, Michel, *Römer*, 149; Wilckens, *Römer*, 1:188; Cranfield, *Romans*, 1:204–5; Käsemann, *Romans*, 95; Dunn, *Romans*, 1:167–68; Byrne, *Romans*, 131; Jewett, *Romans*, 280; Wright, "Letter to the Romans," 470–71; Kruse, *Romans*, 181; Schreiner, *Romans*, 187; and Hultgren, *Romans*, 195. Of course, each of these commentators understands the verse in various ways.

participatory themes. After surveying several Jewish texts that are sometimes claimed to support adamic backgrounds for Paul's theology, he concludes that there is little, if any, support for Jewish thought on Adam to have found its way into Paul's writings. There are two primary reasons for this. First, drawing on the work of Levison and others, Macaskill notes that Jewish thought on Adam was varied and most often shaped to fit a particular author's literary purposes.[107] That is, there is no commonly accepted Adam myth within the literature. Instead, Jewish thinking on Adam developed in various directions with no uniformity. For Macaskill, this means Paul did not draw on such themes with regard to glory (of Christ or believers). Second, Macaskill claims that when glory is ascribed to Adam in Second Temple Jewish literature, "an adamic myth does not shape other motifs, but rather the story of Adam is subordinated to the portrayal of Israel."[108] Thus, according to Macaskill, one should look for backgrounds of glory-language in other Jewish symbols, such as the temple.

Space will not allow engagement with all the texts mentioned by Macaskill. The Greek *Life of Adam and Eve* was treated above and those arguments need not be repeated here. Instead, I will mention a few other texts in dialogue with Macaskill. First, in Sir 49:16, the author uses glory language in reference to Adam: "Shem and Seth and Enosh were honored (ἐδοξάσθησαν), but above every other created living being was Adam." However, as Macaskill notes, within the context, the emphasis is on Israel rather than Adam: Adam is glorious only inasmuch as he is a part of Israel's (glorious) heritage. Further, this passage is unique in Sirach as the only place Adam is said to be glorious. While true, this does not rule out references to Adam in Romans: though Israel remains central, Adam is nevertheless described as having glory.[109] Neither does it mean Paul could not have taken a Jewish theme and shaped it both exegetically through reflection on the OT and Christologically as he reflected on Jesus as the Messiah. Indeed, this is the exact thing Macaskill claims the Jewish texts to be doing: shaping their thoughts on Adam to fit their contexts.[110]

---

107. Macaskill, *Union with Christ*, 137, 143.

108. Ibid., 138. See similar statements on 133, 139, and 143.

109. Levison, *Portraits*, 45, argues that the reference to Adam's glory here must be seen as particular to Sirach rather than a part of a unified Adam tradition. I am arguing that Paul is doing something similar: reframing a Jewish theme (adamic glory) around his gospel.

110. Levison, *Portraits*, 161, concludes similarly: "Paul's writings are an independent

Moreover, this observation may actually serve to support the argument presented here, namely that Paul alludes to the Adam story with Israel's story intermingled in order to show that all people, Jew and Gentile, are united to sin in Adam. Paul may be correcting the Jewish notion of the nation as the possessor of the original glory enjoyed by the first humans. Like Sirach (and other texts), Paul links the stories of Adam and Israel. However, in opposition to Sirach (and other texts), Paul sees this as a union with sin rather than a glorious inheritance. Furthermore, the fact remains that the author of Sirach saw a connection between Adam and glory and this connection is common among other writings.[111] The exact meaning of glory in Sir 49:16 remains elusive, but one need not understand the precise force of the term in order to see the clear connection between Adam, Israel, and glory.

Macaskill notes the references to the "glory of Adam" (כל כבוד אדם) in the Qumran documents (*Community Rule* 4:23; *Damascus Document* 3:20; *Hodayot* 4:15), but concludes that these references provide little evidence of adamic glory, especially as it relates to Paul's writings. He points out that the glory ascribed to Adam in these texts are actually references to God's glory, which was enjoyed by Adam in Eden.[112] For Macaskill, this raises serious problems for Dunn's notion of Adam Christology, which sees Christ's glory as strictly adamic in nature.[113] According to Dunn, the result is that Christ is pictured as glorious only as a new Adam *after his resurrection* rather than as inherently glorious. This is indeed problematic and takes the evidence in both the Jewish writings and Paul too far, as several scholars have shown.[114] Nevertheless, the linking of

---

contribution to biblical interpretation which can be compared fruitfully with other individual authors who employ the figure of Adam to express their *Tendenzen*."

111. While Sir 15 seems to present Adam as sinful, Noffke, "Man of Glory," argues that the seemingly contradictory references to Adam in Sirach (as both glorious and sinful) is probably the result of the author's combination of multiple traditions. Alternatively, Levison, *Portraits*, 46–47, suggests that differing portraits simply reflect "differing contextual emphases."

112. Macaskill, *Union with Christ*, 139. Macaskill also notes the flexibility in the Hebrew word אדם such that the references could simply be to humanity in general. However, the contexts of the passages, which recount much biblical history and contain numerous allusions to Eden, most likely point to a reference to Adam over against a general reference to humanity.

113. See Dunn, *Christology*, 107–13; *Paul*, 200–204.

114. See, for example, Fee's interaction throughout his *Pauline Christology*, especially 390–93. See also Macaskill, "Incarnational Ontology."

glory and Adam in relation to Paul's Christology need not lead to Dunn's conclusions. Paul could very well have been drawing a distinction: Adam failed to continue enjoying God's shared glory while Christ is inherently glorious. Thus, while the glory-language in the Qumran literature may not support Dunn's thesis, it does not rule out adamic backgrounds for Romans. As with other texts, regardless of the exact application, it remains true that Adam and glory are often linked.

In each text noted above, the "glory of Adam" is said to be given to the faithful. The emphasis is unquestionably on (faithful) Israel rather than Adam. For example, in the context of *The Damascus Document* 3:20, the text is recounting the history of Israel with the primary focus on their sin. The immediate context turns from sin and punishment to the hope of restoration for those who are faithful. In this context, the "glory of Adam" is promised to those who live in obedience. Thus, the mention of Adam's glory is for the sole purpose of encouraging right living and is rather undeveloped as a concept. However, contra Macaskill and others, I would argue that this actually confirms the analysis offered of Romans offered above. Like the Qumran texts, Paul's primary point is not the glory (or loss of glory) in Adam. Instead, adamic glory is background for the restoration that takes place in Christ, for both Jews and Gentiles. Moreover, this background highlights a key contrast between Paul and the writings at Qumran: rather than a return to or restoration of Adam's glory, Paul sees union with Christ as an escalated glory, namely that of Christ.[115] Though the glory enjoyed by Adam in Eden is the background for union with Christ, the eschatological climax is not a return to Eden, but a participation in the glory of Christ.[116] As noted with regard to Sirach above, Israel's story is again linked to Adam's in Qumran: Adam's glory will be Israel's. In contrast, Paul argues that Adam's shame is Israel's, along with all those outside of Christ.

The context of the reference to Adam's glory in *Community Rule* 4:23 offers further support to the linking of Adam, glory, and Ps 8 in Rom 3:23. In *Community Rule* 4:7–8, there is an allusion to Ps 8:6. The document claims that the faithful "will receive a crown of glory with a robe of honor, resplendent forever and ever."[117] Kinzer argues that "crown

---

115. Blackwell, "Immortal Glory," 301.

116. This understanding would seem to fit with Paul's contrast of Adam and Christ in Rom 5:12–21, where Christ and Adam are pictured as similar, but not equal, as the gift of grace in Christ far exceeds the trespass of Adam.

117. Quoted from Wise et al., *Dead Sea Scrolls*, 121.

of glory" evokes Ps 8:6, even though the noun "crown" (כליל) is from a different root than the verb "crowned" (צטר) in Ps 8:6.[118] Thus, within the near context, this Qumran document alludes to Ps 8 and draws on the notion of Adam's glory. It should be noted that in both cases, glory is promised to faithful Israel. Nevertheless, it is significant that in a Jewish document predating Paul, Ps 8 and Adam are both used with relation to the restoration of glory. Though we have no evidence that Paul was aware of this document, the *Community Rule* 4 at least shows the conjoining of Adam's glory with Ps 8 was not entirely unprecedented in early Judaism.

In addition to the three occurrences of "all the glory of Adam" cited above, another Qumran text might provide some background for the concept of adamic glory. In *The Words of the Heavenly Lights* (1Q504 Frag 8), the creation of humanity is recounted (or rewritten) for the community:

> 1[...Re]member, O L[o]r[d] that [...] 2 [...]and it is You who lives fo[ever...] 3 [...You have done] wonders of old, and awesome deeds [long ago.] 4 You fashioned [Adam,] our [fa]ther, in the image of [Your] glory; You breathed 5 [the breath of life] into his nostrils, [and filled him] with understanding and knowledge. 6 Y[ou] set him to rule [over the Gar]den of Eden that You had planted. 7 [...] and to walk about in a glorious land [...] 8 [...]he guarded it. You enjoined him not to turn as[ide from Your commands.] 9 [...]flesh is he, and to dust h[e shall return.] 10 [...] It is You who knows [...] 11 [...] for the generations of eternity [...] 12 [...] the living God, and Your hand [...] humankind in the ways of [...] 14 [...to fill the] earth with [wro]ngdoing and to she[d innocent blood...][119]

Following Chazon, Macaskill argues that one must be cautious with this text as it is liturgical in nature, a part of numerous prayer texts that reflect on biblical stories.[120] Further, other biblical characters are also described as glorious. Yet, these points have little bearing on the question of whether or not Paul was alluding to Adam in Rom 3:23. That the text is liturgical does not detract from the fact that Adam is described as being created in glory. Moreover, this text explicitly links the image of God with glory and includes reflection on the sin of Adam and its implications. In short, the

---

118. Kinzer, "All Things Under His Feet," 106. Kinzer suggests that כליל may have been used in order to recall the image of the glorious Adam from Ezek 28:12.

119. Quoted from Wise et al., *Dead Sea Scrolls*, 526.

120. Macaskill, *Union with Christ*, 139, citing Chazon, "Liturgical Document."

text itself would seem to support the argument for an adamic allusion in Paul rather than raising doubt of such an allusion. Indeed, van Kooten argues that the theme of Adam's glory is found in both liturgical writings and the Qumran community's foundational documents and is, therefore, "deeply rooted in the Dead Sea Scrolls."[121]

Other intertestamental books could be mentioned to show that at least some Jewish writers made a similar connection between Adam and glory.[122] The way in which these books linked Adam and glory is not uniform and, as Levison as clearly shown, there was no cohesive body of Adam speculation in the Jewish writings. Moreover, Adam is rarely the main character in these writings, a position most often occupied by Israel (or some subgroup of Israel). Nevertheless, it is important to note that Adam and glory are connected in several writings. The (true) premise of the nonexistence of unified Jewish thought on Adam does not lead to the conclusion that the Adam narratives have a minimal (if any) role in Paul's theology. Having surveyed the literature, Kinzer summarizes his findings with regard to the use of Ps 8 and the Adam narratives:

> The national and eschatological appropriation of Adam and his inheritance was thus characteristic of many Jewish writings at the turn of the Common Era. The motif varies in its meaning and significance in the different works, depending on the overall ideology of the author(s). The motif itself, however, can be found in diverse systems, and was apparently widespread.[123]

Of course, this does not prove with certainty that Paul had Adam in mind in Rom 3:23, but it at least makes it plausible. Further evidence is needed, but I contend such evidence is provided by 1) the connections between

---

121. van Kooten, *Paul's Anthropology*, 21.

122. Though some of texts are probably later than Paul, Blackwell, "Immortal Glory," 288–90, lists the following texts as connecting Adam's sin to the loss of glory: Greek *Life of Adam and Eve* 20–21; *Targum Pseudo-Jonathan* Gen 2:25; 3:7; *3 Baruch* (Greek) 4:16; *Genesis Rabbah* 12:6; and *Apocalypse of Sedrach* 6:5. Blackwell also lists the following texts that link Adam and glory, though not with regard to the loss of glory in sin: *2 Enoch* 30:10–18; *History of the Rechabites* 20:4; *Genesis Rabbah* 20:12; *Leviticus Rabbah* 20:2; *Ecclesiastes Rabbah* 8:1–2. He concludes, "From these many texts, we can easily affirm that Adam was associated with glory in a variety of ancient Jewish texts and that in some traditions his sin is associated with a loss of glory, which easily parallels Paul's argument in Rom 3:23."

123. Kinzer, "All Things Under His Feet," 112.

Rom 1, 3, and 5; 2) the context; and 3) the explanatory power of the Adam allusion.[124]

In addition, Macaskill notes that other figures, such as Seth and Moses, are also considered glorious in the Jewish literature.[125] This fact leads him to doubt that references to glory in Paul are adamic in nature. However, the mere possibility of other referents does not necessarily negate the adamic background, especially if other textual clues point to Adam. The numerous allusions to Adam throughout the letter, along with his explicit naming in Rom 5, provide such textual clues. Of course, other backgrounds are possible, but the consistent clustering of allusions running through Romans gives weight to the adamic backgrounds as most probable. This is especially true since other possible backgrounds find less (if any) textual support in Romans.[126] Indeed, Stuhlmacher has affirmed that Rom 3:23 can be properly understood only in the context of Jewish thought on the consequences of the Adam's sin in Gen 3.[127]

Blackwell, arguing for a social and ontological meaning of glory in Romans, complains that a focus on the "Jewish theological contexts have not only placed their emphasis in the wrong place—radiance—but also ignored the social significance of Paul's language."[128] Blackwell is right to note the differences in Paul's reference to glory and the emphasis on radiance in some Jewish writings. Ignoring the adamic background, particularly in relation to the concept of the people of God, fails to fully appreciate the social significance of the theme of lost glory and the restoration of glory through union with Christ, which results in the reconstitution of the people of God in Christ. In other words, the intertextual interpretation offered here more fully denotes the social ramifications of both sin in Adam and salvation in Christ. Blackwell's attention to the

---

124. With regard to sin and evil, Stone, *Ancient Judaism*, 31–58, argues that Enoch traditions (especially at Qumran) in Jewish literature attribute the entry of evil into the world to angelic beings. By contrast, other writings (such as *4 Ezra*) attribute the current evil state to Adam. Stone places Paul in the latter group.

125. Macaskill, *Union with Christ*, 133, 137.

126. The possible exception to this is the temple imagery running through much of the epistle. These will be pointed out in later chapters of this book. However, though temple imagery is present, it is also true that throughout the OT and other Jewish literature, the temple is linked to Eden. Thus, temple imagery does not necessarily set aside allusions to Adam. See Beale, *Temple and the Church's Mission*, 29–80.

127. Stuhlmacher, *Romans*, 58. So also Wilckens, *Römer*, 1:188. Wilckens notes that this theme is also found in Rom 5.

128. Blackwell, "Immortal Glory," 300.

social consequences of the adamic allusion in Rom 3:23 helps establish the importance of Adam's story in the larger context.

Finally, the understanding of Rom 3:23 presented here fits well within the overall argument of Romans to this point. In Rom 1–3, Paul has argued that Jew and Gentile alike are sinners. In 3:22, Paul prefaces his statement of verse 23 by saying "for there is no distinction" (οὐ γάρ ἐστιν διαστολή). A reference to creation and the fall fit perfectly as these stories clearly demonstrate the universal results of Adam's sin. That is, Jew and Gentile alike are sinners. As Dunn writes,

> The familiarity of the assertion to present-day readers should not be allowed to dull the shocking character of what Paul says: the established character of the phrase "Jew and Gentile/Greek" expressed the axiomatic nature of the Jewish self-understanding of the people of Israel as different. The object of 1:18—3:20, however, had been precisely to destroy the Jewish presumption of special prerogative and defense even before the faithful covenant God (the point reiterated in v. 23). If that special claim on God is not allowed, the way is opened for Paul to expound faith as the only means for anyone, everyone, to receive God's righteousness.[129]

God's intentions for his people had been ruined by sin. Referencing the fall through Ps 8 shows that God's purposes for his people still stand, but before the coming of the Messiah were left unfulfilled. This, then, points forward to union with Christ, which is presented as God's remedy for the sinful predicament of all people.

In sum, while some scholars have doubted the adamic background for Rom 3:23, there are good reasons for holding to this line of interpretation. The textual and thematic links between Rom 3:21–26 and Rom 5:12–21 make the allusion to Adam in 3:23 highly likely. Most scholars notice the significant thematic links between these two sections. Since Adam is explicitly named in Rom 5, it seems probable that Adam was in mind when Rom 3 was composed. Moreover, while the Jewish literature varies in the treatment of the Adam narratives, it remains the case that Adam is often described as glorious or as possessing (and losing) glory. Thus, the conceptual background is present in the literature. Finally, the above exegesis has sought to show the explanatory power of the adamic allusions: the interpretation offered here seems to fit well within Paul's argument in Romans, especially chapters 1–5.

129. Dunn, *Romans*, 1:167.

Romans 4

Many modern interpreters understand Paul's reference to Abraham in Rom 4 to be more than a mere proof-text for justification by faith. Though once viewed in this way,[130] it has been recently shown that Paul is doing much more than simply offering up Abraham as an OT example of one who was justified by believing. Indeed, once Paul's OT references are understood within a narrative framework, his use of the Abraham story becomes much more meaningful and better integrated into his overall argument. This section will not provide a full exegesis of Rom 4, but more narrowly focus on the way in which Paul's use of the Abraham narratives is connected to the story of Adam (and Israel) within Romans and thus further defines the narrative background for union with Christ.

A key term found in Rom 4:20 links the Abraham section of Romans to the previous allusions to the Adam narratives. In 4:20, Paul writes that Abraham, having believed and obeyed, "gave glory to God" (δοὺς δόξαν τῷ θεῷ). The term δόξα was very important in the echoes of Adam in Rom 1 and 3. Now, in the middle of his discussion of Abraham, he again mentions glory, but this time he uses it positively in opposition to the previous negative uses. Many scholars see a link between Abraham's giving glory to God and the failure of humanity to glorify God.[131] Adams writes, "Abraham is portrayed as the reverse image of the disobedient Gentiles."[132] However, few have seen a connection between the Abraham narratives and the allusions to Adam within Paul's argument.

The interpretation offered here is that Paul presents Abraham not as an OT proof of the doctrine of justification by faith, though Abraham is certainly an example of one who trusted in the promises of God. Rather, when Rom 4:20 is considered in relation to the allusions to Adam from Rom 1 and 3, it becomes clear that that Paul is showing God to be faithful in that he is restoring the glory lost by Adam through the promises given to Abraham. Thus, rather than an aside to show OT proof for Paul's doctrine of justification, Rom 4 is an integral part of the overall argument. It

---

130. Wright, "Paul and the Patriarch," 208, lists Conzelmann, *An Outline*; Sanders, *Paul, the Law, and the Jewish People*; Tobin, "What Shall We Say"; and Longenecker, *Introducing*, as examples of those espousing this view.

131. Käsemann, *Romans*, 124–25; Byrne, *Romans*, 154–55; Schreiner, *Romans*, 238.

132. Adams, "Paul's Story," 35. So also Grieb, *Story of Romans*, 52–53.

will be clear that this is also essential for understanding Paul's doctrine of union with Christ.

Sailhamer argues that there is a close connection between the Adam narratives and Abraham narratives in the final canonical text of Genesis. The author (and redactor) has placed the material such that the original intent seems to be to show Abraham and his seed as God's solution to the problem of sin, which has been shown to be a worldwide problem in Gen 3–11. Related to the point being made in this chapter, Sailhamer comments on Gen 12, writing,

> Abraham is here represented as a "new Adam," the "seed of Abraham" as a "second Adam," a new humanity. Those who "bless" him, God will bless; those who "curse" him, God will curse. The way of life and blessing which was once marked by the "tree of the knowledge of good and evil" (2:17) and then by the ark (7:23b), is now marked by identification with Abraham and his seed.[133]

Thus, Paul appears to be reading Gen 15 in the context of Gen 1–3 and in light of the coming of the Messiah. Again, this anticipates the concept of union with Christ, which will be presented as the ultimate fulfillment of the promises given to Abraham and, therefore, the solution to the problem of sin.

Paul's argumentation in Rom 4 seems to be drawing on a similar understanding of the relation between the stories of Adam and Abraham. That is, Paul saw an intimate relationship between the sin of Adam in Gen 3 and the covenant with Abraham in Gen 15 and 17 and this relationship is central to Paul's argument in Romans. Therefore, the use of the term "glory" in Rom 4:20 is intended to recall the lost (exchanged) glory in Adam from Rom 1 and 3 and show that God is restoring that lost glory in Christ, and thus fulfilling the promises given to Abraham. This, then, fits into the overall argument of Romans by demonstrating the righteousness of God: he is the covenant-keeping God, fulfilling his intentions for creation through the family of Abraham, which, in fulfillment of the covenant promises, is a worldwide family composed of all nations.

---

133. Sailhamer, *Pentateuch as Narrative*, 139–40. Similarly, Dempster, *Dominion and Dynasty*, 77, argues for a close connection between the Abraham and Adam narratives. Dempster highlights the verbal correspondences between the call of Abraham with the fivefold repetition of "bless," harking back to the original blessing of creation. See also Goldingay, *Old Testament Theology*, 214.

Adams nicely summarizes the point, noting that "By incorporating the Abraham story, which is the story of how God justifies the ungodly, into the 'story of God and creation,' Paul indicates that God's act of justification does not constitute a departure from the creator's aims; it is a creative act that repairs the fractured relationship between creator and creature and effects the achievement of the creator's original objectives."[134] Though Adams makes no mention of union with Christ, it will be clear that this narrative background plays an important role in Paul's exposition of salvation in Christ.

Thus far, the focus has been on the use of the term "glory" in Rom 4:20 because it provides a clear link to allusions to the Adam narratives from Rom 1. However, Adams notes further connections between Rom 1 and 4, which serve to confirm that Paul saw a close connection between the Adam narratives and the story of Abraham. First, there is a link between τὸν δικαιοῦντα τὸν ἀσεβῆ of Rom 4:5 and ἀσέβειαν καὶ ἀδικίαν in Rom 1:18. Adams believes the verbal linkage is intended to show a change in Abraham from ungodly to righteous, thus linking Abraham with the Gentiles of Rom 1.[135] However, it seems that Paul has something different in mind. Assuming the validity of the Adam allusion in Rom 1, Paul links the Abraham narrative to the Adam narrative in order to show the faithfulness of God in righting the world through Abraham's seed. This, then, lays the foundation for the Paul's concept of union with Christ. In short, Paul will present union with Christ as God's means of 1) keeping the covenant promises to Abraham to create a universal family and 2) restoring everything destroyed through human sinfulness, which started with Adam and continued with Israel.

Second, Adams notes that Paul picks up creational themes again in Rom 4:17, linking back to the mention of God the Creator in Rom 1:20, 25.[136] In Rom 1, Paul clearly identifies the God of Israel as the Creator of the world. All people, Jew and Gentile alike, however, have rejected the revelation of the true God and have worshiped the creation instead. Abraham is shown in Rom 4 as the one through whom God is restoring the world ruined by sin. The textual links between chapters 1 and 4 again show Paul's contextual reading of the Genesis account and his understanding of Christ as the culmination of God's restoration through

---

134. Adams, "Paul's Story," 36.
135. Adams, "Abraham's Faith," 51.
136. Ibid., 52.

Abraham and his seed. The quotation of Gen 17:5 in the first part of Rom 4:17 confirms that Paul has a corporate emphasis in mind here. Abraham is the "father of many nations" since the Gentiles are included in the true people of God and identified as the seed of Abraham by faith. In addition, God's promise to bless all the families of the earth through Abraham (Gen 12:3) is most likely an echo of the original blessing given to humanity in Gen 1:28.[137] Put otherwise, God's promise was to restore the original blessing through Abraham and his seed. All of this shows that God is keeping his covenant promises of restoration through the family of Abraham and that the ultimate fulfillment of such is union with Christ.

Further, the description of God not only as Creator but also as one who "gives life to the dead" probably recalls the resurrection of Christ, which was mentioned in 1:4. This is the first mention of resurrection since chapter 1 and thus links together Paul's Christological opening words with covenant fulfillment themes here in chapter 4.[138] As Hultgren points out, there is a parallel statement in 4:24 concerning the faith of Christians in "the one who raised Jesus our Lord from the dead."[139] Again, this links the faith of Christians with the fulfillment of the promises given to Abraham. The connection to union with Christ will become more explicit later in the letter.

Third, Adams notes the textual link between Rom 4:21 and 1:20.[140] Though a minor point with regard to the argument of this book, the additional textual connection between Rom 1 and 4 supports the notion that these chapters should be interpreted together. Both of these verses make mention of God's power (1:20—δύναμις; 4:21—δυνατός). In chapter 1, Paul argues that the Gentiles have rejected the display of God's power in creation. By contrast, in chapter 4, Paul argues that Abraham was sure of God's power to keep the promise. Again, the focus is on the promise

---

137. Sailhamer, *Pentateuch as Narrative*, 139. See also Wenham, *Genesis*, 1:282.

138. For readers familiar with the OT, the mention of resurrection here could also call to mind the vision of Ezek 37, where God promised to raise his people to life. In Rom 6, Paul links the resurrection of believers to the resurrection of Christ. Thus, Paul incorporates Israel's later story of resurrection as return from exile into the story of Adam and the story of Israel's sin. Those united to Christ fulfill the promise to raise people of God from the dead, and thereby fulfill the promises given to Abraham.

139. Hultgren, *Romans*, 187–88.

140. Adams, "Abraham's Faith," 53.

of God and his power to fulfill it.[141] Paul will show that God is indeed faithful to the promise in the sending of Jesus the Messiah.

In addition, the mention of God's power also recalls the programmatic statement in Rom 1:16–17, where Paul presents the gospel as the "power of God" (δύναμις θεοῦ). Thus, the keeping of the promise to Abraham is linked to the message of the gospel, which fits with the overall argument of Romans as a defense of the righteousness of God. All of this will serve as OT foundations for the doctrine of union with Christ.

In sum, the links between Rom 1 and 4 show an intertextual interpretation of the OT. Paul is reading the story of Abraham in relation to the story of Adam and showing the fulfillment of the promises of God in the gospel. The story of Adam provides the negative background for the problem of human sin in Rom 1 because all humanity is caught up in the disastrous results of Adam's sin. Israel is also a part of the problem since they have failed to live as God's people. Now, in Rom 4, Paul is showing the story of Abraham as God's solution to the problem. In particular, Paul is arguing that God has indeed been faithful to fulfill his promises to Abraham in that those who have the faith of Abraham are a part of his worldwide family. Those united to Christ by faith are the true seed of Abraham. Jew and Gentile alike are now a part of the solution to the universal problem.

CONCLUSION

The analysis offered thus far has shown that the story of Adam is very important in Paul's argument in Rom 1–4. Allusions to Adam are found throughout these chapters and are located strategically within the discussion of the universality of sin. In addition, Paul has masterfully woven the story of Israel, particularly Israel's failure in the wilderness, into the story of Adam in order to show that not only are the Jewish people a part of the problem, but also, in many ways, are a magnification of the problem. It is clear that Paul viewed the sin of Israel as a recapitulation of the sin of Adam. In the following chapters, I will seek to show that all of this is intended to serve as background to Paul's doctrine of union with Christ.

---

141. Holland, *Romans*, 146.

3

The Story of Adam (and Israel) in Romans 5–8

INTRODUCTION

IN CHAPTER 2, I argued that the story of Adam plays an important role in Romans, particularly related to the plight of humanity in sin. In addition, each allusion to Adam includes an additional allusion to the story of Israel in the near context. The primary purpose of the connection between the stories is to show that the Jews are also caught up in the sin of Adam and to show a basic human solidarity in sin that supersedes ethnic identity. This foundational concept will prove to be crucial for a proper understanding of union with Christ in the letter. The present chapter will continue the exegetical analysis of allusions to the Adam and Israel in Rom 5–8.

EXEGETICAL ANALYSIS

Romans 5:12–21

This important and controversial section of Romans has sometimes been interpreted in strictly individualistic terms. If individual status before God were Paul's primary concern here, then union with Christ would also necessarily be an individualistic concept. However, I will argue that a proper exegesis of the text leads to a corporate understanding of Paul's meaning and thus a corporate understanding of union with Christ.¹ As Ridderbos pointed out, the primary intention of the text is not "to give an explanation either of the universality of sin or of the manner of its propagation" but to give "insight here into the nature of the solidarity in sin as the apostle conceived it."² The OT narrative background is central to this line of interpretation and helps explain this passage as necessary groundwork for a proper understanding of union with Christ.

In what follows, it will not be possible to provide a verse-by-verse exegesis of this text. Instead, the exegetical analysis will focus on the role of the Adam narrative, along with the use of Israel's story, with the intention of pointing forward to the later discussion of the way in which this narrative provides the OT background of union with Christ. The exegesis that follows builds on the study of Rom 1 and 3 in the previous chapter in which I argued for the presence of adamic allusions. The following analysis will show the continuity of Paul's discussion in Rom 5:12–21 with these previous allusions to form a coherent narrative argument for human solidarity in Adam apart from Christ. While some interpreters have viewed this section as an aside, the exegesis in chapter 2 of this book demonstrates clearly that the Adam narrative has already played an important role in the argument. Thus, it is not surprising that Paul now more explicitly brings Adam into his discussion at this point. Indeed, as Byrne has noted, "The present section furthers that argument [for hope in 5:1–11], 'unpacking' the instrumentality of Christ with respect to righteousness and (eternal) life, over against the instrumentality of Adam with respect to sin and death."³

Textual and thematic correlations undoubtedly link Rom 5 with Rom 3. Several points are worthy of note. In the opening paragraph of Rom 5 (vv. 1–5), Paul draws the readers' attention to the hope of believers in the justifying work of the faithful Messiah. This paragraph repeats the word "hope" (ἐλπίς) three times. The first occurrence is in verse 2, where Paul says, "we boast in the hope of the glory of God" (καυχώμεθα ἐπ' ἐλπίδι τῆς δόξης τοῦ θεοῦ). The phrase "τῆς δόξης τοῦ θεοῦ" reproduces the

---

1. The intention is not to play individual and corporate aspects against one another. Rather, the argument is simply that Paul's primary meaning is corporate. Nevertheless, it is also true that any corporate group is composed of individuals. Thus, individual aspects are not completely missing.

2. Ridderbos, *Paul*, 95.

3. Byrne, *Romans*, 173.

exact wording of 3:23, which refers to the loss of the glory of God via the sin of Adam, as argued above.[4] In addition, the mention of glory ties the argument to the preceding chapter, where Paul noted that Abraham "gave glory to God" (δοὺς δόξαν τῷ θεῷ).[5]

Further, in Rom 5:5 Paul builds on the theme of hope, stating that "hope does not put to shame" (ἡ δὲ ἐλπὶς οὐ καταισχύνει). Having already stated that believers hope in the glory of God, Paul reminds his readers that this hope will not bring shame upon those who believe.[6] The contrast between honor and shame is again present. People have brought shame upon themselves in sin, despising the glory of God. However, God is restoring this glory through Christ. Thus, at the outset of the chapter, Paul is again drawing attention to the glory of God, but now the point is that the lost glory is being restored in Christ, the last Adam and true seed of Abraham.

Finally, the first paragraph of chapter 5 contains allusions to prophetic promises, which serves to establish a covenantal context for what follows as well as the corporate flavor to the entire argument, particularly the Adam-Christ analogy later in the chapter. Two allusions seem especially worthy of note. First, the phrase "access to this grace" (τὴν προσαγωγὴν . . . εἰς τὴν χάριν ταύτην) in 5:2 uses temple-language to describe grace received through Christ.[7] Unhindered access to God's pres-

---

4. The NRSV translates the last phrase of 5:2 as follows: "We boast in our hope of sharing the glory of God." This translation seems to echo 3:23 and interprets the glory here as shared glory. Jewett, *Romans*, 352, denies that the glory in 5:2 is the shared glory of God, opting instead for a purely sociological interpretation, arguing that Paul's meaning relates to the valuing of God's glory over the elevation of one's group over that of another. However, he understands ὑστεροῦνται τῆς δόξης τοῦ θεοῦ in 3:23 as falling short "of the ultimate honor they were intended to bear, that is, 'the glory of God'"(280). Thus, in 3:23, the phrase refers to the shared glory of God. It would appear to be more consistent to read 5:2 along these same lines. See Moo, *Romans*, 302; Schreiner, *Romans*, 254-55; Fitzmyer, *Romans*, 396; Byrne, *Romans*, 165; Dunn, *Romans*, 1:264.

5. Rom 4:20.

6. The concept of the people of God escaping shame is a clear OT motif. Schreiner, *Romans*, 256, lists Ps 22:5; 25:3, 20; 119:116; and Isa 28:16 as examples. Schreiner further notes that the verb here (καταισχύνει) most likely carries a future orientation, pointing to future salvation. In any case, the main point seems to be that the hope of the glory of God is a surety and will not end in shame for the people of God.

7. Wilckens, *Römer*, 1:289; Käsemann, *Romans*, 133; Wright, "Letter to the Romans," 516; Moo, *Romans*, 300-301. Dunn, *Romans*, 1:247-48, and Fitzmyer, *Romans*, 396, argue that the term is used to express access to a king in the sense of being granted the right to come into the presence of royalty. This meaning is not to be excluded,

ence was lost by Adam, never achieved by Israel, and is being restored in Christ. Second, the last phrase in the paragraph, "the love of God has been poured out in our hearts through the Holy Spirit who has been given to us" (ἡ ἀγάπη τοῦ θεοῦ ἐκκέχυται ἐν ταῖς καρδίαις ἡμῶν διὰ πνεύματος ἁγίου τοῦ δοθέντος ἡμῖν), clearly alludes to the prophetic promises concerning the Spirit of God, especially prophecies of Ezek 36 and Joel 2. This would again place emphasis on the restoration of God's people through the Messiah as well as provide a covenantal context.[8]

In the second paragraph of the chapter (vv. 6–11), Paul expands on the themes of 3:21–26. Parallels can be seen between 3:25 where God "put forth" his son and 5:8 where God "demonstrates his love." In both instances, the reference is to the death of Jesus as the means by which God shows forth his righteousness and reconciles sinners to himself. The argument comes to a climax in vv. 9–11. Reconciliation, while not a prominent OT theme, aptly summarizes the point to which Paul is building. In Adam's sin humanity is separated from the Creator, but through the Messiah's work is being reconciled to God. This is probably to be seen as fulfillment of the OT promise "You will be my people and I will be your God."[9] Combined with the previous allusions to prophetic promises, the corporate nature of the argument is clear: the Messiah has come to restore the people of God.

Thus, the textual and thematic similarities provide close links between chapter 5 and Paul's foregoing argument. This then provides the groundwork for the exposition of Adam and Christ in 5:12–21. The previous allusions to Adam are now made explicit in Paul's "wide-angle" argument in which he sets forth the plan of redemption of God's (corporate) people. The numerous connections between Rom 1, 3, and 5 seem to give more weight to the argument for the existence of adamic allusions in the earlier chapters of Romans. Nevertheless, some scholars maintain that Rom 5 is the first (and only) time in the letter that Paul references

---

especially in light of the fact that the term in the noun form is not used in the LXX. Nevertheless, two factors make the temple allusion probable. First, as Jewett, *Romans*, 349, points out, the verb form προσάγω is used in the LXX to refer to the action of bringing an offering to the altar (Lev 4:14). Second, in OT thought, the temple was to be seen as the throne room of God. Thus, access to grace is the honor of knowing and approaching God because peace has been made (Rom 5:1). In other words, the allusion probably carries both temple and kingship meanings, particularly since the OT does not neatly separate the two themes. See Hultgren, *Romans*, 205.

8. Holland, *Romans*, 155–56.
9. Wright, *Paul and the Faithfulness of God*, 888.

the Adam narratives. For example, Macaskill argues that in Rom 5:12–21, Adam is "not a symbol of lost glory" since glory language is absent from this section. Instead, Adam functions theologically "as the one whose action brought about a set of conditions that would reign over those who followed him."[10] Likewise, while Stowers strongly argued for the absence of adamic allusions in Rom 1 and 3, he gives very little space to Rom 5:12–21, relegating Adam's role to that of an example within Paul's argument, much like Abraham served as an example of faith in Rom 4.[11] However, this line of interpretation downplays the relationships between the two parts of Rom 5 (5:1–11; 5:12–21) and the connections with previous and subsequent sections of the epistle. As noted above, glory/shame language is significant in the first half of Rom 5, which is closely connected to the second half, as indicated by the διὰ τοῦτο of 5:12. Further, the textual connection between 3:23 and 5:12 directly links sin (in Adam) to lost glory. Moreover, much of the argument of Rom 5:12–21 was anticipated earlier in the letter and the theological themes arising in this section will be expanded through the whole of Rom 5–8.[12] Thus, the story of Adam may carry more weight than some interpreters allow.[13]

Beker insightfully reflects on the relationship between Rom 5:12–21 and the preceding argument:

> Jew and Gentile are now subsumed under the one figure of Adam, who by his transgression sealed "all men" (*pantas anthropous*, 5:18) under sin and death. The subject is no longer Jew or Gentile but "the many" (*hoi polloi*, 5:19). The scheme of "the one and the many" with its incorporation motif introduces a universalistic argument that concludes with the confidence and hope of eternal life (5:21). The Jewish argument of Rom 1:18–4:25 has been transcended, and we find ourselves on a new ontological level, the level of existence in Adam and in Christ, which 5:1–11 introduced. Because of "the new age" of "life" that has come in

---

10. Macaskill, *Union with Christ*, 238.

11. Stowers, *Rereading*, 253–55.

12. This claim will be substantiated through the exegetical analysis below and throughout the chapters that follow.

13. It is worth noting that those denying adamic allusions in Rom 1 and 3 typically give less attention to Rom 5:12–21 than to other sections. Stowers was mentioned above. In addition, Fitzmyer, *Romans*, 405–22, gives little space to the actual significance of Adam in Paul's argument, focusing instead on the translation of ἐφ' ᾧ in 5:12 and the concept of original sin.

Christ, the difference between Jew and Gentile is neutralized, for both belong equally to "the old age" that Christ has undone.[14]

One may take issue with some details of Beker's approach and with the assertion that the question of ethnicity is laid aside in chapters 5–8, but his point is apt.[15] The Jew and Gentile question is not completely settled at this point in the letter, and Paul builds on his previous argument in which the universality of sin was demonstrated with allusions to the Adam narrative. Now explicit, the story of Adam is again used to set up Paul's understanding of unity in Christ and flows directly from the purpose of the letter.[16]

Like the previous allusions to the Adam story, in Rom 5, Paul seems to be focusing on the story of Adam's failure in Gen 3. However, rather than focus on the sin itself, Paul centers his discussion on the relationship between Adam's sin and the rest of humanity. In addition, Garlington has pointed to the salvation-historical elements that pervade the entire section of Rom 5–8. He notes the following:

1. Rom 5—"life in Christ vs. death in Adam"

2. Rom 6:1—7:6—"newness of life in Christ vs. death and bondage to sin and the law"

3. Rom 7:7—8:39—"life and liberty in union with Christ and the Spirit vs. the captivity to the flesh, even in spite of indwelling sin and believer's groaning for the redemption of the body"

Garlington summarizes, "In each instance, the motif of the believer's once-for-all break with the past and his entrance into a new state of affairs stands out in prominent relief: an old pattern of existence is broken in order that a new mode of life may begin."[17] Thus, Rom 5:12–21 echoes some of the main themes of previous sections while at the same time setting the

---

14. Beker, *Paul*, 85.

15. Beker is commonly associated with the apocalyptic approach to Pauline theology, which differs at significant points from the reading of Romans offered in this book. The discussion that follows will briefly engage in dialogue with some proponents of the apocalyptic reading since Rom 5:12–21 is a passage that clearly illustrates the differences between a covenantal-narrative approach and the apocalyptic approach.

16. See chapter 1 for a brief discussion of the purpose of Romans as it relates to the argument of this book.

17. Garlington, "Obedience of Faith, Part III," 87.

theological table for the chapters that follow.[18] The entire section of the epistle draws on creational themes, reworked around the coming of the Messiah. The story of Adam (and Israel) plays an important role in the argument and is essential in understanding the central concept of union with Christ running through the section.

At the outset, it should be noted that the primary focus is on the actions of Adam and Christ and the ensuing effects of those actions. Jewett holds "that the main theme is how Christ's life (v. 10) defines the future destiny of believers just as Adam's life defined the future of his descendants."[19] Again, the corporate meaning of the text is emphasized. This is especially important to the argument of this book because Rom 5–8 contain the most explicit references to union with Christ in the entire letter. Thus, it would seem that Paul's use of the Adam narrative at the beginning is foundational for understanding the entire section, particularly his doctrine of union with Christ. The following exegetical analysis will focus on the role of the Adam narrative in the passage and set the stage for the discussion of the next two chapters in which the story of Adam (and Israel) will be shown to be the background for union with Christ.

Verse 12 opens the paragraph by immediately pointing to Adam and his sin. This verse also introduces the theme of death, which, along with sin, is personified and will play important roles throughout the following chapters. As with the previous allusions to Adam in Romans, there are some thematic links to the story of Israel running throughout this passage. That is, while the primary focus is on Adam and Christ, the story of Israel lurks not far beneath the surface. The exegetical analysis that follows will highlight the way in which Paul subtly weaves Israel's story into the discussion of Adam and Christ. I have argued in chapter 2 that Paul saw an intimate connection between the stories of Adam and Israel. This central passage is no exception.

Much of the discussion of 5:12 throughout the history of interpretation has focused on the last phrase (ἐφ' ᾧ πάντες ἥμαρτον). Though important, for the purposes of the present discussion, analysis will be limited to the contribution of this phrase to Paul's overall use of the Adam narrative in the paragraph. Most commentators agree that in verse 12, Paul begins a discussion, but then in verses 13–17 he steps back from

---

18. Michel, *Römer*, 155.
19. Jewett, *Romans*, 370.

the discussion to offer a couple of explanatory notes. He then picks back up his original argument in verse 18.

In verse 12, Paul draws on key terms and phrases, such as sin and death, from the earlier chapters, which helps to link the use of the Adam narrative to the previous allusions discussed above. Of course, the mention of sin draws the reader back to the primary theme of the first 3 chapters of Romans: all people, Jew and Gentile, are sinners. The focus here is on Adam's sin and its universal result. This serves to establish not only the universality of sin, but also the concept of unity in Adam over against unity in Christ, which will be essential to the following discussion of salvation in Christ.[20] As Ridderbos terms it, in this section, Paul shows the "solidarity in sin" of all people.[21]

Clearly, Paul has in mind the primal human being who failed to obey the command of God. The result of his failure was the entrance of death into God's world. The question of whether or not death existed before Adam's sin seems beyond the point. The fundamental issue at hand is the horrendous change brought about by one man's disobedience. Wright links the sin to the vocation of humanity: "The good creation was nevertheless transient: evening and morning, the decay and new life of autumn and spring, pointed on to a future, a purpose, which Genesis implies was the job of the human race to bring about."[22] Thus, Adam's failure was not only with regard to obeying the clear command of God, but failure to fulfill his vocation and usher in God's good intentions for his world.[23]

While I have focused on the participatory and narrative features of the text, the apocalyptic approach to Rom 5 typically emphasizes the cosmic dimensions of Paul's argument, particularly in terms of two aeons: before and after the Christ event. Käsemann's exposition is foundational for this line of interpretation. He identifies Paul's theme as the present life of believers who have through Christ entered "eschatological salvation," which is to be understood in sharp contrast to "the dominant Jewish

---

20. Jewett, *Romans*, 373.
21. Ridderbos, *Paul*, 95. So also Byrne, *Romans*, 176.
22. Wright, "Letter to the Romans," 526.
23. The interpretation of the Genesis text as literal, figurative, symbolic, or mythical lies outside the present purposes. Suffice to say that Paul seems to acknowledge the existence of a literal man who disobeyed God and brought sin into the world. Beyond this primary point, Paul gives few clues as to his understanding of the other elements of the story.

view."²⁴ This approach is, at heart, focused on the concept of the defeat of sin and death and the ushering in of the new age through Christ's death and resurrection. For Käsemann, the rule of Christ is to be stressed over against any concept of union with him.²⁵

Additionally, scholars situated within this school of thought usually give little attention to the narrative continuity with the OT, instead emphasizing eschatological newness of the gospel. The problem is that while the reign of Christ over sin and death is central to this section, Paul also emphasizes the effects of the actions of Adam and Christ on others, a relationship best described as union. That is, one need not pit kingship and eschatology against participatory themes as both feature significantly in Rom 5–8. Moreover, apocalyptic approaches typically downplay the connections between the stories of Adam and Israel, a connection that I have contended is central to Paul's argument. Building on Käsemann, de Boer holds that the cosmic statements of Rom 5:12 and 5:21 frame the passage while the intervening verses merely explain the central concept of cosmic reign.²⁶ Again, though broadly true, such an emphasis misses the role of the OT stories in the argument, particularly as they relate to union with Christ. Thus, the apocalyptic approach of Käsemann and de Boer rightly emphasizes the reign of Christ in victory over sin and death, but misses the key point of unity in Adam for all people apart from Christ. This emphasis then leads to a downplaying of participatory themes.

The controversial phrase that concludes 5:12 fits into the discussion by drawing attention back to 3:23. Paul's use of the phrase πάντες ἥμαρτον connects to 3:23, where the exact terms were used. In chapter 2, I argued that this phrase was is an allusion to the participation of all people in the sin of Adam and the linkage of this sin to the loss of the original glory of humanity. Adam's sin caused all people to lose the derived glory of God. In 5:12, Paul begins his discussion of Adam and Christ by reminding his readers of this point. Death here is linked to the loss of original glory and the failure of Adam to fulfill his original purposes. Again, this serves to set the stage for Paul's argument for the unity of the people of God in Christ. One man's sin brought about the negative unity of all people in sin. That is, the one act of the first man profoundly affected the future of his family. This family includes all descended from Adam, including

---

24. Käsemann, *Romans*, 142.
25. Ibid., 143. Käsemann is specifically combatting notions of corporate personality.
26. de Boer, *Defeat of Death*, 162–63.

Israel. The emphasis should be on "all" in that all people, without exception, are caught up in the sin of Adam.[27] In relation to the purpose of the present argument, one could say that all are united to Adam in sin, which leads to death. The universal nature of the statement serves the purposes of the epistle as well as setting up the exposition of salvation in Christ, which is to follow.

As mentioned above, commentators widely agree that verses 13–17 contain an explanatory aside before Paul continues the original argument in verse 18. Though an aside, these verses nevertheless play an important role in the overall argument of the paragraph, particularly in relation to Paul's use of the Adam narrative and his weaving of the story of Israel into the Adam story. In verses 13–14, Paul immediately brings Israel into the discussion after his reference to Adam in verse 12. Why do this? It is the repeated pattern Paul has utilized through each stage of the argument to move from Adam to Israel. Thus, it is unsurprising that he would again employ this technique at such a pivotal point in the epistle.

The overall purpose of verses 13–14 seems to be to indicate again the culpability of all people as a result of sin. Having already stated that "all sinned" and that death comes to all because of sin, Paul shows the way in which sin and death relate to law. In sum, both Jews and Gentiles are guilty of sin, regardless of whether or not they possess the law. Sin entered the world through Adam and spread to all people, who are united to Adam, sin, and death. All die because all sinned in Adam. This means that sin "is deeper and more pervasive, infecting even those who conform to the Torah."[28]

Paul seems to be subtly pointing out the fact that Israel is also part of the human sin problem. Though all die, "sin is not reckoned where there is no law" (ἁμαρτία δὲ οὐκ ἐλλογεῖται μὴ ὄντος νόμου). While some have focused on the meaning of this verse in relation to the culpability of those who lived between Adam and Moses,[29] it seems that Paul's primary point is to show that Israel is indeed caught up in the sin of Adam. He does this in several ways. First, all Jews would agree that all humanity is descended from Adam, including Israel. Thus, Israel is certainly included in the "all"

---

27. Rapinchuk, "Universal Sin and Salvation." The point is that all, regardless of ethnic identity, are in sin.

28. Jewett, *Romans*, 377.

29. Clearly, Paul intends to say that even those without the law are sinners because they die. Death comes because of sin. Since those who lived between Adam and Moses all died, they were all sinners.

of "all sinned." On the most basic level, none could deny that Israel was affected by Adam's sin.[30] However, the argument pushes further.

Second, Israel would not be counted among those whose sin was "not reckoned" because of the lack of God's law. In verse 14, Paul says that even those who did not have the law died. Their sins were counted against them even though they did not have the law of God as Adam did. However, Israel did indeed have the law and their sin was like that of Adam: having the clear commandments of God yet failing to keep them. In this way, Paul is emphatic that Israel, though intended as a nation to be part of God's solution for the problem of sin, has become a part of the problem. Indeed, their problem is deeper on the account of the law. In other words, if those without the law die as a result of sin, much greater is the culpability of those with the law. In this way, Paul links the breaking of the Torah to the sin of Adam.

Finally, the last phrase of verse 14 is at once both a statement of Adam Christology and a confirmation that corporate Israel is not the one sent to reverse the massive effects of Adam's sin. Adam is a type (τύπος) of the coming one, who is the Messiah. This phrase sets up the Adam-Christ comparison that will follow, but also implies that Israel is just as much in need of a savior as the rest of humanity. This again lays the narrative foundation for the following exposition of salvation in Christ. In short, all people—those with and those without the law—are united to Adam, sin, and death and, therefore, in need of God's grace given through the Messiah Jesus.

In contrast to this reading, de Boer holds that Paul is setting the work of Christ "not only in opposition to Adam and his trespass but *also* to the Law as the presumed remedy to the trespass."[31] Throughout his exposition, de Boer focuses on the role of the Law in Rom 5:13, 20, arguing that the Law itself is "antithetical" to grace.[32] While Paul certainly argues that sin used the Law as a tool to produce disobedience and death (Rom 7:8), there seems to be a more fundamental point in Rom 5 that the overemphasis on the discontinuity of Law and grace causes de Boer to neglect: the unity of all people, Jew and Gentile, in Adam. This emphasis, in turn, also shifts the focus away from the participatory elements that run strongly through the whole of Rom 5–8. Consequently, the apoca-

---

30. This is clear in multiple references to the sin of Adam in early Jewish literature.
31. de Boer, "Paul's Mythologizing Program," 10 (emphasis de Boer's).
32. Ibid., 14.

lyptic interpretation falters as Paul's primary use of the Adam and Israel narratives is misconstrued.

In verses 15–17, Paul shows the way in which Adam was a type of the coming one. Adam and Christ are alike in that their acts of disobedience and obedience had profound effects on those who came after them, or rather, on those who are united to them.[33] Paul seems to offer this clarification so that his readers would not misunderstand and assume that Adam and Christ are exactly alike in every way. Christ did not come to simply restore humanity to the pre-fallen state. Rather, the gift of grace in Christ far outweighs the trespass and its results.[34]

With regard to the story of Adam, Paul's repeated reference is to the story of Adam's sin from Gen 3, highlighting the disobedience of Adam. The primary point is to show that all die because of the sin of Adam, including both Jews and Gentiles. Verse 16 explicitly mentions the judgment that followed the sin of Adam, which clearly refers to death. Being united to Adam results in death. Later in this book, it will be demonstrated that in the same way, yet on an elevated level, union with Christ results in righteousness and life. The story of Adam, which includes the story of Israel, forms the background for union with Christ by showing the unity of humanity in sin and the need for a new union with the Messiah.

Verses 18–21 pick up the argument that was left in verse 12. Paul here completes his original thought regarding the relationship of the sin of all people to the sin of Adam. There are several points that need to be made. First, Paul expands the depth of meaning in these verses by stating that through Adam's sin, all people were "made sinners" (ἁμαρτωλοὶ κατεστάθησαν οἱ πολλοί). In Adam's sin, sin and death entered the world, spread to all, resulting in the sinfulness of those who are united to Adam. This phrasing places strong emphasis on the intimate connection between sinners and Adam.

Second, in verse 20, Paul again makes reference to the law, undoubtedly to draw attention to Israel. Here, the law is given a negative purpose: "to increase the trespass" (ἵνα πλεονάσῃ τὸ παράπτωμα). The intended meaning is that Israel has participated in the sin of Adam and, ironically, increased in trespass on account of the law. That is, the law gave additional opportunities for Israel to sin like Adam, compounding the sin problem. Rather than being the means through which the sin of Adam

---

33. Jewett, *Romans*, 378.

34. This point will be explored further later in chapter 5 below.

would be set aright, the law only led to greater sinning. Clearly this does not portray an overall negative attitude toward the law. Rather, Paul simply points out one negative effect of the law that ultimately led to God's purposes being fulfilled in Christ rather than in national Israel alone.

Finally, the paragraph ends with a reference to kingship: "sin reigned in death" (ἐβασίλευσεν ἡ ἁμαρτία ἐν τῷ θανάτῳ). Having entered the world through Adam's disobedience, sin, here personified, reigned supremely over all Adam's descendants. Those who came after Adam were born into the kingdom of sin, participating in rebellion via their union with their forefather. The effect of this is to show the domination of sin over all people because they are united to sin.

The kingship language of verse 20 leads some, especially those related to the apocalyptic approach, to interpret the entire Adam/Christ discussion in terms of cosmic reign. Whereas I have primarily framed the discussion around two unions (with Adam and with Christ),[35] Käsemann emphasizes the distinction between the reign of sin through Adam and the reign of Christ, who brings eschatological victory.[36] While the kingship language is undoubtedly important, the primary theological emphasis, especially in Rom 6–8, is on union with Christ. Kingship language will appear again in Rom 6, but most fundamental is the identification of believers with the King: they are united, Jew and Gentile together, to the Messiah-King. Likewise, in Rom 5:12–21, the primary emphasis is the union of those outside of Christ in Adam. Moreover, the overemphasis on the complete breaking in of the new age misses much of Paul's narrative argumentation. Throughout Romans, Paul argues for a new identification in Christ, but he does not mean that all things prior to Christ has been completely set aside. Indeed, his gospel is that which is promised beforehand (Rom 1:2; 3:21).

To summarize, Rom 5:12–21 makes explicit and clear that which was previously alluded to in the epistle. Namely, the Adam (and Israel) narrative is essential for rightly understanding salvation in Christ. All people are united together in Adam and his sin. Thus, none are exempted from the penalty of sin, death. Humanity's relationship to Adam's sin is one of intimate union and this union is stronger than any ethnic identity or socio-economic status. It remains to be shown that Paul intended union with Christ to be understood with this background in mind. At

---

35. The above exegesis has focused specifically on union with Adam in sin; union with Christ will be examined in chapter 5 below.

36. Käemann, *Romans*, 158.

this point, suffice to say that believer's union with Christ is presented as trumping all other allegiances, including the former allegiance to sin.

Romans 7:7–13

Romans 7 brings yet another hotly debated passage throughout the history of interpretation. In the wider context, historical debates have included the verses following 7:7–13, with interpreters debating the identity of the "I" throughout the passage. Schreiner lists three primary suggestions as to the "I": 1) Adam in the garden; 2) Israel at Sinai; and 3) Paul himself.[37] As Moo has made clear, though much debate has centered on this issue, the primary point of the text does not concern "human nature, or anthropology, but the Mosaic Law."[38] Thus, while the issue of the identity of the "I" cannot be ignored, there are larger concerns at work in the passage, particularly as it relates to the argument of this book. I will argue here that while the text is primarily about the Mosaic Law, Paul uses particular language to allude to the Adam narrative, thus showing that Israel, like all humanity, is caught up in the sin of Adam. In particular, Paul alludes to both Adam and Israel to show that the sin of Israel recapitulates the sin of Adam.[39] In this way, this passage contains parallels with passages examined above and extends the argument in order to continue building the OT background for union with Christ.

As with the passages studied above, the exegetical analysis is this section will focus on Paul's use of the Adam and Israel stories, particularly as they serve as OT background for union with Christ. While the exegetical analysis below will argue for the presence of allusions to both the Adam and Israel narratives, some interpreters believe that Adam has no role in Paul's argument in Rom 7 or that if present at all, it is a "remote" reference.[40] Before exegetically defending the presence of adamic allusions, it will be helpful to engage alternative positions. Fitzmyer believes that interpretations that detect adamic allusions are "eisegetical," even

---

37. Schreiner, *Romans*, 359. Others have suggested that Paul is here describing the "normal Christian life" in which believers continue to struggle with sin. See Dunn, *Romans*, 1:387–99, and Cranfield, *Romans*, 1:342–47. However, the context, particularly chapters 6 and 8, make such an interpretation highly unlikely.

38. Moo, *Romans*, 424. Moo adds a fourth possible line of interpretation, which sees the passage as a description of the experience of all people.

39. Wright, *Climax*, 197. So also Kruse, *Romans*, 302.

40. Macaskill, *Union with Christ*, 238.

though he admits to a probable allusion to Gen 3:13 in Rom 7:11.[41] Such a view seems to disregard the textual connections with previous chapters as well as the wider context as Rom 7:7-13 falls broadly within the larger argument of Rom 5-8. In addition, I will point out numerous echoes of the story of Gen 3 below in order to demonstrate that the adamic allusion extends beyond verse 11. While some connections to the Genesis account are clearer than others, the clustering of references makes the adamic interpretation plausible. Finally, denial of the adamic allusion causes Fitzmyer and others to miss the real force of Paul's argument, which stands in continuity with Rom 1, 3, and 5: outside of Christ, Jew and Gentile are united in Adam. It seems that the denial of the adamic allusions in Rom 1 and 3 leads to the denial of Adam in Rom 7 without adequate attention given to the individual allusions.

Jewett denies references to both Adam and Israel, opting for an autobiographical approach and arguing that there are elements of the text that cannot be applied completely to Adam or Israel.[42] As an alternative, Jewett gives weight to potential Greco-Roman parallels and concludes that Paul is making use of *prosopopoeia* (speech-in-character), reflecting on "his preconversion experience as a zealot, but with an eye to the current situation in the Roman churches."[43] The denial of allusions to Adam (and Israel) is based on the observation that there are some elements of Rom 7:7-13 that do not completely apply the Genesis narratives or Israel's story. However, this assumes that for an author to allude to an earlier text, he must include all the details of the story. Moreover, such an argument leaves no room for Paul's interpretive use of the Adam narrative. In other words, Paul is not simply retelling the story, but interpreting in light of Israel's story and the gospel. Jewett's position also seems to miss the place of the passage within the overall argument and the connections to other passages. In addition, he does not give enough weight to the clear OT allusions. He acknowledges the probable allusion to Adam in verse 11, but curiously dismisses the force of the allusion for the meaning of the text. These factors make his proposal untenable.

41. Fitzmyer, *Romans*, 464, 468.

42. Jewett, *Romans*, 441-53. Stowers, *Rereading*, 275-80, likewise denies adamic allusions and argues for similarities with Greco-Roman writings instead. However, most commentators recognize the problems of a strictly autobiographical interpretation and credit Kümmel, *Römer*, with changing the tide of interpretation onto a more figurative understanding of the "I."

43. Jewett, *Romans*, 444.

Against the above interpretations, I will argue that Paul alludes to both Adam and Israel in Rom 7:7–13 and that this reading makes better sense of both this particular passage and Paul's wider argument. In beginning this analysis, it will be helpful to first demonstrate the connection between Rom 7:7–13 and other passages containing allusions to both the Adam and Israel narratives. First, there are textual and thematic links between chapters 1 and 7. In order to illustrate his point in 7:7–8, Paul chooses the example of coveting (ἐπιθυμία). While at first blush it may seem to be a random selection, it is interesting that the term first occurs in 1:24, where Paul writes "Therefore God gave them over in the lusts (ἐπιθυμίαις) of their hearts."[44] Within the context, this is the first of three instances in chapter 1 in which Paul says that God "gave over" sinners to their sin, giving it a prominent position within the argument. Thus, using the term again in 7:7 links the discussion to chapter 1.

In addition, there are other key word and thematic links to chapter 1. In explaining the effects of the law upon the "I," Paul notes that the commandment brought about death (7:9, 10, 11). In chapter 1, those committing the litany of sins listed earn death for themselves (1:32). This again serves not only to link the two chapters, but also to show that those with the law are no better off, at least in terms of standing within the people of God, than those without the law. Other prominent terms and themes such as righteousness (7:12), law (7:7–12), and deceit (7:11) also find connections in chapter 1 (1:17, 25, 29).

Second, the key themes of sin and the results of sin echo Rom 3:23, where Paul summarized his argument on the universality of sin: all have sinned in Adam and thus lost the creational glory given by God. In 7:7–13, Paul echoes this argument by expounding on the negative use of the law, arguing that those who have the law die because they fail to keep it. It will be argued below that there is also an allusion to the Adam narrative (with the story of Israel woven into it) in this section, thus linking the loss of the glory of God with death through the law.

Third, the themes introduced in verse 7—law (νόμος) and sin (ἁμαρτία)—immediately link the paragraph back to Rom 5:12–21, where such themes figured prominently. In addition, the following verses discuss the relationship between law, sin, and death, which were major components of the argument in chapter 5. Here, Paul defends the goodness

---

44. The same idea, though with a different term (πλεονεξία), is found in 1:29. The term ἐπιθυμία also occurs in 6:12 and 13:14.

of the law while at the same time reinforcing what he already stated in chapter 5: death is a result of sin. This is again linked to the sin of Adam.

These links between Rom 7:7–13 and the previous allusions to Adam (and Israel) serve to draw together a unified use of these stories in Paul's argument, thereby leading the reader to expect references to both Adam and Israel in the context. That is, given the links between Paul's previous uses of these OT narratives, it is unsurprising to find additional allusions here. With this in mind, it will be argued below that Paul is again showing the solidarity of humanity in sin, thus preparing the way for his argument for the unity of the new humanity in Christ.

The short paragraph of 7:7–13, while somewhat difficult in the particulars of the argument, clearly puts forth the primary idea: death is a result of sin, not the fault of the law. The law in itself is good because it comes directly from God. Thus, any exegetical analysis must proceed from this main point. That this is the primary thrust of the paragraph is clear from verse 7, in which Paul anticipates a possible objection to his argument—that the law is sin since it cannot produce life. Paul answers this challenge via allusions to the Adam and Israel stories.

The immediate reference to the law in verses 7–8 draws the reader's attention to the story of Israel and the giving of the law at Sinai. Specifically, Paul says that he would not have known covetousness if the law had not commanded him not to covet. The terminology here indicates that Paul most likely intends to communicate something more than the law merely giving information about sin. When Paul writes that he would not have "known sin" apart from the Law (τὴν ἁμαρτίαν οὐκ ἔγνων εἰ μὴ διὰ νόμου), he means that the law was the tool used by sin to give an intimate knowledge of sin and this type of knowledge is experiential, knowing sin from the heart.[45] Verse 8 confirms this understanding as Paul pushes the argument further by noting that all kinds of coveting was produced "in me" (ἐν ἐμοί).

Covetousness is an interesting choice of example, since, as mentioned above, the term has connections with Rom 1. In addition, the sin of Adam can be described as coveting, since he reached for that which he did not already possess. Such an understanding was present in Jewish literature, such as in the Greek *Life of Adam and Eve* 19:3, which describes the sin of Adam as "covetousness" (ἐπιθυμία).[46] In addition, other texts,

---

45. Wright, "Letter to the Romans," 562.

46. Dochhorn, "Röm 7,7." As noted in chapter 2 above, while some doubt the usefulness of *GLAE*, Paul was probably drawing on similar traditions. Thus, parallels

such as *4 Ezra* 7:11 and the *Apocalypse of Abraham* 24 link Adam's sin to the breaking of commandments.[47] Finally, Philo claims that "most truly may covetous desire [ἐπιθυμία] be said to be the original passion which is at the bottom of all these mischiefs."[48] Thus, the Jewish literature provides some background for Paul's thinking as he links together Adam, Israel, Law, and sin.

That Paul has Adam in mind is confirmed in Rom 7:9 where he claims to have once been alive apart from the law. Paul is speaking of spiritual life and death in this passage. Adam stands as the clear example of one who lived prior to the law but then died when the commandment came. Created in the image of God, Adam began life without sin. In Gen 2, God commands Adam not to eat the fruit from the tree of the knowledge of good and evil and informs Adam that upon eating, he will die. Thus, the result of sin is ultimately death. Conversely, abstaining from eating this fruit would have resulted in life, to which Paul alludes in verse 10 (εἰς ζωήν). In addition, prior to sin, Adam had free access to the tree of life, which would have presumably given unending life in the garden.[49] This, of course, points back to the discussion of Rom 5, where sin and death entered the world via the disobedience of Adam.

The following verses contain further clues that Paul has Adam in mind in this exposition. Indeed, as Adams notes, "There is little in these verses that does not apply to Adam."[50] In verse 11, Paul writes, "for sin, taking hold of an opportunity, deceived me through the law and through it killed me" (ἡ γὰρ ἁμαρτία ἀφορμὴν λαβοῦσα διὰ τῆς ἐντολῆς ἐξηπάτησέν με καὶ δι᾽ αὐτῆς ἀπέκτεινεν). This verse has clear connections to the Genesis account of Adam's sin. First, the term "deceived" (ἐξαπατάω) is the same term used in the LXX to translate the Hebrew term נָשָׁא in Gen. 3:13, where Eve claims that her disobedience was the result of the serpent's deception.[51] Thus, in Paul's exposition, "sin" takes the place of the

---

between Romans and *GLAE* are not irrelevant.

47. Kidwell, "Adamic Backdrop of Romans," 108, argues that *Jubilees* also looks on Eden retrospectively as if Adam and Eve possessed the Law.

48. *De Specialibus Legibus* 4:85. "These mischiefs" include "thefts, and acts of rapine, and repudiation of debt, and all false accusations, and acts of insolence, and, moreover, all ravishments, and adulteries, and murders, and, in short, all mischiefs, whether private or public, or sacred or profane."

49. Dunn, *Romans*, 1:384.

50. Adams, "Paul's Story," 28.

51. The same term is used in relation to the Genesis account of Eve's sin in 2 Cor

serpent as the deceiver.[52] In Gen 3, the serpent used the commandment given by God in order to deceive Eve. That is, the serpent used the law as a means of deception that led to sin.[53] The identity of personified sin is now clearly revealed: it is the serpent himself. Just as the serpent used the command of God as a tool of deception, so he has used God's commands and laws throughout history as tools to produce sin and death. The veiled reference allows wider application.[54] Adam, Israel, and all people find themselves deceived and therefore united to sin (Satan). Second, this is followed by the result clause: the "I" is killed by sin. This clearly links back to the result of Adam's sin (death). Third, in verses 8–11, Paul changes terminology, using "commandment" (ἐντολή), which would seem to point to Adam since "law" (νόμος) would have more readily alluded to the Mosaic Law.[55] Thus, the progression of Paul's narrative argument fits the story of Adam: life apart from the law (creation) → commandment given → sin → death.

At the same time, Paul continues to use the term "law" (νόμος) and includes additional allusions to the story of Israel, indicating that Jews are not exempt from the charge of sin. First, though I argued above that the example of coveting lends itself to identification with Adam's sin, it is nevertheless a direct quotation from Exod 20:17 in the LXX (οὐκ ἐπιθυμήσεις), which forms the tenth commandment. Second, Watson argues that Paul's statement that he was once alive "apart from the law" (χωρὶς νόμου) alludes to Israel before the giving of the law.[56] If the exodus is pictured as a new creation, Paul's mention of life before law could very well point to Israel's experience.[57] Thus, the giving of the law at Sinai would form a "parallel" to the giving of the commandment to Adam in the garden.[58] Nevertheless, Israel, like Adam, died because of sin through disobedience to the law. Indeed, Dunn convincingly argues that there is an echo of Israel's sin of Exod 32 within this passage, which would build

---

11:3 and 1 Tim 2:14.

52. Dochhorn, "Röm 7,7," 69.

53. Watson, *Paul, Judaism, and the Gentiles*, 283.

54. Wright, "Letter to the Romans," 563–64.

55. Adams, "Paul's Story," 28.

56. Watson, *Paul, Judaism, and the Gentiles*, 282.

57. On the relationship between creation and exodus, see Sailhamer, *Meaning of the Pentateuch*, 572–83; Dempster, *Dominion and Dynasty*, 100–104; Beale, *New Testament Biblical Theology*, 93.

58. Grieb, *Story of Romans*, 74.

on a common Jewish understanding that links the golden calf episode with the sin of Adam.[59]

Third, just as Adam's story ended in death because of sin, so also the story of the exodus generation ended in death in the wilderness.[60] God redeemed Israel from Egypt, giving them life like they had never experienced. Yet, they quickly rebelled and the entire generation died without entering the Promised Land. Alternatively, if one focuses on the specific sin of the golden calf, the end result was also death. Thus, the progression of the story in Rom 7 fits with Israel: life apart from the law (exodus) → law given → sin → death.

Since Paul's discussion of death is an exposition of the OT narratives of Adam and Israel, his understanding of death is shaped by those stories. In Genesis, God told Adam that if he disobeyed the command, he would die (Gen 2:17). However, according to Gen 3, Adam did not physically die upon eating. The immediate results of his disobedience include alienation from God and exile from the garden, though he would physically die. The same basic pattern can be seen in the story of Israel in the wilderness. When they refused to enter the land of promise, God decreed that they would die in the wilderness (Num 14:20–25). For the Israelites, physical death occurred over a period of time, but the immediate results of rebellion include alienation from God and exile from the land. The same can be said of the later exile. Thus, in referencing death, Paul has in mind spiritual death, which eventually results in physical death. The OT does not seem to sharply divide these two types of death since one results directly from the other.[61] Paul saw all people as dead in Adam and sin (exile and alienation from God), leading to physical death.

Fourth, Watson argues that the juxtaposition of life and death, along with the juxtaposition of good and evil in Rom 7:13–25 draws on the final speech of Moses in Deut 30.[62] The LXX translates Deut 30:15 as Ἰδοὺ δέδωκα πρὸ προσώπου σου σήμερον τὴν ζωὴν καὶ τὸν θάνατον, τὸ ἀγαθὸν καὶ τὸ κακόν. This would give the whole of Rom 7:7–25 a covenantal background that would draw attention to both the giving of the law and the failure of Israel.

---

59. Dunn, *Romans*, 1:400.

60. Watson, *Paul, Judaism, and the Gentiles*, 284.

61. See Dempster, *Dominion and Dynasty*, 66–68; Scobie, *Ways of Our God*, 892–93; Wenham, *Genesis*, 1:90–91; Moberly, *Theology of Genesis*, 83–86; and Waltke and Yu, *Old Testament Theology*, 260.

62. Watson, *Paul, Judaism, and the Gentiles*, 285–86.

Thus, while some have argued for an allusion to either Adam or Israel,[63] it would seem that Paul had both in mind with an organic relationship between the two. Indeed, as Keck has pointed out, "The whole passage results from the juxtaposition of, and interplay between (a) the quotation from the Decalogue (v. 7), (b) allusions to Gen 3, and (c) allusions to what Paul said in 5:12-21 about both Adam and the law."[64] Moreover, the criteria set forth in chapter 1 for identifying allusions are met with regard to both Adam and Israel. As in each of the passages analyzed above, Paul alludes to Adam and includes a reference to Israel. The purpose of this technique is to show that Israel is just as much a part of humanity's sin problem as the Gentiles: the sin of Israel is pictured as a recapitulation of Adam's sin. Thus, instead of solving the problem of sin, Israel has ironically made it worse (Rom 7:13).

Paul's purpose here is twofold. First, he defends the law by showing that God's commandments are good and holy. It is the sin of humanity that is evil, not the law itself. Second, Paul again weaves together the stories of Adam and Israel to show that all people are caught up in Adam's sin. As Wright aptly put it, "what is being asserted about Israel is that when the Torah arrived it had the same effect on her as God's commandment in the Garden had on Adam."[65] That Paul saw an intimate connection between the stories of Adam and Israel has been clear from the exegetical analysis above.[66] He builds further upon this idea in 7:7-13, where readers are themselves drawn into the story by Paul's use of the first person. Whether Jew or Gentile, all people find themselves dead in sin.

Watson draws all of this back to the grand purpose of Romans: to drive the readers, particularly Jewish readers, to unity in Christ. Paul "wishes to persuade the Jewish Christians to find their identity exclusively in Christ, and not in the Torah, and his Genesis-inspired argument in Rom 7 aims to persuade his readers that life under the law leads only to insoluble contradiction as the quest for life issues in death and the quest for the good issues in evil."[67] To nuance this slightly, Paul is here laying

---

63. For example, Käsemann, *Romans*, 196, writes "a story is told in vv. 9-11 and that the event depicted can refer strictly only to Adam ... there is nothing in the passage which does not fit Adam, and everything fits Adam alone."

64. Keck, *Romans*, 183. That the stories of Adam and Israel are drawn together in Rom 7:7-12 is recognized by Thielman, "Story of Israel," 191-93.

65. Wright, *Climax*, 197. So also, Byrne, *Romans*, 218.

66. See the discussion in Wells, *Grace and Agency*, 237-40.

67. Watson, *Paul, Judaism, and the Gentiles*, 287.

the foundation for his argument for unity in the church via the concept of union with Christ. Jews and Gentiles alike are dead in sin and cannot find life apart from Christ. That all people find themselves in the same predicament shows a basic unity in sin for all people. In other words, those finding their identity in any other affiliation are actually unified in sin, whether Jew or Gentile.

This section has focused almost exclusively on Rom 7:7–13 because these verses contain the "loudest" echoes of the Adam and Israel stories. Thus, the controversial remaining verses of the chapter have not been treated exegetically here and, for the purposes of this book, such a study is unnecessary. Suffice to say that the last part of the chapter stands in continuity with the first thirteen verses and further illustrates the plight of Israel in union with Adam.[68] That is, while the passage is much debated, the preferable understanding, especially in light of the above exegesis, is that though Israel has the law, they nevertheless remain "in Adam" and in need of rescue like the rest of humanity. These verses set up the solution that will be celebrated in chapter 8: no condemnation in Christ.

Romans 8

Romans 8 contains the last of the commonly recognized allusions to Adam within the letter.[69] While there is no obvious allusion to Adam after Rom 8, the foundational stories of the Hebrew Bible remain important as chapters 9–16 build upon the Paul's argument in chapters 1–8, especially related to the OT stories and union with Christ, while simultaneously transitioning to additional stages in the overall argument.[70] Interestingly, Rom 8 contains two allusions to the story of Adam, but in both cases, the primary concern of the text is to show the restoration of that which was lost or damaged through Adam's sin in Christ. More specifically related to the argument of this book, the allusions of Romans 8 represent a shift in emphasis from sinfulness in Adam to redemption in Christ. As such, this section will be somewhat shorter than the above sections as some of the discussion will be deferred to the following chapters on union with Christ.

---

68. Wright, "Letter to the Romans," 565.

69. An additional allusion is found in 16:18–20, but is not commonly recognized and does not feature significantly in the argument of this book. See below.

70. See chapter 6 below.

Adams identifies the two allusions to the Adam narrative as 8:19-22 and 8:28-30.[71] Each of these passages will be examined below, but it may be helpful to begin by placing them within the overall argument of Rom 8. Following Paul's defense of the law and his exposition of the plight of those living under the law in chapter 7, Paul moves to an explanation of God's solution to the problem of sin in chapter 8. Having already affirmed that the law itself is not sinful, Paul advances his argument by showing that although the law is not the cause of sin, nevertheless sin has rendered the law powerless to give life (8:3). In short, God accomplished redemption through the work of Christ as applied by the Spirit (8:4). Where sin worked through the law to bring about death, there is "no condemnation for those in Christ" (8:1). The result of this is life in the Spirit—a life lived in obedience to God (8:5-11). In 8:12-17, Paul enumerates the blessings of the new life in Christ, namely that those "who are led by the Spirit are the sons of God" (8:14).

This brings the discussion to the first allusion to the Adam narratives in Rom 8. As noted above, the allusions here focus primarily on restoration in Christ rather than sinful solidarity in Adam. Additionally, the allusions in Rom 8 are largely eschatological in nature, pointing to future glory: an allusion to the creation story shows the all-encompassing nature of redemption in Christ, including the restoration of the cosmos. Paul sets up the allusion to Adam by linking the present discussion with previous allusions to Adam via the term "glory" (δόξα) in 8:17 and 8:18. The term, though here pointing forward to the glory to be possessed by believers, links to previous allusions to Adam in Rom 1 and 3, where the term was used to describe that which was lost through Adam's sin. In 1:23, Paul says that people have traded the glory of God for the worship of idols. As argued in chapter 2 above, Paul's reference in 1:23 is to both Gentiles and Jews. Within the argument of the letter, it seems that Paul intends to communicate that all people, Jew and Gentile alike, have failed to adequately reflect the glory of God. Therefore, they are sinful and destined to suffer the coming wrath. In 3:23, Paul brings his universal indictment of sinners full circle, stating that "all sinned and lack the glory of God." Again, the glory here is that of original creation lost by Adam and still lacking in all humans.

In addition to these clear linkages to the lost glory in Adam, Paul already hinted at restoration through Christ in chapter 2, where he used

---

71. Adams, "Paul's Story," 28-29.

OT allusions to argue that Gentile believers are fulfilling new covenant promises and thus glory is being restored. In 4:20, Abraham is pictured as one who "gave glory to God," thus demonstrating that God is righteous to fulfill his original intentions for humanity through the covenant promises given to Abraham. In addition, there is a corporate meaning here reflected in a possible link to Yahweh's promise of restoration of glory as an important aspect of redemption (Isa 35:1–2).[72] Thus, not only does the promise of restoration of glory refer to the lost glory of all people in Adam, but it also refers to the restoration of the glory of God's people. In other words, the fulfillment of Isa 35:1–2 (as well as other OT passages) is taking place in Christ. All of this provides an Adam-Israel context for the following verses.

With the repetition of glory in 8:17–18, the stage is set for the allusion to Adam in 8:19–22. Verse 19 begins by calling the reader's attention to creation, linking back to Rom 1:20, where Paul argued for the sinfulness of humanity despite the clear revelation of God. Romans 8:19–22, like previous allusions to Adam, points to the disastrous effects of Adam's sin. However, the focus here is on the effects of sin upon creation rather than the universality of human sin. Nevertheless, the use of the Adam story serves to set the universality of human sin within the history of the cosmos. Verse 20 makes it clear that Paul is indeed talking about the sin of Adam. The original glory of creation has been diminished, not by creation itself, but "by one who subjected it" (διὰ τὸν ὑποτάξαντα) to "futility" (ματαιότης).[73] Paul is clearly alluding to Gen 3, where the ground is cursed because of Adam's sin. This idea, "which links the bondage of creation again and again to the disobedience and bondage of the people of God" is important throughout the narrative of the Bible.[74]

Further, as Jewett notes, the term ματαιότης links back to 1:21, where the related verb (ματαιόω) was used to describe the state of futility of those who have rejected God's revelation in idolatry.[75] This verbal link to Rom 1 shows that "the primary allusion is to the Adam narratives."[76] In addition, "hope" and "glory" were used together in 5:2 (ἐλπίδι τῆς δόξης

---

72. Jewett, *Romans*, 510–11.

73. The fact that the subjection was done "in hope" means that the one who subjected creation to futility was God, thus placing the emphasis on the curse.

74. Keesmaat, *Paul and His Story*, 106. She specifically points to several passages in the prophetic writings.

75. Jewett, *Romans*, 513.

76. Dunn, *Romans*, 1:470.

τοῦ θεοῦ) leading up to Paul's discussion of Adam and Christ. Again, these key terms and concepts link together the various allusions to Adam (and Israel) throughout Romans.

An additional possible reference to Adam is found in 8:19. There, Paul personifies creation as "eagerly awaiting the revelation of the sons of God" (ἡ γὰρ ἀποκαραδοκία τῆς κτίσεως τὴν ἀποκάλυψιν τῶν υἱῶν τοῦ θεοῦ ἀπεκδέχεται). Paul has already used the term "son(s) of God" in Rom 1:4 to refer to the resurrected Christ, in 8:3 to refer again to Christ, and (in the plural) in 8:14 to refer to Christians. In the OT, "son of God" was used to refer to Israel (Exod 4:22–23) as the special people of God and, more specifically, to the king of Israel as the "son of God."[77] However, though Adam is never specifically called the "son of God" in Genesis, the concept is certainly present. In the genealogy of Gen 5, God is in the father position to Adam. Further, being created in the image of God implied a special relationship between God and Adam: a father-son type of relationship.[78] Thus, Paul's use of the term in Rom 8:19 serves to (1) further link the argument to Adam; (2) link the identity of those united to Christ with Christ himself; and (3) identify believers as the true people of God.

Unsurprisingly, the allusions to Adam in Romans 8 are mixed with allusions to the story of Israel, particularly the story of the exodus. This is especially clear in 8:12–17, the verses that immediately precede the Adam allusions in 8:19–22. This passage is filled with exodus language, which is intended to identify believers in Christ as the "new-exodus people."[79] In verse 14, Paul writes that those "who are led by the Spirit of God are sons of God" (ὅσοι γὰρ πνεύματι θεοῦ ἄγονται, οὗτοι υἱοὶ θεοῦ εἰσιν.). The Spirit within has taken over the role of the pillar that led the Israelites out of Egypt and through the wilderness. As mentioned above, in the narrative of the exodus, God refers to Israel as his "son."[80] Verse 15 then references "slavery" and "fear." For those familiar with the OT, slavery would have certainly brought to mind the plight of the Israelites in Egypt and the fear they experienced in the wilderness. As Wright has written, "There is no question that in Judaism in general any story about slaves and how

---

77. Holland, *Romans*, 272–73.

78. Sailhamer, *Pentateuch as Narrative*, 117. Adam is called the "son of God" in Luke 3:38.

79. Wright, "New Exodus," 29. Keesmaat, *Paul and His Story*, 61–63 notes several other possible textual links to Israel's story, particularly to the exodus tradition. Keesmaat especially notes overtones of Deut 32 and Isa 63.

80. So also Hos 11:1—"Out of Egypt I called my son."

they come to be free must be seen at once as an allusion to the events of the exodus."[81] The slavery in fear mentioned here is countered by the eschatological liberation that is to come in verse 21. Finally, the concept of "heirs" in verse 17 would call to mind the gift of the Promised Land. In sum, this section uses exodus language to identify Christians as the true people of God. Paul uses the narrative of redemption from Egypt to describe salvation in Christ. He immediately follows this with allusions to Adam, again weaving the two stories together.[82]

In short, the purpose of Rom 8:19–22 is to point again to the sweeping effects of Adam's sin. Not only has the first human sin resulted in the original glory of God being lost in humanity, but the creation has also been made subject to decay. Thus, just as believers look forward to complete redemption, so creation also looks forward to a future restoration. All of this will prove important in understanding the sweeping nature of union with Christ.

Allusions to Adam also appear later in chapter 8, particularly in 8:29 with the use of the term "image" (εἰκών). This is an obvious link to the creation account, where Adam and Eve were created in the image (εἰκών) of God. Here Paul uses the term to explain salvation as being "predestined to be conformed to the image of his son" (προώρισεν συμμόρφους τῆς εἰκόνος τοῦ υἱοῦ αὐτοῦ). Thus, the image of God, having been damaged by sin is being restored in Christ. The use of image language serves to link the allusion to Adam here with the allusion in 8:19–22 noted above. The restoration of the image of God is the restoration of the lost glory, a glory to be revealed in believers in the age to come (8:18). However, it should be noted that believers are not simply restored to Adam's original status, but are conformed to the image of the last Adam.

The wording of 8:29 lends further support to the argument put forward thus far—that Paul's allusions to Adam include echoes of the story of Israel and that these allusions provide the OT background for union with Christ. Though the use of image language surely points to the creation account, there are two unique terms in the context that incorporate Israel into the argument. First, rather than announcing believers as being conformed to the image of Christ, he writes that they are being conformed to the image of *his son*. As noted already, sonship in the OT was often used in reference to the people of Israel in relationship

81. Wright, "New Exodus," 29.
82. This will be explored further in chapter 5 below.

with God. Second, believers are being conformed to the image of Christ "so that he might be the firstborn among many brothers" (εἰς τὸ εἶναι αὐτὸν πρωτότοκον ἐν πολλοῖς ἀδελφοῖς). In the OT, "firstborn" could refer to Israel in general (Exod 4:22), which makes clear the corporate aspect of Paul's argument.[83] As Byrne notes, πρωτότοκος also carried messianic intimations, particularly as "derived from its use as an epithet for the Davidic king in LXX Ps 89:28."[84] In any case, πρωτότοκος is never used in the OT or in Jewish writings to refer to Adam, thus making it clear that the allusion is to Israel.[85] A full discussion of the meaning and significance of these terms lies beyond the purposes of this chapter. Suffice to say that these theologically loaded concepts were used for the purpose of weaving together the stories of Adam and Israel. However, in the context of Rom 8, it would seem that Paul is moving from the negative background of these stories to show the full restoration in Christ, which redeems that which was lost in sin for Jew and Gentile alike.

To summarize, in Rom 8, Paul references the stories of Adam and Israel via key OT theological concepts. He freely moves between the Adam narratives and the stories of Israel, particularly the story of the exodus. This fact further confirms that Paul saw an intimate relationship between Adam and Israel and that these stories together will provide the OT narrative background for union with Christ.

Romans 16:18–20

Though this brief passage does not significantly affect the argument of this book, it should nevertheless be briefly mentioned for the sake of completeness. In Rom 16:18–20, Paul alludes to the story of Gen 3 once again as he closes the letter.[86] Having already voiced his greetings to some of the members of the Roman church, he gives one final warning concerning the false teachers and does so in language reminiscent of the account of Adam's sin. Several allusions can be seen. First, in 16:18, Paul accuses the false teachers of being those who "through smooth speech and flattery deceive the hearts of the innocent" (διὰ τῆς χρηστολογίας καὶ εὐλογίας ἐξαπατῶσιν τὰς καρδίας τῶν ἀκάκων). Just as the serpent

---

83. Dunn, *Romans*, 1:485.
84. Byrne, *Romans*, 273.
85. Fee, *Pauline Christology*, 520–21.
86. Garlington, "Obedience of Faith, Part I," 215–16.

deceived (ἀπατάω) Eve with his smooth words (Gen 3:13), so these false teachers seek to deceive God's people. Paul has already alluded to the deception of the serpent in 7:11. Here again, the deception of the false teachers is linked to the deception in the Garden of Eden.

Second, though all know of the Romans' obedience, Paul is concerned that they be "wise toward what is good (ἀγαθόν), pure toward what is evil (κακόν)." Though different terms are used to describe it in the LXX, this probably recalls the tree of the knowledge of good and evil.[87] Unlike Adam and Eve, Paul wants the Roman believers to act wisely in obedience to God.

Finally, Rom 16:20 alludes to Gen 3:15 and the promise of hope given to Adam and Eve after their sin.[88] In Gen 3:15, God promised that the seed of the woman would strike the head of the serpent, indicating mortal wounding and final defeat. At the same time, the serpent will strike the heel of the seed. Interestingly, Paul says that Satan will soon be "crushed" under the feet of the Roman believers. Thus, he has drawn together the striking of the head and the heel and applied them to the church in Rome. The point is that Satan is being crushed through the work of the Messiah and those in the Messiah take part in the victory. Indeed, the second half of verse 20 directly links the victory to the "grace of our Lord Jesus Christ" and most likely recalls the exposition of Christ's victory in Rom 5:12–21.

For the purposes of the present argument, Rom 16:18–20 serves to confirm the importance of the Adam narrative throughout Paul's argument. While Israel is not explicitly drawn into the text at this point, the connections to Rom 7 show continuity of thought. In addition, the position of this allusion at the close of the letter makes a detailed exposition of Adam and Israel unnecessary. Paul's purpose is to encourage the believers to stand in victory against the deceitfulness of the false teachers. Further, at this point in the letter, it has been argued that the church is to be the new, united people of God. Therefore, additional references to the story of Israel are unnecessary. In sum, the final allusion to the Adam narrative supports the thesis argued throughout this chapter and the previous one—that apart from Christ, all are in Adam (and sin). The false teachers are just like the serpent of old, seeking to deceive the people of God with smooth words. Nevertheless, God's people stand united in the

---

87. In the LXX, the tree of the knowledge of good and evil is τοῦ ξύλου τοῦ γινώσκειν καλὸν καὶ πονηρόν (Gen 2:17).

88. Wright, "Letter to the Romans," 765.

Messiah. Thus, this last allusion not only supports the thesis already argued, but also anticipates the argument to come in the next two chapters.

CONCLUSION

At key points throughout the first eight chapters of Romans, Paul draws on the story of Adam and weaves into it the story of Israel in order to set up his central argument—that the true people of God are those united to Christ. The primary point is that all people, Jew and Gentile alike, are united in Adam and under the dominion of sin and death. Through key words and concepts, allusions to Adam (and Israel) are linked together to provide a coherent interpretation of the OT stories in the light of the coming of the Messiah. The law does not give Israel a preferred status before God because through the law, their sin has magnified the general sin problem. The following chapters will show the way in which the stories of Adam and Israel together form the OT background for union with Christ.

4

Adam, Israel, and Union with Christ in Romans 1–4

INTRODUCTION

AN INTERESTING FEATURE OF Paul's argument, particularly related to his use of the Adam and Israel stories, is that references to union with Christ in the near (and not-so-near) context draw on the themes developed through these stories in order to show a unity in Christ that not only trumps ethnic identity but also trumps humanity's union in sin. In short, the stories of Adam and Israel form the OT background for union with Christ by theologically demonstrating a basic human solidarity within the realm of sin and death. Union with Christ is thus the new theological and spiritual solidarity within the realm of righteousness and life.

This chapter and the next re-examine the allusions to Adam and Israel studied in chapters 2 and 3, this time focusing on the relationship of these allusions to references to union with Christ within the contexts. The goal is to show exegetically that there is a connection between Paul's use of these OT stories and his exposition of salvation in Christ. In addition, I argue that attempting to understand union with Christ apart from this background will result in misunderstanding, not just of the theme itself, but of its function within the letter, and, indeed, the overall purpose and argument of Romans.

THE STORY OF ADAM (AND ISRAEL) IN RELATION TO UNION WITH CHRIST

As mentioned above, an interesting feature of Adam (and Israel) allusions in Romans is that they are often followed in the near context of the letter with references to union with Christ. Further, Paul's doctrine of union with Christ draws on the themes developed from his uses of and weaving together of the stories of Adam and Israel.

Table 4.1: Adam (and Israel) and Union with Christ in Near Context

Allusion to Adam and Israel	Key Words and Themes related to Adam and Israel	Union with Christ Reference	Key Words and Themes Related to Union with Christ
1:18–32	creation; exchanged glory; dishonor; shame; image; death; idolatry	2:15–16, 29	new covenant themes: law written on their hearts; circumcision of the heart; glory and honor; "through Christ Jesus" (διὰ Χριστοῦ Ἰησοῦ)
3:23	sin; lacking glory	3:24–26	redemption in Christ; faith of Jesus
4:5, 17, 20, 21	creation; glory	4	covenant; raised for our justification
5:12–21	sin; death; law; condemnation; dominion of death; made sinners	5:12–21; 6:1–14	Grace; dominion of life; justification; baptized into Christ; baptized into his death; united to his death; united to his resurrection

Allusion to Adam and Israel	Key Words and Themes related to Adam and Israel	Union with Christ Reference	Key Words and Themes Related to Union with Christ
7:7–13	sin; commandment; death; law	8:1–17	no condemnation in Christ; life in Christ; indwelling Spirit; Christ in you; adoption
8:19–22	creation; futility; glory	8:23–27	adoption; Spirit; redemption
8:28–30	image	8:28–39	conformed to the image of his Son; love of God in Christ

In nearly every instance of allusions to Adam and Israel, a clear reference to union with Christ is found within the context. Even where clear references to union with Christ are not found, there are theological themes closely related to union with Christ in the near context. In other words, given that this occurs in the context of every instance of Adam and Israel allusions, it could hardly be coincidental. Additionally, given that union with Christ language is pervasive throughout Romans, it is reasonable to assume that when it is not explicitly mentioned, the concept is presupposed or assumed. This chapter and the next will seek to show exegetically that this is indeed the case.

Romans 1:18–32 and the New Covenant Themes of Romans 2

In chapter 2, I argued that Rom 1:18–32 is intended to communicate that all people are subject to wrath because they have failed to glorify God. As such, the needed remedy is much deeper than simply the forgiveness of sins, though this is certainly included.[1] Humanity needs "a means of

---

1. This statement is not intended to pit legal/judicial themes against participatory themes. Such an either/or approach rarely leads to nuanced, balanced understandings of Pauline theology. Rather, the point is simply draw attention to the importance of

undoing the exchange, a means of becoming the righteousness of God that God intended, a means of attaining the glory they lack."[2] In Romans, Paul presents the only solution to the pervasive problem of human sin as the pervasive nature of union with Christ. Because all people find themselves corporately bound together with Adam in sin, redemption must also include a corporate union with other believers in Christ. Christ thus redeems people from their bondage in sin and unites them to God (and each other) in himself.[3]

That Paul is thinking in these terms can be seen through careful attention to the wording of his letter. Indeed, participatory ideas exist within the opening paragraph. Because of the importance of Rom 1:3–4 for Christology, these two verses have often received more attention than the two verses that follow. Though routinely skipped over, verses 5–6 have important implications for the study of the letter. In verse 5, Paul explains that Jesus is the one "through whom" (δι' οὗ) he has received grace and apostleship. Campbell notes that though God is the one who appoints grace and apostleship, the intended meaning here is that these are given through the "mediatorial instrumentality" of Jesus.[4] That is, the grace and apostleship that was given to Paul was received via his union with Christ. As Dunn notes, this points to Jesus as the one who connects heaven and earth.[5]

Further, while detailed examination of "the obedience of faith" (ὑπακοὴν πίστεως) in Rom 1:5 is beyond the bounds of the present discussion, it is worth noting that at least one scholar has detected participatory themes within this phrase. Gorman argues that "the obedience of faith" is "a soteriological term coined by Paul from his Christological convictions: life *in* Christ means fundamentally sharing in the obedience and faithfulness *of* Christ."[6] Of course, this understanding depends on a subjective view of πίστις Χριστοῦ, which will be defended later in this chapter. In any case, the existence of participatory themes this early is the epistle is reasonable, particularly given both the immediate context and the overall thrust of the letter. We have just argued that the phrase δι'

---

participatory nature of salvation in relation to the stories of Adam and Israel.

2. Gorman, "Romans," 22.

3. The following paragraphs are an expansion of Sun, "Seeking (Exchanged) Glory."

4. Campbell, *Paul and Union with Christ*, 259. So also Cranfield, *Romans*, 1:65; Dunn, *Romans*, 1:16; and Moo, *Romans*, 51.

5. Dunn, *Romans*, 1:16. Dunn notes similar meanings in 1:8 and 7:25.

6. Gorman, "Romans," 19.

οὗ most likely conveys union with Christ and will see that Rom 1:6 also points in that direction.

Following closely behind these possible participatory phrases, Paul addresses the members of the church in Rome as those "called to belong to Jesus Christ" (κλητοὶ Ἰησοῦ Χριστοῦ). This has been translated with the word "belong" in order to communicate the genitive of possession.[7] More literally, it would be rendered "called of Jesus Christ," indicating that the believers in Rome were called to be Christ's. Their calling, like Paul's, had a purpose: to be joined to Jesus Christ. While not a direct reference to union with Christ, given that the previous verse was intended to communicate grace and apostleship are received via union with Christ, it is also feasible that Paul had the idea in mind here as well, this time affirming the believers in Rome as those who are also united to Christ.

Though the above union connotations are possible, the primary argument presented in this section is that there is a direct link between the use of the Adam and Israel stories in Rom 1 and the new covenant themes of Rom 2. The opening verses of the epistle allude to union with Christ, but the new covenant themes of Rom 2 provide a conceptual foundation for the doctrine. Any study of Romans must give adequate attention to chapter 2. While sometimes ignored or passed over quickly, scholars are realizing the importance of the chapter within the overall argument. Thus, Rom 2 should form an important piece of the argument of this book.

At the outset, it is readily admitted that Rom 2 does not contain an overt reference to union with Christ. The argumentation of Rom 2 lacks the normal union language of "in Christ" and related phrases. However, it will be argued that (1) there are clear links to OT new covenant promises and (2) the new covenant provides a covenantal context for union with Christ that will be developed later in the epistle. Thus, this section will seek to do three things. First, I argue that Paul's reference to Gentiles who obey the law in 2:14–16 is a reference to Gentile Christians who are members of the new covenant. This will also be linked with the circumcision of the heart in 2:28–29. Second, I will seek to demonstrate that this reference to Gentile believers is closely connected to the use of the Adam narrative in Rom 1. Third, I further argue that the new covenant themes in relation to the Adam (and Israel) allusions provide a foundation for

---

7. Cranfield, *Romans*, 1:68.

later explicit references to union with Christ. In order to make such an argument, a few ground-clearing items must be mentioned.

First, though they are sometimes read in isolation (at least in practice, if not overtly), Rom 1 and 2 are intimately related and must be read as a continuous argument. Stowers notes that "the oldest chapter divisions, the *kephalaia majora* and a system in *Codex Vaticanus*, have no break at 2:1. Both mark off 1:18—2:12 as a section."[8] Of course, chapter divisions are later additions and not a part of the original letter. Nevertheless, the fact that some of the earliest chapter divisions grouped 2:1–12 with 1:18–32 shows that at least some early readers of the epistle read these two sections together. While the primary allusions to the new covenant are in the latter half of Rom 2, this fact at least serves to support a close connection between the two chapters. Further, as Moo points out, 2:12–16 is closely connected with the argument of 2:1–11.[9] Put otherwise, reading chapters 1 and 2 in isolation will result in a misreading of both. Indeed, Grieb argues that 1:18—3:20 should be read as a continuous "story of a world gone wrong."[10] In addition to the narrative continuity, there are key words and themes in chapter 2 that link back to chapter 1. These will be explored further below.

Despite the close relationship between Rom 1 and 2, some interpreters seem to read each chapter independent from the other. An example of failure to adequately integrate the two chapters is the common reading wherein Rom 1:18–32 is understood strictly as an indictment against Gentile sin while Rom 2 is understood as an indictment of Jewish sin. For example, while he views 1:18—3:20 as a unit, Byrne describes the relationship between chapters 1 and 2 as "setting a trap" and "springing the trap."[11] In other words, in 1:18–32, Paul gives a fundamentally traditional Jewish critique of Gentile sin that would have drawn significant agreement from Jewish readers. Having gained agreement on this point, in chapter 2 he turns on the imaginary dialogue partner in order to show

---

8. Stowers, *Rereading*, 12. Stowers is making a very different point than the one presented here. Though not vital, this point does at least give early historical precedence for reading Rom 1 and 2 as a continuous argument.

9. Moo, *Romans*, 144.

10. Grieb, *Story of Romans*, 25.

11. Byrne, *Romans*, 79–80. This is not to say that Byrne and other interpreters argue for a sharp separation between Rom 1 and 2. Rather, the point is that isolated interpretation occurs in practice as interpreters fail to interpret contextually in their exegesis of Rom 2.

that the implied "he" is also sinful before God. Thus, the Paul first attacks Gentile sin in Rom 1 and then Jewish sin in Rom 2. While this is true in broad terms and at least shows a connection between Rom 1 and 2, the exegesis of Rom 1:18–32 in chapter 2 of this book showed that Israel was also subtly included among those facing the wrath of God in Paul's argument via an allusion to Ps 106:20. While Paul undoubtedly gives primary attention to Jewish sin in Rom 2, a firm division between chapters 1 and 2 is untenable. Thus, Byrne unnecessarily divides the two chapters into seemingly separate arguments and comments on Rom 2 largely without reference to the preceding chapter.

Most commentators agree that Paul begins a diatribe in 2:1 in which he engages an imaginary Jewish interlocutor.[12] The change in style to diatribe is undeniable. Nevertheless, just as Israel found her way into the indictment aimed primarily at Gentiles in chapter 1, so now Gentiles find their way into the attack on Jewish sin in chapter 2. Thus, interpreters who read the two chapters in isolation ultimately fail to understand Paul's intention. In short, the change in style and the focus on Jewish sin should not result in an exegetical analysis isolated from chapter 1. Indeed, though Paul transitions, chapter 2 is a part of a continuous argument.

However, the more fundamental problem with isolated reading lies not in the lack of attention to the use of the Israel story in Rom 1. Rather, the main issue, particularly related to the argument of this book, is that such a division prevents interpreters from relating the echoes of the new covenant in chapter 2 with the use of the story of Adam (and Israel) in chapter 1.[13] I will argue below that these two features—new covenant and sin in Adam—are closely related and must be held together to feel the full impact of Paul's argument.

An additional prefatory issue is the identity of the Gentiles in the chapter. While disputed, the evidence seems to support a reference to Gentile believers in Christ who are members of the new covenant in Rom 2:14–16 and 2:29.[14] Though many interpreters reject such an understand-

---

12. See, among others, Jewett, *Romans*, 193–94; Byrne, *Romans*, 79; Dunn, *Romans*, 1:78; Hultgren, *Romans*, 112; Fitzmyer, *Romans*, 297; Wright, "Letter to the Romans," 438; Moo, *Romans*, 126.

13. Gathercole, "Law Unto Themselves," 30, notes the connection between the Gentiles facing the wrath of God in Rom 1 and the Gentile believers of Rom 2. He does not link the allusions to Adam with the allusions to the new covenant or the relationship of all of this to union with Christ.

14. This will be defended below in dialogue with opposing views.

ing, I will argue that the allusions to the OT, along with the context of the chapter within the larger argument of the letter, make this the most defensible interpretation. In any case, fresh exegesis of the text with both the story of Adam (and Israel) and the concept of union with Christ in mind will be necessary to substantiate this point.

It will be helpful to first place 2:14–16 and 2:28–29 within the larger context of chapter 2. Here Paul continues his argument for the universality of sin. As argued in chapter 2 above, 1:18–32, while primarily focused on Gentile sin, has already alluded to the fact that all people, Jew and Gentile, have failed to rightly honor God and are therefore subject to his wrath. Paul made this argument exegetically via allusions to the Adam and Israel narratives. Thus, to the attentive reader (or hearer), Paul has already indicated that all are sinners. However, lest any consider themselves righteous on account of possessing the law, Paul in Rom 2 turns his attention primarily to his Jewish audience. He does this as a continuation of the previous argument, as seen by his use of διό as the first word of the verse, which indicates that what follows is predicated upon what has preceded.[15]

In 2:1–11, Paul engages an imaginary interlocutor who presumably heard Paul's indictment in 1:18–32 and failed to consider himself as a part of the problem.[16] Verses 1–5 call attention to the fact that none can claim superiority because those who judge others actually do the very things they condemn.[17] Just as those who have the revelation of God in nature yet fail to honor God are "without excuse" (ἀναπολογήτους, 1:20), so the interlocutor is also "without excuse" (ἀναπολόγητος, 2:1).[18] The interlocutor should not presume upon the patience of God, ostensibly

---

15. Wallace, *Greek Grammar*, 673.

16. There has been some debate over the identity of the interlocutor as Jewish, Gentile, or representative of both. The position taken here is that the interlocutor is Jewish, but is to be understood as one who is a part of those facing the wrath of God in Rom 1:18–32. The point of the opening verses of Rom 2 is to make clear that while some (Jews or possibly proselyte Gentiles) view themselves as exempt from judgment, all are in need of redemption. While most commentators agree that the interlocutor is Jewish, some have argued for a Gentile interlocutor. For example, see Keck, *Romans*, 74–75; and Stowers, *Rereading*, 11–15, 100–102.

17. This assumes that the interlocutor serves as a representative or example of those who do such things. Jewett, *Romans*, 194, notes a connection with Rom 1 via the use of πράσσεις in 2:1, which was used twice in 1:32 (though in a different form) and is repeated in 2:2–3.

18. Jewett, *Romans*, 196.

based upon the mere possession of the law as a sign of God's favor. Verse 5 is key because it draws immediate attention to the heart, which is foundational for the exposition that follows, particularly in the key verses to be examined below. Here Paul insists that the true problem of humanity is a problem of the heart. The interlocutor and those like him face the wrath of God "because of your hardness and unrepentant heart" (κατὰ δὲ τὴν σκληρότητά σου καὶ ἀμετανόητον καρδίαν). The wording clearly draws on OT themes of the hardness and the stubbornness of Israel.[19] In addition, the mention of wrath (ὀργὴ) links back to 1:18 and therefore communicates that those addressed in chapter 2 are no better off than those facing the wrath (ὀργὴ) of God in chapter 1.

In the remainder of the chapter, Paul's primary purpose is to argue that mere possession of the law makes no difference in terms of one's standing before God, or better, one's status as a covenant member. Perhaps it is more accurate to say that Jewish identity markers do not provide the fundamental basis for marking out the people of God. Verses 12–16, which will be examined in more detail below, continue the argument by focusing on God's judgment and the possession of the law. Far more significant than possessing the law is being a "doer of the law" (2:13). Finally, verses 17–29 put the nails in the coffin by pointing out that boasting about the law results in hypocrisy. The law must be obeyed; otherwise possession of the law leads only to judgment. The same is true of circumcision. All of this leads to the discussion of 2:14–16 and 2:28–29 and the role of these verses within the overall argument.

Before defending the interpretation adopted here exegetically, a brief evaluation of alternative understandings is in order. Byrne holds that Rom 2:14–15 should be viewed as "the kind of comment modern writers might place in a footnote."[20] In other words, these verses are not central to the argument of chapter 2, but rather something of an explanatory note before moving on to the main point. According to Byrne, the purpose of the explanatory note is to show the way in which Gentiles who do not possess the law are still judged on the basis of their actions. Based on this view of the role of the verses within the argument, Byrne believes that the Gentiles to whom Paul refers in 2:14–15 are "righteous Gentiles" who, at least partially, do what the law requires without having knowledge of the

---

19. For example, Deut 9:27, where the same term is used in the LXX. Lucas, "Reorienting," 136, notes that in the wider context of Deut 9, Moses links Jew and Gentile together in ungodliness as ἀσέβεια is used in 9:4 to describe Gentiles.

20. Byrne, *Romans*, 88.

law. That the works of the law are written on their hearts means that they have a sense of morality within.[21] Regarding 2:28–29, Byrne again holds that this is a righteous Gentile who is not a believer in Christ.[22]

Byrne's understanding of the Gentiles of Rom 2 fails to adequately explain the text itself and the role of these Gentiles within the larger argument. In what follows, an alternative and preferable understanding will be defended. At this juncture, a few brief critiques can be mentioned. First, Byrne's interpretation is unable to show the connection between chapters 1 and 2. In Rom 1:18–32, it is very clear that Paul believes the Gentile world will face the wrath of God on the basis of their failure to honor the Creator. It seems contradictory that in the next chapter he would say just the opposite—that there are some Gentiles who uphold the law and honor God. Second, Byrne's interpretation misunderstands Paul's use of the OT in Rom 2. It will be shown below that Paul makes clear references to the new covenant throughout the chapter and that this plays an important role in the argument. Though Byrne admits a possible allusion to the new covenant in 2:15, this makes no difference in his interpretation. Third, Byrne's understanding cannot be reconciled to the overall argument of Romans. Paul will emphatically say in chapter 3 that none are righteous (3:10). Again, it seems contradictory for Paul to say that some Gentiles practice the law here only to later say none keep the law. Indeed, Paul's argument throughout Romans is that the true people of God are those who are united to Christ and that these are the ones who have the ability to obey the law. Thus, exegetically and logically, Byrne's interpretation does not work.[23]

In contrast to this interpretation, the exegesis here will seek to show that Paul's intention was to argue that the true people of God are those who do the law, that is, Christians.[24] Doers of the law, whether Jewish or Gentile, are members of the new covenant. This in turn is argued to be foundational for Paul's later exposition of union with Christ. That is, the references to the new covenant in Rom 2 are of profound importance because they provide a covenantal context for union with Christ. Fur-

21. Ibid.

22. Ibid., 105.

23. Other recent commentators who see the Gentiles as morally upright unbelievers include Moo, *Romans*, 148–51; Holland, *Romans*, 63–64; Dunn, *Romans*, 1:98–100; Hultgren, *Romans*, 117–19; Fitzmyer, *Romans*, 309–11; Stuhlmacher, *Romans*, 43–45; Keck, *Romans*, 80–81.

24. Bird, *Saving Righteousness*, 166.

ther, the pattern of allusions to Adam (and Israel) followed by exposition of union with Christ begins with the references to the new covenant in chapter 2.[25]

In 2:14, Paul defines the people about whom he is talking: Gentiles who do what the law requires. One grammatical issue within this verse needs to be addressed briefly. Paul writes, "ὅταν γὰρ ἔθνη τὰ μὴ νόμον ἔχοντα φύσει τὰ τοῦ νόμου ποιῶσιν," literally, "for when Gentiles who do not have the law by nature do the law." The primary question revolves around the use of φύσει and whether it goes with the first or second half of the clause. If it goes with the first half, it would indicate that Gentiles are people who by nature do not have the law.[26] If with the second, it would mean that these people are Gentiles who by nature do the law.[27] While both interpretations are possible, a third, mediating position could be preferable. Perhaps Paul placed the φύσει in the middle of the clause in order to allow it to pull double-duty. In this case, the term describes both parts of the clause. In other words, the Gentiles of Rom 2:14–16 by nature do not possess the law and also do the law by nature. Regarding the first half, Gentiles are obviously those who do not possess the law by birth. This use of φύσει fits with the identical use of the term in 2:27. Thus, φύσει refers to the ethnic identity of the Gentiles in question.

Nevertheless, linking φύσει with the second half of the sentence adds considerable theological meaning to Paul's argument. Though many scholars arguing for linking φύσει solely with the first half of the phrase do so because it seems impossible that Paul would claim that there are people who naturally obey the law when he has argued vigorously in 1:18–32 that people have turned away from the clear revelation of God for the worship of idols and in 3:10–18 that none obey God, there is another interpretive option that allows for φύσει to describe the doing of the law in the second half of the phrase. Those who by nature do what the law requires fits with the following verse that further defines them as those with the law written on their hearts. That is, they do the law by nature because the law is within and, therefore, obedience to the law comes from the heart. In this way, they by (a renewed) nature do what the law requires. Ironically, then, while not having the law in the sense

---

25. Table 4.1 above shows the pattern throughout Romans.

26. Those linking φύσει with the first half of the verse include Cranfield, *Romans*, 1:156; Gathercole, "Law unto Themselves," 35–37; Wright, "Letter to the Romans," 441–42; Kruse, *Romans*, 130–31; and Jewett, *Romans*, 214.

27. Dunn, *Romans*, 1:98; Bassler, *Divine Impartiality*, 142; Ito, "Romans 2," 33.

that they are Gentiles, they do possess the law in their hearts. Therefore, it seems best to allow this key term to provide meaning to both parts of the sentence. Paul's argument is that Gentiles who do not possess the law by birth naturally obey the law written on their hearts as members of the new covenant.

This then affects the way in which one understands the second half of verse 14. Paul writes "these, though not having the law, are a law to themselves" (οὗτοι νόμον μὴ ἔχοντες ἑαυτοῖς εἰσιν νόμος). Again affirming that these are the same Gentiles who do not have the law, Paul now says that they are a law to themselves. How is this possible? As mentioned above, some have argued that Paul's meaning here is moral Gentiles who are responding to the general revelation of right and wrong that all people possess by virtue of being created in the image of God. However, there are two fatal flaws with this interpretation. First, the word νόμος, while certainly able to express general moral teachings, more readily refers to the Mosaic Law, particularly in the context of Rom 2. If Paul's meaning were something other than the Mosaic Law, the context would need to make this particularly clear. The context provides no such clarity. Second, such an understanding would seem to be in opposition to the general teaching on sin in the first three chapters of the epistle. Paul says that "none is righteous" (3:10); "no one seeks God" (3:11); "no one does good" (3:12) and the list could continue. In short, Paul has clearly stated that all people are sinners turned away from God and lack any natural ability to please God. If this verse were about righteous (unbelieving) Gentiles, it would not square with the rest of Paul's exposition of human sin.

By contrast, the most viable interpretation is that these are Gentiles who have become believers and now live in obedience to the law, which is the law written on their hearts.[28] It would seem from the context of Romans that only those who are believers in Jesus would possess the abil-

---

28. The use of ἔθνη here without the article may also support my argument. If Paul had used the article ("the Gentiles"), he would be referring to Gentiles as a whole: "when the Gentiles..." which would point to Gentiles in general who sometimes obey the law. However, without the article, the meaning is more limited and can be thought of naturally as "Gentile believers": "when [believing] Gentiles...". In other words, Paul's point is the importance of obedience through a changed heart and holds up Gentile Christians as an example over against Jews who, while having the law naturally (as Jews), do not obey it. This use of the noun without the article probably fits into Wallace's category "qualitative noun," which emphasizes the quality rather than the class as a whole. See Wallace, *Greek Grammar*, 244. In this case, the emphasis is on the quality of being Gentile, which fits with my interpretation: they are *Gentile* Christians.

ity to obey the law, especially obeying the law by nature. Rom 1–3 clearly expounds the fact that all people have turned away from God and are unable to do that which pleases God apart from a change in heart. Though Paul's words are probably aimed at Jews, Rom 2:5 has already established that the primary human problem is a heart problem—hardness and unrepentant hearts.[29] Thus, Paul now shows that the answer to this problem is obedience from the heart, which only comes with the law being written on the heart. This focus on the heart then leads to 2:15.

The way in which one understands Rom 2:15 is key not only for interpreting Rom 2, but in many ways for understanding the entire epistle. As mentioned above, those who believe Paul is making reference to moral Gentiles in 2:15 fail to connect Paul's meaning to Rom 1 and to the surrounding context. In contrast to this understanding, I argue that Paul is instead referring to Gentiles who are members of the new covenant. There are several points to be made here.

First, in describing the Gentile believers, Paul describes them as those who have "the work of the law written on their hearts." Regardless of the way in which the details are interpreted, it is important to notice that Paul draws attention to the heart. As mentioned above, this is intended to connect to 2:5 where Paul describes the root problem of unbelieving Jews as "hardness and unrepentant hearts." Thus, the description of these Gentiles as those with the works of the law on their hearts is clearly intended to stand in juxtaposition to those with unrepentant hearts. This means that Paul is setting up a contrast between those who presume upon the kindness of God (2:4) yet practice the evil things they condemn in others (2:1) over against those who have the law on their hearts and thereby do the law. These are the people who seek glory and honor and attain eternal life (2:6). Indeed, the only way that it would be possible for people to seek (ζητοῦσιν) glory, honor, eternal life, and peace (2:7, 10) is through a changed heart since there are no God-seekers (ὁ ἐκζητῶν τὸν θεόν) (3:11).

Second, the wording used here alludes to Jer 31:33. Jeremiah 31:31–34 is a central passage within the prophetic literature related to

---

29. Ito, "Romans 2," argues for a "Deuteronomistic framework" for all of Rom 2. He avers that the blessings and curses of Deut 27–30 provide the interpretive key for the entire passage. He does so through noticing verbal and thematic connections between the two texts. While some of Ito's exposition is overstated, his basic point holds. To nuance his argument, it seems most likely that the prophetic texts that Paul explicitly draws upon (Jer 31; Ezek 36; Isa 52) have intertextual connections to Deut 27–30. That is, Paul could be alluding to Deuteronomy through the prophetic literature.

the promise of a new covenant. While a full exegesis of this text is unnecessary for the present purposes, a few important points should be made. Verse 31 states clearly that the promised new covenant will be made with "the house of Israel and the house of Judah." Verse 32 then clarifies that while there are some similarities between the new covenant and the covenant made with the Israelites at Sinai, it will also be different. Further, the reason for the difference is the sin of Israel in breaking the covenant. Finally, in verses 33–34, Yahweh makes the new covenant promises, which include (1) writing the law on the hearts of his people; (2) a renewed relationship; and (3) that all the covenant people will know Yahweh. These points are important for understanding Paul's allusion to verse 33 in Rom 2:15.

While some have denied an allusion to Jeremiah, the similarity in wording between Rom 2:15 and Jer 31:33 makes it difficult to imagine that Paul, a Jew steeped in the OT, could write such things without the OT passage in mind. Note the parallels:

Table 4.2: Jeremiah 31:33 and Romans 2:15

Jeremiah 31:33 (LXX 38:33)	Romans 2:15
ὅτι αὕτη ἡ διαθήκη, ἣν διαθήσομαι τῷ οἴκῳ Ισραηλ μετὰ τὰς ἡμέρας ἐκείνας, φησὶν κύριος Διδοὺς δώσω **νόμους** μου εἰς τὴν διάνοιαν αὐτῶν καὶ **ἐπὶ καρδίας αὐτῶν γράψω αὐτούς**, καὶ ἔσομαι αὐτοῖς εἰς θεόν, καὶ αὐτοὶ ἔσονταί μοι εἰς λαόν	οἵτινες ἐνδείκνυνται **τὸ ἔργον τοῦ νόμου γραπτὸν ἐν ταῖς καρδίαις αὐτῶν**, συμμαρτυρούσης αὐτῶν τῆς συνειδήσεως καὶ μεταξὺ ἀλλήλων τῶν λογισμῶν κατηγορούντων ἢ καὶ ἀπολογουμένων

Though Rom 2:15 is not a direct quotation of Jer 31:33, the use of the metaphor of writing the law on the hearts of the believers is unique to these two passages, apart from the quotation of Jer 31:31–34 in Heb 8 and 10. That this is a unique manner of speaking and that this is the only place in the OT to use the metaphor of writing in relation to the law in the heart of God's people makes it probable that Paul was drawing on the Jeremiah passage in Rom 2. In addition, the only other time the words "write" or "written," "law," and "heart" are found together in a single OT verse is in Deut 30:10, another new covenant passage that will be alluded to later in Rom 2. Thus, when Paul describes these Gentiles as those with the work of the law written on their hearts, he was describing them as members of the new covenant.[30]

30. Käsemann, *Romans*, 64–65, denies the presence of an allusion to Jer 31. Seifrid,

Though other passages in the prophetic literature indicate that Gentiles will be members of the new covenant,[31] Jer 31 states that the covenant will be with "the house of Israel and the house of Judah." The allusion in Rom 2 is to an OT passage that clearly promises a new covenant for Israel, yet Paul is putting forward Gentiles as those through whom God is keeping his promise. This must have been surprising to Jewish readers (or hearers) in Rome. The "shock value" of this allusion gives support to the interpretation offered here. Paul's purpose is to show the radical nature of the gospel: it is equally for Jew and Gentile alike. The universal nature of his gospel was repeated in 2:9–11. In 2:15, he is showing that the blessing of the gospel—becoming members of the new covenant—is for all. As Jewett summarizes, "Paul is implying that the Jeremiah prophecy has been fulfilled in an unexpected manner as the gospel recruits Gentiles to become the heirs of the divine promise."[32]

William S. Campbell argues that the covenantal relationship can be detected in the way in which Paul addresses the Roman believers in Romans 1:7: ἀγαπητοῖς θεοῦ and κλητοῖς ἁγίοις.[33] If this is true (which appears probable), then Paul has already established a covenantal framework for his argument. Thus, it would be unsurprising that he would allude to the new covenant in chapter 2 in order to show that contrary to the thinking of his imaginary Jewish interlocutor, the true people of God are the members of the new covenant, regardless of ethnic identity.

Third, while the allusion to Jeremiah is probable, Paul appears to have made a couple of alterations to the original text. These must be examined in order to confirm the allusion. First, Paul inserts τὸ ἔργον ("the work") into the verse. Yahweh promised that his law would be written on the hearts of new covenant members, but Paul asserts that it is *the work* of the law that is written on their hearts. Some have taken this difference

---

"Romans," 611, does not mention 2:15 in his discussion of 2:1–16, seemingly intimating that no allusion exists. Though Dunn, *Romans*, 1:100, acknowledges (1) a probable allusion to Jer 31 in Rom 2:15 and (2) that Paul elsewhere alludes to Jer 31 with reference to the new heart given by the Spirit to believers in Christ, he nevertheless denies that Paul is here referring to Gentile believers. Hultgren, *Romans*, 118, also recognizes the allusion to Jer 31, yet dismisses the possibility that Paul is referring to Gentile Christians. His reasoning is that while possible, this interpretation "need not follow." He offers no further defense of his position.

31. For example, Isa 42:6.
32. Jewett, *Romans*, 215. So also Cranfield, *Romans*, 1:159.
33. Campbell, "Covenant and New Covenant," 181.

as evidence that Paul did not have Jer 31 in mind when writing Rom 2.[34] However, it is more likely that this is simply a slight change in order to fit with the context of Paul's argument.[35] Alternatively, Paul inserted τὸ ἔργον in order to link back to 2:6, where judgment is according to works (τὰ ἔργα). In other words, having the work of the law written on their hearts means that the work necessary for final judgment is performed by these believing Gentiles because such work has been written on their hearts and is therefore performed as a result of heart change. In any case, slight changes in OT quotations are a common feature in the Pauline canon and pose no real threat to the feasibility of the interpretation offered here.

Second, there is a difference in preposition: the LXX text of Jer 31:33 uses ἐπὶ, which Paul changes to ἐν. One should not overemphasize the change in preposition. Nevertheless, it is interesting that the author of Hebrews retains the ἐπὶ both times he quotes Jer 31. Therefore, it is doubtful that this is merely an incidental shift in preposition, thus making it at least possible that Paul made the change here to fit with his later use of ἐν Χριστῷ. If so, the wording here would provide a preview of the union with Christ language to come. If Paul is indeed thinking in new covenant terms here, the change in preposition could be the result of a conflation of Jer 31:33 and Ezek 36:26, where God promises to put a new spirit "within you" (ἐν ὑμῖν). As argued below, Paul alludes to Ezekiel later in the chapter, making it possible that he has it in mind here. In any case, the change to ἐν could be related to later union with Christ language.

In sum, the above argument has tried to show that the text of Rom 2:15 meets the criteria of identifying allusions as described in chapter 1 above. In particular, distinctiveness is clearly present: the image of writing on the heart is unique to Jer 31 and Rom 2. Second, recurrence may not be immediately obvious since Paul does not elsewhere allude to or quote Jer 31:33. Nevertheless, I will argue that new covenant themes are present elsewhere in Romans. Third, multiplicity is also apparent: the allusion includes several key words in sequence (writing, law, heart).

---

34. See, for example, Schreiner, "Did Paul Believe"; Lamp, "Paul, the Law"; Mathewson, "Moral Intuitionism." Gathercole, "Law unto Themselves," 41, avers that holding such a position is "to split hairs." See also Caneday, "Judgment, Behavior, and Justification," 178–81, who gives six reasons why denying that Paul is speaking of Gentile new covenant members on the basis of Paul's addition of "works of" is inadequate.

35. On the meaning of the "work of the law," see, in addition to the major commentaries, Moo, "'Law,' 'Works of the Law'"; Cranfield, "'Works of the Law'; Dunn, "Yet Once More"; and Schreiner, "Works of Law."

Finally, I have argued that thematic coherence is also present: both texts are discussing the nature of the new covenant people of God.

Having affirmed that Paul's reference is indeed to the new covenant in 2:15, the rest of the verse, as well as 2:16, must be examined in order to show that this interpretation fits within the context. The second half of verse 15 builds upon the first half. Having claimed that the Gentiles in mind are members of the new covenant with the law written on their hearts, Paul writes, "their conscience also bears witness and their thoughts within themselves accuse and also make self-defense among themselves" (συμμαρτυρούσης αὐτῶν τῆς συνειδήσεως καὶ μεταξὺ ἀλλήλων τῶν λογισμῶν κατηγορούντων ἢ καὶ ἀπολογουμένων).[36] The above exegesis of 2:15a, along with the explanation offered of 2:14, sheds considerable light on the somewhat difficult wording here. Since the Gentile members of the new covenant have the law written upon their hearts, they have renewed consciences and thoughts that serve to lead them in obedience (the work of the law). In 8:16, the same wording is used of the Holy Spirit who "bears witness with our spirit that we are the children of God" (αὐτὸ τὸ πνεῦμα συμμαρτυρεῖ τῷ πνεύματι ἡμῶν ὅτι ἐσμὲν τέκνα θεοῦ). Though unstated in 2:15, the most likely meaning is that the Holy Spirit bears witness in the conscience of believers that they do in fact have the law written on their hearts.[37] The OT promises of the new covenant closely link together the law being put in the hearts of God's people and the giving of the Spirit of God.[38] This proves that they are members of the new covenant and displays the righteousness of God in keeping his covenant promises. When understood in relation to Rom 1, the fact that they have thoughts and conscience battling within shows that they are the people of God. In Rom 1:21, Paul writes that those who have failed to honor God "have been made futile in their thoughts and have their foolish hearts darkened" (ἐματαιώθησαν ἐν τοῖς διαλογισμοῖς αὐτῶν καὶ ἐσκοτίσθη ἡ ἀσύνετος αὐτῶν καρδία). Because of this, "God gave them over" (παραδίδωμι) to their foolishness (1:24, 26, 28). In other words, those

---

36. The phrase μεταξὺ ἀλλήλων τῶν λογισμῶν is difficult to translate. It could be rendered "thoughts among/between themselves" or "thoughts within them." Several English translations (NRSV, ESV) translate it "conflicting thoughts." See Wilckens, *Römer*, 1:136. The translation used here (thoughts within themselves) seems to fit best with the context, which mentions the conscience. This will be reflected in the exegesis below.

37. The Spirit will be mentioned explicitly in 2:29. See below.

38. For example, Ezek 36:26–27.

facing the wrath of God in Rom 1 have no conflicting thoughts because they have been wholly given over by God to their sinful thoughts. By contrast, the Gentile members of the new covenant in Rom 2 have conflicting thoughts, which demonstrates their status as covenant members with the law written on their hearts. They have been rescued from the lot of those "given over" and now via the work of the Spirit have renewed thoughts. Their thoughts accuse them in that they know their covenant membership has been granted on the basis of the righteousness of the Messiah (1:3–4)[39] and their thoughts make a defense of this fact based upon the gospel (1:3–4, 17–18; 2:16). Thus, the second half of the verse shows the outworking of the first half of the verse. That is, because the law is written on the hearts of new covenant members, their conscience and their thoughts serve to lead them in covenant obedience. This, of course, ties together the "doing good" and "seeking glory and honor" from earlier in the chapter.

Verse 16 makes explicit the eschatological flavor of the argument and explains the last word of verse 15—excuse (ἀπολογουμένων). Gentile members of the new covenant are excused, not based on acts of righteousness performed apart from the knowledge of God, but because of their status as the new covenant people of God. They will be excused "according to my gospel through Christ Jesus" (κατὰ τὸ εὐαγγέλιόν μου διὰ Χριστοῦ Ἰησοῦ). The intended meaning here is the final judgment when it will be clear that these Gentile new covenant members are a part of the true people of God. All of this is on the basis of the gospel: the good news that God has in the Messiah-King restored that which was destroyed by sin and renewed the people of God, Jew and Gentile alike. Thus, here in chapter 2, there is a close association between the gospel, which was already proclaimed as the righteousness of God, and the new covenant.

Before continuing the study of Rom 2, and especially 2:28–29, there are a few important summary points that flow from the exegesis above. First, it is important to note that the allusion to Jer 31:33 in 2:15 controls the interpretation of the entire chapter. Failure to adequately identify and explain the allusion will result in failure to follow Paul's argument throughout the chapter. The importance of Paul's use of the central new covenant passage from the prophetic literature cannot be overlooked. Second, the allusion to the new covenant provides a covenantal context

---

39. Jesus is the faithful Messiah as his righteousness is demonstrated through his resurrection. The accusing thoughts result from faith in Paul's gospel as announced in 1:3–4.

early in the epistle for the entire discussion of redemption in Christ. Paul's use of this key OT passage at this stage in the argument can hardly be coincidental. While the new covenant is not specifically mentioned at every point throughout the letter, this early use means that it is at least implied throughout. Third, and related to the second point, the new covenantal context will be particularly important for the concept of union with Christ. I will argue throughout this chapter and the next that Paul brings union with Christ into the discussion following allusions to the story of Adam (and Israel). While union with Christ is not overtly mentioned in Rom 2, the pattern of Adam (and Israel) followed by discussion of salvation in Christ is established here in covenantal terms. Further, there is at least a hint toward this pattern in 2:16, which closes the paragraph with the phrase διὰ Χριστοῦ Ἰησοῦ, which is often used in the Pauline literature to communicate some aspect of union with Christ.[40] Since this is the case, Paul probably attached the phrase to the end of the sentence for proleptic purposes, setting the stage for later discussion. In other words, the sentence could have ended "according to my gospel" without theological or grammatical problem. However, Paul adds "through Christ Jesus" in order to prepare the reader to the later use of the phrase. Finally, as Kruse notes, central to the argument of 2:16 is the impartiality of God.[41] This will be important in the overall argument and fundamental for union within the people of God as they are corporately united to Christ.

In the last two paragraphs of chapter 2 (17–24 and 25–29), Paul sets up a contrast between Gentile members of the new covenant and his imaginary Jewish interlocutor who seemingly considers himself to be a part of the people of God on the basis of the possession of the Mosaic Law and/or his ethnic identity. In 2:17–24, Paul brings charge against the interlocutor for having the knowledge of the law, but failing to obey. The implied contrast with the Gentiles of 2:14–16 is that while the Gentile new covenant members have the law written on their hearts and thus will be excused on the last day, the interlocutor and those like him have the law, but only externally and therefore dishonor God (2:23).

This argument is further established by the quotation of Isa 52:5 in 2:24. In context, Isa 52 announces the coming salvation for the people of God in terms of a second exodus. Verses 3–6 move from exile and slavery to exodus and salvation. As in the first exodus, when God rescues

---

40. Campbell, *Paul and Union with Christ*, 237–66.
41. Kruse, *Romans*, 134–35.

his people a second time, they will "know my name" says Yahweh (52:6). Thus, the results of the second exodus are that God's people will know him and will be restored. The function of verse 5 within the section is to pronounce the primary problem that requires action—the defiling of God's name.

In Rom 2:24, Paul quotes from the LXX:

Table 4.3: Isaiah 52:5 in Romans 2:24

Isaiah 52:5	Romans 2:24
δι' ὑμᾶς διὰ παντὸς τὸ ὄνομά μου βλασφημεῖται ἐν τοῖς ἔθνεσιν	τὸ γὰρ ὄνομα τοῦ θεοῦ δι' ὑμᾶς βλασφημεῖται ἐν τοῖς ἔθνεσιν

The LXX seems to be an interpretive translation of the Hebrew text since the Hebrew does not mention the nations and only focuses on the defilement of God's name. It is interesting that Paul chooses the Isaiah text and that he sticks with the LXX over the Hebrew. This is significant and reflects Paul's desire to use "a citation that brings the Gentiles into the equation."[42] In addition, in Isaiah, the dishonor brought to God's name was on account of the captivity. For Paul, the dishonoring is on account of the failure to obey the law. Paul's use is interpretive since the captivity of the Isaiah text was a result of failure to obey the law. This suits Paul's purposes in Rom 2 since he is contrasting the conduct of those who possess the law over against Gentile members of the new covenant. Those who possess the law yet fail to obey it will be judged.

It is interesting that Paul again frames the issue in terms of honor and shame. In 1:21, the wrath of God is coming against those who know about God via his revelation in creation yet fail to properly glorify him as God (οὐχ ὡς θεὸν ἐδόξασαν). In 1:23, the same is true of those who "exchange the glory of the immortal God for images" (ἤλλαξαν τὴν δόξαν τοῦ ἀφθάρτου θεοῦ ἐν ὁμοιώματι εἰκόνος). As noted in chapter 2 above, this sets the human sin problem in relational terms in that all people are caught up in Adam's sin and have failed to reflect his glory. In 2:7, those who attain eternal life are those who seek glory and honor (δόξαν καὶ τιμὴν καὶ ἀφθαρσίαν ζητοῦσιν). Paul no doubt chose Isa 52:5 as his text in order to place the sin of the interlocutor and those like him within the realm of those who have failed to honor God as God. In short, those addressed by Rom 2:24 are no different from those addressed in 1:18–32,

---

42. Jewett, *Romans*, 231.

for all people, Jew and Gentile, have failed to give glory and honor to God. These stand in stark contrast to the Gentile new covenant members who are forgiven on the basis of the gospel.

Finally, Paul alludes to another important OT passage in Rom 2:24. Ezekiel 36:20 is similar to Isa 52:5 and may have also been in Paul's mind when he was writing Rom 2. Ezekiel 36 stands as an important chapter in the book. In verses 16–21, Yahweh proclaims that the people of Israel have been exiled because they have unfaithful to him. Yahweh says that at the time of the exile, "when they came to the nations, wherever they came, they profaned my holy name." The charge of profaning God's name is then repeated in verses 22–23. The same idea is present as in Isa 52:5— because of their sin, the people of Israel have dishonored God's name among the nations.

If Paul indeed alludes to Ezek 36:20 in Rom 2:24, this would be significant for the interpretation of the chapter because Ezek 36 is particularly important in relation to the new covenant. Like Isa 52, the promises are set within the context of a new exodus. Important for the purposes of the present argument, Ezek 36:25–27 give promises related to the forgiveness of sins and, similar to Jer 31, a new heart. Whereas in Jeremiah Yahweh promised to place his law within the hearts of believers, here he promises to put his Spirit within for the purpose of giving them the ability to obey the law (36:27). Clearly the promises of Jeremiah and Ezekiel are related and constitute the same prophecy of the new covenant. The allusion to Ezek 36 in Rom 2:24 further confirms the exegesis offered above: Paul almost certainly has the promises of the new covenant in mind. The remaining paragraph of chapter will further support this argument.

Before proceeding to Rom 2:25–29, an additional point needs to be made as it contributes to the overall argument of this book. Wright has recently argued that the primary thrust of Paul's indictment of the Jewish nation in the second half of Rom 2 is related to their failure to fulfill their God-given vocation.[43] In Rom 2:19–20, Paul says that his Jewish interlocutor claims to be "a guide to the blind, a light to those in darkness, an instructor to the foolish, a teacher of children" (ὁδηγὸν εἶναι τυφλῶν, φῶς τῶν ἐν σκότει, παιδευτὴν ἀφρόνων, διδάσκαλον νηπίων). Wright argues this echoes the vocational calling that Jews believed to have been given them by God. Paul agreed that this was the vocation of the Jewish people, but is arguing in Romans that they have failed in this vocation.

---

43. Wright, "Romans 2:17—3:9."

Again, in Rom 3:2, Paul says that Jews were "entrusted with the oracles of God" (ἐπιστεύθησαν τὰ λόγια τοῦ θεοῦ), meaning that they were given the words of God for the purpose of mission. That is, God called the people of Israel to be the vessel through which he would bless the world. This is the most likely understanding of Exod 19:6: "you shall be for me a priestly kingdom."[44] Yet, they have failed in this vocation. In fact, not only did they fail to fulfill the vocation, God's name is blasphemed among those to whom Israel was sent (2:24). Nevertheless, God has been faithful to his plan through the work of the Messiah Jesus.[45] Thus, God is creating a worldwide family in Christ, keeping with his promises to Abraham and Israel. For our present purposes, this again brings the story of Israel to the forefront leading up to Paul's exposition of union with Christ. Where Israel failed to bring about the needed restoration of humanity, God is faithful through Christ to bring about full restoration by creating a new people in him.

Turning now to the last paragraph of Rom 2, Paul argues that God is indeed creating a new covenant people. In Rom 2:25–29, Paul turns his attention to circumcision as another Jewish identity marker that does not in itself indicate membership in the people of God. The entire chapter has been focused on the condition of one's heart as the only true marker of new covenant membership. In this final paragraph, Paul says that circumcision is of no value if it is not accompanied by obedience to the law. Indeed, apart from keeping the law, circumcision is considered uncircumcision (2:25). Paul seems to be taking issue with a Jewish assumption that since circumcision is a mark of the Sinai covenant, then those who have been circumcised are certainly a part of the people of God. To be more highly valued is the keeping of the law. Those who keep the law, regardless of ethnic identity, are to be considered the circumcision (2:26). Paul's meaning in verse 26 is that those who obey the law are the true people of God. Since Paul alluded to Ezek 36 in verse 24, this important passage is probably still in mind here, confirming the new covenant context of the entire chapter. In addition, Paul uses the term "reckoned" (λογίζομαι) in 2:26, a term that is normally used in regard to righteousness.[46] Those who are uncircumcised yet obey the law condemn those who possess the law yet fail to obey (2:27) because this behavior

---

44. Sarna, *Exodus*, 104.
45. Wright, "Romans 2:17—3:9," 4.
46. Schreiner, *Romans*, 141; Dunn, *Romans*, 1:122; Cranfield, *Romans*, 1:173. Examples include Rom 3:28 and multiple times in Rom 4.

demonstrates that they do not belong to the true people of God. This leads to Paul's conclusion in 2:28–29.

Romans 2:28–29 contains an addition allusion to the OT that serves to confirm the exegetical analysis above. Paul draws the conclusion to his discussion on circumcision by affirming that true circumcision is not outward, but inward, a circumcision of the heart. This serves a salvation-historical purpose in that Paul avers that physical circumcision was always intended to point forward to a spiritual reality of renewed hearts. It is clear that those who have undergone heart circumcision are new covenant members, including both Jews and Gentiles.[47] In order to make the argument, Paul again draws on the OT.

In Rom 2:29, Paul alludes to several OT passages,[48] which again indicates that throughout chapter 2, the new covenant has been an important aspect of his argument. The primary allusion is to Deut 30:6, where Moses announces that in the future, "the Lord your God will circumcise your heart and the heart of your descendants, so that you will love the Lord your God with all your heart and with all your soul, in order that you may live." In the LXX, the key phrase is translated καὶ περικαθαριεῖ κύριος τὴν καρδίαν σου. Paul's wording closely matches: καὶ περιτομὴ καρδίας. Paul chose to use περιτομὴ over περικαθαριεῖ, probably because περιτομὴ more accurately indicates circumcision specifically and reflects the meaning of the Hebrew מול. In any case, the concept of heart circumcision is unique and thus, it is almost certain that Paul was drawing on Deut 30:6 in Rom 2:29.[49]

In the context of Deuteronomy, chapter 30 looks forward with hope through the despair that comes as a result of the disobedience of the people.[50] Chapter 29 has already affirmed that Israel will be punished by

---

47. Gorman, *Death of the Messiah*, 67.

48. In addition to the passages detailed below, Jewett, *Romans*, 236, notes Lev 26:41; Jer 4:4; 6:10; 9:25; and Ezek 44:7, 9, as OT passages that command God's people to be obedient from a cleansed heart. Having ignored the allusion to Jer 31 in Rom 2:15, Holland, *Romans*, 71, surprisingly mentions Jer 31 in his comments on 2:29. He ignores allusions to Deut 30 in 2:29 and does not relate the one whose heart is circumcised to the one with the law written on the heart.

49. Thus, the criteria of distinctiveness and thematic coherence are clearly met.

50. The authorship and dating of Deuteronomy does not change the argument presented here. Paul was most likely reading the OT canonically—as the accepted Scripture of his time—without thought to historical-critical matters. That is, Paul was reading Deuteronomy within the OT canon and in relation to the prophetic literature. If one were to argue for a late date for authorship, it does not change the way in which

exile for breaking the covenant. In Deut 30, "Moses apparently has in view the promise of the 'new covenant' spoken of in Jer 31:31–34 and Ezek 36:22–28."[51] Moses is convinced that the Sinai covenant will end in failure, but proclaims hope to the people in the form of a new covenant. While the term "new covenant" is not used in Deut 30, the close correlation between Deut 30 and the later prophecies concerning the new covenant indicate that this was the intended meaning and that this was the way in which the prophets understood the promise of Deut 30:6. Further, Paul's addition of "by the Spirit" (ἐν πνεύματι) in 2:29 indicates that he also saw a close connection between the promises of Deut 30:6 and those of Ezek 36. While Deut 30 makes no mention of the work of the Spirit, Ezek 36 emphasizes the gift of God's Spirit into the hearts of God's people. As mentioned above, Paul alluded to Ezek 36 in 2:24 and therefore probably has the verse in mind in 2:29. In short, Paul draws together Deut 30 and Ezek 36 to argue for believers as the true people of God. Moreover, Paul probably also has Deut 10:16 in mind, where Moses commands the people to "Circumcise, then, the foreskin of your heart, and do not be stubborn any longer." This would link the circumcision of the heart in Rom 2:29 to the hardness of heart in 2:5.

Paul has again used an allusion to the OT to draw attention to the new covenant and its fulfillment in believing Gentiles. Within the context of Rom 2, Paul is referring to the same people as 2:15—Gentiles who have the law written on their hearts. Thus, these Gentile believers are the true people of God, members of the new covenant who are circumcised with the true circumcision of the heart. Yet, in 2:29, the meaning is expanded to include all those, Jew and Gentile alike, who have circumcised hearts. This is Paul's redefinition of the "Jew": one who is a Jew inwardly (ὁ ἐν τῷ κρυπτῷ Ἰουδαῖος). That is, a real Jew is one who (1) has the law written on the heart, (2) is circumcised in the heart, and (3) is a member of the new covenant by faith in Christ and the work of the Spirit. While Paul earlier in the chapter (2:12–16) placed primary emphasis on Gentile new covenant members, the change in terminology from Gentile (ἔθνη) to Jew (Ἰουδαῖος), while retaining the emphasis on the heart is intended to communicate that all are equal members of the new covenant in Christ. That Paul uses the term "Jew" (Ἰουδαῖος) to refer to ethnic Jews and ethnic Gentiles who together comprise the true people of God in the new covenant

---

Paul is using Deuteronomy in Rom 2.

51. Sailhamer, *Pentateuch as Narrative*, 473. So also Waltke and Yu, *Old Testament Theology*, 495.

would have been shocking to his readers, but points to the astounding work of God in Christ. Paul's claim that Jews and Gentiles together compose the true people God explains his words in 2:9–10, where he twice used the phrase "the Jew first and also the Greek" (Ἰουδαίου τε πρῶτον καὶ Ἕλληνος/Ἰουδαίῳ τε πρῶτον καὶ Ἕλληνι) with respect to punishment for evil and reward for good. In other words, both Jews and Gentiles have been on the agenda throughout the chapter. Paul will later link the formation of the true people of God more explicitly to union with Christ.

The focus of Rom 2 has come full circle. In 2:5, the primary problem was identified as hardness of heart. The solution is also within the heart: the law being written on the heart via circumcision of the heart by the Spirit. In addition, it is interesting that the chapter closes with a mention of praise. One with a circumcised heart receives his praise, not from people, but from God (οὗ ὁ ἔπαινος οὐκ ἐξ ἀνθρώπων ἀλλ' ἐκ τοῦ θεοῦ). Once again, Paul frames his argument around honor and shame. Circumcision of the heart results in the true honor of new covenant membership. This points forward to union with Christ, in whom the restoration of the honor of God's people is accomplished.

In sum, turning his attention to an imaginary Jewish interlocutor, Paul says the Jews are no better off before God on the basis of ethnic identity. In order to make this argument, he has again alluded to the OT in an interpretive manner. He argues that those who claim superiority on the basis of the possession of the law or on other Jewish ethnic identity markers are mistaken. Instead, the determining factor in regard to membership within the people of God is the change in heart that comes through circumcision of the heart and having the law written upon the heart. In other words, Paul points to the new covenant. Indeed, as Ridderbos has argued, Paul gives a new definition of the people of God in Christ, which is expressed "in terms of the New Covenant."[52]

It is no coincidence that the argument of Rom 2 follows the indictment of 1:18–32. Paul's use of new covenant language to describe righteous Gentiles indicates that in the midst of his extended argument to show the universal nature of sin, he has already begun his exposition of redemption in Christ. More specifically, he is redefining the people of God. Fee aptly summarizes the point in relation to this theme: "One is no longer a part of the people of God by adhering to the boundary markers of Jewishness; one is part of the people of God on the basis of Christ and

---

52. Ridderbos, *Paul*, 334.

the Spirit alone."[53] The Gentiles who have the law written on their hearts and have undergone heart circumcision have been called out (1:7) of the number of those facing the wrath of God described in Rom 1. Thus, Paul has drawn on the story of Israel to set the stage for discussion of union with Christ as the primary marker of the people of God.

Perhaps it is at this point in Romans that one can most clearly see Paul's scriptural argumentation. Paul appears to be reading Deuteronomy through the prophets and interpreting each in light of the other while demonstrating the fulfillment of the OT story in Christ. This is especially true of the concept of the new covenant, which Paul has shown to be rooted in Deuteronomy, interpreted and predicted by the prophets, and, according to Paul, brought to a climax in Christ. Sailhamer insightfully notes the importance of the new covenant in the OT and the way Paul saw it fulfilled in Christ. He writes,

> The purpose of the Pentateuch is to teach its readers about faith and hope in the new covenant. . .In Jer 31:31 the "Mosaic" Sinai covenant is contrasted with the "prophetic" new covenant. There is an "old covenant" established by Moses, and a "new covenant" established by Christ through his sacrificial death on the cross. In Galatians and Romans Paul looks back to the Sinai covenant as something that failed to bring about faith and divine blessing. Nothing was inherently wrong with the Sinai covenant, but something fundamentally wrong with Israel's heart: it needed cleansing and filling with God's love (Deut 30:6). But, as the prophets saw it, Israel had continued to disobey God's law, and they were in danger of divine correction. Ultimately, the need was to have the law written on their hearts instead of tablets of stone (cf. Ezek 36:26–27).[54]

This provides a clear OT narrative background for union with Christ as the story of Israel, intertwined with the story of Adam, is finding its resolution in the coming of the Messiah and the establishment of the people of God in him.

Romans 2 is of considerable importance to the argument of this book because it rests Paul's understanding of redemption, and therefore union with Christ, within a covenantal context. Later sections will show that whenever Paul draws on the story of Adam (and Israel), references to union with Christ can be found within the near context. Further, verbal

---

53. Fee, *God's Empowering Presence*, 493.
54. Sailhamer, *Meaning of the Pentateuch*, 26–27.

connections between sections alluding to Adam (and Israel) and sections discussing union with Christ exist throughout the letter.[55] Thus, it is significant that following the first allusion to the story of Adam (and Israel) in Rom 1, Paul immediately follows up with a reference to the new covenant. This implies that Paul saw union with Christ as covenantal in nature and as the ultimate fulfillment of the promise of a new covenant.

Romans 3:23 in the Context of 3:21–26

Romans 3:21–26 is a densely-packed paragraph filled with numerous theological themes that are important for the message of the epistle. Justification, the righteousness of God, faith, redemption, sin, glory, grace, and atonement all feature prominently in this short passage. Thus, it is not surprising that themes relating to Adam, Israel, and union with Christ are to be found here. Nevertheless, the relationship between these important themes may not be immediately obvious. Few commentators notice the close relationship between them in part because few take seriously the narrative approach to Paul's use of the OT. In short, this section will show the way in which the adamic background of sin, with Israel's story interwoven, helps to explain what actually takes place in redemption. This passage provides a subtle, yet clear link to union with Christ as the believer is moved from the realm of sin in Adam to redemption in Christ.

Following Paul's extended assertion in Rom 1:18—3:20 that all humanity stands equally sinful in Adam, Rom 3:21–26 begins the transition to the next stage of his argument in which he gives full attention to salvation in Christ for Jew and Gentile alike. It should be remembered that this is not a complete transition from discussing sin to discussing salvation since in Rom 2 he has already shown how Gentiles become new covenant members through Jesus Christ (Rom 2:15–16, 29). Nevertheless, Rom 3:21–26 draws the reader's attention more fully to redemption in Christ and begins his sustained argument regarding salvation that will continue through chapter 8.

The transition is signaled in 3:21, where Paul returns to the theme of the righteousness of God, which he proclaims to have been revealed

---

55. Though arguing a different point, Wischmeyer, "Römer 2:1–24," 376, concludes that Paul's argument in Rom 2 moves "im Horizont der neuen Existenz in Christus" linking to later union with Christ language.

"apart from the law." The νυνὶ δέ that opens the verse confirms that Paul is moving to "the next step in his argument."[56] However, this cannot be divorced from the previous argument since in 3:20, Paul asserted that "by the works of the law, no flesh will be declared righteous before him [God]" (ἐξ ἔργων νόμου οὐ δικαιωθήσεται πᾶσα σὰρξ ἐνώπιον αὐτοῦ). Thus, in light of this, the following pericope is intended to explain how it is that people can be righteous through the death of the Messiah. Further, in the context, the νυνὶ δέ probably also carries intimations of eschatological fulfillment in Paul's thinking.[57] That is, the "now" signals not only the movement of the argument, but the "now" in time as the coming of the Messiah brings eschatological hope into reality. All the complex details of this passage cannot be adequately dealt with in this section as the numerous debates on the themes of this passage lie outside the immediate concerns of this book. Thus, discussion will be limited to the adamic reference within the overall argument, the way in which Israel is drawn into the discussion, and the relationship of these OT stories to union with Christ.

Verse 21 opens the passage with key terms that remind the reader (or listener) of themes that were raised in Rom 1. These include the righteousness of God and a reference to the law and the prophets. This serves to link the discussion to follow with the gospel message first mentioned in chapter 1. The righteousness of God (δικαιοσύνη θεοῦ) should be understood as God's faithfulness to bring his purposes for humanity in general and Israel in particular to completion. That is, his righteousness is both his uprightness morally in keeping his word and his relational faithfulness to creational intentions and covenant promises.[58] This important

---

56. Kruse, *Romans*, 178.

57. Woyke, "'Einst' Und 'Jetzt.'"

58. Dunn, *Romans*, 1:40–42, equates δικαιοσύνη θεοῦ with God's covenant faithfulness to Israel. While this meaning is not to be denied, the use of the phrase in Paul needs a more nuanced understanding to include additional aspects. The wording used above with regard to God's intentions to humanity is intended to broaden the meaning to incorporate concepts of creational purposes that, though including Israel's covenants, are not limited to them. Kruse, *Romans*, 80, summarizes a multifaceted understanding of the δικαιοσύνη θεοῦ as "God acting in accordance with his own nature for the sake of his name." Wright, *Paul and the Faithfulness of God*, 795–804, provides an extended discussion of the term and Paul's use of it with the Jewish background in mind. Contra Moo, *Romans*, 222, who defines δικαιοσύνη θεοῦ narrowly as the "saving activity of God." The saving activity of God should be seen as one outworking of his righteousness rather than the whole of his righteousness. This fits with Hays's argument that δικαιοσύνη θεοῦ in 3:22 must be understood with regard to his use of the

term features prominently throughout the paragraph, which links back to 3:5 and 1:17. A detailed examination of this term is unnecessary at this point. Instead, the primary interest here is the relation of δικαιοσύνη θεοῦ to union with Christ. This will be explored further below.

The righteousness of God, however defined, is the righteousness that was (1) revealed apart from the law and (2) witnessed to through the law and the prophets. The phrase "apart from the law" (χωρὶς νόμου) has caused some debate. The wider discussion of this need not detain the argument of this book. In short, Paul most likely has in mind here covenantal concepts.[59] That is, the righteousness of God has been revealed outside the bounds of the old covenant. Gentiles need not adhere to the demands of the Mosaic Law, particularly identity markers such as circumcision, because the righteousness of God, his faithfulness to his creation and covenant intentions and promises, has been manifested apart from the law. This paves the way for union with Christ through the work of the Spirit to become the new identity marker of the true people of God, a truth that becomes clear later in the letter. Further, this understanding squares with Rom 2, where the law is written on the hearts of new covenant members. In other words, Paul's intention here is not to disparage the law, but rather to continue his argument that status as a new covenant member is not dependent upon possession of the law outwardly since the eschatological righteousness of God has been revealed apart from the law.

Important to the argument of this book is the notion that Paul here evokes the story of Israel via mention of the law, a story Paul has interpreted as entangled with the story of Adam in Rom 1. As argued in chapter 2 above, the primary echo of the Adam story is found in 3:23, with allusions to Israel's story following closely behind. Nevertheless, it is important to note that the pericope begins with evocations of the wider stories. The negative force of "apart from the law" confirms this understanding since God's righteousness is not limited to the Mosaic covenant. God's righteousness is displayed for all, as Paul will immediately argue,

---

term in 3:5. Hays argues that in 3:5, Paul uses the term "as a functional equivalent of 'the faithfulness of God' (3:3) and 'the truthfulness of God'" (3:7). See Hays, *Conversion of the Imagination*, 54–55. In context, these terms refer properly to God's faithfulness to Israel in keeping covenant promises. However, the reference to "Jews and Greeks" in 3:9 followed by the universal tone of the OT quotations of 3:10–18 set the entire chapter in broader terms. Thus, it is fair to say that here, as elsewhere, δικαιοσύνη θεοῦ refers to God's faithfulness to his creational and covenant purposes.

59. So Moo, *Romans*, 223.

Adam, Israel, and Union with Christ in Romans 1-4

through the death of the Messiah. Again, this sets the argument in covenantal terms.

Yet Paul's argument here is not that the gospel of the Messiah is to be understood to be in opposition to the old covenant since the revelation of God's righteousness was "witnessed to by the law and the prophets" (μαρτυρουμένη ὑπὸ τοῦ νόμου καὶ τῶν προφητῶν). Of course, the letter began in 1:1–4 with a proclamation of the gospel, which was "promised beforehand through his prophets in the holy scriptures" (διὰ τῶν προφητῶν αὐτοῦ ἐν γραφαῖς ἁγίαις). Thus, throughout Romans, Paul has been expounding upon the gospel, which for him is not an entirely new message but the culmination of God's redemptive purposes. The coming of the Messiah is the unveiling of the gospel, which is the righteousness of God.

Though the term "gospel" is not used in 3:21–26, the concept is certainly present since Paul is picking up themes from his two mentions of the gospel from Rom 1. Here, as in 1:16–17, the righteousness of God is linked closely with the gospel of the Messiah. In other words, it is clear that the gospel story is the demonstration of God's righteousness. The rest of the passage (3:22–26) makes plain the content of the gospel. The verbal and thematic connections between 3:21–26 and Rom 1 give further weight to the argument of this book that the stories of Adam and Israel are the OT background for union with Christ. As has been shown above, references to Adam and Israel are followed in Romans by references to union with Christ. In this section I will argue that this is true of Rom 3:21–26, but the connections with the previous sections implies that there is a unified argument in Romans in regard to these OT stories and the theme of union with Christ. That is, using key words and themes to point back to Rom 1, which contains the first allusion to Adam (and Israel) within the epistle, sets the stage for the argument of this pericope.

Romans 3:22 has been the source of much scholarly debate, centered on the phrase διὰ πίστεως Ἰησοῦ Χριστοῦ. However, it is important to realize that the verse begins with a repetition of the phrase "the righteousness of God" (δικαιοσύνη δὲ θεοῦ). Therefore, one's interpretation of the controverted phrase διὰ πίστεως Ἰησοῦ Χριστοῦ must be able to explain the way in which it relates to the righteousness of God. Indeed, the δέ indicates that the following is offered as explanation of the preceding, namely the way in which God's righteousness has been revealed apart from the law.

The phrase διὰ πίστεως Ἰησοῦ Χριστοῦ can be rendered "through the faith/faithfulness of Jesus Christ" (subjective genitive) or "through faith in Jesus Christ" (objective genitive).[60] Within the context of the verse, the subjective genitive is most likely.[61] This interpretation seems to make better sense of the overall argument and is consistent with Paul's other uses of the phrase.[62] Thus understood, 3:22 teaches that Jesus has been faithful where all others have sinned. He is "the perfectly faithful human being."[63] The faithfulness of Jesus the Messiah demonstrates the righteousness of God because in Jesus, God is redeeming the world. Jesus is faithful where Adam and all who came after him failed, including Israel. Thus, in the faithfulness of Jesus, God is bringing to apex his original intentions for creation and fulfilling the covenant promises to create a worldwide family for Abraham.

Two further reasons for holding to the subjective genitive could be mentioned. First, the phrase following διὰ πίστεως Ἰησοῦ Χριστοῦ points to faith in Jesus (εἰς πάντας τοὺς πιστεύοντας). That is, if one were to take the first phrase as "faith in Jesus" the second seems merely redundant.[64] However, taking the subjective option makes more sense and fits within the flow of the argument, particularly when narrative undertones are detected. Thus, in 3:21–22, Paul is saying that God has displayed his righteousness through the faithful Messiah and the benefit of this is given to those who place their faith in him. This will prove important in the analysis of 3:23–24 below.

Second, the subjective understanding fits with the participatory themes found in the near context as well as the rest of the letter. Taking πίστεως here to refer to the faithfulness of Jesus and πιστεύοντας to refer to the faith of Christians intimates a close relationship between Jesus and his people. This makes the most sense of the wording of the phrase εἰς πάντας τοὺς πιστεύοντας. Thus, God's righteousness is displayed through

---

60. Within the major commentaries, only Wright, "Letter to the Romans," 470, argues for the subjective genitive. Those arguing for the objective genitive include Schreiner, *Romans*, 182–83; Kruse, *Romans*, 181; Jewett, *Romans*, 275; Fitzmyer, *Romans*, 345; Dunn, *Romans*, 1:177–78; Moo, *Romans*, 224–26; and Byrne, *Romans*, 124.

61. As with δικαιοσύνη θεοῦ, it is beyond the bounds of this book to fully enter the debates concerning this phrase. More to the point is the relationship of the phrase to union with Christ, which will be pursued below. For a recent scholarly discussion, see Bird and Sprinkle, *Faith of Jesus Christ*.

62. See the discussion in Gorman, *Cruciformity*, 110–21.

63. Hays, "ΠΙΣΤΙΣ," 45.

64. Williams, "Again *Pistis Christou*," 436.

the faithfulness of Jesus to all who believe. The righteousness of God for believers is his faithfulness to keep his promises and fulfill his intentions for creation. This is revealed to believers through the faithfulness of the Messiah, which calls them to believe in him. This is available to "all" (πάντας), without distinction. In other words, the Messiah's faithfulness is the revelation of God's righteousness and this is for Jew and Gentile alike, who in Christ form the true people of God. For those who are in Christ, faith is participation in Jesus's story, who is the faithful Son of God.

The exegetical analysis of 3:23 offered in chapter 2 demonstrated that Paul was alluding to the story of Adam's sin. In addition, I argued that the use of glory language draws in the story of Israel, which corporately lost the glory of God during the exile. As Paul is expounding on the revelation of God's righteousness through Christ, attention is drawn again to the failure of Adam and Israel to adequately reflect God's glory to the world and fulfill God's intentions for humanity. This is set in direct contrast to the faithful Messiah, through whom God is restoring his people. The story of Adam is brought to a climax and completion through Christ, the second Adam and faithful Messiah. God's intention to create a people for himself is now being fulfilled in the faithful human being. Thus, the story of Jesus provides the bridge between the OT stories and the story of the church as the people of God. His story completes the stories of Adam and Israel. As believers are incorporated into his story through faith, they become members of the true people of God.[65]

The combination of "all" in relation to believe and the lack of distinction between sinners in 3:22-23 supports the argument here. Just as the righteousness of God revealed through Jesus is for all, Jew and Gentile alike, who believe, so there is no distinction among those who have sinned and lack the glory of God. Paul's wording here summarizes the foregoing argument: all without distinction are "in Adam." Outside of Christ, there is a basic human solidarity in sin. Likewise, the work of the faithful Messiah is for the benefit of all those who are "in Christ."

This, then, leads directly into the rest of the passage and helps to explain the relationship between the story of Adam (and Israel) and union with Christ in Rom 3:21-26. I argued in chapter 2 that 3:23 contains a reference to the sin of Adam through an allusion to Ps 8. Paul is saying that because of sin, humanity in Adam has lost the original glory given by

---

65. See Gorman, *Cruciformity*, 115-19; Campbell, *Deliverance of God*, 647.

God. If this exegesis is correct, then 3:24 follows with an interesting reference to union with Christ as God's solution to the plight of humanity in Adam. In many ways, this discussion anticipates the longer discussion of Adam and Christ in Rom 5:12–21. In short, Paul says in summary form here what he will expand in Rom 5.

However, Wright points out that while Paul has made it clear that all people lack the glory of God because of the sin of Adam, he "does not at once announce that the glory has been restored ... Instead, he announces the necessary step toward it: they are 'justified.'"[66] Here Paul draws in the forensic metaphor, stating that "all who believe" are declared to be in the right, or more fittingly, to be members of the true people of God. This fits with the interpretation offered in chapter 2, where the "all" of 3:23 includes Christians. That is, believers have not yet been glorified and still lack the glory of God as it was originally given to Adam. Nevertheless, believers are being justified in the present because of the work of the faithful Messiah. They have not yet attained to the full restoration of the lost glory in Adam.

Though the primary point here is not in regard to the nature and meaning of justification, it is important to note that Paul gives further explanation of the justifying work of God as done "freely" (δωρεάν) and "by his grace" (τῇ αὐτοῦ χάριτι). This helps to explain the way in which the death of the Messiah displays the righteousness of God. All of this takes place at God's initiative as a result of his gift of grace. This clarification removes any thought of privilege, whether based on ethnic identity or perceived moral uprightness. Indeed, Paul will later emphatically say that all boasting is excluded (3:27). Thus, the justification of humanity through Christ is the unveiling of the righteousness of God because it is his gracious keeping of his covenant promises.

Jewett argues that Paul's use of δικαιούμενοι here should be understood as "being set right."[67] He carries this further by linking to Ps 30:1–2 in the LXX, which calls upon God for deliverance from shame.[68] Thus, Jewett holds that being set right here is a restoration of honor. While one may take issue with the details of Jewett's exegesis, especially his overemphasis on social meanings, he rightly draws attention to the honor and

---

66. Wright, "Letter to the Romans," 470.
67. Jewett, *Romans*, 280–81.
68. Ps 30:2 LXX: Ἐπὶ σοί, κύριε, ἤλπισα, μὴ καταισχυνθείην εἰς τὸν αἰῶνα, ἐν τῇ δικαιοσύνῃ σου ῥῦσαί με καὶ ἐξελοῦ με.

shame dimensions of Paul's argument.⁶⁹ Perhaps the idea of restoration fits better with the concept of redemption in the second half of verse 24. Nevertheless, the fact that much of Paul's exposition of sin in Adam was couched in terms of shame, the restoration here makes the most sense in terms of honor. This is especially true in the immediate context, where verse 23 has announced that all people lack the glory of God and therefore live in dishonor. Justification, then, proclaims that believers in Christ are covenant members, a part of God's family in Christ, and therefore honored members of the people of God, "whose praise is not from people but from God" (Rom 2:29).

All of this comes together in second half of Rom 3:24—"through the redemption that is in Christ Jesus" (διὰ τῆς ἀπολυτρώσεως τῆς ἐν Χριστῷ Ἰησοῦ). That is, in the faithful Messiah, God has himself fulfilled all that was intended for humanity. He has, as it were, redeemed the world that was ruined through sin. The faithful one has accomplished the task originally given to Adam and later given to Israel. Redemption is found only in the Messiah as the second Adam and as the true Israel. Again, all of this serves as a preview of what Paul will expand upon in Rom 5.

To Jewish ears, "redemption" would almost certainly evoke an exodus motif.⁷⁰ A reference to the exodus adds additional support to the argument being presented here. The new exodus was the great hope of Israel in exile. This hope has now become reality in Christ. The exodus motif places the emphasis upon the people of God rather than on the individual. Just as God redeemed Israel from Egypt in the first exodus, so now God has definitively redeemed "all who believe" through the work of the faithful Messiah. Relating this to the foregoing argument of this book, the evocation of the exodus motif draws the story of Israel into the picture once again. Like the rest of humanity, Israel remains in slavery to sin, but the faithful Messiah has led the long-awaited redemption for all those in him. This motif will be seen again in Rom 6–8, which will be examined in chapter 5 below.

---

69. Jewett's meaning with regard to honor and shame is almost always social: the Christian gospel overturns Roman and/or Jewish notions of social honor and shame. While social aspects are not denied, honor and shame are being used in this book to denote a more cosmic level: humanity has shamed God and itself through sin. Jesus restores the glory and honor God intended for humanity through his death and resurrection.

70. Kruse, *Romans*, 174; Wright, "Letter to the Romans," 471; Schreiner, *Romans*, 189.

What is often neglected or denied here is the clear reference to union with Christ in the phrase "in Christ Jesus" (ἐν Χριστῷ Ἰησοῦ). This is the first use of the phrase in Romans (and in the canonical Pauline corpus) and should therefore be given close attention. Many interpreters limit "redemption that is in Christ Jesus" to an instrumental meaning, that Jesus is simply the one through whom redemption is made.[71] While the phrase certainly puts forward the concept of redemption through the work of Christ, the use of "in Christ" most likely also carries another meaning: redemption is found in union with Christ.[72] That is, in this central passage in Romans, Paul is calling attention to a central theme: union with Christ. As Fitzmyer puts it, "All who are 'in Christ Jesus' have become partakers of the uprightness that comes from God through him. Through Christ a human being becomes a member of the people that God has acquired for himself, a member of the new people of God."[73]

This should be understood in relation to the point made above concerning 3:22. God's righteousness is revealed through the faithful Messiah to all who believe. The intimate relationship between the Messiah's faithfulness and the faith of Christians is now explained as redemption in Christ, thus carrying the relationship beyond faithfulness and faith to personal incorporation into Christ. That is, believers only experience the redemption accomplished by Jesus in union with him and thus in participation in his story.

Cranfield denies the reference to union with Christ, stating that the meaning is "the accomplishment of the redeeming action in the past, not of the availability of redemption in the present through union with Christ."[74] Campbell agrees that there is no clear reference to union with Christ here, arguing for a meaning of association. That is, the redemption "is not any kind of redemption ... it is the redemption associated with Christ."[75] Campbell's understanding is correct as far as it goes, but seems to ignore the wider context of Paul's argument.[76] This book has argued

---

71. Cranfield, *Romans*, 1:208. Moo, *Romans*, 230, is unclear, but emphasizes that redemption is effective through faith. Kruse, *Romans*, 184–85 seems to ignore the phrase "in Christ" altogether.

72. Dunn, *Romans*, 1:180; Byrne, *Romans*, 132.

73. Fitzmyer, *Romans*, 348.

74. Cranfield, *Romans*, 1:208.

75. Campbell, *Paul and Union with Christ*, 74. Campbell (114) also argues for an instrumental meaning with reference to justification.

76. One might ask if there was some other type of redemption that Paul needed to

that one of the primary purposes of Romans is the unity of Jew and Gentile in Christ. Paul has been showing the common human conundrum in sin and has now moved to the common salvation of believers in Christ. Thus, using the phrase "in Christ" here moves beyond mere instrumental or associational meaning to conveying the truth of redemption via union with Christ. Certainly it is only the redemption that is associated with Christ that provides for justification, but there is more going on that merely this. Indeed, Dunn links the use of the phrase here with later uses in Rom 6 to indicate that though the instrumental or associational meaning is present, there is deeper level of meaning than attributing the means of salvation to Christ's death and resurrection. He writes, "it is only by participation in Christ in his death and new life that redemption from sin can begin to be experienced now."[77]

Putting all of this together, then, there are several points to be made. First, within this passage, there is a clear link between the shameful state of humanity in Adam and the redemption of honor in Christ. Interpreters routinely miss this, even when affirming the reference to union with Christ in 3:24. It is hard to imagine that Paul did not see a connection between the story of Adam and union with Christ if there is a reference to the former in 3:23 and a reference to the latter one verse later. Paul seems to be saying that that which was lost in Adam is now being redeemed in Christ. Thus it seems that Paul was reading the OT text in a manner similar to Dempster's take on the promise of Gen 3:15. He writes, "The seed of the woman will restore the lost glory ... The realization of the kingdom of God is linked to the future of the human race."[78] This fits nicely with the argument here: the faithful human being has redeemed the glory lost through sin. It is interesting that the same pattern reappears in Rom 5–6, as well as 7–8.

Second, the exodus overtones allude to the corporate meaning of redemption and justification, particularly in relation to union with Christ. That is, the allusion to the exodus ties the theology of the passage to the story of God's people. Paul fascinatingly weaves together the story of Adam and the story of Israel while putting forward union with Christ as the climax of both. This is not to deny that individual believers are united

---

argue against. To use the phrase to merely qualify true redemption as only the redemption associated with Christ would seem to imply that there was some other kind of redemption. In any case, there seems to be more to the phrase than Campbell allows.

77. Dunn, *Romans*, 1:170.
78. Dempster, *Dominion and Dynasty*, 69.

to Christ, but to draw attention to the primarily corporate nature of the doctrine via the allusions to Israel's story. Again, it is interesting that we find a similar pattern in Rom 5–6 and 7–8.

Third, the repetition of "all" (πάντες) in 3:22 and 3:23 is intended to address a primary issue recurring throughout Romans: the question of unity between Jew and Gentile. This, along with the insistence that there is no distinction (3:22b), points to the importance of this question for Paul in regard to the gospel and the identity of the people of God. These issues have been clear throughout Romans in Paul's repeated use of "Jew" and "Gentile," "circumcised" and "uncircumcised." The use of these terms plays on the common Jewish categorizations of humanity. Paul's argument takes a more cosmic approach in dividing people by their union with either Adam or Christ.

Fourth, all of this fits with the rest of the passage. In verse 25, Paul refers to the work of God in Christ as ἱλαστήριον. It is beyond the bounds of the present study to fully investigate the interpretive options of this word, but most scholars agree that it is at least in some way related to the OT sacrificial system, particularly that of Lev 16 and the day of atonement.[79] Whatever the exact meaning, the use of the term in the context again adds to the corporate flavor of the text and reminds the reader that Paul is discussing redemption in the context of the people of God. God has in Christ dealt with the sin of his people so that a new people might be created in him. While the debate regarding the meaning of ἱλαστήριον cannot be adequately adjudicated here, the use of this term is interesting in the context and may suggest divine presence in Christ, which could lend support to seeing union with Christ within the passage. Most commentators recognize that ἱλαστήριον is used in Lev 16:2 in reference to the mercy seat, the top of the ark of the covenant, which is the place where God met with his people to deal with their sin. Thus, the mercy seat represented the place of God's special presence. If Jesus is here pictured as the mercy seat, it could intimate that he represents God's presence with his people or the place where God deals with the sin of his people. This may provide a conceptual foundation for union with Christ. That is, just as the mercy seat was the place where God was present with his people, so God's presence is always with his people via union with Christ.

This, along with the use of πάρεσιν in the second half of the verse, confirms the corporate interpretation of the passage. The term πάρεσιν,

---

79. For a recent discussion, see Kruse, *Romans*, 188–91.

which most interpreters take as "passing over," most likely alludes to God's withholding punishment against sin as a demonstration of his covenant faithfulness.[80] These OT references build on the concept of the righteousness of God to confirm that "the emphasis of the whole passage is on God's action in putting forward Jesus the Messiah who enacts the faith-obedience that Israel failed to render, who thereby glorifies God as faithless human creatures had failed to do and constitutes, through his resurrection, the beginning of a new humanity."[81]

Finally, verse 26 brings the paragraph to a close with another reference the righteousness of God and to πίστεως Ἰησοῦ. For the purposes of the present argument, we need only to pay attention to this last phrase. This time, Paul references the faith of/faith in Jesus with the Greek preposition ἐκ, thus the phrase ἐκ πίστεως Ἰησοῦ. As with verse 22, scholars have debated the meaning of this phrase. However, given the exegesis above, it seems clear that the translation "faith of Jesus" best fits the context. Matera summarizes the options, writing, "Thus 3:26 can be taken in several ways: God justifies those who believe in Jesus; God justifies those who rely on the faithfulness of Jesus; God justifies those who manifest the faithfulness of Jesus in their lives."[82] To these should be added "God justifies those who are united to Jesus and share a faith like his." Thus, Paul's meaning here is that through the death of Jesus, God has redeemed his people to himself. Those who are the true people of God are those united to Christ by faith and this faith is the same faith of Jesus himself. The basis for justification is the faithfulness of Jesus, which, in context, is contrasted to the unfaithfulness of Adam.[83] Justified believers are incorporated into the story of Jesus, which fulfills the story of Adam and Israel.

Verses 25–26 have twice reminded the reader that God did all of this in order to display his righteousness. The presence of union with Christ language in this passage, even if not the primary theme, raises the

---

80. Dunn, *Romans*, 1:173–74; Jewett, *Romans*, 289–90. Holland, *Romans*, 91–96 believes πάρεσιν echoes the Passover in Egypt. However, the term is only used here in the entire Greek Bible and such an association rests solely on thematic overlap. While possible in light of the exodus motif present in the context, it is far from certain. See the recent study by Holmes, "Utterly Incapacitated," in which Holmes argues that the term refers to the incapacitated state resulting from sin and the escape from such a state through the death of Christ.

81. Hays, "ΠΙΣΤΙΣ," 46.

82. Matera, *Romans*, 93–94.

83. Stowers, *Rereading*, 201, agrees with the instrumental reading (justification on the basis of Jesus's faithfulness) but denies the reference to Adam.

question as to the relationship between the righteousness of God and union with Christ. In brief, union with Christ is both the goal of redemption and the manifestation of God's righteousness because in creating a new people in Christ, God is (1) bringing his original intentions for humanity into reality and (2) fulfilling his promise to Abraham to rescue the world through his seed and to create a worldwide family. Thus, the righteousness of God and union with Christ have an inextricable relationship as one depends upon the other. Further, all of this is set within the grand story of Adam, Israel, Christ, and his people.

That his argument is focused on the unity of the people of God in Christ is supported in Rom 3:27–31. Paul here notes that on the basis of his foregoing argument, all human boasting is excluded. God is not the God of the Jews only, but also the Gentiles (3:29) because there is only one true God. Thus, the oneness of God demands the oneness of his people. This oneness is found in Christ since the Jewish identity markers cannot apply to all alike.[84] This leads then to the discussion of Abraham and his heritage in the new covenant people of God in Christ.

Romans 4

In chapter 2, I argued that Rom 4 is integral to the argument of the epistle because of the numerous links between Paul's use of the Abraham story and his previous use of the Adam and Israel stories. That is, rather than simply taking Rom 4 as a brief aside or proof text, Paul is showing that God has acted in Christ to fulfill the promises given to Abraham, which were intended to set to right the world ruined through sin. Thus understood, Paul's reference to Abraham fits within the overall argument and provides further OT background for union with Christ.

The present section will continue the argument of the chapter by focusing on Abraham as the ancestor of those "in Christ." Since Rom 4 contains no overt reference to union with Christ, the discussion here will be brief and argue that the Abraham narrative forms further background for the more explicit discussion of union with Christ later in the letter. That is, union with Christ is the fulfillment of God's promises to create a worldwide family for Abraham. This will be demonstrated by analyzing the textual and thematic connections to union with Christ passages to show that Paul's use of the Abraham story is essential background. In

---

84. Ridderbos, *Paul*, 339.

addition, it will be argued that this further provides a covenantal context within which to understand union with Christ.

First, textual and verbal links to Paul's previous argument show a continuous line of thought that will lead to discussion of union with Christ. Rom 4:1 begins the chapter by linking the forthcoming argument to what has immediately preceded. Paul writes "Τί οὖν ἐροῦμεν," with the οὖν implying something like, "in light of what I have just said, what shall we say?" This is essential because the argument of Romans 4 builds on the assertion of the oneness of God in 3:30, which makes him the God of both the Jews and the Gentiles. Having argued that the true people of God are those who have the faith of Jesus (3:26), the question naturally turns to Abraham, the OT father of the people of God. In 3:27–30, Paul has levelled the field, as it were, to show that status as a covenant member is not boast-worthy since it is not based on ethnicity, possession of the law, or works (whether identity markers or performance of deeds). Rather, covenant status is established on faith in Christ. Even Abraham himself has nothing to boast about before God (4:2). If this is the case, then Paul must show that the promises to Abraham are not set aside, but rather fulfilled in Christ and those united to him.

In 4:3, Paul quotes Gen 15:6, which sets the entire chapter within the context of God's covenant with Abraham. He is dealing with the issue of the Abrahamic covenant in light of his assertion that the (1) Jews and Gentiles are on equal standing in regard to covenant membership and (2) that God is indeed God of all, Jew and Gentile alike. In addition, verse 3 contains Paul's first use of the term λογίζομαι in the chapter, a term that will be repeated more than ten times in Rom 4, making it very prominent within the argument. This is not the first time Paul has used the term in Romans. In 2:26, Paul argued that for Gentiles who keep the requirements of the law, their uncircumcision is reckoned as circumcision (ἡ ἀκροβυστία αὐτοῦ εἰς περιτομὴν λογισθήσεται). That is, though the Gentiles in question are uncircumcised, they are reckoned as members of the people of God. Earlier in this chapter, I argued that these are the same Gentiles who have the works of the law written on their hearts (Rom 2:15). Thus, uncircumcised Gentiles are reckoned as covenant members on the basis of their obedience to the law, which they do as a result of a circumcised heart. This point is further confirmed by Paul's reference to the justification of the "ungodly" in verse 5, which points back to 1:18–32. In short, Abraham was called out from among the ungodly and was marked out by faith in God. The true people of God are likewise marked by the same faith.

Therefore, the repeated use of the key term λογίζομαι, which already featured prominently in Rom 2, links the argument of Rom 4 with Paul's previous assertions concerning justification and covenant membership. The above argument sought to show a relationship between Paul's contention concerning the Gentiles in Rom 1 and 2. By use of λογίζομαι, Paul has now linked his discussion of Abraham to his former discussion of sinfulness in Adam remedied in Christ. Of course, the use of this key term started in chapter 4 with a quotation from Gen 15:6 and other uses throughout the chapter should be understood as referring to that important OT passage as well. Thus, it might be that Paul already set up this discussion with a preliminary use of λογίζομαι in 2:26. That is, he used the term there in anticipation of the exposition on Abraham in chapter 4. In addition, the term will be used again in 6:11, which is situated in one of the most explicit union with Christ passages in the epistle. Paul has tied together his argument through the Abraham story and thereby laid the foundation for more detailed expositions of union with Christ to follow. Further, the verbal link back to Rom 2:26 ties together the covenant with Abraham to the new covenant and thereby presents the new covenant as the fulfillment of the Abrahamic covenant.

Second, the primary purpose of Rom 4 is to show the worldwide (Jew and Gentile) family of Abraham was God's intention from the beginning. This worldwide family is defined by faith. Having already identified God as the God of all (3:29), Paul denies that Abraham is to be considered the father of any *according to the flesh* (κατὰ σάρκα). In other words, Christians are the true seed of Abraham in Christ and do not simply become fleshly descendants through circumcision.[85] This, then, sets the stage for the rest of the argument in which Paul will repeatedly show that the true seed of Abraham are those who have faith in Christ.

In Rom 4:9–12, Paul again draws the main point into focus. In this short paragraph, Paul asks whether the blessing of not having one's sins counted against him/her is a blessing only for those who are circumcised, the Jews. He emphatically denies this since the reckoning of Abraham's faith as righteousness occurred prior to circumcision, thereby giving faith priority over circumcision. Paul asserts that this is no mere matter of coincidence, but was purposeful: in order for him to be the father of all

---

85. Wright, "Paul and the Patriarch," 225–31. See also Hays, *Conversion of the Imagination*, 61–84.

who believe (εἰς τὸ εἶναι αὐτὸν πατέρα πάντων τῶν πιστευόντων).[86] Thus, Abraham's true fatherhood is over those who share in his faith without respect to ethnicity. Again, it is clear that Paul is here defining the true people of God as Jews and Gentiles who together share the same faith as Abraham. The language of circumcision calls to mind the argument of 2:25–29, where true circumcision is of the heart and is the true marker of the new covenant people of God.[87] This definition will later center on union with Christ.

In Rom 4:13 and again in 4:16–18, Paul explicitly mentions the promise of a worldwide family. Curiously, in 4:13, Paul interprets the promise given to Abraham to be that he would "inherit the world" (τὸ κληρονόμον αὐτὸν εἶναι κόσμου). He is most likely drawing together the worldwide scope of the promises from Gen 12:3, 18:18, and 22:18. This is expanded through the prophetic literature, the Psalms, and several Jewish writings and interpreted by Paul as viewed through the lens of the arrival of the Messiah, who has ushered in the kingdom of God.[88] In any case, the primary point is clear: the use of worldwide language hammers home that what is now taking place in Christ was God's original intention. Union with Christ is no *ad hoc*, contrived notion to serve Paul's circumstantial needs. Rather, it is the culmination of God's creational and covenantal purposes.

In Rom 4:16–18, Paul further builds on this point by again quoting Genesis. This time, he draws on Gen 17 and the changing of Abram's name to Abraham, which summarizes the promise: he will be the father of many nations. He also alludes to Gen 15, as well as the creation story in Rom 4:17. The allusion to creation serves to set the promises to Abraham within the wider context of God's purposes for the created world. Again, the point is faith: Abraham believed that he would become the father of many nations, the father of a worldwide family, and now those who believe become members of this family. By making his argument as an exposition of the Abraham story with allusions to creation, Paul shows the reality of a multi-ethnic people of God to be the glorious display of the righteousness of God. In 4:17, the one in whom Abraham believed is the God "who gives life to the dead and calls non-existent things into

---

86. Rom 4:11.

87. Barclay, "Paul and Philo," 555–56.

88. Kruse, *Romans*, 213. Forman, "Politics of Promise," argues that Paul is here alluding to Isa 54:1–3 and thereby applying God's encouragement to Israel in exile to the church in Rome as they were living in the shadow of the empire.

being" (οὗ ζῳοποιοῦντος τοὺς νεκροὺς καὶ καλοῦντος τὰ μὴ ὄντα ὡς ὄντα). This designation is important since Paul views the united community of Jewish and Gentile believers "as a result of the new creation."[89] Thus, Jews and Gentiles are united to each other in union with Christ, which is no "plan B," but the exact eschatological outcome planned by God from the very beginning. God's purposes in creation and covenant coalesce in their fulfillment in the death and resurrection of Christ, through which God is creating his people.

Finally, in Rom 4:24–25, Paul makes the entire argument explicitly Christological. Specifically, Paul draws attention to the death and resurrection of Christ and to the God who raised him as the object of the faith he has argued marks the people of God throughout the chapter. There are several interpretive issues in these last two verses of Rom 4, most of which lie beyond the immediate purpose of the present argument. There are two primary points that need to be made in relation to the argument of this chapter. First, Paul defines the people of God as those who believe in the God who raised Jesus from the dead. Just as Abraham believed God and it was reckoned as righteousness (covenant membership), so now those who trust in God through Jesus are also reckoned as covenant members. This is true of all people, Jew and Gentile alike. Second, the mention of Jesus's death and resurrection anticipates the argument of Rom 6, where union with Christ is explicit.

The final phrase of verse 25 has caused considerable debate. Paul says Jesus "was raised for our justification" (ἠγέρθη διὰ τὴν δικαίωσιν ἡμῶν). Interpreters have mused over the relationship between the resurrection of Jesus and the justification of believers. It will be argued here that union with Christ is the key to understanding Paul's meaning. The way in which Paul words this phrase makes it somewhat difficult to adjudicate his exact meaning. It stands in parallel to the previous phrase, which says Jesus "was handed over for our trespasses" (παρεδόθη διὰ τὰ παραπτώματα ἡμῶν). This part of the verse seems straightforward enough: he was handed over because of our trespasses, meaning that our trespasses were the cause of his being handed over.

Most interpreters recognize the allusion to Isa 53:12 and the link back to Rom 3:25.[90] However, the relationship between Christ's resurrection and the justification of believers remains unclear. Most interpreters

---

89. Moxnes, *Theology in Conflict*, 253.
90. Moo, *Romans*, 288.

steer away from a causal meaning of the second διά, seeking to deny that our justification was the cause of Jesus's resurrection. It is possible that Paul continues to draw on Isa 53 in regard to resurrection since verses 10–12 seem to indicate that the servant will see life after his suffering and that he makes people righteous. Moo holds that this is difficult to maintain since the allusion is not immediately obvious. Thus, he argues that the second use of διά in the verse should be understood to be prospective: he was raised for the purpose of our justification.[91] This understanding of the διά makes sense of the wording, yet there is more going on in the verse.

A few further points need to be made. First, this mention of Christ's resurrection needs to be understood in relation to the previous mention in Rom 1:4. There, Paul says that Jesus was "designated the Son of God" (ὁρισθέντος υἱοῦ θεοῦ) by his resurrection. Whatever the nuances of the wording, it is clear that the resurrection was in some sense the vindication of Jesus as the true Son of God. Just as the resurrection was his vindication, so it is also the vindication of believers as the true people of God. In that sense, it could therefore be said that Jesus's resurrection is our justification. Thus, some causal meaning of διά can be maintained.[92] Perhaps the honor/shame motif aids in understanding. Jesus's resurrection was the vindication of his honor before both God and humanity. However, in 4:25, Paul is stating that he was raised because of the honor of his people. In other words, Jesus's resurrection restores the honor of humanity lost through sin. Further, this restoration of honor results in God's honor because it shows his righteousness—his faithfulness to the covenant promises given to Abraham.

Second, while the allusion to Isa 53:12 may not be as clear as other Pauline allusions, it is nevertheless probable. One thing is clear: the servant of Isa 53 acted on behalf of others. Accordingly, the death of Christ and the benefits of his resurrection are on behalf of others. Third, the communication of benefits takes place in union with Christ. While not immediately clear in Rom 4, it will become clear in Rom 6:5, where Paul says believers are united to Christ's resurrection. In other words, Christ's resurrection is also the resurrection of believers.[93] Bird argues similarly,

---

91. Moo, *Romans*, 288–89. So also Bird, *Saving Righteousness*, 50–52.

92. Schreiner, *Romans*, 244.

93. Kirk, *Unlocking Romans*, 79, draws attention to Rom 8:10, where there is another parallel use of διά and explicitly focuses on union with Christ in the phrase Χριστὸς ἐν ὑμῖν.

commenting "Though faith, believers are incorporated or identified with the risen and justified Messiah, and they are justified by virtue of their participation in him."[94] This will be explored further in chapter 5 below. Fourth, as Dunn notes, one should not seek to drive a wedge between the two statements of verse 25. Indeed, they are "two sides of the same theological assertion."[95] The death and resurrection of Jesus must be held together as one act.

Finally, though often overlooked, it is important to note the first-person plural pronouns Paul uses in verses 24–25.[96] The OT Scripture was written also "for *us*" (δι' ἡμᾶς); Jesus is "*our* Lord" (τὸν κύριον ἡμῶν); Jesus was handed over for "*our* trespasses" (παραπτώματα ἡμῶν) and raised for "*our* justification" (τὴν δικαίωσιν ἡμῶν). Paul is forging a new identity of the people of God in Christ. The pronouns here refer to all believers, Jew and Gentile in Christ, who together are the true seed of Abraham and true people of God. The Ἰουδαῖος and ἔθνος of 3:29, the περιτομή and ἀκροβυστία of 4:9–12 have become "us" and "our" in Christ.

In both Rom 1 and 3, the story of Israel has been intertwined with the story of Adam. Humanity outside of Christ shares a common unity in sin, which transcends ethnic identity. This leads to union with Christ, the concept around which Paul will define the true people of God. A further stone is laid in the foundation of this argument through Rom 4. The towering OT figure Abraham is brought into the argument to show that the joining of Jew and Gentile in Christ is the fulfillment of God's promises to Abraham and thus displays God's righteousness in keeping those promises. In other words, the story of God's people begins with failure in Adam, moves to promise in Abraham, failure again in Israel, and finally to fulfillment in Christ. Union with Christ cannot be properly understood apart from this background.

CONCLUSION

This chapter has begun the argument for a close connection between the stories of Adam and Israel and union with Christ. Thus far, we have dealt with the mostly implicit references to union with Christ in the first four chapters of Romans. Nevertheless, the exegesis of key passages from Rom

---

94. Bird, *Saving Righteousness*, 77.
95. Dunn, *Romans*, 1:241.
96. Moxnes, *Theology in Conflict*, 44.

1–4 is essential to the overall argument of this book because of the foundational nature of Paul's exposition to this point. While interpreters have often studied the "in Christ" language of chapters 5–8 in isolation from chapters 1–4, such an approach leads to faulty conclusions, especially regarding the OT background of union with Christ. With the foundation of Rom 1–4 laid, we now turn to the more direct references to union with Christ in Rom 5–8.

5

Adam, Israel, and Union with Christ in Romans 5–8

INTRODUCTION

THE PREVIOUS CHAPTER BEGAN the main argument of this book—that there is a close link between Paul's use of the Adam and Israel stories and his exposition of union with Christ. Having surveyed the mostly implicit notions of union with Christ in Rom 1–4, this chapter will continue the argument with exegetical analysis of union with Christ language in Rom 5–8, while demonstrating that these references to union with Christ are textually and thematically linked to Paul's allusions to Adam and Israel in these chapters.

EXEGETICAL ANALYSIS

Adam, Israel, and Union with Christ in Romans 5–6

Romans 5 is the most obvious point of connection between the story of Adam and union with Christ, for this is the one place in the letter where Adam is explicitly named. However, it has already been intimated that the argument of Rom 5 builds upon and expands that which Paul has already said about Adam and Israel via the previous allusions. Nevertheless, it remains the case that Rom 5 is important not only within the argument of Romans, but for understanding Paul's use of the Adam stories, especially as this relates to union with Christ. In addition, Rom 5 begins the concentrated references to union with Christ found within the middle section of the epistle. Given these facts, Rom 5 must be given careful attention.

This section will explore the relationship between the stories of Adam and Israel and union with Christ in Rom 5-6. Special attention will be given to Paul's union with Christ references throughout these two chapters, emphasizing textual and thematic connections to allusions to Adam and Israel in the surrounding context. In addition, I will argue that the explicit references to union with Christ in these chapters confirm the implicit notions of union detected in Rom 2-4. Textual and thematic connections between the allusions to Adam in Rom 5 and those of the previous chapters have already been noted.[1] Now it remains to show further links as related to union with Christ. In sum, as we move forward through Romans, the unified theme of humanity in Adam and new humanity redeemed in Christ will become clear.

Romans 5:1–11

While the explicit mention of Adam occurs in Rom 5:12-21, the first eleven verses of the chapter are crucial to understanding the flow of the argument. In chapter 3 above, I enumerated the connections between the two halves of Rom 5, particularly related to the use of the Adam story. The same is true in regard to union with Christ, especially as Rom 5 follows on Paul's exposition of the Abraham narratives in Rom 4. Therefore, it will be necessary to briefly examine Rom 5:1-11 in order to rightly understand the broader argument and the role of union with Christ. Chapter 5 begins the application of Paul's teaching on justification and faith found in chapters 3 and 4 to the church in Rome. That is, in Rom 5-8 Paul demonstrates the importance of the chapters 3:21 through chapter 4 for the church: they are the people of God in Christ. Union with Christ is essential in this exposition.

Paul's discussion builds upon the argument of chapter 4 via the initial phrase δικαιωθέντες οὖν ἐκ πίστεως in verse 1. The οὖν implies that

---

1. See chapter 3.

the argument follows from what has preceded and the idea of "justified by faith" was an important theme of Rom 3:21—4:25. In Rom 5:1–11, Paul details some of the positive outcomes of justification. These include peace, hope, reconciliation, and rescue from wrath. Though not the primary focus of the section, throughout Rom 5:1–11 Paul uses language that is distinctive of union with Christ. Most commentators detect some sort of transition in Rom 5, bridging to following major pieces of Paul's argument. Given that union with Christ features significantly in chapters 6–8, one would expect to find anticipatory hints of union with Christ in chapter 5.

In 5:1, Paul harks back to what he said in chapters 3–4 about justification, namely that believers are justified "of faith" (ἐκ πίστεως).[2] This phrase was used in 3:26, where those who are justified are "of the faith of Jesus" (ἐκ πίστεως Ἰησοῦ). It appears again in 3:30 in reference to believers, who are to have the same faith/faithfulness as Jesus and in 4:16 (twice) in reference to becoming part of Abraham's family by sharing his faith. In 5:1, Paul is probably referring back to these previous uses of ἐκ πίστεως and thus to the faithfulness of Jesus the Messiah.[3] That is, believers in Jesus are justified by his faithful, redemptive work.[4] As such, δικαιωθέντες . . . ἐκ πίστεως anticipates the argument of the second half of the chapter, where Jesus's faithfulness is contrasted with Adam's (and Israel's) unfaithfulness. Having affirmed again that one is a covenant member through Jesus's faithfulness, Paul continues, "we have peace with God *through our Lord Jesus Christ*" (εἰρήνην ἔχομεν πρὸς τὸν θεὸν διὰ τοῦ κυρίου ἡμῶν Ἰησοῦ Χριστοῦ). It is interesting that this follows closely after the discussion of Abraham, which was shown to have some intimations of union with Christ in chapter 4 of this book. Here Paul says that the peace we have with God is on account of the justification that comes through Jesus. The way this happens is not immediately apparent.

Campbell argues that this use of διά is best taken as communicating instrumentality.[5] That is, Jesus is the one through whom believers receive

---

2. Again, justification here is taken to be "declared to be a covenant member" or "declared to be in right relationship with God." Thus, the blessings of justification are relational and, as will be shown, are received via union with Christ.

3. Though I came to this understanding independently, Young, "Paul's Ethnic Discourse," also argues for a subjective understanding of ἐκ πίστεως in Rom 5:1 with reference to Jesus's faithfulness.

4. See the similar use of the phrase in Gal 2:16.

5. Campbell, *Paul and Union with Christ*, 239–40.

the peace that has be granted by God; peace with God is received via union with Christ. In this verse, "peace" most likely draws attention to the hoped for "covenant of peace" promised in Ezekiel.[6] Thus, Paul again places the discussion of justification and redemption in Christ in the context of the new covenant. Further, the close link between justification and peace with God through Christ also implies a connection between justification and union with Christ. This understanding of the prepositional phrase διὰ τοῦ κυρίου ἡμῶν Ἰησοῦ Χριστοῦ gives further support to the interpretation of ἐκ πίστεως above since the peace with God is clearly obtained through the faithfulness of Jesus the Messiah.

Verse 2 follows closely with another use of διά, this time in the form of δι' οὗ, "through whom." Just as Paul claimed that Jesus was the one "through whom" (δι' οὗ) he received grace and apostleship (Rom 1:5), so now Jesus is the one through whom believers receive "access to this grace" (τὴν προσαγωγὴν ... εἰς τὴν χάριν ταύτην). In chapter 3, I argued that the language here possibly alludes to access to the presence of God in the temple. The phrase δι' οὗ affirms that the access is again obtained through Christ, that is, via union with Christ. The limited access to God's presence in the temple is now replaced by continuous access to grace for the believer united to Christ. If Paul intended for the temple language to be detected, he would be drawing the story of Israel into the discussion and arguing that the true people of God have no need of a temple building for access to grace since the temple as the location of God's presence with his people is replaced by Christ.[7] As such, this is the second time that Paul alluded to God's presence with his people in Christ, as seen in the study of ἱλαστήριον in chapter 4 above.

In the second half of verse 2, Paul draws attention to boasting (linking back to 3:27), but this time in a positive sense. Whereas earlier in the letter Paul abhorred boasting, even claiming that Abraham had nothing to boast about before God (4:2), now he revels in boasting. However, it is essential to note that which causes Paul to boast: "in hope of the glory of God" (καυχώμεθα ἐπ' ἐλπίδι τῆς δόξης τοῦ θεοῦ). His boasting is in his hope, which is the hope of the restoration of God's glory in Christ.[8] The hope of God's glory is given through Christ since the δι' οὗ from the be-

---

6. Dunn, *Romans*, 1:263. The identification of an allusion to Ezek 36 here fits the criteria of distinctiveness, recurrence, and thematic coherence as defined in chapter 1.

7. Such an interpretation is consistent with Jesus's self-identification with the temple in, for example, John 2:13–22.

8. Byrne, *Romans*, 165.

ginning of the verse links to this clause. I argued in chapter 3 that the glory of this verse is intended to point back to Rom 3:23. Paul's point is that the loss of the shared glory of God in Adam is being restored via union with Christ. Placing this within the context of the entire chapter confirms the point since throughout Rom 5, union with Christ is at the forefront of the argument.

Verses 3–5 continue the themes of boasting and hope as Paul encourages the Roman Christians to boast in their suffering because in the end, they are "not put to shame" (οὐ καταισχύνει). Believers have their shame before God removed by the death of Jesus and are restored to their honorable position of being God's people. Paul here most likely draws on the Psalms, such as the LXX of Ps 21:6, applying it to the Roman believers as the people of God. Instead of shame, hope will be produced "because the love of God has been poured in our hearts through the Holy Spirit given to us" (ὅτι ἡ ἀγάπη τοῦ θεοῦ ἐκκέχυται ἐν ταῖς καρδίαις ἡμῶν διὰ πνεύματος ἁγίου τοῦ δοθέντος ἡμῖν). This last part of the sentence needs to be given brief attention because it probably has both new covenant themes and intimations of union with Christ seeping through. The imagery here points to Ezek 36:26, an important new covenant text where, in the midst of exile, God promised "A new heart I will give you, and a new spirit I will put within you." Then, in verse 28, the classic covenant promise is added: "you shall be my people, and I will be your God." Thus, when Paul writes that believers have hope because of the love of God poured into their hearts through the Spirit, this is the hope of the new covenant fulfilled. Of course, this links back to the new covenant promises to which Paul alluded in Rom 2. Additionally, the image of "pouring" may reference Isa 44:3, where God promises to pour out his Spirit.[9] Further, the wording that this love has been poured in the hearts of believers anticipates later union with Christ themes, especially Paul's assertion in 8:39 that nothing can separate believers from "the love of God in Christ Jesus our Lord" (τῆς ἀγάπης τοῦ θεοῦ τῆς ἐν Χριστῷ Ἰησοῦ τῷ κυρίῳ ἡμῶν). Thus, the hope is sure because believers are in inseparable union with Christ.

Verses 6–11 give attention to the story of Jesus's death, particularly concerning the representative nature of his death on the cross. In verse 6, Paul highlights the fact that Jesus died for those who were ungodly, linking back to Rom 4:5 and the justification of the ungodly. Paul here fills out the way in which the ungodly are justified: through the death of Jesus. In

---

9. Fitzmyer, *Romans*, 398.

verses 9–11, Paul makes subtle references to union with Christ by the use of particular prepositional phrases. While none of these phrases point exclusively to union with Christ, the all probably carry such a meaning, especially when heavily concentrated within the 3 verses. In each case, Paul communicates that various blessings of salvation are enjoyed in union with Christ. Believers united to Christ are rescued from the wrath of God *through him*—"δι' αὐτοῦ" (5:9). The wrath faced by all people (1:18; 2:5) is escaped because of the death of Jesus and via union with him. Reconciliation is accomplished *through the death of his son*—"διὰ τοῦ θανάτου τοῦ υἱοῦ αὐτοῦ" (5:10). This is so because believers are united to the death of Jesus (Rom 6:5) and thus enjoy the benefits of his death. Since we are reconciled, we are saved *by his life*—"ἐν τῇ ζωῇ αὐτοῦ" (5:10), which again points forward to Rom 6.[10] Finally, verse 11 summarizes the section by drawing attention again to boasting and reconciliation, both of which take place *through our Lord Jesus Christ*—"διὰ τοῦ κυρίου ἡμῶν Ἰησοῦ Χριστοῦ," that is, through union with Christ. In short, believers are incorporated into the story of Jesus and within that story find peace, reconciliation, and salvation.[11]

Throughout Rom 5:1–11, Paul continues the pattern began at the end of chapter 4 of using first-person plural pronouns to describe himself in relation to his audience. The rhetorical function is to highlight the unity of believers in Christ—Paul, as well as Jewish and Gentile readers, included.[12] Paul has made the transition from showing general human solidarity in sin to redeemed solidarity in Christ. All of this leads to the second half of the chapter, where union with Christ themes become more explicit alongside clear references to Adam (and Israel).

---

10. Moo, *Romans*, 312, contends that the phrases here are intended to communicate an instrumental meaning such that union with Christ is not in view. However, this interpretation focuses narrowly on one possible meaning of the terms without consideration to the wider meaning, especially as these verses set up 5:12–21 and 6:1–11, which contain very explicit union with Christ language. Further, instrumentality does not necessarily rule out union with Christ since the benefits of Christ's death and resurrection are only received through union. See Jewett, *Romans*, 366–67.

11. Hays, "Christ Died," 59.

12. McDonald, "Romans 5:1–11."

Romans 5:12-21

From the opening of the letter up to 5:11, Paul has rarely written unambiguously about union with Christ. Nevertheless, there have been numerous hints to this important theme and, as has been argued, union with Christ may be detected below the surface even when it is not explicit. One may ask why Paul has withheld direct exposition of union with Christ, especially if it is regarded as a central theme in the letter. Above, I suggested that the transition to first-person plural pronouns at the end of chapter 4 and into chapter 5 have the rhetorical function of encouraging the unity of believers in Christ. A similar point could be made with regard to the implicit nature of union with Christ in Rom 1:1—5:11. Most likely, the clustered union with Christ language in 5:12—8:39 serves the rhetorical structure of the argument. That is, first 5 chapters, more specifically chapters 1-4 with 5:1-11 as a "bridge,"[13] Paul has made the case that outside of Christ, there is a basic human solidarity in sin. While the structure does not break down quite this cleanly,[14] it is fair to say that Paul has been building up an argument for the universal nature of sin as union with Adam, which includes both Jews and Gentiles. Having done so, 5:12-21 marks the transition to showing the universal nature of God's purposes in Christ to create a multi-ethnic people of God. As Hays argues, "the action of Jesus is narrated as an event that delivers humanity from a state of bondage to a state of righteousness and life."[15] It is the story of Jesus that brings the stories of Adam and Israel to completion as the people of God are reconstituted in him.

In chapter 3, I analyzed Rom 5:12-21 with a primary focus on the way in which Paul uses the story of Adam (and Israel) within the argument. In this section, we return to these verses with a view toward the role of union with Christ within the same argument. It will be shown that there is a close relationship between the use of the Adam story (with Israel's story woven within) and union with Christ in this central section and this relationship aids readers in understanding the less explicit allusions to Adam in relation to union with Christ found earlier in the letter.

---

13. Ibid.

14. There are expositions of redemption in Christ in 2:15-16; 3:21-26; and throughout chapter 4. The point here is that these expositions serve as a contrast to sin in Adam and point forward to the fuller treatment of chapters 5-8.

15. Hays, "Christ Died," 60.

Further, I argued that careful attention to the corporate nature of Paul's exposition in Rom 5:12–21 aids readers in understanding his use of the OT stories. Likewise, the corporate nature of the argument also helps in understanding union with Christ. This presupposition allows for some corrective to overly individualistic understandings of union with Christ.[16] While Paul's theology certainly intimates that individual believers are united to Christ, the concept is primarily corporate, especially in Romans where Paul has been arguing for the unity of the church in Christ. The following exegesis will substantiate this claim.

Having again argued that all people are caught up in the sin of Adam in 5:12–14, Paul moves to his exposition of Christ and his role in the restoration of humanity in verses 15–17. As argued in chapter 3, verses 12–14 draw on the previous allusions to Adam and Israel, thus making explicit that which was implicit in earlier chapters. As such, it would not be surprising if the same were true of his reference to union with Christ. Verse 15 begins the discussion of the action of Christ and its effect on believers by drawing attention to the grace that is found in "the one man Jesus Christ" (τοῦ ἑνὸς ἀνθρώπου Ἰησοῦ Χριστοῦ). As death spread to all via union with Adam, so those united to Christ are receivers of grace. While the use of the preposition διά in 5:1–11 intimates that the blessings of salvation are received through union with the Christ, the idea of receiving grace through Jesus is communicated in 5:12–21 in expanded form. Thus, when Paul writes that "the grace of God and the gift in the grace of the one man Jesus Christ abounds to many" (ἡ χάρις τοῦ θεοῦ καὶ ἡ δωρεὰ ἐν χάριτι τῇ τοῦ ἑνὸς ἀνθρώπου Ἰησοῦ Χριστοῦ εἰς τοὺς πολλοὺς ἐπερίσσευσεν), there is a clear thematic connection to the previous section. It must be kept in mind that Paul is here focused on an analogy between the actions of Adam and the actions of Christ, as well as the effects of those actions upon humanity. In verse 15, Paul draws attention to the fact that there is an analogous relationship between the two, but neither their persons nor their actions can be described as completely parallel. He does this through the terms πολλῷ μᾶλλον ("much more") and ἐπερίσσευσεν ("abounds"). While commentators usually draw attention to the Christological implications of this, the rhetorical function within the letter should not be missed. Throughout the argument, Paul has been encouraging the Roman church toward unity in Christ despite ethnic differences. Having shown that there is a basic human solidarity in

---

16. For example, Johnson, *One with Christ*, gives very little, if any, attention to the corporate nature of the doctrine, especially in the Pauline corpus.

sin that encompasses all people, Jew and Gentile alike, Paul is here saying that there exists a greater unity in Christ for all those who are united to him. Just as the unity in sin transcends ethnic boundaries, much more the unity in Christ transcends ethnic divisions.[17] As Dunn writes, "Here the implication is clearly that God's response to Adam's trespass sought not merely to make up the ground which had been lost but also to bring to completion the destiny of which Adam had fallen short."[18] More pointedly, the obedience of Jesus creates a renewed humanity in him, composed of Jews and Gentiles. In Jesus, the true human being, renewed humanity is fulfilling the original God-given intentions, which Adam failed to realize.

This point is clarified further in verse 16. The gift that comes through the faithfulness of Jesus is greater than the condemnation that came through the sin of Adam because the obedience of Jesus overcomes the results of Adam's trespass. Adam's sin brought about the ruin of God's world and the separation of his people. Sin also ushered in condemnation, which spread to all people, including Jews and Gentiles. Through the faithfulness of Jesus, restoration is taking place. Paul again introduces justification into the argument, which is clearly corporate within the context. Justification in this verse must be understood in relation to the previous uses of the term. Interestingly, the same pattern found in condensed form in 3:23–24 is found here in expanded form. In 3:23, Paul argued that all people are caught up in Adam's sin and therefore lack the shared glory of original creation. Immediately following in 3:24, Paul announced that this lost glory is redeemed in Christ through his blood and, therefore, people are justified by grace. The same is true here. In Rom 5:12–14 and again in 5:15–16, Paul announces the result of Adam's sin for all people, followed by an immediate reference to justification in Christ. This again draws attention to the redefinition of the people of God as those who are united to Christ.[19] The corporate dimension here is hard to miss. Understood this way, the sin of Adam leads to the condemnation of all people and thus the failure of all to be God's people. Conversely, the faithfulness of Jesus has resulted in the reconstitution of the people of

---

17. Thus, the "all humanity" (πάντας ἀνθρώπους) of verse 18 refers to all people, regardless of ethnic identity rather than all in the sense of universalism. See Rapinchuk, "Universal Sin and Salvation."

18. Dunn, *Romans*, 1:280.

19. Stuhlmacher, *Romans*, 87, notes that justification takes place as believers "participate" in the atoning death of Christ.

God in him. This is the meaning of justification: people are declared to be in the right and thus to be the people of God in Christ.

Verse 17 continues the argument via the kingship motif. Through the sin of Adam, all people dwell in the kingdom of sin and death. The language of "reigning" (βασιλεύω) elevates the existential aspect to the surface. Life outside of Christ is marked by the domination of sin over people. In other words, being in Adam results kingship of sin, which in turn reigns over all aspects of life. The contrast to life in Christ carries the same effect. Rhetorically, it points to uniting of God's people under King Jesus, which points back to the opening of the letter (1:3–4), where the gospel is announced as the coming of the Davidic king. The reign of Christ and those in him invades the kingdom of sin.[20] However, Paul's wording here is not so straightforward. Literally translated, he writes "those who receive the abundance of grace and the gift of righteousness shall reign in life through the one man Jesus Christ" (οἱ τὴν περισσείαν τῆς χάριτος καὶ τῆς δωρεᾶς τῆς δικαιοσύνης λαμβάνοντες ἐν ζωῇ βασιλεύσουσιν διὰ τοῦ ἑνὸς Ἰησοῦ Χριστοῦ). Bypassing some of the details here, the final phrase holds the key to understanding Paul's meaning. Death reigned over all people through the sin of Adam. However, because of the faithfulness of Jesus, people have been freed from the kingship of sin and death and shall reign in life *through the one man Jesus Christ*. At first glance, it may seem that the two parts of the verse are incongruous, but this is not the case. Believers are not freed from the reign of sin and death on their own. Rather, reigning in life is via union with Christ.[21] As Dunn notes, the future tense "shall reign" gives the eschatological flavor to Paul's exposition.[22] Christians shall reign because they are united to the true king, the one man Jesus Christ. As such, humanity in Christ is restored to the position of dominion given by God at creation.[23] This takes place in union with Christ, an idea that will become more explicit in Rom 6.

Verses 18–21 close the chapter by reinforcing the point through a series of comparisons between Christ's act of righteousness and Adam's act of sin. It is important to recognize that the comparisons here are between the *actions* of Adam and Jesus rather than their persons. More specifically, Jesus is presented as the true human being, the one who

---

20. Käsemann, *Romans*, 142; Jewett, *Romans*, 383.

21. 2 Tim 2:12 makes a similar point: believers "will reign with him" (συμβασιλεύσομεν).

22. Dunn, *Romans*, 1:282.

23. Leithart, "Adam, Moses, and Jesus," 263.

perfectly fulfills all God intended for humanity. Jesus succeeds where Adam, Israel, and, indeed, all people have failed. This echoes back to Rom 3 as the obedience of Christ in 5:19 is parallel to the faithfulness of Christ in 3:22.[24] In 3:22, Paul wrote that righteousness comes to God's people through "the faithfulness of Jesus Christ" (διὰ πίστεως Ἰησοῦ Χριστοῦ). As noted already, this is in the context of Paul's discussion of sin and is followed by his affirmation that "all sinned and lack the glory of God." In Rom 5:18–21, Paul explains πίστεως Ἰησοῦ Χριστοῦ as the story of Jesus's obedience.

In verses 18–19, Paul describes the faithfulness of Jesus as an "act of righteousness" (δικαιώματος) and "obedience" (ὑπακοῆς). Of course, the theme of righteousness/justification has been in view since Rom 3:26. Here, drawing on the same theme of righteousness/justification coming through the work of Jesus, Paul argues that through the righteous act and obedience of Jesus, those who believe in him obtain "justification life" (δικαίωσιν ζωῆς) and are "made righteous" (δίκαιοι κατασταθήσονται). This is contrasted with obtaining death and being made sinners through Adam's disobedience. Justification is linked closely with life here because the declaration of justification brings life as people are brought out of the realm of condemnation in Adam and carried into the realm of righteousness in Christ.[25] Further, Paul makes this abundantly clear in the second contrast as those rightly related to Jesus are "made righteous." While some have attempted to interpret this as moral uprightness, the immediate context, as well as the overarching argument, makes clear that Paul is describing the status of the true people of God. Here Paul makes explicit what he has already alluded to throughout chapters 1–4: the world is not made up of Jews and Gentiles, but of those "in Adam" and "in Christ." Verse 20 brings the law into the argument and thus affirms that the Jews cannot claim to be the true people of God solely on the basis of possession of the law. Indeed, the law ironically caused sin to abound. Nevertheless, "grace abounded all the more" (ὑπερεπερίσσευσεν ἡ χάρις), leading to "eternal life *through Jesus Christ our Lord*" (εἰς ζωὴν αἰώνιον διὰ Ἰησοῦ Χριστοῦ τοῦ κυρίου ἡμῶν). This last phrase makes clear the way in which the above blessings are received and enjoyed by Christians: through union with Christ. This serves to set the entire argument

---

24. Johnson, "Romans 3:21–26," 89.
25. Campbell, *Paul and Union with Christ*, 346.

in terms of union—union with Adam leading to death and union with Christ leading to life. The following table illustrates the comparison.

Table 5.1: Union with Adam and Union with Christ in Rom 5:12–21

Union with Adam	Union with Christ
Death earned through sin	Life gifted through grace
One man's disobedience brought sin and death	One man's obedience brought life and justification
Death reigns through sin	Believers reign in life through Christ
All people (πάντες ἥμαρτον)	Those in Christ (λαμβάνοντες)
Sin abounds	Grace super-abounds

Drawing the various threads together, a few concluding points can be made. First, the entire argument of Rom 5:12–21 should be read as an expansion of Rom 3:21–26. Paul alluded to Adam's sin and its effect on all people in 3:23 and explains it further in 5:12–21. It is no coincidence that union with Christ language follows closely behind. In 3:21–26, the faithfulness of Jesus was an important theme further expounded in 5:12–21. In particular, Jesus's faithful obedience in fulfillment of everything God intended for humanity brings about the restoration of the people of God. Wright summarizes the point: "in Christ the human project, begun in Adam but never completed, has been brought to its intended goal."[26] The way in which this takes place is through union with Christ. Therefore, the righteousness of Jesus is also the righteousness of his people as they participate in his faithful obedience through union with him. Again Paul draws in the story of Jesus as that which completes the stories of Adam and Israel.

Second, in order to rightly understand this section, one must give careful attention to the prepositional phrases. Each time Paul mentions a benefit of Jesus's faithfulness, it is expressed via the prepositions εἰς or διά, used here to indicate union with Christ. That is, his righteous act translates into the justification and eternal life for his people only through union with him. This is highly significant for Paul's argument, particularly as it relates to his call for Christian unity for the sake of mission. For Paul, faith in Christ is no mere cold mental assent to a set of propositions, but a life-giving union with the faithful man, Jesus Christ. This has

---

26. Wright, "Letter to the Romans," 524.

enormous implications for the unity of the first century house church(es) of Rome (and today), for mission, and for discipleship.

Third, the argument of this section, while important on its own, sets up the following discussion running through chapters 6–8. The fact that union with Christ has taken center stage in the argument will become increasingly clear, starting with the next pericope, Rom 6:1–11. The exegesis above highlighted several words and themes that point forward to the extended discussion of union with Christ in Rom 6–8. Paul's emphasis on righteousness and eternal life through the faithfulness of Jesus lays the foundation for the very clear union with Christ language to follow.

Romans 6:1–11

It is no coincidence that Rom 6:1–11, which contains some of the clearest union with Christ language in the entire letter, follows Rom 5:12–21, which contains the most explicit reference to Adam (with Israel's story drawn into the discussion). This book has argued that union with Christ and the stories of Adam and Israel are closely related in the argument of Romans. Nowhere is this more readily observable than Rom 5:12—6:11. Unsurprisingly, Rom 6 is filled with allusions to Israel's story, thus linking together Adam, Israel, and union with Christ.

The first eleven verses of Rom 6 contain some of the most explicit language related to union with Christ in the entire epistle. Indeed, Rom 6:5 uses the language of union (σύμφυτοι) in describing the relationship between believers and the resurrection of Jesus. The primary point of this passage is to argue for a fundamental identification of believers with Christ. Paul's argument is that any other primary identification is identification with sin (and Adam).[27] Thus, the emphasis on union with Christ in this section feeds into Paul's goal of encouraging the Roman believers toward unity for the sake of mission. They are united with Christ and therefore should be united with one another. Paul builds this argument upon the foregoing Adam/Christ analogy, but the centrality of identification points back to Rom 1:6, where he described believers as those who "are called to belong to Jesus Christ" (κλητοὶ Ἰησοῦ Χριστοῦ). As argued in chapter 4, the language of belonging most likely implies union with

---

27. This is not to say that ethnic identities are erased for believers but rather that identification with Christ is more fundamental that one's social or racial identity. See Barclay, "Neither Jew nor Greek," 211.

Christ. In Rom 6, Paul makes this implication explicit as he demonstrates the real identification of believers with Christ in his death, burial, and resurrection life.

Paul begins this argument with a reference to baptism, utilizing the image to combat the possible objection to his gospel as promoting sin since in Rom 5:20 he stated that "where sin abounds, grace abounds all the more" (οὗ δὲ ἐπλεόνασεν ἡ ἁμαρτία, ὑπερεπερίσσευσεν ἡ χάρις). Contra this misunderstanding, Paul argues that it is impossible for believers to continue in sin because those identified with Christ have died to sin and therefore cannot continue to live in it (Rom 6:2). Though sinful behavior is undoubtedly involved, Paul's point relates more readily to the fundamental identity of the church in Rome. Since believers no longer give their allegiance to sin as they did in Adam, their new identity is in Christ. Thus, believers do not continue in sinful behavior because they are no longer in Adam, but in Christ, which results in "newness of life" (Rom 6:4). By implication and in keeping with the overall purpose of Romans in general and the use of union with Christ in particular, Paul is calling the believers in Rome to find their primary identity in Christ and his church. Thus, the breaking free of sin is also a breaking free from the former allegiance to ethnicity or social status through embracing solidarity in Christ over any other group identification. That is, the old union with Adam, which includes all people, Jew and Gentile alike, is no longer effective.

Many commentators understand this passage as representing the movement of believers from the old age of sin into the new age in Christ. Thus, the event is historical and eschatological.[28] While this highlights the salvation-history aspect of Paul's argument, it misses the more fundamental theme of participation in Christ's death and resurrection as a breaking away from the former union with Adam. Thus, rather than simply a movement in time or realm, Paul is saying that a change in allegiance and identity has taken place in Christ. Further, the emphasis on union with Christ's death and resurrection recalls the opening programmatic verses of Romans, where Jesus is identified as the resurrected Son of God and Davidic king (Rom 1:3–4). Thus, to be united to his death, and thus to his resurrection, is to identify with Jesus as king.[29] All of this serves the greater purpose of Romans: unity among believers for mission.

---

28. So Hultgren, *Romans*, 242–43.

29. Wright, *Paul and the Faithfulness of God*, 828–29, has argued that OT concepts of corporate solidarity and of the representational nature of Israel's king forms partial

In verse 3, Paul makes union with Christ central to his argument and therefore the believer's new identification. Baptism signifies this as the believer is "baptized into Christ Jesus" (ἐβαπτίσθημεν εἰς Χριστὸν Ἰησοῦν). This includes being "baptized into his death" (εἰς τὸν θάνατον αὐτοῦ ἐβαπτίσθημεν). Campbell argues that Paul's reference here is to identification, specifically identification with Christ's death. He writes, "To be baptized into Christ refers to a dynamic action that results in a new state—identification with Christ."[30] Keck goes further: "For Paul, being baptized 'into' someone makes one a participant in that person's significance by entering into it, by sharing it, and so accepting that person's significance as authoritative for one's life."[31] Thus, union with Christ is identification with his death in the sense of being marked out as one who belongs to Christ and claims his death to sin as one's own death. Baptism identifies one with the story of Jesus, here specifically his death, such that his story becomes one's own.[32] Verse 4 extends the identification to resurrection and new life. Here again the story of Jesus is the point of connection between the OT stories and the people of God in Christ. As Fowl notes, "the story of Christ's life, death, and resurrection in which sin is defeated defines the community [of believers]."[33]

Romans 6:1–4 must be interpreted in relation to the preceding argument of Rom 5:12–21. In putting forth baptism as a sign of the new identification with Christ, Paul is essentially presenting Christ as the new Adam.[34] All people are identified with Adam and his death, but believers in Christ have been removed from the kingship of death and have been baptized into Christ such that now they not only share in Adam's death (they will still die), but also share in Christ's death.[35] Thus, sin and death no longer reign over the community of believers in Rome, but Christ reigns in life, which is their new identity together in him.

---

backgrounds for Paul's "in Christ" language. Wright cites particularly 1 Sam 17 and 2 Sam 19–20. See also his earlier statement in Wright, *Climax*, 46–49. While this is possible, it is not clear in the text of Rom 6. Nevertheless, the conceptual background, along with the identification of Jesus as the Davidic king in Rom 1:3–4, make the connection thematically reasonable.

30. Campbell, *Paul and Union with Christ*, 207.
31. Keck, *Romans*, 158.
32. Gorman, *Cruciformity*, 176–77.
33. Fowl, "Some Uses of Story," 298.
34. Schreiner, *Romans*, 307.
35. Dunn, *Romans*, 329.

Interestingly, Paul again draws on themes of honor and shame in this section. Believers are baptized into the shameful death of Christ.³⁶ However, just as Jesus was raised "through the glory of the Father" (διὰ τῆς δόξης τοῦ πατρός), so also those "in Christ" will also experience this glory in resurrected new life. Again, at a key moment in the argument, Paul couches his discussion in terms of honor/glory to describe the results of the believers' union with Christ. Readers naturally link this glory to previous references to glory in the letter, particularly to the lost glory in Adam of 3:23. Ironically, uniting to the shameful death of Christ leads to resurrection through the glory of the Father. Presumably, Paul means that believers also share in this glory since they are also united to Christ's resurrection. In addition, the glory language fits well with the recurring exodus motif throughout the chapter. In Exod 14:4, Yahweh proclaimed the purpose of the exodus and the crossing of the sea to be "so that I will gain glory for myself over Pharaoh." Likewise, the resurrection of Christ, in which the believer participates, is also by and for the glory of God.³⁷

Further, Beale argues for an echo of Ezek 36 in Rom 6:3–4, noting that in the context, Paul has used to the image of baptism to illustrate the new identity in Christ, combined with the notions of resurrection and newness of life (καινότητι ζωῆς). Unique in the LXX is Ezek 36:25–28 in drawing together images of "clean water" (ὕδωρ καθαρόν) and the giving of a "new heart and a new spirit" (καρδίαν καινὴν καὶ πνεῦμα καινὸν δώσω ἐν ὑμῖν).³⁸ If this echo is indeed present, which seems reasonable, this would draw new covenant overtones into the discussion.³⁹ The death of Jesus and the co-crucifixion with him results in believers entering into the new covenant, which creates the new people of God in Christ. Further echoes of Ezek 36 can be seen in Rom 6–8, which will be explored in the discussion below.

The next section, Rom 6:5–11, builds on this with clear focus on union with Christ and echoes of Israel's story. Union with Christ language provides the bookends of the paragraph. Verse 5 opens the paragraph with "for if we have been united to the likeness of his death" (εἰ γὰρ σύμφυτοι γεγόναμεν τῷ ὁμοιώματι τοῦ θανάτου αὐτοῦ), which is one of the

---

36. Jewett, *Romans*, 398.
37. Holland, *Romans*, 184.
38. Beale, *New Testament Biblical Theology*, 253.
39. The criteria of recurrence and thematic coherence are clearly discernible here.

few places in which Paul uses the explicit language of "union" (σύμφυτος).[40] The section then ends with one of the most common phrases Paul used to communicate union with Christ: "in Christ Jesus" (ἐν Χριστῷ Ἰησοῦ). These two clear references serve to frame the paragraph by emphasizing union with Christ. Having introduced the notion in Rom 6:1–4 with the image of baptism, verses 5–11 continue the thought with images of kingship, slavery and liberation, life and death.

In Rom 6:4, Paul drew attention to the relationship between the resurrection of Christ and the "newness of life" (καινότητι ζωῆς) given to believers. The implicit notion of union with Christ's resurrection is then made explicit in verse 5. As believers are united to his death, so they will be united to his resurrection. Interpreters must pay close attention to the verbs in this verse as Paul moves from the perfect tense-form (γεγόναμεν) in regard to union with Christ's death to future tense-form (ἐσόμεθα) in regard to union with his resurrection.[41] This seems to serve two purposes in Paul's exposition. First, the fact that believers "have become" united to the death of Christ makes sure the future union with his resurrection. This is probably intended to encourage the believers with the guarantee of future resurrection. The concept of assurance will resurface in chapter 8. Second, the future orientation of union with Christ's resurrection leads into ethical discussion. Indeed, Paul has already described life in Christ as the ability to "walk in newness of life" (Rom 6:4), which builds on his assertion that believers can no longer continue in sin because of their union with Christ's death (Rom 6:2). Thus, the future orientation is used as a motivator for the Roman believers to live in light of their union with Christ. In other words, union with Christ is the primary marker of the new covenant people of God (along with the gift of the Spirit—Rom 8) and therefore this union profoundly affects the lifestyle of Christians. The identification with Christ in his death and resurrection serves to put an end to old relationships (in Adam) and to enter into new, covenantal relationships with Christ and his people.[42] Paul will follow this with echoes of exodus to further emphasize the point.

In Rom 6:6–7, Paul draws on slavery images in order to further his argument, which undoubtedly carries overtones of the exodus event.[43]

---

40. This is the only use of the term in the NT. Jewett, *Romans*, 400, notes multiple secular uses of the term including biological, horticultural, and social uses.

41. Kruse, *Romans*, 262.

42. Jewett, *Romans*, 401.

43. Many commentators recognize the exodus language in Rom 6:12–23, but few

In verse 6, Paul argues that by virtue of co-crucifixion with Christ, "the body of sin" (τὸ σῶμα τῆς ἁμαρτίας) has been destroyed and, therefore, "we are no longer to serve sin" (τοῦ μηκέτι δουλεύειν ἡμᾶς τῇ ἁμαρτίᾳ). There are several points that need to be made here. First, as Moo points out, the "old man" crucified with Christ links back to Rom 5:12–21 and thus relates to the former union with Adam in sin.[44] That this is the case makes it clear that Adam is still in the picture in these verses. Second, the destruction of the "body of sin" comes by crucifixion with Christ. This links Paul's discussion here with the previous verses. Thus, the importation of the exodus language to come is closely connected to both union with Christ and the identification with his death. That is, there is an unmistakable emphasis on the death of Christ. Third, co-crucifixion results in the end of the believer's slavery to sin. Perhaps the exodus language along with the emphasis on identification with the death of Christ is intended to evoke memories of the Passover event.[45] On the night of the last plague, the blood of the lamb placed on the doorposts marked out the Israelite homes (Exod 11–12). What is sometimes missed is the purpose of the blood. Exodus 11:7 states that by the blood on the doorpost, "the Lord makes a distinction between Egypt and Israel." Likewise, co-crucifixion marks out the true people of God: those who are united to Christ.[46] Therefore, just as the last plague results in the people of Israel no longer serving as slaves of Pharaoh, so also believers in Jesus no longer serve sin. Fourth, the connections with previous themes and the exodus language also make clear that the "body of sin" and the "old self" should be understood as corporate entities rather than an individual's physical body.[47] The primary point is the severing of the former union with Adam

---

notice the way Rom 6:6–7 sets up this emphasis on liberation from sin in the remainder of the chapter. Thielman, "Story of Israel," 185, writes, "Echoes of the story of Israel in 6:1–11 are attenuated at best, but in 6:12–23 they resound more clearly." While surely louder later in the chapter, I will argue that the echo is clear in 6:6–7.

44. Moo, *Romans*, 374.

45. Goodrich, "From Slaves of Sin to Slaves of God," argues that Paul's slavery language in Rom 6 is influenced by Hellenistic cultural themes. He believes OT exodus themes lie in the background, but do not form the primary meaning of slavery for Paul. However, this seems to ignore (1) Paul's consistent use of exodus language throughout Romans and (2) the function of Rom 6 within the overall argument. Thus, as argued here, exodus themes play a larger role than Goodrich seems to allow.

46. Paul refers to Jesus as "our Passover lamb" (τὸ πάσχα ἡμῶν) in 1 Cor 5:7.

47. Dunn, *Romans*, 332; Jewett, *Romans*, 403–4; Holland, *Romans*, 185–90. See also Tannehill, *Dying and Rising with Christ*.

and the creation of a new union with Christ. This process also entails union with a community: those who are "in Christ."

In verse 7, identification with the death of Christ means that the believer "has been set free/vindicated from sin" (δεδικαίωται ἀπὸ τῆς ἁμαρτίας). At first glance, this verse appears as a restatement or summary of what has already been said: those united to Christ's death are no longer enslaved to sin.[48] Yet, Paul uses the verb δικαιόω here, which seems somewhat odd. Perhaps the apparent oddity results from the contemporary debate among Pauline scholars, which pits forensic categories against participatory language.[49] For Paul, no such dichotomy exists. His use of δικαιόω in this verse draws in the forensic notion of declaration into his discussion of participation in the death and resurrection of Christ through baptism.[50] As Schnelle puts it, "participation in the Christ event is the condition for salvation in the court."[51] In other words, those united to Christ have been "vindicated from sin" (δεδικαίωται ἀπὸ τῆς ἁμαρτίας). That is, the death sentence resulting from sin and union with Adam no longer applies.

Yet, there seems to be more going on in this short verse. The previous verse, as well as the verses that follow, draw on exodus themes of liberation from slavery. One may ask how it is that Paul fits vindication language into the discussion. Indeed, Schreiner notes that "It is quite difficult, though, to discern the logical relationship between the two verses [Rom 6:6–7]."[52] The answer lies in the OT background. As mentioned already, throughout Rom 6, Paul draws on exodus imagery in his explanation of new life in Christ.[53] Since this is the case for the surrounding verses, there is good reason to believe that Paul is likewise drawing on exodus themes in verse 7. At the exodus, Israel was set free from the slavery. No longer bound to Pharaoh, they were instead bound to Yahweh. It

---

48. Hultgren, *Romans*, 249, holds that Rom 6:7 is simply a "recap" of what has preceded.

49. For a summary of the various positions and the scholars that hold to them, see Westerholm, *Perspectives Old and New on Paul*.

50. Contra Moo, *Romans*, 376–77, who believes δικαιόω is used to indicate "set free from" rather than "justified."

51. "die Teilhabe am Christusgeschehen ist die Voraussetzung für die Rettung im Gericht," Schnelle, "Transformation Und Partizipation," 74.

52. Schreiner, *Romans*, 318

53. The following discussion is an expansion of Sun, "Difficult Texts."

could be said that they were justified from Pharaoh.⁵⁴ In the same way, the believer is "justified from sin" in the sense of being no longer bound to sin and thus legally and rightfully bound to Christ. Themes of redemption and justification have already been linked closely together in Rom 3:24 as discussed in chapter 4 above. Here again, Paul binds these themes together in his fuller exposition of union with Christ.

The prophetic literature may have influenced Paul's thinking in these verses as well. The themes of exodus and justification are wed together in Isa 40–55, a text frequently cited or alluded to in Paul's writings. The second exodus theme is widely recognized in Isaiah,⁵⁵ as is the restoration promised in the servant songs. One example will suffice to show the connection: Isa 52–53. These chapters have a number of thematic connections with Rom 6. First, the new exodus theme is very clear. In Isa 52:3–6, Yahweh uses explicit exodus language in promising to restore the people of Israel. They "shall be redeemed without money" (52:3).⁵⁶ At the time of the new exodus, the people of Israel "shall know my [Yahweh's] name" (52:5). In addition, the promises of 52:12 echo the first exodus with the people leaving and Yahweh going before them.

Second, Isa 52:7 contains foundational teaching for Paul's gospel as it announces the "good news." The Isaiah background for the use of the term "gospel" is undoubtedly important, but perhaps the latter part of Isa 52:7 is more immediately applicable to Rom 6. The "good news" as announced through Isaiah is simply "Your God reigns" (LXX: Βασιλεύσει σου ὁ θεός). In Rom 6:12, using the same terms, Paul commands the Roman believers to not allow sin to reign (βασιλευέτω) over them. Instead, since they are united to Christ, grace and righteousness reign (Rom 5:17, 21).

Third, it is clear that at least part of the servant's mission is to redeem his people through suffering and therefore "make many righteous" (Isa 53:11). The LXX of Isa 53:11 has clear verbal links to Rom 6:7 in the use of δικαιόω (δικαιῶσαι δίκαιον εὖ δουλεύοντα πολλοῖς). Whatever the exact meaning of this verse, it is clear that it has to do with the forgiveness of sin and setting to rights the people of God. Thus, in Isa 52–53 there is a clear linkage of exodus themes and righteousness language.⁵⁷ Accord-

54. Holland, *Romans*, 91.

55. Watts, "Consolation or Confrontation"; Watts, "Echoes from the Past."

56. The LXX translates this as λυτρόω, which is related to the term Paul used in Rom 3:24 (ἀπολύτρωσις).

57. Ceresko, "Rhetorical Strategy," argues for additional exodus motifs within the

ingly, it is unsurprising that Paul would use δικαιόω in this context as he identifies Jesus as the servant who leads the new exodus. Those united to him are thus "justified from sin" and freed from sin's lordship. In short, an allusion to Isa 52–53 fits all the criteria I identified in chapter 1: (1) distinctiveness: Isa 52–53 draws together exodus themes and justification; (2) recurrence: both themes are found elsewhere in Paul, especially in Romans; (3) multiplicity: numerous elements of the source text are found in Rom 6; (4) thematic coherence: an allusion to Isa 52–53 fits nicely within Paul's argument.

If Paul here indeed echoes themes from Isa 52–53 in Rom 6:6–7, the "one who has died" (ὁ ἀποθανών) in verse 7 probably refers to Christ in the first instance and to believers secondarily through union with his death.[58] This makes good sense in the context since there is a mingling of the death of Christ with the death (with Christ) of believers. Further, the focus of the entire passage is that there is a change in identity and union: believers are no longer united to Adam (and sin) and therefore do not find their primary identity anywhere other than in Christ. Thus, they are to "walk in newness of life" because of this new union. Jesus is the one whose death and resurrection bring about this new identity. He is the first to be vindicated from sin: the vindication of others is directly dependent on his death to sin and resurrection to life. Therefore, Rom 6:7 most likely refers fundamentally to the death of Jesus as the servant of Isa 52–53, who, as demonstrated above, leads in the new exodus. Again, the story of Jesus is pictured as the climax of the OT story as those baptized into Christ become God's people through entering the story of the faithful Messiah.

The above exegesis makes clear that Paul was drawing on exodus themes in his exposition of union with Christ in Rom 6. However, it is equally important to realize that the new exodus accomplished through the death of the Messiah Jesus is redemption from the slavery to sin, which was brought about through union with Adam. Thus, Paul has drawn together the stories of Adam and Israel, intimately intertwined, as

---

servant song of Isa 52:12—53:13, not in departure from Egypt language, but rather in echoing the suffering of Israel in Egypt.

58. Ridderbos, *Paul*, 66; Kirk, *Unlocking Romans*, 113–15. Moo, *Romans*, 377, followed by Schreiner, *Romans*, 319, rejects this interpretation because it "introduces a shift in subject for which the context has not prepared us." This seems to ignore the continuing argument from Rom 5, which Moo himself recognizes in his comments on Rom 6:6.

the OT background for union with Christ. The new exodus is a breaking of the former union with sin and Adam as well as the formation of a new union with Christ and with his people. Within the context of Rom 6, the net result is a powerful argument for holy living and unity among those in Christ, which leads to participation in mission. The rest of the chapter fills out this argument, all couched in exodus terms alongside clear union with Christ language.

Verses 8–11 continue the discussion with a focus on new life in Christ, filling out Paul's meaning from 6:4. The language of verse 8 serves to confirm the interpretation offered above regarding the identification of the "one who died" (ὁ ἀποθανών) as primarily referring to Jesus and, secondarily, to those who have died with him. In verse 8, Paul writes "now if we died with Christ, we believe that we also will live with him" (εἰ δὲ ἀπεθάνομεν σὺν Χριστῷ, πιστεύομεν ὅτι καὶ συζήσομεν αὐτῷ). Thus, Paul has Christ's death in view in verse 7 and builds upon this in verse 8 in relation to the participation in his death by believers. Here Paul uses two σύν- compounds, which communicate union with Christ.[59]

The close identification of the believer with Jesus in his death and resurrection life is further expounded in verses 9–11. The death and resurrection of Christ is first given attention in verses 9–10, in which Paul announces the victory of Jesus over death. The resurrection of Christ demonstrates his eternal defeat of death, resulting in resurrection life. As such, death no longer "has dominion over him" (θάνατος αὐτοῦ οὐκέτι κυριεύει). Paul's wording here aids the reader in connecting this part of the argument with the preceding verses and the OT background echoed throughout: Adam and exodus. This is particularly seen in Paul's use of κυριεύω. This word is closely related to the LXX translation of Gen 1:28, where Adam and Eve are given "dominion" (κατακυριεύω).[60] If this lies in the background, which is possible given the use of the Adam story in the near context, then Jesus is pictured as the new Adam who has defeated the enemy unleashed in the world through the sin of the first Adam.[61] Whereas the first Adam failed to obtain dominion over all things, Jesus not only reigns over all things, but also has reversed the consequences of the Adam's failure. Perhaps Paul's statement that Christ "died to sin" (τῇ

---

59. Campbell, *Paul and Union with Christ*, 217–37.

60. Or commanded to obtain dominion as the Greek verb implies.

61. Dunn, *Romans*, 1:323, notes that κυριεύω functions as a virtual synonym with βασιλεύω, which was used in Rom 5:14, 17. This lends further support to the claim that Adam is in the not-so-distant background.

ἁμαρτίᾳ ἀπέθανεν) reflects Jesus's identification with humanity in his incarnation.[62] Wright links this to Rom 8:3 and the coming of the Messiah "in the likeness of sinful flesh" (ἐν ὁμοιώματι σαρκὸς ἁμαρτίας).[63] If this is correct, then the emphasis on union with Christ is made all the more clear. Jesus, as Israel's Messiah, has identified with his people in order to reverse the effects of sin and thereby fulfill the task given to Adam and Israel. As Byrne points out, this is alluded to in Paul's statement that "he lives to God."[64]

Of course, Paul has already powerfully argued that all people, Jew and Gentile alike, are caught up in Adam's failure through their union with him. Now, those who have died with Christ are bound to him and share in his victory over death. Therefore, Paul writes that believers must "consider yourselves dead to sin but alive to God in Christ Jesus" (λογίζεσθε ἑαυτοὺς [εἶναι] νεκροὺς μὲν τῇ ἁμαρτίᾳ ζῶντας δὲ τῷ θεῷ ἐν Χριστῷ Ἰησοῦ). By virtue of death with Christ, believers are to live as if they were dead to sin. In other words, sin and death no longer rule over them. As the Israelites were set free from the reign of Pharaoh, so those who have died with Christ are no longer under the dominion of death. Paul wants the Roman believers to fully understand the transfer that has taken place: they are no longer in Adam, but in Christ. The "in Christ" language is significant, indicating the new life attained through union with Christ. Verse 11 serves as the conclusion to Paul's answer to the potential objection of verse 1: believers do not continue in sin because they are "in Christ." Thus, Rom 6:1–11 has built an argument for right living in union with Christ via echoes of OT narratives of Adam and Israel. This is consistent with the reading of Romans offered throughout this book.

Romans 6:12–23

The rest of Rom 6 expands on verses 1–11 using kingship and slavery metaphors. In Rom 6:12–14, Paul encourages the Roman Christians toward righteous living. This should be understood as the outworking of their union with Christ. As argued above, Paul has already made use of the kingship motif, arguing in verse 9 that "death no longer has

---

62. Though not drawing on Rom 6, Letham, *Union with Christ*, 21, writes, "The basis of our union with Christ is Christ's union with us in the incarnation."

63. Wright, "Letter to the Romans," 540.

64. Byrne, *Romans*, 193.

dominion over him [Christ]." Likewise, those who are "in Christ" share in his victory over death. Then, in verses 10-12, Paul continues this line of thought, applying it to the life of the community. Sin is again presented in the role of Pharaoh and union with Christ as the outcome of the new exodus. Those united to Christ are no longer slaves to sin as the union, which they had in Adam, has been broken through the gospel. In verse 13, Paul defines believers as those who are "out of death to life" (ἐκ νεκρῶν ζῶντας). This harks back to the first half of the chapter in which Paul expounded union with Christ as union with his death and resurrection. Because of this, those who are in Christ are not to turn back to the former slavery to sin, just as the Israelites were not to turn back to the former slavery to Pharaoh.[65]

The last words of verse 14 have been a cause of debate among many interpreters. Having repeated his charge that believers not allow sin to have dominion over them, Paul announces the grounds for this: "for you are not under law but under grace" (οὐ γάρ ἐστε ὑπὸ νόμον ἀλλὰ ὑπὸ χάριν). For the purposes of this book, there are two points that need to be made. First, though the introduction of law (νόμος) at this point in the argument may at first seem strange, careful attention to the narrative undercurrent running throughout Romans sheds considerable light on Paul's meaning. As argued in chapters 2 and 3 of this book, Paul has the OT narratives of Adam and Israel, as well as the Abrahamic covenant, running beneath the surface of his entire argument. Thus, a reference to law is not out of place here. Indeed, law has turned up in the argument several times, particularly in relation to union with Christ. For example, I argued in chapter 2 that in Rom 3:21-26, which is clearly related to the argument of Rom 5-8, drew together echoes of Adam and Israel. In that context, Paul says the revelation of God's righteousness takes place "apart from the law" (χωρὶς νόμου).[66] In chapter 4, I argued that the reference to law in 3:21 is a reference to the Sinai covenant. Likewise, rather than setting the content of the law over against the content of the gospel, Paul here says that those in Christ are no longer under the regulations of the Sinai covenant. Further, as with the rest of the chapter, this statement should be seen as further expounding on the content of Rom 5:12-21, especially verse 20 where Paul claimed that the law was given that "the trespass might increase." Thus, for Paul, being "under law" essentially means the

---

65. Holland, *Romans*, 195.
66. See also Rom 2:12-16, 25-29; 5:20.

same thing as being "in Adam." Those "in Christ" are no longer in this situation. Rather, they are the new covenant people of God. This again, as mentioned above, provides a covenantal context for Paul's understanding of union with Christ.[67]

Second, the placing of "grace" (χάρις) in opposition to law must also be understood within the narrative argumentation of the epistle. Interestingly, Paul has often referred to grace as something that is received in union with Christ. In Rom 1:5, Christ is the one "through whom" (δι' οὗ) Paul has received grace and apostleship. In 3:24, justification is by grace, which is received "through the redemption which is in Christ Jesus" (διὰ τῆς ἀπολυτρώσεως τῆς ἐν Χριστῷ Ἰησοῦ). In 5:2, access to grace is obtained "through him" (δι' οὗ). Finally, the Adam/Christ analogy of 5:12–21 notes several times that as death came through Adam, grace comes through Jesus (5:15, 17, 20, 21). Thus, the attentive reader knows that grace is received through union with Christ, which is the status of the new covenant people of God. Understood this way, Paul's notion that those in Christ are no longer under law but under grace serves as a pregnant summation of his argument. The mention of law at this point levels the ground, as it were, by removing any hint of Jewish privilege via the possession of the law.[68] Instead, Jew and Gentile stand together as the new covenant people of God.

The rest of Rom 6 presses the issue further by use of the slavery metaphor. There are few direct references to union with Christ in this section making in-depth analysis here unnecessary. Two points will suffice. First, it must be acknowledged that while union with Christ language is less common from Rom 6:15–23, the concept is not completely absent. Throughout the section, Paul uses the slavery metaphor to indicate that believers belong to God rather than to sin. Again, this echoes Rom 5:12–21, and shows a complete severing of the former union with sin in Adam. In addition, the slavery metaphor points back to Rom 1:6, where Paul described the Roman believers as those who "called to belong to Jesus Christ" (κλητοὶ Ἰησοῦ Χριστοῦ). Barclay aptly summarizes the point:

> The gift of God in Jesus Christ has established not liberation from authority or demand, but a new allegiance, a new responsibility, a new "slavery" under the rule of grace. Although not

---

67. Kruse, *Romans*, 269, recognizes the covenantal emphasis of Paul's contrast.
68. Dunn, *Romans*, 1:352.

itself an imperative, grace is imperatival: it bears within itself the imperative to obey.[69]

Thus, the content of Rom 6:15–23 should be understood as further explanation of union with Christ for the purpose of encouraging the believers to live in light of this union. Moreover,, the mention of "obedience from the heart" (ὑπηκούσατε . . . ἐκ καρδίας) in Rom 6:17 most likely ties back to previous uses of "heart" language in 2:15, 29 and 5:5, which I argued has direct connections to the concept of union with Christ in fulfillment of prophetic promises.[70]

Second, the first point is confirmed in Rom 6:23, which contains very explicit union with Christ language. In summarizing the preceding argument, Paul writes that the "free gift of God is eternal life in Christ Jesus our lord" (τὸ δὲ χάρισμα τοῦ θεοῦ ζωὴ αἰώνιος ἐν Χριστῷ Ἰησοῦ τῷ κυρίῳ ἡμῶν). This brings the whole argument to a conclusion, showing that the end result of the believers' union with Christ is eternal life. Further, this eternal life is found only in Jesus "our lord." This makes clear that believers belong to Jesus and give full allegiance to him as lord. Having been set free from the lordship of sin in Adam, those in Christ are the new covenant people of God under the lordship of Christ. This is the location of the church's unity and the foundation for mission: they are all, Jew and Gentile alike, in Christ.

Adam, Israel, and Union with Christ in Romans 7–8

Romans 7

In chapter 3, I argued that Rom 7:7–13 is best understood as alluding to both Adam and Israel, which serves to highlight a key component of the argument of this book: throughout Romans, the Adam and Israel narratives are closely intertwined and together form the background for union with Christ. In this section, I will continue to build the case by showing that the allusions to Adam and Israel found in Rom 7:7–13 are connected to union with Christ in the near context. At the outset, it must

---

69. Barclay, "Under Grace," 60.

70. Kruse, *Romans*, 281, links Paul's use of καρδία in 6:17 with Jer 31:33, which serves to place the argument in new covenant terms. This fits with previous uses of καρδία, particularly in Rom 2.

be emphasized that Rom 7 cannot be properly interpreted if studied in isolation from the surrounding context. Indeed, the argument in Rom 7 builds on and continues the argument from Rom 6.[71] This is clear from the first words of chapter 7: "Ἢ ἀγνοεῖτε (Or, do you not know . . .). Clearly Paul intends this to be read as a continuation of the previous argument. In addition, Rom 7:1 contains a key term found several times in chapter 6: κυριεύω. This serves to demonstrate the close connection between the foregoing argument and the whole of chapter 7.[72] Further, Macaskill argues that Paul's placement of the marriage metaphor of Rom 7 in close proximity to the baptism discussion of Rom 6 suggests that both communicate the close identification of believers with Christ as the "covenant representative."[73] Since union with Christ is explicitly linked to baptism in Rom 6, one would expect union themes to be present in Rom 7.

While Rom 7 is not the most important chapter for the study of union with Christ within the epistle, it nevertheless contains a few significant references to the doctrine. Of particular importance is Rom 7:4, where Paul writes, "so then, my brothers, you also have been put to death to the law through the body of Christ, into belonging to another, to the one who was raised from the dead, that we might bear fruit to God" (ὥστε, ἀδελφοί μου, καὶ ὑμεῖς ἐθανατώθητε τῷ νόμῳ διὰ τοῦ σώματος τοῦ Χριστοῦ, εἰς τὸ γενέσθαι ὑμᾶς ἑτέρῳ, τῷ ἐκ νεκρῶν ἐγερθέντι, ἵνα καρποφορήσωμεν τῷ θεῷ.). In the context, Paul has used the marriage metaphor to further illustrate the breaking of the former union with Adam in sin and the formation of the new union with Christ in faith. The OT prophets used marriage as a metaphor to describe the relationship between Yahweh and Israel.[74] Paul's use of the metaphor at this point further highlights (1) the corporate nature of his argument and (2) the redefinition of the people of God in Christ. In order to apply the image of marriage to the relationship between Christ and the church, Paul argues that there was a previous union with "sinful flesh" (Rom 7:5) that is now broken. He argues that the

---

71. Contra Käsemann, *Romans*, 187, who believes that these verses "represent a fresh start." For further connections between Rom 6:1–23 and 7:1–6, see Kirk, *Unlocking Romans*, 120–21. Earnshaw, "Reconsidering Paul's Marriage Analogy," 72, argues that Rom 7:1–4 and 6:1–11 are "parallel passages as far as the underlying structure of thought is concerned."

72. Jewett, *Romans*, 430, notes, "This verbal choice signals that Paul intends to place the law in a parallel category [as sin and death] as a force from which believers have been freed." Again, this serves to connect Rom 7 to the argument of Rom 6.

73. Macaskill, *Union with Christ*, 196.

74. For example, Hos 1–2.

law of marriage is no longer binding when a spouse dies because death renders the remaining spouse free to marry again. Likewise, death has caused the dissolution of the former union with Adam, rendering people free to be joined to Christ.[75] Thus, those who believe are no longer bound to sin in Adam, but are bound to Christ.

Within Rom 7:4, there are two important descriptors of union with Christ that require attention. To start, Paul says that believers "have been put to death to the law through the body of Christ."[76] This statement is significant in that Paul ties together several union themes that appeared earlier in the letter and will appear again later. First, the mention of death undoubtedly links back to Rom 6, where Paul described believers as having "died to sin" (6:2), baptized into the death of Christ (6:3), buried with Christ (6:4), united to the death of Christ (6:5), and crucified with him (6:6). All of the references to death in chapter 6 relate directly to union with Christ. In other words, from Rom 6, the theme of death is clearly intended to communicate the believers' union with the death of Christ. Thus, when Paul again references death in Rom 7:4, the concept of union with the death of Christ is most likely still close at hand.

Second, it is not just death that Paul references here; it is death to the law. This helps shed light on the somewhat cryptic mention of law in Rom 6:14, which was examined above. It seems that Paul is picking up this theme again here and further explaining what it means to no longer be "under law." This is clear from Rom 7:1, where Paul states that in the verses to come he is speaking to "those who know the law" (γινώσκουσιν ... νόμον). That is, this section is addressed primarily to Jewish believers or Gentile believers previously connected to the Jewish synagogue. Thus, Paul is saying that being united to the death of Christ has freed those under the law from their union with Adam. While this connection may not seem immediately obvious, we have argued throughout this book that Paul has gone to great lengths to show that all people, Jew and Gentile alike, are "in Adam." This is why "under law" means something similar to "in Adam." The Mosaic Law is no longer the primary identifier of the seed

75. Earnshaw, "Reconsidering," argues that the two marriages both refer to the believer's union with Christ: the first marriage is the union with his death, while the second marriage is the union with his resurrection. While possible, it seems more likely that the first marriage is the union with Adam, which is broken via participation in Christ's death.

76. Though somewhat awkward in English, the passive has been retained in order to show the parallel use of the passive in the second half of the sentence. See Dunn, *Romans*, 1:361.

of Abraham, the true people of God. Rather, those who are "in Christ" have died to the law and are no longer bound to it.

Third, this death to the law takes place "through the body of the Messiah" (διὰ τοῦ σώματος τοῦ Χριστοῦ). While the phrase "body of the Messiah" can in other contexts convey the concept of union with Christ on its own, Paul appears to be using it differently in this verse.[77] Here the "body of the Messiah" most readily refers to the actual physical body of Jesus since the immediate reference is to death. That is, just as Rom 6:1–4 emphasized union with the death of Jesus, here the death that believers have died to the law comes via the death of Jesus and the believers' union with him. Though "body of the Messiah" does not here in itself communicate union with Christ, the preposition διὰ alerts the reader to the concept. Paul uses the same phrasing several times to indicate the reception of a blessing or attainment of a status or position has occurred through union with Christ.[78] The same is true here: death to the law takes place via union with Christ, specifically union with his death. Thus, Paul's meaning here is closely related to that of Rom 6: because of one's union with Christ's death, the old union with Adam in sin is broken. With regard to the marriage metaphor, Paul seems to be saying that since a death has taken place, those in Christ are no longer legally bound to that which he/she was formerly bound.

The additional union with Christ terminology is found in Paul's description of believers as those "belonging to another, to the one who has been raised from the dead." Belonging to the resurrected Christ is the purpose of being put to death to the law.[79] The concept of belonging to Christ has been present in the letter from chapter 1 and is especially prominent in the slavery metaphor of Rom 6, as argued above. The language in Rom 7:4 makes explicit the implicit notion, as γίνομαι is used with the dative ἑτέρῳ to communicate belonging to someone.[80] This intimates close relationship, which is unsurprising given the consistent use of union language and themes throughout the contours of Paul's argument. Further, the one to whom believers now belong is "the one who was raised from the dead." Again, this connects back to Rom 6, where believers are those united not only to the death of Christ, but also to his

---

77. In Romans, an obvious example is Rom 12:3–8, where body (σῶμα) is used in the corporate sense.

78. See especially Rom 5:1–11 and the discussion of these verses above.

79. As Dunn, *Romans*, 1:362 notes, εἰς plus the infinitive communicates purpose.

80. BDAG, 199.

resurrection. Thus, the close identification of believers with Christ is now described as belonging to the resurrected Messiah.

At the end of verse 4, Paul includes yet another purpose clause: "in order that we might bear fruit to God" (ἵνα καρποφορήσωμεν τῷ θεῷ). The purpose of being put to death with regard to the law was to belong to Christ. Belonging to Christ results in bearing fruit to God. Though the terms are not the same,[81] there is a possible allusion to the creational mandate given to Adam to "be fruitful and multiply."[82] Contextually, an echo of the Adam narrative makes good sense and fits with the additional allusions found in Rom 7:7–13. Further, as argued above, this section of the epistle must be understood as explanation of Rom 5:12–21, where Adam featured prominently. If Paul indeed alludes to Adam here, then he is showing that humanity is being renewed in Christ, the last Adam. All those who belong to the risen Jesus are members of the true people of God. In Christ, the renewed people of God, the true seed of Abraham, are fulfilling the original commission given to Adam.[83] Or, perhaps better, God is fulfilling the original commission through keeping his covenant promises to Abraham.[84] This point demonstrates that Rom 7 is not an aside, but fits within the larger argument of Romans by showing the δικαιοσύνη of God. Accordingly, "bearing fruit" also connects to the purpose of Romans: to unite the church for mission. As Stuhlmacher argues, the phrase "derives from the Christian mission."[85] The unity found in the corporate belonging to Christ should result in participation in mission.

The above exposition has focused on the direct references to union with Christ in the passage. However, the concept cannot be properly interpreted without placing it within the context of Rom 7:1–6 as a whole.

---

81. In the LXX, "be fruitful" in Gen 1:28 is translated αὐξάνεσθε.

82. Wright, *Paul and the Faithfulness of God*, 1010; Holland, *Romans*, 229.

83. Busch, "Figure of Eve," 13, suggests that the "bearing fruit to death" (τὸ καρποφορῆσαι τῷ θανάτῳ) in Rom 7:5 echoes the story of Adam and Eve's sin in Gen 3. If this is the case, a contrast with "bearing fruit to God" through belonging to Christ in verse 6 is established and further supports the contention of this book that the Adam narratives form the background for union with Christ. Further, an echo of Gen 3 coupled with the references to law in this section fits with the other references to Adam in Romans, which usually link with an allusion to Israel's story. See also Krauter, "Eva in Röm 7."

84. Beyond the thematic, covenantal links to Abraham in this section, there is also a link to Rom 4 via the resurrection. In 4:24–25, Paul states that faith is "in the one who raised the Lord Jesus from the dead" and that Jesus was "raised for our justification."

85. Stuhlmacher, *Romans*, 104.

Thus, a brief summarization is in order. An initial observation is that this section focuses on the Law of Moses, which connects with previous references to the law, particularly in Rom 2, 3, and 5. The primary point is that those who are in Christ, who compose the true people of God, are not marked out by the law, but by union with Christ. Thus, Jewish Christians are not to find their identity in their ethnicity or in possession of the law. This is because one who has died with Christ (Rom 6:8) has died to the law, which thereby breaks the union with Adam. However, just as Christ was raised from the dead, so those who are united to his resurrection now have "the new life of the Spirit" (Rom 7:6). This "new person" belongs to Christ.[86] The marriage metaphor, thus understood, is not nearly as confusing as sometimes assumed. Neither should Rom 7:1–6 be seen as a digression from the main point. Rather, it is integral to the argument of the letter, not least in relation to union with Christ. Just as in Rom 6, the union with Christ language of 7:4 indicates participation in the death of Christ. The last two verses of the section (7:5–6) further contrast the lives of those in Adam and those in Christ, which echoes the point of Rom 6: death and resurrection with Christ leads one to "walk in newness of life" (6:4). Finally, one should not overlook the mention of the Spirit in verse 6. As with previous mentions of the Spirit, such as Rom 2:29, Paul's language here is more proleptic than explanatory and will be revisited in Rom 8. Nevertheless, the wording here most likely evokes new covenant themes from Jer 31 and Ezek 36.[87] The contrast between the "newness of the Spirit" (καινότητι πνεύματος) and the "oldness of the letter" (παλαιότητι γράμματος) makes the allusion to the new covenant all the more feasible.[88]

In chapter 3, I argued that Rom 7:7–12 alluded to both the Adam and Israel stories in order to show that those outside of Christ, Jew and Gentile alike, are all "in Adam." This immediately follows the discussion of Rom 7:1–6, which gives further support for the argument of this book. As seen throughout the epistle, there are multiple connections between union with Christ and the OT narratives of Adam and Israel. Thus, it is unsurprising to find more of the same in Rom 7. What is often missed

---

86. Though he does not focus on union with Christ as such, Röhser, "Paulus Und Die Herrschaft Der Sünde," argues that Paul here pictures believers as not in the "dominion of sin."

87. Dunn, *Romans*, 1:366.

88. Beale, *New Testament Biblical Theology*, 235, links the "newness of the Spirit" (καινότητι πνεύματος) with "new spirit" (πνεῦμα καινὸν) Ezek 36:26.

is the central place given to union with Christ in Paul's argument. Yet, as the above exegesis of Rom 7:4 shows, Paul's point is incomprehensible apart from careful attention given to the concept of union—with Adam and with Christ.

Romans 8

The eighth chapter of Romans is one of the most significant chapters in the Pauline corpus and, perhaps, in the entire NT. It is certainly central to the argument of the epistle as it draws together the numerous themes running through the first seven chapters, including justification, the Spirit, sin, death, and glory. And, at the center of it all: union with Christ. That is, in Rom 8, Paul expounds on the terse statements from earlier in the epistle, as will be shown below. Unsurprisingly, we also find OT themes that have played important roles in Paul's previous arguments. Crucial for our purposes, both the Adam and Israel narratives feature prominent in the chapter as well.[89] Particularly important are the new exodus and new covenant themes and the way in which they relate to union with Christ. As mentioned in chapter 3 above, it is interesting that Paul's use of the Adam narratives in Rom 8 differ from previous uses in that the focus throughout the chapter is on the work of Christ and the Spirit in restoring that which was lost through Adam's sin. Paul also leverages the stories of Israel in order to show the restoration in Christ and the Spirit fulfills God's promises and intentions for his covenant people. The study below will proceed through Rom 8 giving careful attention to the language and themes of union with Christ.

ROMANS 8:1–11

The initial paragraph of the chapter serves the purposes of linking the forthcoming argument to the previous sections as well as setting the stage for the discussion to come. Although the commonly recognized allusions to Adam do not occur until later in the chapter (vv. 19–22; 28–30), the key theological themes found in the opening paragraph indicate that Paul is still building on his argument in 5:12–21.[90] For example, in 5:12–21,

---

89. See chapter 3.
90. Keck, *Romans*, 194, holds that Rom 8:1–30 "is the climax of the discussion begun at 5:12."

Paul shows that sin entered the world through Adam's sin and that death followed from sin (5:12), bringing condemnation to all (5:16). Likewise, in 8:1–11, Paul writes that having the mind set on the (sinful) flesh leads to death (8:6), but there is no condemnation for those in Christ (8:1). While there is a transition into fuller exposition of the work of God in Christ, there are clear connections to the forgoing texts such that chapter 8 must be read as a part of the continuous argument of the epistle, particularly chapters 5–8. Thus, any references to union with Christ in this section (and chapter) must be interpreted in relation to the argument as a whole.

The first two verses of Rom 8 draw attention to union with Christ as both verses contain the most common phrase related to the concept: ἐν Χριστῷ. That the paragraph begins with consecutive references to union with Christ is determinative for the entire chapter. In verse 1, Paul writes, "therefore, there is now no condemnation for those who are in Christ Jesus" (Οὐδὲν ἄρα νῦν κατάκριμα τοῖς ἐν Χριστῷ Ἰησοῦ). It is obvious that the final phrase is significant for the argument of this book, but nearly every word in the sentence serves an important purpose. The ἄρα ("therefore" or "consequently") shows that what follows is intended to continue and build upon what has preceded. While it may be tempting to understand the connection to be merely with the argument of chapter 7, especially with the reference to the law in verse 2, it should be remembered that Rom 8 brings to conclusion the section started in 5:12. In other words, rather than simply building on Rom 7, chapter 8 is yet another step in the longer, complex argument. Nevertheless, the announcement of "no condemnation" following the confession of serving sin in 7:25 is somewhat startling. This is because, in typically Pauline style, a loaded statement is made followed by explanation. As will be immediately clear, in this chapter, Paul moves the discussion forward by focusing on the work of the Spirit in the lives of those who are "in Christ." Yet, this is contingent on the previous argument in which Paul demonstrated all people to be involved in one of two unions: with Adam or with Christ. Most immediately, Paul averred in Rom 7:25 that God has set him, and by implication other believers, free from the body of death "through Jesus the Messiah our Lord" (διὰ Ἰησοῦ Χριστοῦ τοῦ κυρίου ἡμῶν). Being set free from the "body of death" undoubtedly sums up what the Messiah has done for those who are united to him in relation to the condemnation that comes through sin as exacerbated by the law (Rom 5:12; 6:7, 18). Though Paul still struggles with sin (Rom 7:25), as a result of the work of the Messiah, there is no condemnation for him.

Romans 8:1 also features the small, but significant word νῦν. Here, as in Rom 3:21, this term signals not only the place of the present section within the argument ("now" as a turning point in the letter), but functions to place the content of the present argument within the movement of history.[91] This is confirmed in the verses that follow in which Paul will describe the accomplishment of God through the death of Christ. In other words, "now" refers to the present moment in the history of God's people, namely after the death and resurrection of the Messiah. The combination of ἄρα with νῦν connects Rom 8:1 closely to Rom 5:18. Referring to the effects of Adam's sin, Paul writes Ἄρα οὖν ὡς δι' ἑνὸς παραπτώματος εἰς πάντας ἀνθρώπους εἰς κατάκριμα. The verbal parallels between this verse and 8:1 show that the "no condemnation" in Christ is the answer to the condemnation that spread to all people through Adam.

Finally, the main content of verse 1 is no "condemnation for those in Christ Jesus" (κατάκριμα τοῖς ἐν Χριστῷ Ἰησοῦ). Of course, as mentioned already, this is not the first time these concepts ("condemnation" and "in Christ") have appeared in Romans. Significant for the present discussion are the references to condemnation in chapters 2 and 5.[92] In chapter 2, Paul used the verb form of condemn (κατακρίνω) in order to show that all people, Jew and Gentile alike, are bound together in sin (or "in Adam"). To the Jewish interlocutor who would pass judgment on those described in Rom 1:18–32, Paul says that he/they also stand condemned because he/they practice the same things.[93] In Rom 2:25–29, Paul argues that those who obey the law, whether physically circumcised or not, are the true people of God. In verse 27, those who are not physically circumcised, yet obey the law, will condemn (κρίνω) those who are physically circumcised yet do not obey the law. Thus, in Rom 2, condemnation comes to those who fail to keep the law. Similarly, in Rom 5, condemnation (κατάκριμα) comes to those who are bound to Adam (5:16, 18).[94] In both Rom 2 and 5,

---

91. Dunn, *Romans*, 1:415, labels the word "eschatological." So also Jewett, *Romans*, 479.

92. Though see also Rom 3:7, 8, where Paul uses κρίνω and κρίμα respectively. It should be noted that while related, κρίνω and κατακρίνω are not to be equated. While κρίνω can be either positive or negative (judgment for or against), κατακρίνω is negative in that it includes the concept of punishment.

93. See the discussion in chapter 4 above.

94. Lowe, "There Is No Condemnation," 233, notes that the noun is found only in

condemnation is a result of sin. Yet, more fundamental to the argument of Romans is the fact that condemnation comes to those who are united to Adam. This sets up the deep contrast with those who are united to Christ since the verdict of "no condemnation" is restricted to those who are "in Christ." As Keck notes, the genius of this verse is in the combination of participatory and forensic language.[95] Thus, when Paul announces climatically that there is no longer condemnation for those in Christ, it is intended to encourage the Roman believers in their new declared status via union with the Messiah and thereby demonstrate a unity among those for whom condemnation has been removed. Looking back, there is no condemnation because of the justification that comes through the Messiah (5:16) and because believers have died with Christ (6:3). Looking forward, the following verses will tease this out further, highlighting the work of God in Christ and the giving of the Spirit.

The γὰρ in verse 2 signals that what follows further expounds the content of verse 1. Here again, union with Christ proves important for the argument. There are several sticky issues related to the interpretation of Rom 8:2–4. While we must deal with these briefly, the focus will remain on the function of union with Christ in the argument. In verse 2, Paul explains that there is no condemnation because "the law of the Spirit of life in Christ Jesus has set you free from the law of sin and death" (ὁ γὰρ νόμος τοῦ πνεύματος τῆς ζωῆς ἐν Χριστῷ Ἰησοῦ ἠλευθέρωσέν σε ἀπὸ τοῦ νόμου τῆς ἁμαρτίας καὶ τοῦ θανάτου). The main words in this verse hark back to previous arguments, especially with the use of "set free" language. Interestingly, Paul sets up a contrast between two laws: that of the "spirit of life" and that "of sin and death." While the introduction of "law of" into the sentence could cause some confusion, the basic contrast is clear. Sin and death link directly to Rom 5:12–21, where Adam's sin brought death into the world, which spread to all people via their union with him. Those "in Christ" have been set free from sin and death because they died with Christ (Rom 6:3–4). However, Paul here draws in the work of the Spirit, pointing back to Rom 2:29 where the Spirit was mentioned, though in a veiled manner. Those who are "in Christ" are filled with the Spirit. The former union with Adam resulted in being filled with sin leading to death, but now those united with Christ are filled with the Spirit, who gives life.

Rom 5:16, 18, and 8:1 in the entire NT. This obsvervation further supports the close connection between the two chapters.

95. Keck, *Romans*, 195.

The issue of the law in verse 2 must be briefly mentioned. Paul says that those in Christ are set free from the law of sin in death by the law of the Spirit. It should be immediately recognized that the law here is the Mosaic Law rather than some unspecified standard or rule.[96] Indeed, throughout Romans, νόμος has normally referred to the Mosaic Law. Further, this makes much better sense of the passage and fits with the wider context. In short, Paul's argument here is that the law indeed has brought life, but not in the way one might expect. When viewed from the perspective of sinful flesh (in union with Adam), the law could only lead to more sin resulting in condemnation. However, when viewed from the perspective of the Spirit of life (in union with Christ), freedom from sin and death is attained and "the righteousness of the law is fulfilled" (8:4). Thus, the law is not evil in itself, as Paul has emphatically stated in Rom 7. Sinful humanity is simply unable to keep the law, preventing the law from bringing life. Now, for those in Christ, the Spirit gives life. Careful attention to union with Christ clarifies an otherwise difficult text. Dunn rightly conceives the two laws as two perspectives on the Mosaic Law, but views the distinction as being between two epochs: flesh and Spirit.[97] However, given the repetition of "in Christ" and the overall thrust of union language in the broader (Rom 5–8) and nearer (Rom 8) context, the more reasonable association is between the two unions: "in Adam" vs. "in Christ." For humanity in Adam, the law could only lead to sin and death. However, in Christ, the righteousness of the law has been fulfilled by the Spirit of life (Rom 8:4).

Having again set the argument in terms of union (with Adam or Christ), in verses 3–4, Paul extends the discussion to show the reason those in Christ need no longer fear condemnation. God in Christ has done what was impossible for the law to do: deal with the problem of sin. Paul is clear that this is not because the law itself was somehow deficient. Rather, it was "weakened by the flesh" (ἐν ᾧ ἠσθένει διὰ τῆς σαρκός). Indeed, Paul has already said that rather than dealing with sin, the law actually exacerbated the sin problem (Rom 5:20). However, the death of Christ removes this problem in that God condemned sin in his flesh (κατέκρινεν τὴν ἁμαρτίαν ἐν τῇ σαρκί). That is, the sin that infected all humanity, Jew and Gentile alike, in Adam has now been condemned in

---

96. Schreiner, *Romans*, 400. Contra Kruse, *Romans*, 324.
97. Dunn, *Romans*, 1:416–17. See also Dunn, *Theology of Paul*, 645–67.

the Messiah's flesh. Thus, the condemnation that was over the heads of all those in Adam has been removed for those who are "in Christ."

A further point, which could be highly significant for the theology of union with Christ, is also made in verse 3: the sending of the son "in the likeness of sinful flesh" (ἐν ὁμοιώματι σαρκὸς ἁμαρτίας). This statement probably reflects on the incarnation and thus shows that God sent his Son to be united to humanity so that humanity might be united to him.[98] The point is that Jesus took on flesh, perfectly obeyed God, and thus died as a representative for his people. Thus, "what was true of him was true of them."[99] Paul adds that Jesus was sent περὶ ἁμαρτίας, most likely referring to the death of Jesus as a sin offering, particularly in view of the description of Jesus's death in Rom 3:25.[100] Verse 4 then follows with the purpose statement of the sentence: "in order that the righteousness of the law might be fulfilled in us" (ἵνα τὸ δικαίωμα τοῦ νόμου πληρωθῇ ἐν ἡμῖν). Eastman aptly summarizes the point: "Paul unites forensic and participatory themes here in Rom 8:1–4 by stressing the participation of the divine Son in human dereliction and culpability under sin, which in turn opens the way for human participation in the life of the Son."[101] In short, the faithful Messiah's obedience (Rom 5:19) has resulted in justification for those who participate in his death and resurrection.[102] Finally, the "us" is further defined as those "who walk not according to the flesh but according to the Spirit" (τοῖς μὴ κατὰ σάρκα περιπατοῦσιν ἀλλὰ κατὰ πνεῦμα). This is a life dominated by the Spirit rather than (sinful) flesh. By the Spirit, people are incorporated into the story of Jesus, the faithful Son of God.[103]

The above exegesis of Rom 8:2–4 has merely attempted to summarize the meaning and link these verses to Paul's previous argument while emphasizing union with Christ. However, it needs to be pointed out that

---

98. Keck, *Romans*, 198.
99. Wright, "Letter to the Romans," 578.
100. Kruse, *Romans*, 326; Keck, *Romans*, 199.
101. Eastman, "Oneself in Another," 107.
102. The translation and meaning of δικαίωμα is debated, but within the context, it seems most likely to refer to a "righteous declaration" rather than "righteous requirement." That is, Paul's meaning is related more to status than to action. This would fit with the declaration of "no condemnation" in verse 1. However, the declared status does result in action: walking according to the Spirit. Jewett, *Romans*, 485, notes that the only occurrence of the exact wording in the LXX is in Num 31:21, where it refers to a ruling.
103. Campbell, "Story of Jesus," 107.

Adam, Israel, and Union with Christ in Romans 5-8

all of this is highly reliant on the OT. Just as the discussion of freedom from sin in Christ in Rom 6 drew on exodus themes, so here Paul echoes notions of liberty that seem to combine new exodus language with the coming of the Spirit. The Spirit giving life probably evokes Ezek 37:5, the only LXX text that links the Spirit and life "in an eschatological context."[104] In the vision of the dry bones found in Ezek 37, Yahweh promises that he will give his people πνεῦμα ζωῆς. Thus, Paul is arguing that this promise of restoration via the Spirit has been fulfilled in those who are "in Christ." The link to Ezek 37 is confirmed in Rom 8:11, where Paul mentions the resurrection. Perhaps the echo of Ezekiel sheds light on Rom 8:2, for in Ezek 36, Yahweh promised that when he gives his Spirit to his people, they will "follow my statutes (LXX: δικαιώμασίν) and be careful to observe my ordinances" (36:27). Thus, in the new covenant, the Spirit gives life and causes covenant members to live in obedience ("walking according to the Spirit").[105] Stuhlmacher sums up the point well:

> On the basis of Jer 31:31ff. (and Ezek 36:27), this means that, for the sake of the sacrificial death of Jesus, God no longer considers sinners to belong to those who have deviated from the Law (cf. Jer 31:32, 34). Rather, they now participate in the obedience of Christ in the power of the Holy Spirit, who indwells them...In other words, Christ has placed those who belong to him in the reality of the Law of the new covenant.[106]

Again, union with Christ features prominently in the argument and is linked directly to the OT story, here particularly the story of Israel's restoration in the new covenant. Further support for a reference to the new covenant is found in the textual connections between Rom 8:4 and 2:26.[107] In both verses, Paul argues that "the righteous demands/righteousness of the law" (2:26—τὰ δικαιώματα τοῦ νόμου; 8:4—τὸ δικαίωμα τοῦ νόμου) is kept (2:26—φυλάσσῃ) or fulfilled (8:4—πληρωθῇ) in new covenant believers.[108] These new covenant references come in the midst of numerous links to the Adam narrative alluded to earlier in the epistle. The pattern present throughout Romans is observed once more: union

---

104. Beale, *New Testament Biblical Theology*, 253.

105. This also fits with Paul's previous allusions to the new covenant, not least in Rom 2:15, 29. See the discussion in chapter 4.

106. Stuhlmacher, *Romans*, 120.

107. Blackwell, *Christosis*, 123.

108. On Rom 2:25–29, see the argument in chapter 4 above.

with Christ is to be understood against the background of the Adam and Israel narratives.

In verses 5–8, Paul shows the clear distinction between those who are "in Christ" and those who are "in Adam." The descriptor "being according to the flesh" (κατὰ σάρκα ὄντες) is another way of saying "in Adam." In Rom 5, Paul argues that life in Adam leads to death (vv. 12, 14, 17, 21). In 8:6, setting the mind on the flesh leads to death (τὸ γὰρ φρόνημα τῆς σαρκὸς θάνατος).[109] By contrast, setting the mind on the things of the Spirit leads to life and peace (τὸ δὲ φρόνημα τοῦ πνεύματος ζωὴ καὶ εἰρήνη).[110] Again, this wording connects back to Rom 5, where Paul argued that the faithfulness of the Messiah leads to "eternal life" (ζωὴν αἰώνιον) for those who call him Lord. Further, in Rom 5:1, Paul says "we have peace with God through our Lord Jesus Christ" (εἰρήνην ἔχομεν πρὸς τὸν θεὸν διὰ τοῦ κυρίου ἡμῶν Ἰησοῦ Χριστοῦ). Life and peace come through Jesus. The addition of "peace" in both 5:1 and 8:6 carries overtones of the new covenant, the covenant of peace (Isa 54:10), which places union with Christ within the covenantal context as seen already in much of Paul's argument. Understood this way, the contrast between "flesh" and "spirit" in Rom 8 could be described as a contrast between two unions: with Adam (flesh) and with Christ (Spirit). This becomes increasingly clear in the next short paragraph (Rom 8:9–11).

The concept of union, which is implied in Rom 8:5–8, is made explicit in vv. 9–11. Indeed, these three verses are filled with some of the clearest references to union with Christ in the entire epistle. First, Paul asserts that the Roman believers are not "in the flesh since God's Spirit dwells in you" (Ὑμεῖς δὲ οὐκ ἐστὲ ἐν σαρκὶ ἀλλὰ ἐν πνεύματι, εἴπερ πνεῦμα θεοῦ οἰκεῖ ἐν ὑμῖν). Using temple language, Paul marks out those who are "in Christ" as those in whom the Spirit dwells. Temple themes connect the concept of union with Christ directly to the OT story, this time in a clearly eschatological way. The prophetic literature, especially Ezekiel, contains promises of God's return to dwell among his people in a new

---

109. Holland, *Romans*, 259, notes the echo of God's warning to Adam and Eve in the Garden (Gen 2:17) and the choice Moses gave Israel between "life and death" (Deut 30:15, 19). Thielman, "Story of Israel," 182, argues that the contrast between flesh/death and Spirit/life echoes Deut 28, thus showing life in Christ as the eschatological fulfillment of blessings promised in the OT.

110. As Jewett, *Romans*, 486, points out, φρόνημα refers not merely to the things people think about, but to "mind-set" or "basic orientation." Dunn, *Romans*, 1:425–26, argues that the term means "to have a settled way of understanding" or "to maintain an attitude."

temple. Paul sees this fulfilled in the people of God in Christ. That is, the promise that God would dwell among his people in the new temple is fulfilled in that he does indeed dwell *within* his people. In addition, Paul says negatively that "any who do not have the Spirit of Christ are not his" (τις πνεῦμα Χριστοῦ οὐκ ἔχει, οὗτος οὐκ ἔστιν αὐτοῦ). The close correlation between Christ and the Spirit shows that possession of the Spirit is essentially the same thing as union with Christ. To have the Spirit is to be united to Christ. Indeed, as Fee notes, "the presence or absence of the Spirit is the one thing that distinguishes those who are Christ's from those who are not."[111] Thus, the Spirit is the mark of the people of God in Christ, which again ties union with Christ to OT promises (Ezek 36:26).

Second, in verse 10, Paul links together "Christ in you" (Χριστὸς ἐν ὑμῖν) with "spirit is life" (πνεῦμα ζωή) and "righteousness" (δικαιοσύνην). There is much that could be said about this verse, particularly with regard to the syntax, but for our purposes, one primary point needs to be made: union with Christ language is closely related to the major theological themes of the epistle. Clearly "Christ in you" communicates union with Christ.[112] The plural "you" (ὑμῖν), along with echoes of the temple, highlight the corporate nature of the doctrine. Further, the emphasis lies on the fact that Christ is in all equally, Jew and Gentile alike, while also stressing the church's position as his corporate people. The placing of union with Christ language in conjunction with themes such as "life," "spirit," and "righteousness" shows its importance in the argument of the epistle. To comment briefly on the meaning of verse 10, Paul argues that since Christ is in his people (via the Spirit, v. 9), though the body dies as a result of sin (in Adam),[113] life is given through the Spirit on account of righteousness. If Paul is consistent with his use of δικαιοσύνην, then we must see his meaning here the declaration of covenant membership.[114] In other words, because the Roman believers, Jewish and Gentile alike, have been declared to be covenant members, the Messiah dwells within them

---

111. Fee, *God's Empowering Presence*, 553.

112. Ibid., 548–49, argues that "Christ in you" is "simply shorthand for 'the Spirit of Christ in you.'" This is almost certainly correct, but as argued in this section, it also points to union with Christ via the indwelling of the Spirit. This accounts for the use of "Christ in you" as well as "spirit of Christ" in v. 9. Fee draws attention to the connections between Rom 8:10–11 and Rom 6:4–14, but makes no mention of union with Christ.

113. Rom 5:12. Thus, here refers to the sin of Adam. So Barclay, "Under Grace," 66. See the discussion in Dunn, *Romans*, 1:430–31.

114. Wright, *Paul and the Faithfulness of God*, 901.

by the Spirit of God and this results in life. Perhaps it is better to say that the indwelling of the Spirit is the mark of the believers' union with Christ and therefore of new covenant membership, which points back to the circumcision of the heart performed by the Spirit in Rom 2:29.

Third, Rom 8:11, pointing back to Rom 6:4-5, ties the life given in Christ by the Spirit to the resurrection. The Spirit, which has previously been described as the "Spirit of God" and the "Spirit of Christ," is now named "the Spirit of him who raised Jesus from the dead" (τὸ πνεῦμα τοῦ ἐγείραντος τὸν Ἰησοῦν ἐκ νεκρῶν). This life-giving, resurrection Spirit dwells within believers and is the one through whom God "will give life to your mortal bodies" (ζωοποιήσει καὶ τὰ θνητὰ σώματα ὑμῶν). This last phrase almost certainly refers to resurrection, which again is linked to Jesus's resurrection through participation.[115]

The last three verses of Rom 8:1-11 have brought this part of the argument to a climax, placing union with Christ at the center of Paul's meaning. The emphasis on union in these verses confirms the above point, namely that the contrast is between two unions: with Adam and with Christ.[116] Paul's wording in these verses gives further support to this proposal as he describes unbelievers as being "in the flesh" (ἐν σαρκὶ) over against believers being "in the Spirit" (ἐν πνεύματι). These phrases clearly parallel the "in Christ Jesus" (ἐν Χριστῷ Ἰησοῦ) language of Rom 8:1. Each particular union encompasses the entire person. "Being of the flesh" (κατὰ σάρκα ὄντες) leads to "fleshly thinking" (ἧς σαρκὸς φρονοῦσιν), which in turn leads to death. This is a restatement and expansion of what it means to be "in Adam." Conversely, "being of the Spirit" (κατὰ πνεῦμα) leads to "spiritual thinking" (τοῦ πνεύματος), which in turn leads to life. This is a restatement and expansion of what it means to be "in Christ." In addition, the repeated mention of the law throughout the section in combination with temple language serves to draw Israel's story into the picture. Jews, no less than Gentiles, are also in need of the change in union. Further, Paul's use of plural pronouns in verses 9-11 draws attention to his communal focus: the people of God in Christ.[117]

---

115. Schnelle, "Transformation und Partizipation," 70.

116. Dunn, *Romans*, 1:428, describes the change from "in the flesh" to "in the Spirit" as a "change in orientation and motive centers." Though this is certainly included, the more fundamental change is that of union: from "in Adam" to "in Christ." Other changes, such as "motive center" proceed from the change in union.

117. Eastman, "Oneself in Another," 112-13. So also Jewett, *Romans*, 490.

ROMANS 8:12-17

Having affirmed that the Roman believers, Jew and Gentile alike, are free from the threat of condemnation through the work of Christ (Rom 8:3), that their lives therefore are to reflect their "spiritual" being (Rom 8:5-8), and that true life has been attained in Christ (Rom 8:9-11), Paul elaborates on the status of believers in Christ in verses 12-17. At first glance, this passage seems to have few, if any, direct references to union with Christ. Indeed, the primary theological metaphor is adoption. However, if interpreted within the wider context of the chapter, union themes show themselves important, even where not explicitly mentioned. In Rom 8:12-17, union with Christ is seen in sonship language, the presence of the Spirit, and in the prepositional phrase "with Christ." These verses echo OT stories, thereby linking union with Christ yet again to the Adam and Israel narratives.

First, sonship language in this section probably communicates union with Christ, though perhaps in an indirect way. Verse 12 opens this section with the transitional Ἄρα οὖν, thereby connecting the content of verses 12-13 to the previous 11 verses. Thus, Rom 8:12-17 must be interpreted in light of what has preceded. In verses 14-17, Paul emphasizes the status of sonship for believers. However, in Rom 8:3, Paul identifies Jesus as the Son of God, a title which he has already associated with Jesus in 1:4, 1:9, 5:10 and will again associate with Jesus in 8:29, 32. Thus, the most fundamental referent of "son of God" is Jesus.[118] Nevertheless, believers in Jesus are called "sons of God" in this section. Theologically, this is only possible via union with Christ. That is, believers attain the status of "sons of God" only through participation in Christ's sonship.[119]

Second, the concept of sonship in Christ need not rest solely on theological conjecture, for Paul links the status of sonship directly to the presence of the Spirit (8:14). Following closely after Rom 8:5-11, it is clear that being "led by the Spirit of God" (πνεύματι θεοῦ ἄγονται) is essentially the same thing as "being according to the Spirit" (κατὰ πνεῦμα),[120] having "the mindset of the Spirit" (φρόνημα τοῦ πνεύματος),[121] and having "the Spirit of God dwell in you" (οἰκεῖ ἐν ὑμῖν).[122] Further, in verses

---

118. Stuhlmacher, *Romans*, 129.
119. Dunn, *Romans*, 463.
120. Rom 8:5.
121. Rom 8:5-6.
122. Rom 8:9, 11.

9–11, possession of the Spirit was closely related to union with Christ such that Paul can smoothly alternate between the Spirit and Christ as the one "in you."

We can now draw these two exegetical points together (Christ as the Son of God and the Spirit as the mediator of union with Christ). Since Jesus is the Son of God, to call believers in Jesus "sons of God" implies a close relationship between Christ and Christians. Paul fills in the details of this close relationship by claiming that believers are "led by the Spirit." Thus, it is the presence of the Spirit that makes believers sons of God. However, according to Rom 8:1–11, to have the Spirit is to be "in Christ." Therefore, being led by the Spirit = being in Christ = being sons of God.

The nature of sonship in Christ by the Spirit is further expanded in verse 15. Again, the focus is on the Spirit, whose presence both creates and assures the status of sonship. This time, the Spirit is called πνεῦμα υἱοθεσίας, the Spirit of adoption. The metaphor of adoption is intended to communicate the relationship established between God and those who are "in Christ." Connecting with the argument of this book, the idea of adoption communicates the creation of a previously unattained status. That is, an adopted child is taken from outside a family and placed within the family. Likewise, the adopted sons of God in Christ by the Spirit are taken from the family "in Adam" and placed in the family "in Christ." Thus, the Spirit gives believers the ability to call God "Abba, Father" (αββα ὁ πατήρ), mirroring the Father-Son relationship between God and Jesus.[123]

Echoes of the OT in verses 14–15 are essential for understanding Paul's meaning. In verse 14, Paul writes that believers are "led by the Spirit," evoking the memory of the exodus as in Rom 6. After the escape from Egypt, the people of Israel were led through the wilderness by the cloud and the fire (Exod 13:17–22). Instead of being led by a cloud, those in Christ are led by the Spirit dwelling within them.[124] The image of slavery in verse 15 further confirms the echo of the exodus account in verse 14. Paul encourages the believers in Rome by reminding them that the Spirit is not the "spirit of slavery again into fear" (πνεῦμα δουλείας πάλιν εἰς φόβον), but the "spirit of adoption" (πνεῦμα υἱοθεσίας). The contrast

---

123. Jesus prays to ἀββα ὁ πατήρ in Mark 8:36. See Macaskill, "Incarnational Ontology," 97–98, who notes that the sonship of believers is determined by the sonship of Jesus, but cautions against making a one-to-one correspondence since Jesus is *inherently* the Son of God while believers are *adopted* sons of God.

124. Wright, "Letter to the Romans," 593.

between slavery and sonship undoubtedly echoes the exodus account in which the people of Israel were taken out of the slavery and established as the people of God. Indeed, in the exodus story, God referred to Israel as "my son" (Exod 4:23). Of course, the image of slavery points back to Rom 6, where the metaphor featured prominently. Interestingly, in Rom 6, the exodus background was closely related to Paul's understanding of union with Christ. The reader should expect the same here. The implication is that just as the people of Israel were rescued from Egypt and established as God's people, so now via the death and resurrection of the faithful Messiah, those in him are rescued from sin (in Adam) and established as the new covenant people of God. Finally, the term "sons of God" probably evokes the OT stories of Adam and Israel. As noted above, the corporate people of Israel were called the "son of God." Keesmaat detects multiple echoes of Deut 32 in Rom 8:14–17 such that she argues, "In Rom 8 Paul is taking the characteristics of Israel found in Deut 32 (and elsewhere) and applying them to the church, the new community in Christ."[125] In other words, Paul is claiming that those in Christ, Jew and Gentile together, are the people of God. However, it must be remembered that the genealogy of Gen 5 pictures Adam as the son of God. Now those in Christ are the eschatological people of God, bringing the story of sonship, from Adam, through Israel, to its climax.[126]

Third, an additional reference to union with Christ is found in verse 17. In this verse, Paul uses three συν- compounds, two expressing the benefits of being in Christ and one introducing a main topic of the next section. Having affirmed that the Spirit confirms sonship within the hearts of believers (8:16), Paul takes the status to its logical conclusion: sons are heirs. However, since Jesus is the Son of God, believers are only heirs inasmuch as they are in him. Thus, Paul clarifies by saying we are "coheirs with Christ" (συγκληρονόμοι . . . Χριστοῦ). The status of heir, like the status of adopted son, is found only in union with Christ. Further, as coheirs, "we suffer with him in order that we also might be glorified with him" (συμπάσχομεν ἵνα καὶ συνδοξασθῶμεν). Both suffering and glory will be explained further in verses 18–30. The important point here is that suffering and glory are both "with Christ." The idea of participation, here applied to inheritance, was also prominent in Rom 6:1–11, where Paul argued that believers have died, been buried, and will

---

125. Keesmaat, "Exodus and the Intertextual Transformation," 39.
126. Dunn, *Romans*, 1:499–500. As Dunn notes, such claims give rise to the discussion of Rom 9–11.

be raised "with Christ." Thus, Rom 8:12–17, while not containing the key phrase ἐν Χριστῷ, is still best understood as further explanation of union with Christ, focusing primarily on the privileges of that union.[127] Moreover, the subtle references to the story of Christ earlier in the epistle, as well as in chapter 8, provide further subtext for union with Christ, especially with regard to suffering with him. As Douglas Campbell puts it, "Just as Jesus faithfully endured suffering to the point of death and then received a triumphant and glorious resurrection, so too Christians who maintain their loyalty to God and to Christ until the end will receive a resurrection."[128] In short, his story—the story that completes the OT story—is the story of those united to him.

Throughout the epistle, Paul has presented a case for unity in Christ for the sake of mission. In 8:12–17, he brings the argument to a head, boldly announcing that all those in Christ are sons of God, coheirs with Christ, destined to be glorified with him. Sonship in Christ transcends ethnic and social divisions as "it defines the varied groups of believers in Rome as God's family, adopted by him through the Spirit into a position of extraordinary honor."[129] Union with Christ takes central stage as those in Christ are the true people of God, the true family of God, the seed of Abraham,[130] thus bringing the OT stories of Adam and Israel to its climax in the last Adam, Israel's Messiah.

Romans 8:18–30

In the last two sections of Rom 8 (vv. 18–30 and 31–39), Paul teases out some of the implications of union with Christ, particularly focusing on suffering and future hope, followed by joyous celebration. While explicit union with Christ language is slight compared to the first 17 verses of the chapter,[131] two points stand out as important. First, as argued in chapter 3, verses 18–30 contain two allusions to the Adam narratives mixed with

---

127. Byrne, *Romans*, 251, rightly notes that Paul's vision of union with Christ in this passage includes participation in the totality of Christ's work—both sufferings and rewards.

128. Campbell, "Story of Jesus," 122.

129. Jewett, *Romans*, 497.

130. Rom 4:13. See Ridderbos, *Paul*, 203.

131. Since union with Christ is less explicit in the argument of Rom 8:18–30, this discussion in this section will be brief and the overall argument of the paragraph will not be summarized.

allusions to Israel's story. The allusions to Adam in these verses stand somewhat in contrast to previous allusions in that they primarily point forward to renewal rather than focusing on the plight of humanity in Adam. In verses 19–23, Paul reflects on the suffering of believers in relation to the suffering of creation. Creation's suffering is a result of subjection to futility, which is closely related to Adam's sin. Thus, the created world is personified to broaden the ramifications of Adam's sin beyond humanity to all things.[132] I have argued throughout this book that outside of Christ, all people are united to Adam. Paul's picture of creation in Rom 8 shows that the universal problem of sin in Adam dramatically affects the entire created world. Nevertheless, the focus of this section is future hope and, as will be demonstrated below, this hope is for those who are "in Christ." An additional allusion to Adam is found in verse 29 by way of the term εἰκών and possibly through reference to Christ as πρωτότοκος.[133] The allusions in verse 29, like those in verses 19–22, also point to renewal in Christ. This leads to the second point.

Second, the few references within these verses are significant in that there are clear textual links to previous union themes.[134] The most obvious and important of these connecting themes is glory (δόξα). In verse 18, Paul argues that the present suffering of believers cannot compare to "the glory to be revealed in us" (δόξαν ἀποκαλυφθῆναι εἰς ἡμᾶς). In verse 21, the creation is awaiting "the freedom of the glory of the children of God" (τὴν ἐλευθερίαν τῆς δόξης τῶν τέκνων τοῦ θεοῦ). Finally, the list of blessings in Christ in verse 30 ends with "glorified" (ἐδόξασεν). Thus, it is certain that the concept of glory is important in this section of Romans. Indeed, glory is central to Paul's encouragement for believers in the midst of suffering. The point is that though they may suffer in this life, this suffering is with Christ (Rom 8:17) and will give way to glorification in Christ (Rom 8:30).

Glory has been an important theme in Romans and, indeed, in the argument of this book. At several key moments, Paul has linked glory language together with union language, including both the loss of glory in Adam (Rom 1:23; 3:23) and the restoration of glory in Christ (Rom 3:24; 5:2). In other places, glory language was not linked directly to union

---

132. Moo, "Romans 8:19–22," 88, argues, "The story of Adam and the story of Israel, brought to a climax in the story of Christ, is also the story of God's purposes for all creation."

133. See the discussion in chapter 3.

134. Kirk, *Unlocking Romans*, 137.

with Christ, but the true people of God are described as those who attained glory (Rom 2:7, 10) or gave glory to God (Rom 4:20). These previous references to glory have been addressed earlier in this book and we need not repeat the arguments here. Suffice to say that the restoration of lost glory is at least part of Christ's work of redemption.[135] In other words, the glory forfeited by Adam (and thus by those in Adam, Israel included) is restored through the faithfulness of the Messiah (and thus restored in those who are in Christ). Accordingly, references to glory in Rom 8:18–30 must be read within the wider context of glory language in the epistle.

The first mention of glory in this section confirms the point. In Rom 8:18, Paul presents "glory to be revealed in us" as the hope of suffering believers. The previous verse makes clear that this glory is not to be earned or obtained by the believer alone, but with Christ (συνδοξασθῶμεν). As argued above, this means that glory is only received via union with Christ. Therefore, the additional reference to glory in verse 18 must refer to glory in union with Christ as well. Interestingly, in this verse, glory is revealed "in us" (εἰς ἡμᾶς). While Paul has not used the preposition εἰς to refer to the indwelling of Christ or the Spirit in Rom 8, preferring ἐν, the meanings of these prepositions are clearly related, particularly when referencing union with Christ.[136] Thus, glory revealed εἰς ἡμᾶς most likely refers glory restored via union with Christ. If Paul's use of glory in this verse is consistent with his previous uses, then this is the full restoration of the original glory given to humanity at creation but lost in Adam. As Scroggs notes, "Christ is not only the true humanity; he also mediates this true humanity to the believer."[137] Additional references to glory in Rom 8 follow this same pattern: glory is restored in Christ. This restoration should be understood not only in relation to the glory given to humanity at creation, but also to the restoration promised to Israel in the prophetic literature (Isa 35:1–2; Ezek 43:1–5). The hope of Israel in exile was the return of God's glory, a glory that will flood the earth (Isa 6:3).[138] Here again, the stories of Adam and Israel overlap and are brought to

---

135. Fee, *Pauline Christology*, 251.
136. Campbell, *Paul and Union with Christ*, 200–203.
137. Scroggs, *Last Adam*, 102.
138. Jewett, *Romans*, 510–11. Jewett especially notes passages in Isaiah and Ezekiel.

their goals in Christ as those united to him form the true, eschatological people of God.[139]

In addition to the glory theme running through Rom 8, one may also point to the repeated reference to believers as sons/children of God (vv. 19, 21, 23). As argued above, the sonship of believers is an adopted sonship, a status achieved only via union with Christ, the true Son of God (Rom 8:14–17). Indeed, adoption is again referenced in verse 23, this time with a focus on the full adoption that awaits those who are in Christ. The completion of adoption is linked to "the redemption of our bodies" (τὴν ἀπολύτρωσιν τοῦ σώματος ἡμῶν), which is a reference to resurrection. Of course, resurrection is in union with Christ (Rom 6:5) and is effected through the indwelling Spirit (Rom 8:11). "Redemption" was last mentioned in Rom 3:24, where it is explicitly "in Christ" and, as argued in chapter 4 above, evokes memory of the exodus. Thus, in the midst of reflection on the restoration of glory lost in Adam, Paul has again drawn in the story of Israel via exodus allusions coupled with repeated references to the "children of God." Family metaphors emphasize the unity of those in Christ as Jewish and Gentile believers are equally new-exodus children of God and have an equal share in future glory.[140] Further, the mark of the people of God is the possession of the Spirit (8:23–27), whose presence was essentially equated with union with Christ earlier in the chapter (8:9–11) and guarantees full adoption as the "firstfruits" (τὴν ἀπαρχήν).

Finally, in Rom 8:29, Paul describes the restoration in Christ as being "conformed to the image of his Son" (συμμόρφους τῆς εἰκόνος τοῦ υἱοῦ αὐτοῦ). As argued in chapter 3 above, "image" most likely alludes to Adam, who was created in the image of God. The restoration of the image of God in Christ is not a return to the original image that Adam bore. Rather, it is conformity to the image of the Messiah. Significantly, Paul refers to Jesus in this verse as the Son of God, thus tying together the argument of the entire section. That is, conformity to the image of Jesus should not be seen as an additional picture of redemption, but as another angle from which to view the same picture. Therefore, conformity

---

139. A similar concept is found in Col 1:27, where the mystery of the gospel revealed to the Gentiles is "Christ in you, the hope of glory" (ὅ ἐστιν Χριστὸς ἐν ὑμῖν, ἡ ἐλπὶς τῆς δόξης). Here, explicit union with Christ language is used in conjunction with future glory.

140. Dunn, *Romans*, 1:489.

to this image is closely related to adoption in Christ.[141] It is, via union with Christ, to grow into one's status as a new covenant member. In other words, Paul views sanctification as growing to resemble Jesus in union with him by the power of the Spirit.[142] Paul's use of yet another συν- compound further links the discussion to his forgoing argument. The adjective συμμόρφους refers to something being "similar in form" to something else.[143] The true people of God are those "predestined" (προώρισεν) to be like the true Son of God, the true human being, Jesus the Messiah. As such, he is the "firstborn" (πρωτότοκον) in the family and all "brothers" (ἀδελφοῖς) achieve sonship only via union with him.[144] That is, God creates his people in Christ, restoring the glorious image "because in one man, Jesus Christ, that image of God has come to full expression, not for himself alone but as a relationship he can share with others."[145] The conformity of believers to Jesus links back to Rom 8:3 where Paul states that he came "in the likeness of sinful flesh." Thus, as Bonhoeffer famously remarked, Christ "became like human beings, so that we would be like him."[146] In so doing, his shared image creates the new covenant, communal identity in Christ.[147]

Romans 8:31-39

Paul's majestic conclusion to Rom 8 includes few direct references to union with Christ, but the concept flavors the entire paragraph. Throughout this book, I have sought to demonstrate the importance of union with Christ in the argument of Romans. While Romans may not be a "treatise on theosis," union with Christ has played a key role in the argument, even

---

141. There is a link between sonship and image in Gen 5:1–3. See Sailhamer, *Pentateuch as Narrative*, 117; Hamilton, *Genesis*, 255.

142. Paul makes similar claims in 1 Cor 15:49, which also links the restoration of the image of God to glory. Jesus is called the image of God in 2 Cor 4:4 and Col 1:15. Both of these verses have union with Christ language in the near context. In addition, 2 Cor 3:18 connects "image" and "glory" in the context of the new covenant.

143. BDAG, 958.

144. Kirk, *Unlocking Romans*, 141, labels this "derived" glory. See also Fitzmyer, *Romans*, 525. As argued in chapter 3 above, "firstborn" is a title given to Israel (Exod 4:22) and to the Davidic king (Ps 89:27) in the OT.

145. Dunn, *Romans*, 1:495. See also Ridderbos, *Paul*, 77.

146. Bonhoeffer, *Discipleship*, 285.

147. Adams, "Paul's Story," 39.

when it is not explicitly mentioned.[148] It is unsurprising that the concept would pervade this last paragraph of the central chapter of the epistle. In what follows, we will only briefly examine the ways in which union with Christ features both explicitly and implicitly through these verses.

The rhetorical question in verse 31 sets up the exposition to follow of God's love for the Roman church. Paul begins his encouragement with a reminder that God is "for us" (ὑπὲρ ἡμῶν). If this is the case, then no enemy is to be feared since none can stand against God (Rom 16:20). In the context, God is "for us" because "we" are his children in Christ, thus picturing God's fatherly love and protection. Paul uses the same phrase (ὑπὲρ ἡμῶν) in Rom 5:8 in describing Christ's death "for us," which demonstrates God's love.[149] The one true God is for "us"—Jews and Gentiles together in Christ—as one family.[150] The familial tone is confirmed in verse 32, where Paul argues that God will "freely give us all things with him" (σὺν αὐτῷ τὰ πάντα ἡμῖν χαρίσεται). Paul's reasoning is that since God gave his own Son, which was of inestimable value, he will surely give believers much more. The "all things" refers back to the inheritance believers receive as "co-heirs with Christ" (Rom 8:17). Jewett argues that the phrase τὰ πάντα connotes the universe, meaning that those "in Christ" will inherit the "entire creation."[151] Jewett is correct in identifying creation as the primary referent, but he denies that Paul also has salvation in mind. However, in context, "all things" most likely includes the blessings of salvation, most notably, glorification (Rom 8:17, 18, 30).[152] As argued above, glorification is a reference to union with Christ, in which Paul is arguing that those "in Christ" are the true people of God, the seed of Abraham, who inherit the blessings promised to the forefather. Paul's use of σύν in verse 32 confirms the point, as this preposition has been key throughout the chapter, especially as related to union with Christ.

Verses 33–34 deepen the argument as Paul's readers are described as "God's elect" (ἐκλεκτῶν θεοῦ) whose condemnation is removed by the death and resurrection of the Messiah. Paul's rhetorical question concerning condemnation (τίς ὁ κατακρινῶν;) serves to link this stage of the argument back to Rom 8:1, where Paul boldly proclaimed that there is

---

148. See Gorman, "Romans."
149. Jewett, *Romans*, 536.
150. Dunn, *Romans*, 1:500.
151. Jewett, *Romans*, 538. So also Dunn, *Romans*, 1:502.
152. Schreiner, *Romans*, 461.

"no condemnation for those in Christ" (Οὐδὲν ἄρα νῦν κατάκριμα τοῖς ἐν Χριστῷ Ἰησοῦ). The repeated mention of Christ's death and resurrection with reference to condemnation support the understanding that Paul is here still thinking in terms of union with Christ. His point is clear: those in Christ need not fear condemnation because they are the elect of God. Thus, in the celebration of God's love, Paul subtly redefines the people of God as those who are "in Christ."

Many commentators recognize an allusion to Isa 50:8 (LXX) in Rom 8:33–34.[153] A detailed exegesis of the OT text in comparison with Romans is unnecessary at this point. However, there are two important observations to be mentioned. First, the Isaiah text concerns the vindication of Yahweh's servant. The context is the third "servant song" and announces that though the servant will suffer, he will be vindicated and "not be put to shame" (Isa 50:7). Second, Paul applies the prophecy to the church. The application of the servant's vindication to the church deepens the theological understanding of union with Christ such that what is true of the servant, is also true of those who are "in Christ." Jesus's resurrection is his vindication (Rom 1:3–4), but the vindication of believers comes via identification with Jesus in his death and resurrection (Rom 6:1–11).[154] Indeed, the death and resurrection of Christ is clearly the grounds for "no condemnation" (Rom 8:1, 32). Thus, the vindication of the servant (Jesus) is also vindication for his people as they participate in his story.

Finally, verses 35–39 paint a beautiful picture of the inseparable bond between the Messiah and those who are in him.[155] Paul argues that no created thing "will be able to separate us from the love of God that is in Christ Jesus our Lord" (δυνήσεται ἡμᾶς χωρίσαι ἀπὸ τῆς ἀγάπης τοῦ θεοῦ τῆς ἐν Χριστῷ Ἰησοῦ τῷ κυρίῳ ἡμῶν). Two prepositions in these verses draw attention to union with Christ. First, in verse 37, Paul argues that none stand against the true people of God because "we completely prevail *through* the one who loves us" (ὑπερνικῶμεν διὰ τοῦ ἀγαπήσαντος ἡμᾶς). Paul has used prepositional phrases with διά several times in Romans to communicate union with Christ, particularly in Rom 5:1–11, where the

---

153. Dunn, *Romans*, 1:503; Byrne, *Romans*, 276; Jewett, *Romans*, 541; Wright, "Letter to the Romans," 610. For a chart showing the verbal connections between the two texts, see Beale, *New Testament Biblical Theology*, 501.

154. Beale, *New Testament Biblical Theology*, 502.

155. On Paul's quotation of Ps 44:23 (LXX 43:23), see Hays, *Echoes*, 57–63, who argues that Paul reads the Psalm as a prophecy of the suffering of God's eschatological people.

work of God in Christ was also the key theme. Here again, believers are victorious, not on their own, but through Jesus. Again, the language connects back to the opening verses of Rom 8, where Paul argued that God had accomplished all that the flesh-weakened law could not in condemning sin through the death of the Messiah. Thus, none can condemn. Second, the chapter ends with an additional prepositional phrase: in Christ Jesus our Lord (ἐν Χριστῷ Ἰησοῦ τῷ κυρίῳ ἡμῶν). Thus, the argument of the whole chapter has come full circle. Paul began with "in Christ" and ends with "in Christ." God's love cannot be separated from his people because it cannot be separated from his Son. And, his Son cannot be separated from those who are in him, Jew and Gentile alike.

CONCLUSION

This book has argued that an important aspect of Paul's argument is the close connection between the OT Adam and Israel stories and union with Christ. In Rom 5–8, Paul has shown that there exists a new people of God: those who are "in Christ." These chapters overflow with union language ("in Christ"; "with Christ") and with allusions to the OT stories. The above argument shows that these two facets of Paul's discussion are intimately related such that the stories of Adam and Israel form the OT background of union with Christ. These chapters have clearly put forward an argument for the redefinition of the people of God in the Messiah. Therefore, Paul is calling the believers in Rome to find their identity as the people of God in the Messiah over against social or ethnic identities. Those who are "in Christ" are the true seed of Abraham, the children of God. For Paul, true identity is found in union with Christ.

6

Union with Christ in Romans 9–16

INTRODUCTION

THE TWO PREVIOUS CHAPTERS form the "meat" of the argument presented in this book. Though our study of Rom 1–8 has argued for a consistent use of the Adam and Israel narratives in relation to union with Christ, it remains to be seen whether this pattern holds true for the rest of the epistle. In chapters 2–3, the discussion was limited Rom 1–8 (with the exception of Rom 16:18–20) because these chapters contain all of the commonly recognized allusions to Adam. However, it cannot be said that Paul's references to union with Christ are limited to Rom 1–8. Indeed, if union with Christ is as important as I have argued, then one would expect the concept to be present, if not prominent, in the second half of the letter. Within the constraints of this chapter, detailed exegesis of Rom 9–16 will not be possible. Instead, the task here is to explicate the role of union with Christ in the argument of Rom 9–16 and to show the references to union with Christ in these chapters to be in continuity with Paul's earlier union with Christ language.[1]

---

1. Though there are many connections between Rom 9–11 and the rest of the epistle, the following discussion will be limited to those links related to union with Christ. See Stenschke, "Römer 9–11."

UNION WITH CHRIST IN ROMANS 9-11

Before examining the role of union with Christ within Rom 9-11, it will be helpful to summarize the broad argument of these chapters. In this way, we can adequately ascertain the function of union with Christ within Paul's discussion. Much recent scholarship argues that Rom 9-11 stands as something of a theological climax within the letter.[2] Assuming this is at least broadly true, it will be apparent that these three chapters are in continuity with the argument of Rom 1-8.[3] Of course, Paul's meaning is widely debated and I cannot attempt a full exegetical examination here. I will summarize the broad strokes with references to the relevant literature.

The celebration of Rom 8:31-39 gives rise to the question "what of Israel?" or, perhaps, "what of God's promises to Israel?" since Paul has just proclaimed that those who are "in Christ" are the ones to inherit the promises to the patriarchs. Through the first eight chapters, Paul has presented a powerful argument that the true people of God are those who are "in Christ," Jew and Gentile alike. Conversely, all other people are "in Adam," Jew and Gentile alike. The problem is that most Jews, the physical descendants of Abraham, rejected Jesus as the Messiah, giving the appearance (at least to some observers) that God had cast aside the Jewish people and therefore left former promises unfulfilled. As Keck remarks, some may suppose that "the Jews' No to the gospel is God's No to the Jews as his people."[4] It is this misunderstanding Paul addresses.

Paul's argument draws heavily on the OT, thus showing God's work in Christ to be consistent with his work throughout Jewish history. However, as Kruse points out, Paul's argument is primarily addressed to Gentile believers, which suggests that Paul may have perceived the potential for division within the church if Gentile Christians "looked down on Jews and Jewish believers."[5] This can be seen clearly in Rom 11:13, where Paul states directly that he is speaking to Gentiles. Thus understood, the

---

2. See, among others, Dunn, *Romans*, 2:518-21; Hays, *Echoes*, 63-83; Fitzmyer, *Romans*, 539-43; Wright, "Letter to the Romans," 620-26; Keck, *Romans*, 223-26.

3. Even when not viewing Rom 9-11 as central or climactic, most scholars see these chapters as integral to the message of the epistle. See Longenecker, *Introducing Romans*, 409-21.

4. Keck, *Romans*, 224.

5. Kruse, *Romans*, 367.

argument of these chapters fits within the overall purpose of the letter: to encourage the unity of the church for the purpose of mission.

Briefly stated, the primary purpose of Rom 9–11 is to demonstrate the faithfulness of God to his covenant promises despite the widespread unbelief of Jews. Therefore, "God's dealing with Israel and the nations in the present age is fully consistent with God's modus operandi in the past and with his declared purposes."[6] The first five verses of the section serve as an introduction in which Paul states the problem: his kinsmen have rejected Christ despite being the ones to whom the ancient promises and blessings were given and despite the fact that the Messiah, God himself, came from them. In Rom 9:6–29, Paul draws on and redefines the story of Israel, highlighting the consistency of God's sovereign choices. In 9:30—10:21, Paul shows that bringing the Gentiles into the people of God was always a part of God's purposes and now serves to make the Jews jealous so that they may indeed believe. In 11:1–32, Paul argues that while many Gentiles believe the gospel and most Jews reject the gospel, this does not mean that God has rejected his people. Instead, God is still at work to bring the Jews to himself as attested to by the existence of a remnant of believing Jews. Finally, the section ends in praise of God's glory in 11:33-36.[7]

Romans 9:1–5

Having sketched the main argument of Rom 9–11, we can examine the references to union with Christ and their function within the discussion. Interestingly, though union with Christ may not play the central role in chapters 9–11 as in previous chapters, there is a reference to the concept in the first verse of chapter 9. Romans 9:1, while seemingly minor in regard to the argument of this book, serves as a clear example of the importance of union with Christ for Paul. In what may appear superfluous, Paul claims the truthfulness of his words by describing himself as "speaking the truth in Christ" (Ἀλήθειαν λέγω ἐν Χριστῷ). While this statement makes no great theological contribution to the argument of the letter, it demonstrates the all-encompassing nature of union with Christ. That is, Paul wants to communicate that he speaks as one "in Christ" just as the

---

6. Hays, *Echoes*, 64.

7. The basic structure outlined here is similar to that of Hays, *Echoes*, 64, and Longenecker, *Introducing*, 412–13.

Roman believers are "in Christ."[8] In addition, the use of "in Christ" links chapter 9 to the preceding argument as the last words of Rom 8 were "in Christ Jesus our Lord" (ἐν Χριστῷ Ἰησοῦ τῷ κυρίῳ ἡμῶν). Further, Paul echoes the close link between Christ and the Spirit in Rom 8:9–11 when he writes that his "conscience bears witness together with me in the Holy Spirit" (συμμαρτυρούσης μοι τῆς συνειδήσεώς μου ἐν πνεύματι ἁγίῳ). The use of the συν- compound along with "in the Holy Spirit" most likely evokes notions of union with Christ. Thus, Paul sets his forthcoming argument in the context of the unity of believers (Paul himself included) in Christ.

In the remaining verses of the introductory section (9:1–5), Paul makes several more references to union with Christ, connecting chapters 9–11 to the preceding argument. In expressing his desire for the Jews to believe the gospel, Paul says that he would be willing to be "apart from Christ" (ἀπὸ τοῦ Χριστοῦ) if that would result in their salvation.[9] This language seems to stand in contrast to being "in Christ." In other words, the implication is that Paul is presently "in Christ" but would be "apart from Christ" if it was possible in order for his kinsmen to be "in Christ." Of course, this is not possible since Paul has already proclaimed that "nothing can separate us from the love of God in Christ Jesus our Lord" (Rom 8:39).[10]

Via key terms and themes, verses 4–5 then connect to previous sections, most notably chapter 8. In verse 4, Paul notes that the Jews are God's chosen people, given "the adoption, the glory, the covenants, the giving of the law, the worship, and the promises" (ἡ υἱοθεσία καὶ ἡ δόξα καὶ αἱ διαθῆκαι καὶ ἡ νομοθεσία καὶ ἡ λατρεία καὶ αἱ ἐπαγγελίαι). The clear connections to Rom 1–8 in these verses anticipate the full argument of chapters 9–11. The possession of these blessings means that God has not forgotten the Jews, but the fact each has been attributed to the people of God in Christ previews the forthcoming argument: God is faithful to his promises in the gospel. That is, Paul has already claimed that those "in Christ" are adopted children of God (Rom 8:14–17); will be glorified

---

8. Moo, *Romans*, 556; Kruse, *Romans*, 367. Contra Dunn, *Romans*, 523, who denies a reference to union with Christ, instead insisting that Paul is "speaking primarily in terms of religious experience."

9. That he is speaking of Jews is clear from the phrase "kinsmen according to the flesh" (τῶν συγγενῶν μου κατὰ σάρκα), which stands in distinction from his brothers and sisters in Christ.

10. Johnson, "Romans 9–11," 223.

with Christ (Rom 8:17–18); are new covenant members (Rom 2:15, 25–29); have the law fulfilled in them (Rom 8:4); and are the ones in whom God is keeping his promise to give Abraham a worldwide family (Rom 4). While the term "worship" (ἡ λατρεία) has not been used, it is clear in Paul's celebratory sections (Rom 7:25; 8:31–39) as well as in his use of temple language to describe the presence of the Spirit in believers (Rom 8:9–11) that those in Christ are true worshippers.[11] Thus, that the blessings were given to Israel affirms their special status, but the links with Rom 1–8 show that Paul is also affirming the status of those "in Christ" as the true people of God.

Finally, in Rom 9:5, Paul brings the attention back to the Messiah, who is the central focus of the entire letter since it is through him that God displays his righteousness. This verse continues to annunciate the blessings of Israel, including the patriarchs. Central to these blessings is that "from them, according to the flesh, came the Messiah, who is God over all, blessed forever, amen" (ἐξ ὧν ὁ Χριστὸς τὸ κατὰ σάρκα, ὁ ὢν ἐπὶ πάντων θεὸς εὐλογητὸς εἰς τοὺς αἰῶνας, ἀμήν). While controversial, there are a couple of significant points for our purposes. First, Paul's language connects to earlier parts of the letter. That the Messiah came from Israel "according to the flesh" echoes Rom 1:3–4. In Rom 1:3, Jesus the Messiah is identified as "of the seed of David according to the flesh" (ἐκ σπέρματος Δαυὶδ κατὰ σάρκα), which affirms Jesus as Israel's Messiah.[12] Thus, the use of κατὰ σάρκα in Rom 9:5 serves to set the stage for the discussion to follow by showing Jesus as ethnically Jewish, but the Messiah for all who are united to him. In addition, the coming of the Messiah points back to Rom 8:3, where Paul wrote that Jesus was "sent in the likeness of sinful flesh" (ἐν ὁμοιώματι σαρκὸς ἁμαρτίας). The net result is theologically significant, particularly related to the argument of this book: Jesus is Israel's Messiah who comes for all people, regardless of ethnicity.

Second, scholars debate the grammar of Rom 9:5, especially related to the phrase "God over all" (ἐπὶ πάντων θεός). Taken at face value, it seems most likely that Paul is identifying the Messiah as God.[13] This is

---

11. Perhaps this worship stands in contrast to those Paul denounced in Rom 1:25 who "worship and serve the created things rather than the Creator" (ἐλάτρευσαν τῇ κτίσει παρὰ τὸν κτίσαντα).

12. Kruse, *Romans*, 372.

13. So Jewett, *Romans*, 567–69; Holland, *Romans*, 304–5; Fitzmyer, *Romans*, 548–49; Schreiner, *Romans*, 486–89; Moo, *Romans*, 565–68. Contra Byrne, *Romans*, 288; Hultgren, *Romans*, 353–55; Dunn, *Romans*, 2:528–29.

the most obvious meaning of the syntax and fits with the Christology of the letter as a whole. However, just as significant for the argument of this book is that the Messiah is not just identified as "God" but "God over all." This identification serves the larger purposes because as "God over all," he is equally God over the Jews and the Gentiles who are "in Christ." Paul argued for the universal reign of God in Rom 3:29–30 on the basis of the oneness of God. Here, the one Messiah, though coming from the Jews, is "God over all." Thus, while not explicitly mentioning union with Christ, Paul's meaning is best understood with the concept in mind.

Romans 9:6–29

Following the introductory verses, which have alluded to union with Christ, Paul begins to address the problem he raised by immediately defending the faithfulness of God. According to Paul, despite the unbelief of many Jews, "it is not as if the word of God has failed" (Οὐχ οἷον δὲ ὅτι ἐκπέπτωκεν ὁ λόγος τοῦ θεοῦ). This is because God has engaged in "a process of selectivity that constituted Israel's identity from the very beginning."[14] Namely, "not all from Israel are Israel" (οὐ γὰρ πάντες οἱ ἐξ Ἰσραὴλ οὗτοι Ἰσραήλ). That is, it has never been the case that all ethnic Jews were a part of the true people of God—those who are faithful to God. The two categories of "Israel" echoes the dual notion of "Jew" in Rom 2:28–29, a passage I argued is foundational for Paul's understanding of union with Christ.[15]

The discussion of election in this section of Romans makes clear that God's choice of a people was never based upon ethnicity alone, for not all of Abraham's children were in the chosen line (9:7–9). Biology is secondary to the promises of God, for only "the children of the promise are considered the seed" (τὰ τέκνα τῆς ἐπαγγελίας λογίζεται εἰς σπέρμα).[16] These "children of the promise" are also "the children of God" (τέκνα τοῦ θεοῦ), terminology which points back to Rom 8:21. Paul's discussion in Rom 8 centered on the true people of God as those who are "in Christ."[17] This conceptual background brings union with Christ into the discussion in Rom 9, where Paul is defending the faithfulness of God. Thus,

14. Barclay, "I Will Have Mercy," 98.
15. See chapter 4 above.
16. Jewett, *Romans*, 575.
17. Fitzmyer, *Romans*, 561.

the Jews' collective rejection of the gospel (and the entry of the Gentiles into the people of God) does not demonstrate God's unfaithfulness; it is consistent with his work throughout the history of Israel.

As Barclay has shown, the quotation of Exod 33:19 in Rom 9:15 is central to Paul's argument.[18] This quotation places God's mercy as the creative power behind election. That is, it is via mercy that God calls his people into existence. The Exodus quotation, of course, is taken from within the golden calf narrative, which we have already argued was important to Paul throughout Romans.[19] In particular, Paul alludes to the golden calf incident in order to show that Jews, no less than Gentiles, are "in Adam" as references to the story from Exod 32–34 are placed alongside allusions to Adam's sin. Accordingly, the quotation signals a connection with previous allusions to the story, but this time Paul references God's act of mercy-giving, which (re)creates his people. In 9:16, Paul makes it clear that the creation of the people of God is not a result of human activity, but the mercy of God alone. Rhetorically, this serves as a reminder one is a member of the new people of God in Christ solely on the basis of God's mercy, thus encouraging unity while at the same time spurring the Roman believers to participate in God's mercy-giving mission.

The remainder of the section teases out the implications of God's sovereign mercy, especially as it relates to the inclusion of the Gentiles within the people of God. Significant for the argument of this book are verses 23–24. Having affirmed that God has the authority to create people for his purposes (9:19–22), Paul argues that creating "vessels of wrath" is "in order to make known the riches of his glory upon vessels of mercy, which he prepared beforehand for glory" (ἵνα γνωρίσῃ τὸν πλοῦτον τῆς δόξης αὐτοῦ ἐπὶ σκεύη ἐλέους ἃ προητοίμασεν εἰς δόξαν). The destruction of the vessels of wrath is reminiscent of the death that results from being "in Adam" (Rom 5:12). However, the point here is that the wrath displayed highlights the mercy of God. Further, Paul makes clear that the "vessels of mercy" include Jews and Gentiles alike (Rom 9:24) and that this was always a part of God's purposes for Israel.[20]

These vessels of mercy are the ones whom God has "called" (ἐκάλεσεν), which links back to Rom 1:6, where Paul described the church

18. Barclay, "I Will Have Mercy," 98–106.

19. For example, in chapter 2 I argued that Paul alluded to the story in Rom 1:23, and in chapter 3 I argued that he again alluded to it in Rom 7:7–13.

20. Dunn, *Romans*, 2:569.

in Rome as the "called of Jesus Christ" (κλητοὶ Ἰησοῦ Χριστοῦ). In addition, in Rom 4:17, Paul presented the God in whom Abraham believed as the one who "calls into being things that are not" (καλοῦντος τὰ μὴ ὄντα ὡς ὄντα), clearly linking calling and promise. Now, in Rom 9:24, Jews and Gentiles in Christ are those "whom he has called." In other words, those who are "in Christ" are the promised seed, which was a primary point in Rom 4. This is the activity of God alone, who calls his people into existence.[21] In the verses that follow, Paul quotes from Hosea and Isaiah in order to show that the inclusion of the Gentiles and the salvation of the remnant of Israel were both significant parts of God's plan all along.

One additional element of verses 23–24 deserves attention: glory. As noted throughout this book, the concept of glory is closely related to union with Christ as the original glory given to Adam, but lost in sin, is being restored in Christ. Thus, while union with Christ language is not specifically mentioned in these verses, the insertion of the key term "glory" most likely points back to earlier uses of the term. Here, Paul focuses on the mercy of God as the means through which people are set apart for glory—the glory lost in Adam, but restored in Christ. This is the same glory that is redeemed by the blood of Christ (Rom 3:24), hoped for (Rom 5:2), and is to be revealed in those in Christ (Rom 8:18). In 9:23, God's glory is shared with those in Christ. Far from being earned or deserved, this restoration of glory comes only by the mercy of God.

Thus, in this first main section of Rom 9–11, Paul focuses on God's mercy and sovereign choice of his people. This is order to show that the current status of ethnic Jews vis-à-vis the church is entirely consistent with God's work throughout history. Barclay aptly sums up:

> [I]t is simply an application of the same merciful creation that calls others also (the nations) into salvific existence. In other words, non-Jews are not "bolted on" to Israel by some fresh divine decision, or by some "extension" of the terms of the original covenant promise, but are called into being as the "people of God" by the very same means by which Israel herself was created and has been perpetually recreated. Because Paul understands "mercy" in Israel's history to go "all the way down," the inclusion of non-Jews is entirely consistent with God's creative purposes from the beginning of Israel's history, right through to the present day.[22]

21. Barclay, "I Will Have Mercy," 99.
22. Ibid., 102.

Yet, it is important to note that Paul's continuous use of Israel's story, including the redefinition of "Israel," shows that as the Gentiles are "in the Messiah," they are entering Israel's story.[23] Paul is arguing that Israel's story, which is also the story of the world since they are the ones through whom God would bless the world, reaches its climax in Jesus and the true seed of Abraham in him. This idea, founded upon the concept of union with Christ, is central for the unity of the church as it combats any feeling of superiority among Jewish or Gentile believers.

Romans 9:30—10:21

Having defended the righteousness of God in Rom 9:6-29, Paul turns again to the plight of the Jewish people, focusing on their unbelief. In Rom 9:30—10:4, Paul insists that the problem lies in the fact that the Jewish people as a whole have not sought righteousness by faith. Instead, they zealously sought a righteousness of their own via the law. In contrast, the Gentiles have attained righteousness, which they were not actively seeking, by faith (Rom 9:30). In Rom 10:5-21, faith remains important: true righteousness is "of faith" (ἐκ πίστεως—10:6); to be saved, one must "believe in your heart" (πιστεύσῃς ἐν τῇ καρδίᾳ σου—10:9); those who believe are "not put to shame" (οὐ καταισχυνθήσεται—10:11); "faith" (ἡ πίστις) is the call of the gospel (10:14-17). Like the previous section, Rom 9:30—10:21 contains no direct reference to union with Christ, but it is again in the conceptual background. The fundamental way in which union with Christ can be seen in the background is via the emphasis on faith.

The importance of faith in Romans is clear from the first chapter as Paul identifies the goal of his apostleship as "the obedience of faith" (ὑπακοὴν πίστεως) among the Gentiles (1:5) and in that the first OT quotation explicitly mentions faith (1:17, quoting Hab 2:4). A thorough examination of faith in the epistle is beyond the bounds of the present discussion. However, important for our purposes is the fact that in Rom 1-8, faith is closely linked to union with Christ. While all references to faith could be understood as participatory in nature, Rom 3:21-26 serves as a clear example of the close connection between faith and union.[24] As

---

23. Wright, *Paul and the Faithfulness of God*, 1186-87.

24. On faith as participatory in nature, see Hay, "Paul's Understanding of Faith." Campbell, "Faith and Participation."

argued in chapter 4 above, faith in these verses refers first to the faithfulness of Jesus and secondarily to human faith as participation in his faithfulness. Paul moves from the faithfulness of Jesus (πίστεως Ἰησοῦ Χριστοῦ) to the faith of believers (πάντας τοὺς πιστεύοντας) in verse 22. The faithfulness of Jesus the Messiah restores the glory lost in Adam (Rom 3:23–24). Finally, Paul writes that "the one who is of the faith of Jesus" (ἐκ πίστεως Ἰησοῦ) is justified (Rom 3:26). The close connection between the faith of Jesus and that of believers is best expressed as union with Christ: believers" faith is participation in the faithfulness of Jesus.

Interestingly, faith-language is largely absent from Rom 5–8. This should not be interpreted to mean that Paul has no interest in faith in these chapters, but rather that the discussion of faith in Rom 3–4 is foundational for the participatory nature of salvation expounded in Rom 5–8. Indeed, Rom 5:1 opens the section with a reaffirmation of justification of faith/faithfulness (Δικαιωθέντες οὖν ἐκ πίστεως), which is a key concept upon which the three chapters are built.[25] Further, I argued in chapter 4 that the discussion of Rom 5:12–21 is an unpacking of the dense argument of Rom 3:21–26, particularly as it relates to the faithfulness of Jesus in contrast to the failure of Adam. Additionally, Rom 5:12–21 is foundational for Rom 6–8, which indicates that "baptism into Christ" includes participation in his faithfulness. Indeed, the call of Rom 6:12–23 and 8:1–11 is to live faithfully in union with Christ. Thus, when Paul again picks up the theme of faith in Rom 9, the discussion (1) echoes discussions of faith from Rom 1, 3, and 4 and (2) builds on the concept of union with Christ, which was prominent in Rom 5–8.

Returning to Rom 9:30—10:21, Paul's emphasis on faith must be understood within the wider context of the epistle. As such, faith in this section is by nature participatory, despite the lack of explicit union with Christ language. Though phrases such as "in Christ" are absent in these verses, there are a number of clues pointing to the concept of union with Christ. First, there is a close relationship between righteousness (δικαιοσύνη) and faith (πίστις). In Rom 9:30–32, Paul argues that the Jews were unable to "reach the law" (εἰς νόμον οὐκ ἔφθασεν) because they did not pursue it by faith. It should be pointed out that Paul is not saying here that the law is deficient, but that the Jews' pursuit of righteousness via the law was deficient due to their lack of faith. In contrast, Gentiles have attained righteousness—covenant membership—by faith, even

---

25. See the discussion on Rom 5:1 in chapter 5 above.

though they were not seeking it.²⁶ A similar link between righteousness and faith is found in Rom 10:6, where Paul personifies "the righteousness of faith" (ἡ . . . ἐκ πίστεως δικαιοσύνη).²⁷ Thus, righteousness and faith go hand-in-hand.

That righteousness and faith are closely related is not a new concept at this point in the epistle. As mentioned above, faith and righteousness are wed very early, namely Rom 1:17. The righteousness of God is revealed ἐκ πίστεως εἰς πίστιν. I have already drawn attention to Rom 3:21–26, but it bears repeating here that the righteousness of God is revealed "through the faithfulness of Jesus Christ to all who believe" (διὰ πίστεως Ἰησοῦ Χριστοῦ εἰς πάντας τοὺς πιστεύοντας). Again, the righteousness of God is closely tied to faith—that of Jesus and, by extension via participation, of believers. The rest of the paragraph makes clear that one is justified (δικαιόω) through faith in the faithful Messiah. At the heart of this argument is 3:24, in which Paul argues that restoration is by "the redemption that is in Christ Jesus" (διὰ τῆς ἀπολυτρώσεως τῆς ἐν Χριστῷ Ἰησοῦ), explicitly linking righteousness, faith, and union with Christ. Beyond Rom 3, there are obvious connections between righteousness and faith in Rom 4. As stated above, faith-language gives way to an emphasis on participation in Christ in Rom 5–8, but the relationship between faith and union remains central to Paul's understanding of both concepts. That is, participation in Christ is participation in his faithfulness by faith.

The intimate relationship between faith and righteousness in Rom 1–8 helps to explain Paul's insistence on this relationship in Rom 9–10, especially when one realizes that union with Christ is the glue holding them together. Righteousness (new covenant membership) is only attained "in Christ." That Paul is thinking in terms of new covenant membership is clear from the repeated use of righteousness language along with the quotations from Deut 30 in Rom 10:6–8.²⁸ Thus, Gentiles have attained the status of covenant member via faith—participatory faith in Christ. Further, according to Rom 10:3, faith as the true mark of new covenant membership for Jews and Gentiles alike, displays the "righteousness of God" (δικαιοσύνη τοῦ θεοῦ). God's faithfulness to his purposes and promises in Christ is the object of Jewish ignorance. As a result,

---

26. Though differing on the meaning of "righteousness," Moo, *Romans*, 619, argues that Paul's central meaning here is that the Gentiles are "being included in God's true spiritual people" on the basis of faith.

27. This verse will be treated below.

28. See the discussion below.

they failed to attain the righteousness of God (τὴν τοῦ θεοῦ δικαιοσύνην), preferring instead a righteousness through the law that would be theirs alone. Israel has in effect made "righteousness a function of Jewish identity rather than of God's gracious outreach to and through faith."[29]

Second, faith in Rom 9:30—10:21 is explicitly Christocentric. The reason the Jews were unable to attain righteousness is because it was not pursued in faith as evidenced by the fact that they have "stumbled over the stumbling stone" (προσέκοψαν τῷ λίθῳ τοῦ προσκόμματος).[30] In Rom 9:33, Paul quotes Isa 28:16, a prophecy about the coming Messiah promising that "those believing in him will not be put to shame" (ὁ πιστεύων ἐπ' αὐτῷ οὐ καταισχυνθήσεται), while announcing that some will stumble over him. In the context of Isa 28, Yahweh announces judgment on his people but also promises restoration through the coming "stone." Paul quotes the same verse again in Rom 10:11, which in the context clearly identifies the stone as Jesus.[31] Thus, the primary problem is that the Jews did not pursue the law by faith, leading to their rejection of Jesus. The implication is that had they pursued the law by faith, they would have believed in Jesus since he is the τέλος of the law (Rom 10:4). Perhaps it could be said that Christ is the τέλος of Israel's story.[32] Faith in Jesus removes the shameful status of those in Adam while conferring on them the honorable status of "children of God" (Rom 8:16).[33]

Having identified Jesus as the referent of the stone from Isa 28:16, Paul gives a Christological interpretation of Deut 30:12; 14, introduced with a portion of Deut 9:4, in Rom 10:6–8.[34] In the original context, Deut 30 focuses on the future hope of Israel and the choice Moses laid before

29. Dunn, *Romans*, 2:577.

30. Rom 9:32.

31. Watson, *Paul, Judaism, and the Gentiles*, 329, argues that the stone refers to the "divine gift of righteousness, received through faith." Israel stumbled because this righteousness is given to all, Jew and Gentile alike. While possible, especially if the "righteousness of their own" in Rom 10:3 implies a righteousness for Jews alone, Paul clearly interprets the stone as Jesus himself in Rom 10:11. It is doubtful that Paul would interpret the same image differently a mere eleven verses later.

32. Wright, *Paul and the Faithfulness of God*, 1172.

33. Jewett, *Romans*, 614.

34. The use of Deut 9:4 is significant in that the rest of the verse reads, "It is because of my righteousness that the Lord has brought me in to occupy this land." Moses reminds Israel that they have no righteousness of their own. Likewise, those outside of Christ (not "in Christ") also have no righteousness of their own. See Jewett, *Romans*, 626.

the people: life and death. Life is to be found in faith and obedience. Paul's use of the passage in Rom 10 places Christ at the center: believe in him and find life and honor.[35] This is because Jesus is Lord and the confession of him as such is the life-giving faith Paul so desperately desires for Israel. For Paul, it is in Jesus that God has fulfilled his promises to Abraham and is bringing about the restoration of Deut 30. Thus, Paul's Christological interpretation of Deut 30 asserts "that the real meaning of Deut 30 is disclosed not in lawkeeping but in Christian preaching."[36] In this way, Christ is the τέλος of the law because God has sent the Messiah and raised him from the dead. The mark of the true people of God is union with Christ through faith rather than law possession or performance.[37]

The Christocentric faith of Rom 9:30—10:21 has multiple connections to Rom 1–8 and therefore to explicit union with Christ language. As argued throughout this book, Paul has used the honor/shame motif to describe life in Adam versus life in Christ. The dual quotation of Isa 28:16 again brings shame into the discussion in the affirmation of "no shame" for those who believe in Christ. In Rom 1–8, Paul has often used the motif to describe the restoration that takes place in Christ, particularly in the use of glory language. Especially important in the near context is Rom 8:18 and 21. Thus, Paul's appropriation of Isa 28:16 in Rom 9:33 and 10:11 is linked to his discussion of redemption of glory in Christ. In short, those "in Christ" will not be put to shame because they are the true people of God.

An additional connection to Rom 1–8 in relation to Paul's Christological focus in Rom 9:30—10:21 is his use of Deut 30. As argued in chapter 4 above, Paul alludes to Deut 30:6 in Rom 2:29, showing that true circumcision is of the heart by the Spirit. In chapter 4, I argued that this use of Deut 30:6 is important for union with Christ as it (1) provides a (new) covenantal context for Paul's soteriological discussion and (2) defines the true people of God as those who have experienced heart change. In Rom 9–10, Paul again draws on Deut 30, this time focusing on faith in Christ. In Rom 10:6–8, the conflation of verses from Deuteronomy shows that the Messiah has already come and the people of God are therefore identified by connection to him by faith.[38] Further, Paul's addition of the

---

35. Deut 30:11–14 was also important in other early Jewish writings. See Dunn, *Romans*, 2:603–7.

36. Hays, *Echoes*, 82.

37. Fitzmyer, *Romans*, 590.

38. As Jewett, *Romans*, 627, notes, Paul's argument here combats the notion that

Spirit in Rom 2:29 proleptically affirms the role of the Holy Spirit. In Rom 8, Paul unpacks the work of the Spirit, emphasizing the Spirit as the one who unites believers to Christ. Drawing all of this together, while "in Christ" and related phrases are not used in Rom 9:30—10:21, the concept can be detected beneath the surface of the argument through Paul's OT narrative-based Christology. As in Rom 1–8, the focus on Christ as the τέλος of the OT story calls people, Jew and Gentile alike, to participate in his story through faith.

Third, discussion of faith throughout this section is focused on the heart (καρδία), particularly in Rom 10 where the term is used five times. In verse 1, Paul repeats his concern for Israel, this time expressing their salvation as his "heart's desire" (ἡ μὲν εὐδοκία τῆς ἐμῆς καρδίας). However, the remaining uses of καρδία in chapter 10 are clustered in verses 6–10. In verse 6, Paul keeps the attention on the heart in his quotation of "the righteousness of faith," which says "do not say in your heart" (μὴ εἴπῃς ἐν τῇ καρδίᾳ σου) followed by a conflation of Deut 9:4, 30:12, and 30:14. In verse 8, Paul proclaims that the word of the gospel is "in your heart" (ἐν τῇ καρδίᾳ σου). Finally, in verses 9–10, Paul makes clear that true faith is located in the heart of the believer. In order to be saved (εἰς σωτηρίαν), one must believe in one's heart that Jesus is raised from the dead, "for with the heart one believes" (καρδίᾳ γὰρ πιστεύεται). Thus, in calling people, Jews and Gentiles alike, to true faith, Paul places a heavy emphasis on the heart. This faith moves beyond intellectual assent to a change of heart: "a total reorientation of a person and his or her relationships."[39] Within the broader context of the letter, this means finding one's primary identity in Christ.

While one may question the meaning of the heart language in Rom 10, it is clear that the emphasis on the heart connects the argument of 9:30—10:21 to multiple earlier passages. As mentioned above, the heart was central to the discussion in Rom 2, particularly related to the two allusions to the new covenant (Rom 2:15; 29).[40] In Rom 2, the primary topic of discussion was the spiritual failure of the Jews. As Paul's attention turns again specifically to the Jews in Rom 9–11, the central section focuses on the heart. In Rom 5:5, Paul avers that for those in Christ, "the love of God has been poured in our hearts by the Holy Spirit who was given to us"

Israel's obedience to the law would quicken the coming of the Messiah.

39. Jewett, *Romans*, 629.
40. See chapter 4 above.

(ἡ ἀγάπη τοῦ θεοῦ ἐκκέχυται ἐν ταῖς καρδίαις ἡμῶν διὰ πνεύματος ἁγίου τοῦ δοθέντος ἡμῖν). Like Rom 2:29, the work of the Holy Spirit is on the heart of the believer. In Rom 6:17, Paul holds that as a result of union with Christ, the believers' obedience comes from the heart (ἐκ καρδίας). Finally, in Rom 8:27, God is described as "the one who searches hearts" (ὁ ἐραυνῶν τὰς καρδίας). In the context, the emphasis on the heart comes in the midst of explicit discussion of union with Christ in Rom 6 and 8. Thus, in each use of καρδία in Rom 1–8, there is a clear connection to union with Christ.

The use of καρδία in the first 8 chapters of the epistle directly affects the way it is used in Rom 10. The emphasis on the heart defines the true people of God as those who inwardly believe the gospel. That is, the mark of the new covenant people of God is not ethnicity or possession of the law, but the circumcision of the heart, expressed here as true faith coming from one's heart. This is the mark that "penetrated far below matters of race and of ritual."[41] The placement of heart language alongside justification and the Spirit further links to previous union with Christ language, here expressed as "salvation" (σωτηρία). Further, faith from the heart is accompanied by the confession of Jesus as Lord, which announces one's belonging to Jesus as the resurrected Messiah.[42] Conceptually, this links back to Rom 5–6, where believers are those who are joined to Christ. Thus, salvation should be understood as union with Christ.

Finally, faith levels the ground ethnically: it is equally for Jew and Gentile alike. Paul argues that Israel's problem (at least in part) is that they sought to establish their own righteousness (Rom 10:3). It is most likely that "their own" (τὴν ἰδίαν) includes the ethnocentric attitude that rejects the worldwide new covenant righteous status available to all. In other words, Israel as a whole has viewed covenant status as dependent upon the law and therefore unavailable to Gentiles.[43] To combat this notion, Paul makes explicit in verses 11–13 what has been implied in the previous verses: the faith he proclaims is for all. In verse 11, Paul quotes a portion of Isa 28:16, which was quoted in 9:33. However, there is one key change in this second quotation: the addition of πᾶς. Where the quotation of in 9:33 simply reads "ὁ πιστεύων," in 10:11, Paul augments the verse to read "πᾶς ὁ πιστεύων." The change places the emphasis on "all,"

---

41. Dunn, *Romans*, 2:593.
42. Ibid., 2:607.
43. Byrne, *Romans*, 314.

especially as Paul clarifies in verse 12, writing "for there is no distinction between Jew and Greek, for the same Lord is over all" (οὐ γάρ ἐστιν διαστολὴ Ἰουδαίου τε καὶ Ἕλληνος, ὁ γὰρ αὐτὸς κύριος πάντων). In verse 13, Paul quotes Joel 3:5, which also uses the word πᾶς, affirming that "all who call on the name of the Lord will be saved." A fundamental piece of my argument has been that in Romans, union with Christ is Paul's primary tool for encouraging church unity. This is true in Rom 10—those who in faith call on the name of Jesus as Lord are the united people of God.

These four points link Paul's discussion of faith in Rom 9:30—10:21 to the forgoing argument, making it clear that union with Christ, while less explicit, is beneath the surface tying together Paul's argument. Righteousness and faith are closely related throughout Romans and is always salted with participatory overtones, requiring the connection between faith and righteousness in Rom 9-10 to be understood as participatory as well. Participation in the faithfulness of Jesus the Messiah is the mark of the true people of God.

Romans 11:1–36

Paul's exegetical argument that "salvation" is available to all through faith in Rom 10 is followed by an assertion of God's faithfulness to Israel in Rom 11. Here Paul not only affirms that God has not cast aside his people completely, but also that the work of God in Christ actually involves drawing the Gentiles into Israel's story.[44] Thus, far from a total rejection of Israel, the saving work of God in Christ involves bringing the story of God's people to its climax in the Messiah. Indeed, Paul affirms that God will not forget the people "who him foreknew" (ὃν προέγνω).[45] Further, Israel's rejection of the gospel is not absolute (all Israelites without exception). In Rom 11:1-10, which serves to both summarize the preceding argument of chapters 9-10 and to bridge into the next section (Rom 11:11-32), Paul argues that though Israel as a whole has rejected Jesus as the Messiah, this does not mean that there are no believing Jews.[46]

44. Longenecker, "Sharing," 61.

45. The use of "foreknew" in Rom 11:2 harks back to 8:29-30, where Paul argued that though God's people in Christ presently suffer, God is faithful to conform them to the image of his son and to glorify them. In Rom 11, Paul is highlighting God's faithfulness to his people despite their sin. Wagner, *Heralds of the Good News*, 231–32.

46. Dunn, *Romans*, 2:635-36.

He offers himself as exhibit A: an Israelite from the tribe of Benjamin who believes Jesus to be the Messiah (Rom 11:1). Then, in verses 2-6, Paul draws on the story of Elijah as another proof of God's faithfulness through the remnant. As in the time of Elijah when God sovereignly kept 7,000 for himself who had not worshiped idols, so in the present God has kept for himself a number of Jews who have believed the gospel. However, Paul is clear that those who are kept for God are "chosen by grace" (ἐκλογὴν χάριτος γέγονεν), and are not new covenant people on the basis of works (ἔργων). Throughout Romans, grace is received through Jesus (1:5, 7; 3:24; 5:2, 15, 17, 20, 21). Though God has not rejected his people, they become new covenant members by grace only, in the same way as the Gentiles. The remnant exists by the sovereign election of God in grace and "the rest were hardened" (οἱ δὲ λοιποὶ ἐπωρώθησαν), just as Pharaoh was hardened (Rom 9:17-18). That this is in keeping with God's work throughout Israel's history is clear from the Scriptures, here particularly Deuteronomy, Isaiah, and Psalms, which Paul quotes in verses 8-10.

Following the affirmation that God has not rejected his people, Paul expounds on the way in which God is using the present situation to draw Israel back into his saving purposes. In verses 11-12, Paul uses the term "trespass" (παράπτωμα) to describe Israel's stumbling. This is significant in that the same word is used six times in Rom 5:15-21 to describe the sin of Adam. Thus, with this subtle allusion, Paul again affirms that Israel is no less "in Adam" than the Gentiles.[47] In spite of this, Paul asserts that the Jewish rejection of the gospel is actually part and parcel of the plan of God. Twice Paul says that Israel's rejection of Jesus results in the salvation of Gentiles (11:11, 15). Nevertheless, the salvation of Gentiles ironically serves to bring Israel to jealously "and save some of them" (καὶ σώσω τινὰς ἐξ αὐτῶν—11:14). Indeed, Paul believes that if blessing comes to the world through Israel's rejection, their acceptance would lead to even greater blessings (11:12, 15). Within this argument, there is a possible echo of union with Christ in Paul's use of resurrection language in verse 15. Paul writes, "for if their rejection led to the reconciliation of the world, what will be the result of their acceptance if not life from the dead?" (εἰ γὰρ ἡ ἀποβολὴ αὐτῶν καταλλαγὴ κόσμου, τίς ἡ πρόσλημψις εἰ μὴ ζωὴ ἐκ νεκρῶν;). This seemingly isolated reference to resurrection should be understood in relation to earlier resurrection language, particularly in chapter 6. Throughout Romans, references to resurrection

---

47. Wright, "Letter to the Romans," 681.

relate to (1) Christ's resurrection and (2) believers' co-resurrection with Christ. That is, whenever Paul mentions the resurrection of humans, *it is always in union with Christ*. The clearest example of this is in Rom 6, the central resurrection passage in the epistle. In chapter 5 above, I discussed Paul's argument regarding of the resurrection of believers in Christ. The key point is that those united Christ have been crucified with him and therefore will be raised with him.[48] Jesus's resurrection was prominent in Rom 10:9, where Paul proclaimed that all who believe in his resurrection "will be saved." Then, in Rom 11:15 Paul describes the restoration of Israel as "life from the dead" (ζωὴ ἐκ νεκρῶν). Given the close link between Jesus's resurrection and that of believers earlier in the epistle and the contextual nearness of Rom 10:9 and 11:15, it seems most likely that the resurrection-restoration of Israel is to be understood in relation to the resurrection of Jesus. Accordingly, when Paul uses the image of resurrection in Rom 11:15, undertones of union with Christ, especially union with his resurrection, are present.

Having argued that the rejection of the gospel by Israel is in keeping with God's plan, Paul uses the image of the olive tree in Rom 11:17–24 to further clarify. Paul argues that both Jews and Gentiles in Christ are joined to the same root (11:17). However, Gentile believers are like a "wild olive tree" (ἀγριέλαιος) that has been in-grafted. That is, they are not "natural branches" (κατὰ φύσιν κλάδων) and therefore must understand their position in Christ as completely dependent upon the grace of God (11:21–22). Further, if God is able to bring in wild olive trees, he is also able to restore broken off branches to the tree (11:23–24). Indeed, Paul asserts that God will graft the natural branches "into their own olive tree" (τῇ ἰδίᾳ ἐλαίᾳ).

While explicit union with Christ language is absent from Rom 11:17–24 (and largely absent from chapter 11), the image of the olive tree is curious in that it involves an agricultural analogy that includes the concept of joining together, or uniting, branches and trees. That is, assuming Paul had other images at his disposal, his choice of this particular analogy seems to intentionally connect on a conceptual level to union themes. As union with Christ communicates an intimate connection between Jesus and believers, so the image of the olive tree communicates live-giving connections between the branches and the tree. Further, the

---

48. Barclay, "Paul's Story," 152, notes the congruence of Rom 11:15 and Rom 6:1–11 in "the pattern of the cocrucifixion and new creation that molds every believer."

most plausible identification of the "root" in the analogy is the Messiah.[49] Therefore, the image explicitly pictures believers being joined to Christ.[50] Paul even uses participatory language in verse 17, writing that Gentiles have been grafted in so as to "share in the riches of the root of the olive tree" (συγκοινωνὸς τῆς ῥίζης τῆς πιότητος τῆς ἐλαίας ἐγένου). As Dunn notes, συγκοινωνὸς is most often used by Paul with reference to sharing in Christ or the Holy Spirit.[51] The emphasis on faith as the condition for Israel to be grafted back into the tree in verse 23 confirms the presence of union with Christ themes. As noted above, faith is the mark of the new people of God in Christ and is explicitly participatory through Romans. Thus, while union with Christ may not be the primary meaning of the olive tree analogy, the imagery certainly points in this direction and supports the contention that union with Christ is fundamental to Paul's argument, even when not explicitly mentioned.

In this section, I have argued that while union with Christ does not feature as prominently in Rom 9–11 as it did in chapters 5–8, a close reading of the text reveals the presence of union themes running beneath the surface. This is especially true in the numerous textual connections between chapters 9–11 and chapters 1–8. In short, while Paul's language in Rom 9–11 includes few direct references to union with Christ, it is clear that his argument in this section builds upon and echoes his earlier discussion, especially pertaining to union with Christ.

UNION WITH CHRIST IN ROMANS 12–16

The beginning of Rom 12 marks a turning point in Paul's argument. In chapters 1–11, Paul focuses on the righteousness of God and the identification of the true people of God. In the remaining chapters, Paul turns to issues of application, addressing the way in which those who are "in Christ" should live both in relation to one another and to outsiders. Of course, this should not be taken to imply that Paul is done with theological argumentation as the last section of Romans is suffused with theological reflection. One of the major theological themes running through

---

49. Khobnya, "Root."

50. The quotation of Isa 59:20–21 in Rom 11:26–27 lends support to the messianic interpretation of the root as it shows Israel's hope in the promised "deliverer" whom Paul believes to be Jesus.

51. Dunn, *Romans*, 2:661. For example, 1 Cor 9:23.

chapters 1–11 comes to center stage in chapters 12–16: the unity of Jew and Gentile in Christ. Much of the outworking of faith in these chapters revolves around this central issue. Unsurprisingly, the concept of union with Christ is highly significant.

In what follows, a verse-by-verse commentary will not be possible or necessary. I will focus on the function of union with Christ, both explicitly and implicitly, in Paul's instructions to the Roman church. In short, where union with Christ language is absent, the argument makes clear that it is presupposed and therefore foundational. Not only is union with Christ the implicit conceptual underpinning for the ethical discourse, but images of the doctrine feature prominently within these final chapters. These include the image of the church as the body of Christ in Rom 12:3–8 and the clothing metaphor in 13:14. Finally, and related to the point above concerning the close relation between theology and ethics, the theological content of Rom 12–16 is intimately connected to union with Christ themes from earlier in the letter. All of this will be substantiated below.

The last major section of Romans begins with a call to worship and transformation. The use of "therefore" (οὖν) in Rom 12:1 indicates that Paul sees the forthcoming instruction to be built upon the preceding argument, further confirmed by his basis for the appeal: "the mercies of God" (τῶν οἰκτιρμῶν τοῦ θεοῦ), which connects thematically to chapters 9–11.[52] In Rom 12:1–2, Paul encourages the believers in Rome to live in light of their union with Christ. As such, they are to live as "living sacrifices" (θυσίαν ζῶσαν), not "conformed to this age but transformed by the renewing of the mind" (μὴ συσχηματίζεσθε τῷ αἰῶνι τούτῳ, ἀλλὰ μεταμορφοῦσθε τῇ ἀνακαινώσει τοῦ νοός). The idea of a "living sacrifice" evokes Paul's discussion of the work of Christ earlier in the letter, as he has used sacrificial language with reference to Christ's death in 3:24–25, 5:6–11, and 8:3. Just as Christ faithfully died to redeem his people, so those in Christ are to live faithfully as those having "died with Christ" (6:3–4). Moreover, Paul has been clear that union with Christ brings life to the believer (5:10, 17–18; 6:4, 23; 8:2, 6, 11). In addition, the juxtaposition of "this age" with being "transformed" is conceptually linked to the idea of being "in Adam" (conformed) and to being "in Christ" (transformed). Thus, "living sacrifice" is the natural outflow of life in Christ. True worship, which formerly belonged to Israel (Rom 9:4), is

---

52. Ibid., 2:709.

now transformed in Christ, for Jew and Gentile alike.[53] In this way, those in Christ are "to become the antithesis of adamic humanity depicted in chapters 1–3."[54]

Following these introductory verses, Paul uses an image that is perhaps most clearly communicative of union with Christ: the body of Christ. That this metaphor reflects union with Christ is clear from Paul's affirmation in verse 5 that the church is "one body in Christ" (ἓν σῶμά ἐσμεν ἐν Χριστῷ). Concerning union with Christ, there are a few key aspects of the concept communicated through the image of the body. First, the church as one body in Christ means that there is an intimate connection between believers and Jesus. Paul presents union with Christ as more than a mere concept, but as the closest of relationships, able to be compared with the unity of the physical body. In Rom 8, Paul emphasized the role of the Holy Spirit, showing that the Spirit's dwelling within the hearts of believers is Christ dwelling within. The picture of the body intimates that as the human body is bound together, so believers are likewise bound together with Christ. Ridderbos states well: "it is certainly clear that Paul here again does not infer that the church is the body from its own existence as community, but precisely from Christ and from the bond that joins the church to him."[55]

Second, the image of the body of Christ is inherently corporate: union with Christ is also union with other believers. Paul uses the first person plural throughout the discussion to emphasize that the church is united together in Christ. That is, the purpose of the metaphor is not so much to communicate that individual believers are united to Christ as much as to communicate the corporate union in which believers are together united to Christ. As Barclay puts it, "Paul imagines a community so interdependent that all are figured, individually, as *organs of one another* (12:5): everyone is essential to everyone else."[56] In this way, this image communicates powerfully the intimate unity of the church, which is one of Paul's primary uses for union with Christ in the epistle.[57] Thus, the image of the body of Christ encourages unity among Jews and Gentiles in Christ.

---

53. Wright, "Letter to the Romans," 704.
54. Gorman, *Becoming the Gospel*, 289.
55. Ridderbos, *Paul*, 371.
56. Barclay, *Paul and the Gift*, 510–11 (emphasis Barclay's).
57. Stuhlmacher, *Romans*, 193.

Third, Paul argues through the body of Christ metaphor that unity in Christ does not disparage diversity. In addition to arguing for unity as one body in Christ, Paul also upholds the diversity within the church through an emphasis on the "many members" (πολλὰ μέλη) who "do not have the same function" (οὐ τὴν αὐτὴν ἔχει πρᾶξιν). Thus, while believers are bound together in Christ, this does not mean that individuals lose their identity. Rather, as the body is made up of differing parts, so the church is composed of a diversity of people. While Paul's primary emphasis is on differing gifts, the unity in diversity also applies to ethnic identity. Believers are bound together in Christ, trumping individual differences, yet the differences are not thereby erased.[58]

The body of Christ metaphor sets the stage for the rest of the discussion of Rom 12–16. In the following verses, Paul applies the basic idea to real life in relation to the community of faith and the outside world. In 12:9—13:7, life in Christ is teased out in blessing others, first those among "the saints" (12:9–13), then among those who may be considered enemies (12:14–21), and finally in living as a good citizen (13:1–7). In 13:8–10, Paul calls upon the Roman church to love others and thereby be counted as one who has "fulfilled the law" (νόμον πεπλήρωκεν). Fulfilling the law harks back to Rom 2:15, where Paul wrote that new covenant members have the law "written on their hearts" and 8:4, where Paul argued that through the death of Christ, those united to him have "the righteousness of the law fulfilled" (τὸ δικαίωμα τοῦ νόμου πληρωθῇ) in them. Thus, fulfilling the law through love takes place only in union with Christ.

Chapter 13 ends with a further call to holy living as the reality of the end of the ages draws near. Within this context, the last verse of chapter 13 contains another metaphor for union with Christ, though Paul only mentions it in passing. In Rom 13:14, Paul exhorts the believers to "put on the Lord Jesus Christ" (ἐνδύσασθε τὸν κύριον Ἰησοῦν Χριστὸν).[59] Several points should be made. First, in the context, the command stands in opposition to sinfulness reminiscent of the indictment of Rom 1:18–32. Since the Roman believers are being "conformed to the image of his Son" (Rom 8:29), they must not live as those still "in Adam."[60] That is, putting

---

58. Dunn, *Romans*, 2:733.

59. Similar clothing metaphors within the Pauline corpus are found in 1 Cor 15:51–54; 2 Cor 5:1–4; Gal 3:26–27; Col 3:9–10; 3:12; Eph 4:20–24; 6:10. See the discussion in Campbell, *Paul and Union with Christ*, 310–23.

60. Dunn, *Romans*, 2:790–91.

on the Lord Jesus means living out one's union with him by imitating his life of obedience. Interestingly, Paul encourages the Roman believers to put on Christ "and do not make provision for the flesh into lust" (καὶ τῆς σαρκὸς πρόνοιαν μὴ ποιεῖσθε εἰς ἐπιθυμίας). The ἐπιθυμίας links back to Rom 1:24 and 7:11, two passages alluding to the sin of Adam and Israel. Thus, union with Christ is here presented as the answer to the problem of human sin. Second, Paul inserts "Lord" here to emphasize allegiance. Echoing the baptism metaphor of Rom 6, putting on the Lord means to be marked out by living under his lordship. Finally, the clothing metaphor implies that union with Christ suffuses every part of the believer. As clothing covers the body, so Christ covers the believer and thus deeply affects the ethical behavior of those in Christ.[61] Barclay aptly summarizes these points: "'Putting on the Lord Jesus Christ' (13:14) enlists every organ of the moribund body for a new allegiance, whose social shape reflects the capacity of the Christ-gift to question every norm."[62]

Though there are no clear references to union with Christ in Rom 14, the concept almost certainly provides the conceptual foundation for Paul's instruction. In this chapter, Paul discusses some of the practical applications of the unity and diversity as taught through the body metaphor of 12:3–8.[63] The primary issue in Rom 14 is the difference of opinion on non-essential matters such as the observation of days and diets. Paul argues that the unity of the church and their identity in Christ supersedes individual preferences. Significantly, Paul does not call for uniformity on these matters, but for tolerance within the body of Christ. Thus, the unity of the church in Christ does not result in erasure of diversity. For Paul, union with Christ issues in unity as "putting on Christ" results in caring for others.

As many scholars note, Rom 15:1–13 must be read in conjunction with chapter 14 as these verses continue the discussion of the strong and the weak (15:1–7) before concluding the major theological argument of the letter in 15:8–13.[64] This last paragraph of the subsection (15:8–13)

---

61. Moo, *Romans*, 825–26.

62. Barclay, *Paul and the Gift*, 511.

63. Much scholarly discussion on Rom 14 revolves around "the weak" and "the strong." While important, a full discussion of this issue is outside the bounds of the present discussion. For recent discussion, see Longenecker, *Introducing*, 433–38; Barclay, "Faith and Self-Detachment"; and the relevant sections of major commentaries.

64. For example, Kruse, *Romans*, 526, views this section as a part of the wider argument of Rom 14:1—15:13.

requires some attention as it ties together the main themes of the letter. Having encouraged the Roman Christians toward love for one another, Paul turns to a scriptural and theological argument, which roots the unity of the church in the Messiah. Since verse 8 begins with "for" (γὰρ), it is clear that this paragraph builds on and explains the preceding argument. In 15:7, Paul encouraged the believers to "welcome one another just as also Christ welcomed you to the glory of God" (προσλαμβάνεσθε ἀλλήλους, καθὼς καὶ ὁ Χριστὸς προσελάβετο ὑμᾶς εἰς δόξαν τοῦ θεοῦ).[65] Rom 15:8–9a explains the meaning of Christ's welcoming of believers. Here Paul mentions Jews and Gentiles explicitly for the first time since chapter 11. The emphasis of these verses is the mission of the Messiah as the servant who came to fulfill the promises given to the patriarchs so that the mercy of God might spread to the Gentiles, thus demonstrating "the truthfulness of God" (ἀληθείας θεοῦ). God's truthfulness, like his righteousness, points to his faithfulness.[66] Thus Paul shows the consistency of God's work in Christ through Israel for the world.[67] The unity of God's saving work has created, and continues to create, a new people in the Messiah.

Echoing Rom 4 and 9–11, Paul again confirms that this was God's plan from the beginning: to bless the world through Israel and thereby create a worldwide people of God. This is so that the Gentiles "might glorify God" (δοξάσαι τὸν θεόν), which stands in opposition to those who fail to glorify God in 1:18–32.[68] The reference to Christ as "a servant to the circumcised" (Χριστὸν διάκονον γεγενῆσθαι περιτομῆς) implies that believers are also to be servants, not least to one another, in Christ. The assertion concerning God's truthfulness to Israel for the nations is followed by a string of OT passages focusing on the inclusion of the Gentiles in the people of God, climaxing in the quotation of Isa 11:10 in Rom 15:12, a passage that promises the Davidic king will come and bring hope to the Gentiles. This points back to the opening of the letter (Rom 1:3–4) and draws Paul's argument together. The "root of Jesse" has come and in him

---

65. Wagner, "The Christ, Servant of Jew and Gentile," 475, points out that εἰς δόξαν τοῦ θεοῦ most likely refers to the reception of the Gentiles by the Messiah rather than the mutual reception of believers.

66. Käsemann, *Romans*, 385; Dunn, *Romans*, 2:847; Moo, *Romans*, 877.

67. As Hultgren, *Romans*, 532, notes, Paul often uses εἰς + infinitive to express purpose. Here, the construction is used to summarize the dual purpose of the Messiah's coming.

68. Dunn, *Romans*, 852. See also Gorman, *Becoming the Gospel*, 293.

God has created a new people through faith in the Messiah for his glory. As Hays remarks, Paul "draws back the curtain and reveals a collection of passages that explicitly embody his vision for a church composed of Jews and Gentiles glorifying God together."[69] It is here, at the close of the main argument, that Paul draws together the key stories running through Romans: those of Adam, Israel, Christ, and the church.[70]

After summarizing the great theme of the people of God in Christ, Paul closes the letter by announcing his plans for travel through Rome to Spain and then sending greetings to his contacts. Interestingly, throughout the greetings, he repeats phrases such as "in Christ Jesus" (ἐν Χριστῷ Ἰησοῦ), "in Christ" (ἐν Χριστῷ), and "in the Lord" (ἐν κυρίῳ) with reference to believers in the church. The repetition of union with Christ language at the close of the letter demonstrates the importance of the concept, not least in the fact that it appears to be common parlance for believers: they are those who are "in Christ."

CONCLUSION

References to union with Christ are less frequent in Rom 9–16 than in the first half of the letter. As to the reasons for this, one can only speculate. Perhaps the concept of the new people of God in Christ had been so adequately expounded in Rom 1–8 that Paul could merely assume it rather than state it explicitly in these final chapters. If this is the case, then the teaching of Rom 9–16 can only be rightly understood as an outworking of union with Christ. Thus, the discussion of Israel in chapters 9–11 shows that union with Christ is the demonstration of the righteousness of God in that he has been faithful to give Abraham a worldwide family, which does include the remnant of Israel. In addition, the ethical and communal teaching of chapters 12–16 is aimed at giving instruction on how to live together as the community in Christ. Paul's discussion is nearly incomprehensible if detached from its theological foundation: union with Christ.

---

69. Hays, *Echoes*, 71.
70. Longenecker, "Sharing," 63–64.

7

Conclusion

INTRODUCTION

THE PRECEDING CHAPTERS HAVE traced the theme of union with Christ through the argument of Romans and showed the way in which this theme is related to Paul's use of the OT. Specifically, I have argued that a close reading of Romans, with careful attention given to the narrative use of the OT, reveals that the stories of Adam and Israel together form the OT background for union with Christ. Further, the relationship between these stories and union with Christ is essential for Paul's purposes in writing the epistle: to encourage the unity of Jew and Gentile in Christ for service and mission.[1] Union with Christ is Paul's primary theological tool for encouraging this unity and his use of the OT is fundamental for his deployment of this tool.

To conclude our examination, this final chapter will briefly summarize the argument of the entire book and offer a few reflections on the way in which the foregoing study brings clarity to the concept of union with Christ.

---

1. As noted in chapter 1, this is one of Paul's purposes in writing, though he probably had others.

SUMMARY OF THE ARGUMENT

The primary aim of this book is to examine a possible OT background for union with Christ within the argument of Romans. Utilizing a narrative approach to Paul's use of the OT, I have argued that the stories of Adam and Israel are intimately linked both exegetically and thematically to union with Christ. As such, these foundational stories together form the OT background for union with Christ. Moreover, I have argued that Paul understands the stories of Adam and Israel as intimately related such that together they form one continuous metanarrative. Rather than isolated *stories*, the Adam and Israel narratives are pieces of a unified *story*. The integration of these narratives can be seen from the first chapter of Romans and each additional occurrence of an allusion to Adam: an allusion to Israel's story, usually related to Israel's sin, is found within the near context.

Following the introductory chapter in which I surveyed the relevant literature, briefly discussed some background issues, and described my chosen methodology, the bulk of this book has been an exegetical study of Romans. In chapter 2, I examined potential allusions to the Adam narratives in Rom 1–4. Through exegetical analysis alongside some investigation into relevant Jewish literature, I concluded that Paul alludes to Adam in Rom 1:18–32 and Rom 3:23. In Rom 1, Paul primarily focuses on the sinful rebellion of humanity with numerous allusions to the story of Adam's sin in Gen 3. Paul draws on the story in order to begin building his case for the universal plight of humanity, Jew and Gentile alike, in Adam. Paul continues this line of argument in much of Rom 1–3 and in 3:23 proclaims that all people without exception lack the glory of God.[2] Important to my argument is the observation that each time Paul alludes to Adam, there is a corresponding allusion to Israel's story in the near context. This was shown to be true in both Rom 1 and 3. In addition, Paul's use of the Abraham narratives in Rom 4 is closely related to the previous allusions to Adam (and Israel).

In chapter 3, I continued the examination of Paul's use of the OT stories in Rom 5–8. Whereas Paul's use of the Adam narrative was allusive in Rom 1 and 3, he makes more obvious and explicit use of the story in Rom 5. Though some have argued that this is the one and only place in Romans in which Paul draws on the Adam story, verbal and thematic

---

2. In dialogue with opposing views, I concluded that "glory" in Rom 3:23 is most likely an allusion to Adam. See the discussion in chapter 2 above.

connections with Rom 1:18–32 and 3:21–26 suggest that Rom 5:12–21 stands in continuity with the more subtle allusions in previous chapters. Thus, the explicit mention of Adam in Rom 5 lends weight to the argument for the existence of adamic allusions in Rom 1 and 3 and sets the stage for additional allusions in Rom 7 and 8. As noted above with regard to Rom 1–4, an allusion to Israel's story, usually emphasizing Israel's sin, is found in the near context of allusions to Adam.

The recognition of the connection between Adam and Israel in Romans raises questions as to Paul's purpose in weaving the stories together. The contention of this book is that the linking of the Adam and Israel narratives is Paul's exegetical argument that all people, regardless of ethnic identity, are "in Adam." Thus, there is a basic solidarity among all humanity in Adam, which is equivalent to being "in sin," being "of the flesh," and being "under law." This solidarity provides the conceptual precursor to union with Christ and serves to elucidate Paul's vision of humanity as divided between those who are "in Adam" and those who are "in Christ."

In chapters 4–5, I returned to the previously studied sections of Romans, this time with a focus on the role of union with Christ, particularly in relation to the aforementioned OT stories. I argued in these chapters that references to Adam (and Israel) in Romans are often followed by references to union with Christ. In chapter 4, I examined references to union with Christ in Rom 1–4. While union with Christ language in these chapters is sparse and normally subtle, it is not completely absent. I further argued that Rom 2 is foundational for union with Christ since (1) the argument follows closely after Paul's first allusion to Adam in Rom 1 and (2) the new covenant language in the chapter provides a covenantal framework for redemption in Christ. Further, Rom 3:21–26 contains some of Paul's central, though tightly packed, teaching on redemption. I argued that this passage reflects the pattern of Adam (and Israel) followed by union with Christ language that marks Paul's teaching on the topic. The use of the Abraham narrative in Rom 4 further bolsters the covenantal context for redemption in Christ while also reflecting a few subtle references to union themes.

In chapter 5, I continued the argument with a re-examination of Rom 5–8. In these chapters, the subtleness of Paul's union language gives way to more explicit exposition. In Rom 5, the Adam-Christ analogy makes plain the "tale of two unions." That is, all people are either in Adam or in Christ. As Christ restores that which sin destroyed, believers in him move from the realm of "in Adam" to the realm of "in Christ." In Rom 6,

Paul makes this argument via the symbol of baptism and via allusions to the exodus story, which leads into ethical living: those dead to sin cannot continue in it (6:2). In Rom 7, Paul continues with a reflection on the law and the way sin makes use of it: binding those under the law to sin in Adam. Finally, in Rom 8 Paul draws his exposition to a climax as he celebrates the redemption in Christ, which makes people God's children through the work of the Spirit uniting people to Christ. Here the narrative movement from "in Adam" to "in Christ" is most clearly observed.

Chapter 6 concluded the exegetical investigation by briefly examining references to union with Christ in Rom 9–16. The primary argument of this chapter was that union with Christ is foundational for Paul's reflection on Israel in Rom 9–11 and for his ethical and ecclesiological teaching in Rom 12–16. Numerous links between these chapters and Rom 1–8 suggest that while union with Christ language is less prominent in the second half of the letter, Paul's argumentation is scarcely understandable without this central concept in mind. In Rom 9–11, Paul argues that while many Jews have rejected Jesus as the Messiah, the engrafting of the Gentiles into the people of God is part and parcel of God's plan of redemption. Far from failing to keep his covenant promises, God is fulfilling these promises through Jesus and is creating Abraham's worldwide family in Christ. In Rom 12–16, Paul demonstrates the outworking of union with Christ in church life. Fundamental to this teaching is the new identity of believers: they are the people of God in Christ. As such, social status and ethnicity are set aside for the more fundamental identity as a people, Jew and Gentile together, united to Christ.

NARRATIVE METHODOLOGY, THE OLD TESTAMENT, AND UNION WITH CHRIST

In this book, I have utilized a narrative approach to the study of Romans with an emphasis on union with Christ. In chapter 1, I argued for the reasonableness of the narrative approach based on the similar uses of the OT in Jewish literature and the explicit references to OT stories in Romans. Nevertheless, I noted that only the results of the study could prove the usefulness of the methodology. Having completed the exegetical analysis of Romans using the described methodology, I believe the narrative approach has brought some clarity to the study of union with Christ. I offer the following points as fruit from this study.

First, the narrative approach recognizes an OT background for union with Christ where previous studies have demurred the possibility of OT backgrounds. As noted in the introduction, in an otherwise excellent study of union with Christ in Paul, Campbell claims that union with Christ is "boldly innovative" and lacks OT antecedents.[3] Other studies rarely consider potential OT backgrounds. Of course, it is not the case that other methodologies are incapable of discerning OT backgrounds. Indeed, Macaskill considers a number of possibilities.[4] Nevertheless, the narrative approach has proved to be capable of shedding light on a potential background for union with Christ and has done so exegetically. That is, the narrative approach is able to give attention to foundational stories in Romans and shows the relationship between these stories and the doctrine of union with Christ.[5] The methodology elucidates the importance of the OT stories in relation to union with Christ where other methodologies may miss the connection.

Second, the narrative approach highlights the corporate nature of union with Christ. In chapters 2–3 above, I explored Paul's use of the Adam and Israel narratives, concluding that Paul saw an intimate relationship between these OT stories and exploited this relationship in order to show a basic human solidarity in sin. Moreover, I have argued that these stories provide the OT background for union with Christ in Romans. As such, the OT background is primarily corporate in nature. This paves the way for a fundamentally corporate understanding of union with Christ. Some treatments of union with Christ, especially those more systematic in nature, have emphasized the individual aspects of union and neglected the corporate nature of the doctrine. While it is undoubtedly true that individual believers are united to Christ, the narrative approach to Romans has illuminated the importance of the corporate aspect. Thus, union with Christ is not only soteriological in nature, but also ecclesiological. That is, union with Christ is the primary theological theme for defining the true people of God: God's people are all those, Jew and Gentile alike, in Christ.

---

3. Campbell, *Paul and Union with Christ*, 417.
4. Macaskill, *Union with Christ*, especially chapters 4 and 5.
5. Hays, *Faith of Jesus Christ*, refers to the foundational stories as the "substructure" of Paul's theology. Wright, *Paul and the Faithfulness of God*, holds that the stories are Paul's "worldview" narratives. In any case, one must reckon with these narratives in order to understand Paul's theology. I have argued that the concept of union with Christ is no exception to this observation.

Third, the narrative approach situates union with Christ within the stories of Israel, Christ, and the church. More pointedly, union with Christ can be viewed as a sort of "intersection" for these stories, each of which is important in Paul's theology. As noted above, the narrative approach sheds considerable light upon the way in which Paul utilizes and draws together the various stories. Specifically, Paul draws on the stories of Adam and Israel to show human solidarity in sin. He references the story of Jesus in numerous places (for example, Rom 1:3–4; 3:24–25; 4:24–25; 5:15–21; 6:4, 9; 8:3) as the climax of the stories of both Adam and Israel. Finally, those united to Christ enter the story of God's people and become children of God through union with his Son. Thus, union with Christ as the defining characteristic of the true people of God is inextricable from the wider biblical narrative. That is, the narrative approach is able to place union with Christ within the biblical story rather than viewing it as an isolated doctrine. I have argued that Paul probably viewed union with Christ as closely related to Israel's story, even if the Christ event and subsequent giving of the Spirit moved the narrative in surprising directions.[6]

Fourth, the narrative approach has clarified the function of union with Christ within the argument of Romans. While many studies have considered Paul's theology of union, few have investigated the importance of the doctrine within the argument of a particular letter. In addition, studies on Romans often focus on other topics, such as justification, similarities with other Jewish writings, or faith. The narrative approach utilized in this book has allowed us to see the importance of the doctrine within Paul's argument by linking the doctrine to the OT narratives. The end result is that union with Christ plays a more important role in Romans than is sometimes recognized. In short, union with Christ is Paul's primary theological tool for encouraging unity in the Roman church for the purpose of mission. As noted already, union with Christ is intimately connected to the narrative (sub)structure of the epistle. Accordingly, union with Christ must be viewed as a central theological concept. The narrative approach of this book has made this clear.

Fifth, and finally, the narrative approach clarifies the meaning of union with Christ. In the introductory chapter, I briefly noted some proposed definitions of union with Christ in recent scholarship. Throughout

---

6. This, of course, stands in contrast to some "apocalyptic" approaches that argue for more discontinuity between Paul's gospel and Israel's story. See the discussion in chapter 1.

the exegetical analysis above, I have reflected on some of the key themes from those definitions as they arose from the text of Romans, especially the covenantal and participatory themes related to union with Christ. Space will not allow a full discussion of all possible definitions of union with Christ. Nevertheless, based on the exegetical analysis of this book, a tentative definition may be offered: *union with Christ is a covenantal bond on the basis of faith that results in the spiritual joining of believers to Christ and one another via the indwelling of the Holy Spirit. It involves the participation of believers in the story of Christ, whose story completes the stories of Adam and Israel, and thereby results in justification, the restoration of the shared glory of God, and the creation of the true people of God in Christ.* The narrative approach has brought clarity to a doctrine sometimes considered too mystical to properly define. While tentative, the above definition attempts to include the major theological themes related to union with Christ in Romans and incorporate the narrative background. The OT background of union with Christ gives further clarification to its meaning by placing the doctrine within the narrative of scripture and, more specifically, by drawing attention to the covenantal nature of the bond between believers and their Messiah.

CONCLUSION

The concept of union with Christ is unquestionably central to Paul's argument in Romans. It is a rich, multifaceted doctrine with tremendous implications for Christian life, community, and ministry. For the Christian life, being united to Christ means living under his lordship in intimate relationship. Within the Christian community, union with Christ binds together people from varying backgrounds in unity superseding all differences. In ministry, the doctrine gives prominent place to the ongoing founding of new communities that display the faithfulness of God. Union with Christ is the climax of the story of redemption, beginning with creation and the sin of humanity, through the calling and falling of Israel, to the triumphant death and resurrection of Jesus, and finally culminating in the creation of a multi-ethnic people awaiting his return—a new people in Christ.

Bibliography

Aageson, James W. "'Control' in Pauline Language and Culture: A Study of Rom 6." *NTS* 42.1 (1996) 75–89.

———. "Scripture and Structure in the Development of the Argument in Romans 9–11." *CBQ* 48 (1986) 265–89.

Abasciano, Brian J. "Diamonds in the Rough: A Reply to Christopher Stanley Concerning the Reader Competency of Paul's Original Audiences." *NovT* 49 (2007) 153–83.

Achtemeier, Paul J. *Romans*. Interpretation. Atlanta: John Knox, 1985.

Adams, Edward. "Abraham's Faith and Gentile Disobedience: Textual Links between Romans 1 and 4." *JSNT* 65 (1997) 47–66.

———. "Paul's Story of God and Creation: The Story of How God Fulfills His Purposes in Creation." In *Narrative Dynamics in Paul: A Critical Assessment*, edited by Bruce Longenecker, 19–43. Louisville, KY: Westminster John Knox, 2002.

Adeyẹmi, Femi. "Paul's 'Positive' Statements About the Mosaic Law." *BibSac* 164 (2007) 49–58.

Anderson, Chip. "Romans 1:1–5 and the Occasion of the Letter: The Solution to the Two-Congregation Problem in Rome." *TJ* 14 (1993) 25–40.

Bauer, Walter, Frederick W. Danker, W. F. Arndt, and F. W. Gingrich. *Greek-English Lexicon of the New Testament and Other Early Christian Literature*. 3rd ed. Chicago: University of Chicago Press, 2000.

Bailey, Daniel P. "Jesus as the Mercy Seat: The Semantics and Theology of Paul's Use of Hilasterion in Romans 3:25." *TynB* 51.1 (2000) 155–58.

Barclay, John M. G. "Faith and Self-Detachment from Cultural Norms: A Study in Romans 14–15." *ZNW* 104 (2013) 192–208.

———. "Grace and the Transformation of Agency in Christ." In *Redefining First-Century Jewish and Christian Identities: Essays in Honor of Ed Parish Sanders*, edited by Fabian E. Udoh, 372–89. Notre Dame: University of Notre Dame Press, 2008.

———. "'I Will Have Mercy on Whom I Have Mercy': The Golden Calf and Divine Mercy in Romans 9–11 and Second Temple Judaism." *EC* 1.1 (2010) 82–106.

———. "Is It Good News That God Is Impartial?: A Response to Robert Jewett." *JSNT* 31.1 (2008) 89–111.

———. "'Neither Jew nor Greek': Multiculturalism and the New Perspective on Paul." In *Ethnicity in the Bible*, edited by Mark C. Brett, 197–214. Leiden: Brill, 2002.

———. *Paul and the Gift*. Grand Rapids: Eerdmans, 2015.

———. "Paul and Philo on Circumcision: Romans 2:25–9 in Social and Cultural Context." *NTS* 44.4 (1998) 536–56.

———. "Paul's Story: Theology as Testimony." In *Narrative Dynamics in Paul: A Critical Assessment*, edited by Bruce Longenecker, 133–56. Louisville, KY: Westminster John Knox, 2002.

———. "Under Grace: The Christ-Gift and the Construction of a Christian Habitus." In *Apocalyptic Paul: Cosmos and Anthropos in Romans 5–8*, edited by Beverly Roberts Gaventa, 59–76. Waco, TX: Baylor University Press, 2013.

Barrett, C. K. *From First Adam to Last*. New York: Scribner, 1962.

Bassler, Jouette M. *Divine Impartiality: Paul and a Theological Axiom*. Chico, CA: Scholars, 1982.

Bauckham, Richard. "The Story of the Earth According to Paul: Romans 8:18–23." *RevExp* 108.1 (2011) 91–97.

Beale, G. K. *Handbook on the New Testament Use of the Old Testament: Exegesis and Interpretation*. Grand Rapids: Baker, 2012.

———. *A New Testament Biblical Theology: The Unfolding of the Old Testament in the New*. Grand Rapids: Baker, 2011.

———. *The Temple and the Church's Mission: A Biblical Theology of the Dwelling Place of God*. NSBT. Downers Grove, IL: IVP, 2004.

———. *We Become What We Worship: A Biblical Theology of Idolatry*. Downers Grove, IL: IVP, 2008.

———, ed. *The Right Doctrine from the Wrong Texts?: Essays on the Use of the Old Testament in the New*. Grand Rapids: Baker, 1994.

Beale, G. K., and D. A. Carson, eds. *Commentary on the New Testament Use of the Old Testament*. Grand Rapids: Baker, 2007.

Beker, Johan Christiaan. *Paul the Apostle: The Triumph of God in Life and Thought*. Philadelphia: Fortress, 1980.

Berkley, Timothy W. *From a Broken Covenant to Circumcision of the Heart: Pauline Intertextual Exegesis in Romans 2:17–29*. SBLDS. Atlanta: SBL, 2000.

Bernstein, Moshe J. "'Rewritten Bible': A Generic Category Which Has Outlived Its Usefulness?" *Textus* 22 (2005) 169–96.

Bird, Michael F. "The Letter to the Romans." In *All Things to All Cultures: Paul Among Jews, Greeks, and Romans*, edited by Mark Harding and Alanna Nobbs, 177–204. Grand Rapids: Eerdmans, 2013.

———. *The Saving Righteousness of God: Studies on Paul, Justification and the New Perspective*. Paternoster Biblical Monographs. Eugene, OR: Wipf & Stock, 2007.

Bird, Michael F., and Preston M. Sprinkle, eds. *The Faith of Jesus Christ: Exegetical, Biblical, and Theological Studies*. Peabody, MA: Hendrickson, 2010.

Black, C. Clifton. "Pauline Perspectives on Death in Romans 5–8." *JBL* 103.3 (1984) 413–33.

Blackwell, Ben C. *Christosis: Pauline Soteriology in Light of Deification in Irenaeus and Cyril of Alexandria*. WUNT. Tübingen: Mohr Siebeck, 2011.

———. "Immortal Glory and the Problem of Death in Romans 3:23." *JSNT* 32 (2010) 285–308.

Blackwell, Ben C., et al., eds. *Reading Romans in Context: Paul and Second Temple Judaism*. Grand Rapids: Zondervan, 2015.

Boers, Hendrickus. "The Structure and Meaning of Romans 6:1–14." *CBQ* 63 (2001) 664–82.

Bonhoeffer, Dietrich. *Discipleship*. Translated by Barbara Green and Reinhard Krauss. Dietrich Bonhoeffer Works 4. Minneapolis, MN: Fortress, 2001.

Bousset, Wilhelm. *Kyrios Christos: A History of the Belief in Christ from the Beginnings of Christianity to Irenaeus*. Translated by John E. Steely. Nashville: Abingdon, 1970 [1913; 1920].

Braaten, Laurie J. "The Groaning Creation: The Biblical Background for Romans 8:22." *BR* 50 (2005) 19–39.

Brady, Monica. "Biblical Interpretation in the 'Pseudo-Ezekiel' Fragments (4Q383–391) from Cave Four." In *Biblical Interpretation at Qumran*, edited by Matthias Henze, 88–109. Grand Rapids: Eerdmans, 2005.

Brett, Mark C., ed. *Ethnicity in the Bible*. Leiden: Brill, 2002.

Brooke, George J. *The Dead Sea Scrolls and the New Testament*. Minneapolis: Fortress, 2005.

———. *Exegesis at Qumran: 4QFlorilegium in Its Jewish Context*. JSOTSupp. Sheffield: JSOT, 1985.

———. *Reading the Dead Sea Scrolls: Essays in Method*. Atlanta: SBL, 2013.

———. "Rewritten Bible." In vol. 2 of *Encyclopedia of the Dead Sea Scrolls*, edited by Lawrence H. Shiffman and James C. VanderKam, 777–81. Oxford: Oxford University Press, 2000.

Bryan, Christopher. *A Preface to Romans: Notes on the Epistle in Its Literary and Cultural Setting*. Oxford: Oxford University Press, 2000.

Busch, Austin. "The Figure of Eve in Romans 7:5–25." *BI* 12.1 (2004) 1–36.

Byrne, Brendan. *Romans*. SP. Collegeville, MN: Liturgical, 1996.

Byron, John. *Slavery Metaphors in Early Judaism and Pauline Christianity: A Traditio-Historical and Exegetical Examination*. WUNT 2. Tübingen: Mohr Siebeck, 2003.

Calhoun, Robert M. *Paul's Definitions of the Gospel in Romans 1*. WUNT. Tübingen: Mohr Siebeck, 2011.

Callan, Terrance. *Dying and Rising with Christ: The Theology of Paul the Apostle*. New York: Paulist, 2006.

Campbell, Constantine R. *Basics of Verbal Aspect in Greek*. Grand Rapids: Zondervan, 2008.

———. *Paul and Union with Christ: An Exegetical and Theological Study*. Grand Rapids: Zondervan, 2012.

Campbell, Douglas A. *The Deliverance of God: An Apocalyptic Rereading of Justification in Paul*. Grand Rapids: Eerdmans, 2009.

———. "Faith and Participation in Paul." In *"In Christ" in Paul*, edited by Michael J. Thate et al., 37–61. Tübingen: Mohr Siebeck, 2014.

———. *The Quest for Paul's Gospel: A Suggested Strategy*. London: T. & T. Clark, 2005.

———. "The Story of Jesus in Romans and Galatians." In *Narrative Dynamics in Paul: A Critical Assessment*, edited by Bruce Longenecker, 97–124. Louisville, KY: Westminster John Knox, 2002.

Campbell, William S. "Covenant and New Covenant." In *Dictionary of Paul and His Letters*, edited by Gerald F. Hawthorne et al., 179–83. Leicester, UK: IVP, 1993.

———. *Paul and the Creation of Christian Identity*. LNTS. London: T. & T. Clark, 2006.

———. *Paul's Gospel in an Intercultural Context: Jew and Gentile in the Letter to the Romans*. New York: P. Lang, 1992.

———. "The Rationale for Gentile Inclusion and Identity in Paul." *CTR* 9 (2012) 23–38.

———. *Unity and Diversity in Christ: Interpreting Paul in Context*. Eugene, OR: Cascade, 2013.

Caneday, Ardel B. "Judgment, Behavior, and Justification According to Paul's Gospel in Romans 2." *JSPL* 1.2 (2011) 153–92.

———. "'They Exchanged the Glory of God for the Likeness of an Image': Idolatrous Adam and Israel as Representatives in Paul's Letter to the Romans." *SBJT* 11.3 (2007) 34–45.

Caragounis, Chrys C. "Romans 5:15–16 in the Context of 5:12–21: Contrast or Comparison?" *NTS* 31.1 (1985) 142–48.

Ceresko, Anthony R. "The Rhetorical Strategy of the Fourth Servant Song (Isaiah 52:13—53:12): Poetry and the Exodus-New Exodus." *CBQ* 56 (1994) 42–55.

Charlesworth, James H., ed. *The Old Testament Pseudepigrapha*. 2 vols. Peabody, MA: Hendrickson, 1983.

Childs, Brevard S. *Biblical Theology of the Old and New Testaments: Theological Reflection on the Christian Bible*. Minneapolis: Fortress, 1993.

Cirafesi, Wally V. "'To Fall Short' or 'To Lack?' Reconsidering the Meaning and Translation of 'ΥΣΤΕΡΕΩ' in Romans 3:23." *ExpT* 123.9 (2012) 429–34.

Clarke, Andrew D. "The Good and the Just in Romans 5:7." *TynB* 41.1 (1990) 128–42.

Collins, John J. *The Scepter and the Star: Messianism in Light of the Dead Sea Scrolls*. 2nd ed. Grand Rapids: Eerdmans, 2010.

Constantineanu, Corneliu. *Social Significance of Reconciliation in Paul's Theology: Narrative Readings in Romans*. LNTS. London: T. & T. Clark, 2010.

Craigie, Peter C. *Psalms 1–50*. WBC 19. Waco, TX: Word, 1983.

Cranfield, C. E. B. *The Epistle to the Romans*. 2 vols. ICC. London: T. & T. Clark, 1975.

———. "'The Works of the Law' in the Epistle to the Romans." *JSNT* 14.43 (1991) 89–101.

Cranford, Michael. "Abraham in Romans 4: The Father of All Who Believe." *NTS* 41.1 (1995) 71–88.

Das, A. Andrew. "Paul of Tarshish: Isaiah 66:19 and the Spanish Mission of Romans 15:24, 28." *NTS* 54 (2008) 60–73.

———. "Paul and Works of Obedience in Second Temple Judaism: Romans 4:4–5 as a 'New Perspective' Case Study." *CBQ* 71 (2009) 795–812.

———. "'Praise the Lord, All You Gentiles': The Encoded Audience of Romans 15:7–13." *JSNT* 34 (2011) 90–110.

———. *Solving the Romans Debate*. Minneapolis: Fortress, 2007.

Davies, W. D. *Paul and Rabbinic Judaism: Some Rabbinic Elements in Pauline Theology*. London: SPCK, 1948.

de Boer, Martinus C. *The Defeat of Death: Apocalyptic Eschatology in 1 Corinthians 15 and Romans 5*. JSNTSup. Sheffield: JSOT, 1988.

———. "N. T. Wright's Great Story and Its Relationship to Paul's Gospel." *JSPL* 4.1 (2014) 49–57.

———. "Paul's Mythologizing Program in Romans 5–8." In *Apocalyptic Paul: Cosmos and Anthropos in Romans 5–8*, edited by Beverly Roberts Gaventa, 1–20. Waco: Baylor University Press, 2013.

Deissmann, Adolf. *Die Neutestamentliche Formel "in Christo Jesu."* Marburg: N. G. Elwert, 1892.

———. *St. Paul: A Study in Social and Religious History*. Translated by Lionel R. M. Strachan. London: Hodder and Stoughton, 1912.

de Jonge, Martinus, and Johannes Tromp. *The Life of Adam and Eve and Related Literature*. Sheffield: Academic, 1997.

Dempster, Stephen G. *Dominion and Dynasty: A Biblical Theology of the Hebrew Bible*. NSBT. Downers Grove, IL: IVP, 2003.

Dochhorn, Jan. "Röm 7,7 Und Das Zehnte Gebot: Ein Beitrag Zur Schriftauslegung Und Zur Jüdischen Vorgeschichte Des Paulus." *ZNW* 100.1 (2009) 59–77.

Donaldson, Terence L. *Paul and the Gentiles: Remapping the Apostle's Convictional World*. Minneapolis: Fortress, 1997.

Donfried, Karl P. *The Romans Debate*. Rev. and exp. ed. Grand Rapids: Baker, 2011.

Dryden, J. de Waal. "Immortality in Romans 2:6–11." *JTI* 7 (2013) 295–310.

Du Toit, Andrie. "Paulus Oecumenicus: Interculturality in the Shaping of Paul's Theology." *NTS* 55 (2009) 121–43.

Dunn, James D. G. *Christology in the Making: A New Testament Inquiry into the Origins of the Doctrine of the Incarnation*. 2nd ed. London: SCM, 1989.

———. *The New Perspective on Paul: Collected Essays*. WUNT. Tübingen: Mohr Siebeck, 2005.

———. *Romans*. 2 vols. WBC. Dallas: Word, 1988.

———. *The Theology of Paul the Apostle*. Grand Rapids: Eerdmans, 1998.

———. "Yet Once More—'The Works of the Law': A Response." *JSNT* 46 (1992) 99–117.

———, ed. *Paul and the Mosaic Law*. Grand Rapids: Eerdmans, 2001.

Dunson, Ben. "Do Bible Words Have Bible Meaning? Distinguishing between Imputation as Word and Doctrine." *WTJ* 75 (2013) 239–60.

———. "Faith in Romans: The Salvation of the Individual or Life in Community?" *JSNT* 34 (2011) 19–46.

Earnshaw, John D. "Reconsidering Paul's Marriage Analogy in Romans 7:1–4." *NTS* 40.1 (1994) 68–88.

Eastman, Susan. "Israel and the Mercy of God: A Re-Reading of Galatians 6:16 and Romans 9–11." *NTS* 56 (2010) 367–95.

———. "Oneself in Another: Participation and the Spirit in Romans 8." In *"In Christ" in Paul*, edited by Michael J. Thate et al., 103–25. Tübingen: Mohr Siebeck, 2014.

———. "Whose Apocalypse? The Identity of the Sons of God in Romans 8:19." *JBL* 121.2 (2002) 263–77.

Ehrensperger, Kathy, and J. Brian Tucker, eds. *Reading Paul in Context: Explorations in Identity Formation: Essays in Honor of William S. Campbell*. London: T. & T. Clark, 2010.

Elliott, Neil. *The Arrogance of Nations: Reading Romans in the Shadow of Empire*. Minneapolis: Fortress, 2008.

———. *The Rhetoric of Romans: Argumentative Constraint and Strategy and Paul's Dialogue with Judaism*. JSNTSup 45. Sheffield: JSOT, 1990.

Enderlein, Steven E. "The Faithfulness of the Second Adam in Romans 3:21–26: A Response to Porter and Cirafesi." *JSPL* 3.1 (2013) 11–24.

———. "To Fall Short or Lack the Glory of God? The Translation and Implications of Romans 3:23." *JSPL* 1.2 (2011) 213–24.

Engberg-Pedersen, Troels. "The Material Spirit: Cosmology and Ethics in Paul." *NTS* 55.2 (2009) 179–97.

Enns, Peter. *Exodus Retold: Ancient Exegesis of the Departure from Egypt in Wis 10:15–21 and 19:1–6*. Atlanta: Scholars, 1997.

———. "Pseudo-Solomon and His Scripture: Biblical Interpretation in the Wisdom of Solomon." In *A Companion to Biblical Interpretation in Early Judaism*, edited by Matthias Henze, 389–412. Grand Rapids: Eerdmans, 2012.

Ensor, Peter. "The Meaning of 'We . . . Died to Sin' in Romans 6:2." *ExpT* 126.5 (2015) 221–30.

Esler, Philip F. *Conflict and Identity in Romans: The Social Setting of Paul's Letter*. Minneapolis: Fortress, 2003.

———. "Sodom Tradition in Romans 1:18–32." *BTB* 34 (2004) 2–16.

Evans, Craig A., ed. *The Interpretation of Scripture in Early Judaism and Christianity*. JSPSup. Sheffield: Academic, 2000.

Fee, Gordon D. *God's Empowering Presence: The Holy Spirit in the Letters of Paul*. Peabody, MA: Hendrickson, 1994.

———. *Pauline Christology: An Exegetical-Theological Study*. Peabody, MA: Hendrickson, 2007.

Fishbane, Michael A. *Biblical Interpretation in Ancient Israel*. Oxford: Clarendon, 1985.

Fisk, Bruce N. "Paul Among the Storytellers: Reading Romans 11 in the Context of Rewritten Bible." In *Paul and Scripture: Extending the Conversation*, edited by Christopher D. Stanley, 55–94. Atlanta: SBL, 2012.

Fitzmyer, Joseph A. *Romans: A New Translation with Introduction and Commentary*. AB. New York: Doubleday, 1993.

Flemming, Dean E. *Contextualization in the New Testament: Patterns for Theology and Mission*. Leicester: Apollos, 2005.

Forman, Mark. "The Politics of Promise: Echoes of Isaiah 54 in Romans 4:19–21." *JSNT* 31.3 (2009) 301–24.

Foster, Robert L. "The Justice of the Gentiles: Revisiting the Purpose of Romans." *CBQ* 76 (2014) 684–703.

Fowl, Stephen E. "Some Uses of Story in Moral Discourse: Reflections on Paul's Moral Discourse and Our Own." *MT* 4.4 (1988) 293–308.

———. *The Story of Christ in the Ethics of Paul: An Analysis of the Function of the Hymnic Material in the Pauline Corpus*. JSNTSup 36. Sheffield: JSOT, 1990.

Freedman, David Noel, ed., *The Anchor Bible Dictionary*. 6 vols. New York: Doubleday, 1992.

Frishman, Judith, and Lucas van Rompay, eds. *The Book of Genesis in Jewish and Oriental Christian Interpretation: A Collection of Essays*. Lovanii: Peeters, 1997.

Garlington, Don B. "The New Perspective on Paul: An Appraisal Two Decades Later." *CTR* 2.2 (2005) 17–38.

———. "The Obedience of Faith in the Letter to the Romans, Part I: The Meaning of hupakoe pisteos (Rom 1:5; 16:26)." *WTJ* 52 (1990) 201–24.

———. "The Obedience of Faith in the Letter to the Romans, Part II: The Obedience of Faith and Judgment by Works." *WTJ* 53 (1991) 47–72.

———. "The Obedience of Faith in the Letter to the Romans, Part III: The Obedience of Christ and the Obedience of the Christian." *WTJ* 55 (1993) 87–112.

———. "Romans 7:14–25 and the Creation Theology of Paul." *TJ* 11 (1990) 197–235.

Garroway, Joshua D. "The Circumcision of Christ: Romans 15:7–13." *JSNT* 34.4 (2012) 303–22.

Gathercole, Simon J. "A Law Unto Themselves: The Gentiles in Romans 2:14–15 Revisited." *JSNT* 24.3 (2002) 27–49.

———. "Romans 1-5 and the 'Weak' and the 'Strong': Pauline Theology, Pastoral Rhetoric, and the Purpose of Romans." *RevExp* 100 (2003) 35-51.

———. *Where Is Boasting?: Early Jewish Soteriology and Paul's Response in Romans 1-5*. Grand Rapids: Eerdmans, 2002.

Gaventa, Beverly Roberts, ed. *Apocalyptic Paul: Cosmos and Anthropos in Romans 5-8*. Waco, TX: Baylor University Press, 2013.

———. "The Cosmic Power of Sin in Paul's Letter to the Romans: Toward a Widescreen Edition." *Interpretation* 58.3 (2004) 229-40.

Gieniusz, Andrzej. "'Debtors to the Spirit' in Romans 8:12? Reasons for the Silence." *NTS* 59 (2013) 61-72.

Gignilliat, Mark. *Paul and Isaiah's Servants: Paul's Theological Reading of Isaiah 40-66 in 2 Corinthians 5:14—6:10*. London: T. & T. Clark, 2007.

Goldingay, John. *Old Testament Theology*. Vol. 1, *Israel's Gospel*. Downers Grove, IL: IVP, 2003.

———. *Psalms*. 3 vols. Grand Rapids: Baker, 2006-2008.

Goodrich, John K. "From Slaves of Sin to Slaves of God: Reconsidering the Origin of Paul's Slavery Metaphor in Romans 6." *BBR* 23.4 (2013) 509-30.

———. "Sold under Sin: Echoes of Exile in Romans 7:14-25." *NTS* 59 (2013) 476-95.

Gorman, Michael J. *Apostle of the Crucified Lord: A Theological Introduction to Paul and His Letters*. Grand Rapids: Eerdmans, 2004.

———. *Becoming the Gospel: Paul, Participation, and Mission*. Grand Rapids: Eerdmans, 2015.

———. *Cruciformity: Paul's Narrative Spirituality of the Cross*. Grand Rapids: Eerdmans, 2001.

———. *The Death of the Messiah and the Birth of the New Covenant: The (Not-So) New Model of the Atonement*. Cambridge: James Clarke, 2014.

———. *Inhabiting the Cruciform God: Kenosis, Justification, and Theosis in Paul's Narrative Soteriology*. Grand Rapids: Eerdmans, 2009.

———. "Romans: The First Christian Treatise on Theosis." *JTI* 5.1 (2011) 13-34.

Grappe, Christian. "Qui me délivrera de ce corps de mort?: L'esprit de vie! Romains 7,24 et 8,2 comme éléments de typologie adamique." *Biblica* 83.4 (2002) 472-92.

Grieb, A. Katherine. *The Story of Romans: A Narrative Defense of God's Righteousness*. Louisville, KY: Westminster John Knox, 2002.

Grogan, Geoffrey. *Psalms*. Two Horizons Old Testament Commentary. Grand Rapids: Eerdmans, 2008.

Guerra, Anthony J. "Romans 4 as Apologetic Theology." *HTR* 81.3 (1988) 251-70.

Haacker, Klaus. *The Theology of Paul's Letter to the Romans*. New Testament Theology. Cambridge: Cambridge University Press, 2003.

Hamilton, Victor P. *The Book of Genesis: Chapters 1-17*. NICOT. Grand Rapids: Eerdmans, 1990.

Harding, Mark, and Alanna Nobbs, eds. *All Things to All Cultures: Paul Among Jews, Greeks, and Romans*. Grand Rapids: Eerdmans, 2013.

Harris, Murray J. *Prepositions and Theology in the Greek New Testament: An Essential Reference Resource for Exegesis*. Grand Rapids: Zondervan, 2012.

Hart, John F. "Paul as Weak in Faith in Romans 7:7-25." *BibSac* 170 (2013) 317-43.

Hawthorne, Gerald F., et al., eds. *Dictionary of Paul and His Letters*. Downers Grove, IL: IVP, 1993.

Hay, David M. "Paul's Understanding of Faith as Participation." In *Paul and His Theology*, edited by Stanley E. Porter, 45–76. Leiden: Brill, 2006.
Hay, David M., and E. Elizabeth Johnson, eds. *Pauline Theology*. Vol. 3, *Romans*. Atlanta: SBL, 1995.
———, eds. *Pauline Theology*. Vol. 4, *Looking Back, Looking Forward*. Atlanta: Scholars, 1997.
Hays, Richard B. "Adam, Israel, Christ—The Question of Covenant in the Theology of Romans: A Response to Leander E. Keck and N. T. Wright." In *Pauline Theology*. Vol. 4, *Romans*, edited by David M. Hay and E. Elizabeth Johnson, 68–86. Atlanta: Scholars, 1997.
———. "Can Narrative Criticism Recover the Theological Unity of Scripture?" *JTI* 2 (2008) 193–211.
———. "Christ Died for the Ungodly: Narrative Soteriology in Paul?" *HBT* 26.1 (2004) 48–68.
———. *The Conversion of the Imagination: Paul as Interpreter of Israel's Scripture*. Grand Rapids: Eerdmans, 2005.
———. *Echoes of Scripture in the Letters of Paul*. New Haven: Yale University Press, 1989.
———. *The Faith of Jesus Christ: The Narrative Substructure of Galatians 3:1—4:11*. 2nd ed. Grand Rapids: Eerdmans, 2002.
———. "Is Paul's Gospel Narratable?" *JSNT* 27.2 (2004) 217–39.
———. "ΠΙΣΤΙΣ and Pauline Christology: What Is at Stake?" In *Pauline Theology*. Vol. 3, *Looking Back, Looking Forward*, edited by David M. Hay and E. Elizabeth Johnson, 35–60. Atlanta: Scholars, 1995.
Henze, Matthias, ed. *Biblical Exegesis at Qumran*. Grand Rapids: Eerdmans, 2005.
———, ed. *A Companion to Biblical Interpretation in Early Judaism*. Grand Rapids: Eerdmans, 2012.
Hodge, Caroline Johnson. *If Sons, Then Heirs: A Study of Kinship and Ethnicity in the Letters of Paul*. New York: Oxford University Press, 2007.
Holland, Tom. *Romans: The Divine Marriage: A Biblical Theological Commentary*. Eugene, OR: Pickwick, 2011.
Holmes, Christopher T. "Utterly Incapacitated: The Neglected Meaning of ΠΑΡΕΣΙΣ in Romans 3:25." *NovT* 55 (2013) 349–66.
Hooker, Morna D. "Adam in Romans 1." *NTS* 6 (1960) 297–306.
———. "Conformity to Christ." *Theology* 116 (2013) 83–92.
———. *From Adam to Christ: Essays on Paul*. Cambridge: Cambridge University Press, 1990.
Horrell, David G. "From Ἀδελφοί to Οἶκος Θεοῦ: Social Transformation in Pauline Christianity." *JBL* 120.2 (2001) 293–311.
———. *Solidarity and Difference: A Contemporary Reading of Paul's Ethics*. 2nd ed. London: T. & T. Clark, 2015.
———. "Solidarity and Difference: Pauline Morality in Romans 14:1—15:13." *Studies in Christian Ethics* 15.2 (2002) 60–78.
Horsley, Richard A. "Paul and Slavery: A Critical Alternative to Recent Readings." *Semeia* 83/84 (1998) 153–200.
Horton, Michael S. *Covenant and Salvation: Union with Christ*. Louisville, KY: Westminster John Knox, 2007.

Hübner, Hans. *Biblische Theologie des Neuen Testaments*. 2 vols. Göttingen: Vandenhoeck & Ruprecht, 1990–1993.

Hughes, Julie A. *Scriptural Allusions and Exegesis in the Hodayot*. Leiden: Brill, 2006.

Hultgren, Arland J. *Paul's Letter to the Romans: A Commentary*. Grand Rapids: Eerdmans, 2011.

Hultgren, Stephen. "The Origin of Paul's Doctrine of the Two Adams in 1 Corinthians 15:45–49." *JSNT* 25 (2003) 343–70.

Hunt, Cherryl, et al. "An Environmental Mantra? Ecological Interest in Romans 8:19–23 and a Modest Proposal for Its Narrative Interpretation." *JTS* 59 (2008) 546–79.

Hyldahl, Niels. "A Reminiscence of the Old Testament at Romans i.23." *NTS* 2 (1955–56) 285–88.

Isaac, E. "1 (Ethiopic Apocalypse of) Enoch." In vol. 1 of *The Old Testament Pseudepigrapha*, edited by James H. Charlesworth, 5–89. Peabody, MA: Hendrickson, 1983.

Ito, Akio. "Romans 2: A Deuteronomistic Reading." *JSNT* 59 (1995) 21–37.

Jackson, T. Ryan. *New Creation in Paul's Letters: A Study of the Historical and Social Setting of a Pauline Concept*. WUNT 2. Tübingen: Mohr Siebeck, 2010.

Jervis, L. Ann. *The Purpose of Romans: A Comparative Letter Structure Investigation*. JSNTSup 55. Sheffield: JSOT, 1991.

Jewett, Robert. "Honor and Shame in the Argument of Romans." In *Putting Body and Soul Together: Essays in Honor of Robin Scroggs*, edited by Virginia Wiles et al., 257–72. Valley Forge, PA: Trinity, 1997.

———. "The Law and the Coexistence of Jews and Gentiles in Romans." *Interpretation* 39 (1985) 341–56.

———. "Major Impulses in the Theological Interpretation of Romans since Barth." *Interpretation* 34 (1980) 17–31.

———. *Romans: A Commentary*. Hermeneia. Minneapolis: Fortress, 2007.

———. "Romans as an Ambassadorial Letter." *Interpretation* 36 (1982) 5–20.

Jipp, Joshua W. "Ancient, Modern, and Future Interpretations of Romans 1:3–4: Reception History and Biblical Interpretation." *JTI* 3 (2009) 241–59.

———. "Rereading the Story of Abraham, Isaac, and 'Us' in Romans 4." *JSNT* 32 (2009) 217–42.

Johnson, M. D. "Life of Adam and Eve: A New Translation and Introduction." In vol. 2 of *The Old Testament Pseudepigrapha*, edited by James H. Charlesworth, 249–95. Peabody, MA: Hendrickson, 1983.

Johnson, Marcus Peter. *One with Christ: An Evangelical Theology of Salvation*. Wheaton: Crossway, 2013.

Johnston, J. William. "Which 'All' Sinned?: Rom 3:23–24 Reconsidered." *NovT* 53 (2011) 153–64.

Juncker, Günther H. "'Children of Promise': Spiritual Paternity and Patriarch Typology in Galatians and Romans." *BBR* 17 (2007) 131–60.

Käsemann, Ernst. *Commentary on Romans*. Translated by Geoffrey William Bromiley. Grand Rapids: Eerdmans, 1980.

Keck, Leander E. *Romans*. ANTC. Nashville: Abingdon, 2005.

Keener, Craig S. *Romans*. NCC. Eugene, OR: Cascade, 2009.

Keesmaat, Sylvia C. "Exodus and the Intertextual Transformation of Tradition in Romans 8:14–30." *JSNT* 54 (1994) 29–56.

———. *Paul and His Story: (Re)-Interpreting the Exodus Tradition*. JSNTSup 181. Sheffield: Academic, 1999.

Khobnya, Svetlana. "'The Root' in Paul's Olive Tree Metaphor (Romans 11:16–24)." *TynB* 64.2 (2013) 257–73.

Kidwell, Brian. "The Adamic Backdrop of Romans." *CTR* 11 (2013) 103–20.

Kim, Seyoon. *Paul and the New Perspective: Second Thoughts on the Origin of Paul's Gospel*. Grand Rapids: Eerdmans, 2001.

———. "Paul's Common Paraenesis (1 Thess. 4–5; Phil. 2–4; and Rom. 12–13): The Correspondence between Romans 1:18–32 and 12:1–2, and the Unity of Romans 12–13." *TynB* 62 (2011) 109–39.

Kinzer, Mark S. "'All Things Under His Feet': Psalm 8 in the New Testament and in Other Jewish Literature of Late Antiquity." PhD diss., University of Michigan, 1995.

Kirk, J. R. Daniel. "Reconsidering Dikaioma in Romans 5:16." *JBL* 126 (2007) 787–92.

———. *Unlocking Romans: Resurrection and the Justification of God*. Grand Rapids: Eerdmans, 2008.

Kister, Menahem. "Romans 5:12–21 against the Background of Torah-Theology and Hebrew Usage." *HTR* 100 (2007) 391–424.

Kraut, Judah. "The Birds and the Babes: The Structure and Meaning of Psalm 8." *JQR* 100 (2010) 10–24.

Krauter, Stefan. "Eva in Röm 7." *ZNW* 99.1 (2008) 1–17.

Kreitzer, L. Joseph. "Christ and Second Adam in Paul." *Communio Viatorum* 32 (1989) 55–101.

Kruse, Colin G. *Paul's Letter to the Romans*. PNTC. Grand Rapids: Eerdmans, 2012.

Kugel, James L. "The Beginnings of Biblical Interpretation." In *A Companion to Biblical Interpretation in Early Judaism*, edited by Matthias Henze, 3–26. Grand Rapids: Eerdmans, 2012.

Kümmel, Werner Georg. *Römer 7 Und Die Bekehrung Des Paulus, Untersuchungen Zum Neuen Testament*. Leipzig: J.C. Hinrichsche Buchhandlung, 1929.

Lambrecht, Jan. "Romans 4: A Critique of N. T. Wright." *JSNT* 36 (2013) 189–94.

Lamp, Jeffery S. "Paul, the Law, Jews, and Gentiles: A Contextual and Exegetical Reading of Romans 2:12–16." *JETS* 42 (1999) 37–51.

Lee, Kye Won. *Living in Union with Christ: The Practical Theology of Thomas F. Torrance*. New York: Peter Lang, 2003.

Légasse, Simon. *L'épître De Paul Aux Romains*. Paris: Éditions du Cerf, 2002.

Leithart, Peter J. "Adam, Moses, and Jesus: A Reading of Romans 5:12–14." *CTJ* 43 (2008) 257–73.

Letham, Robert. *Union with Christ: In Scripture, History, and Theology*. Phillipsburg, NJ: P&R, 2011.

Levison, John R. "Adam and Eve, Life of." In vol. 1 of *The Anchor Bible Dictionary*, edited by David Noel Freedman, 64–66. New York: Doubleday, 1992.

———. "Adam and Eve in Romans 1:18–25 and the Greek Life of Adam and Eve." *NTS* 50 (2004) 519–34.

———. *Portraits of Adam in Early Judaism: From Sirach to 2 Baruch*. JSPSup. Sheffield: JSOT, 1988.

Lincicum, David. *Paul and the Early Jewish Encounter with Deuteronomy*. WUNT 2. Tübingen: Mohr Siebeck, 2010.

Linebaugh, Jonathan A. "Announcing the Human: Rethinking the Relationship between Wisdom of Solomon 13–15 and Romans 1:18–2:11." *NTS* 57 (2011) 214–37.

———. *God, Grace, and Righteousness in Wisdom of Solomon and Paul's Letter to the Romans: Texts in Conversation*. Leiden: Brill, 2013.

Litwa, M. David. *We Are Being Transformed: Deification in Paul's Soteriology*. BZNW 187. Berlin: Walter de Gruyter, 2012.

Longacre, Robert E., and Wilber B. Wallis. "Soteriology and Eschatology in Romans." *JETS* 41 (1998) 367–82.

Longenecker, Bruce, ed. *Narrative Dynamics in Paul: A Critical Assessment*. Louisville, KY: Westminster John Knox, 2002.

———. "ΠΙΣΤΙΣ in Romans 3.25: Neglected Evidence for the 'Faithfulness of Christ'?" *NTS* 39.3 (1993) 478–80.

Longenecker, Richard N. *Biblical Exegesis in the Apostolic Period*. 2nd ed. Grand Rapids: Eerdmans, 1999.

———. *Introducing Romans: Critical Issues in Paul's Most Famous Letter*. Grand Rapids: Eerdmans, 2011.

———. "Prolegomena to Paul's Use of Scripture in Romans." *BBR* 7 (1997) 145–68.

———. "Sharing in Their Spiritual Blessings?: The Stories of Israel in Romans and Galatians." In *Narrative Dynamics in Paul: A Critical Assessment*, edited by Bruce W. Longenecker, 58–84. Louisville: Westminster John Knox, 2002.

Lowe, Bruce A. "Oh Dia! How Is Romans 4:25 to Be Understood?" *JTS* 57 (2006) 149–57.

Lowe, Chuck. "'There Is No Condemnation' (Romans 8:1): But Why Not?" *JETS* 42 (1999) 231–50.

Lucas, Alec J. "Reorienting the Structural Paradigm and Social Significance of Romans 1:18–32." *JBL* 131 (2012) 121–41.

Macaskill, Grant. "Incarnational Ontology and the Theology of Participation in Paul." In *In Christ in Paul*, edited by Michael J. Thate et al., 87–101. WUNT 2. Tübingen: Mohr Siebeck, 2014.

———. *Union with Christ in the New Testament*. Oxford: Oxford University Press, 2014.

Marshall, I. Howard. *New Testament Theology: Many Witnesses, One Gospel*. Downers Grove, IL: IVP, 2004.

Martyn, J. Luis. *Theological Issues in the Letters of Paul*. Nashville, Abingdom, 1997.

Matera, Frank J. *Romans*. Paideia. Grand Rapids: Baker, 2010.

Mathewson, Mark D. "Moral Intuitionism and the Law Inscribed on Our Hearts." *JETS* 42 (1999) 629–43.

McDonald, Patricia M. "Romans 5:1–11 as a Rhetorical Bridge." *JSNT* 40 (1990) 81–96.

McFarland, Orrey. "Whose Abraham, Which Promise? Genesis 15:6 in Philo's De Virtutibus and Romans 4." *JSNT* 35 (2012) 107–29.

Meech, John L. *Paul in Israel's Story: Self and Community at the Cross*. New York: Oxford University Press, 2006.

Melanchthon, Philipp. *Commentary on Romans*. Translated by Fred Kramer. St. Louis: Concordia, 1992.

Michel, Otto. *Der Brief an die Römer*. Göttingen: Vandenhoeck & Ruprecht, 1978 [1955].

Moberly, R.W.L. *The Theology of the Book of Genesis*. Old Testament Theology. Cambridge: Cambridge University Press, 2009.

Moo, Douglas J. "'Law,' 'Works of the Law,' and Legalism in Paul." *WTJ* 45 (1983) 73–100.

———. *The Epistle to the Romans*. NICNT. Grand Rapids: Eerdmans, 1996.

Moo, Jonathan. "Romans 8:19–22 and Isaiah's Cosmic Covenant." *NTS* 54 (2008) 74–89.

Mounce, Robert H. *Romans*. NAC. Nashville: Broadman & Holman, 1995.

Moxnes, Halvor. "Honor and Righteousness in Romans." *JSNT* 10 (1988) 61–78.

———. "Honor, Shame, and the Outside World in Paul's Letter to the Romans." In *The Social World of Formative Christianity and Judaism: Essays in Tribute to Howard Clark Kee*, edited by Jacob Neusner et al., 207–18. Philadelphia: Fortress, 1988.

———. *Theology in Conflict: Studies in Paul's Understanding of God in Romans*. Leiden: Brill, 1980.

Moyise, Steve. *Paul and Scripture: Studying the New Testament Use of the Old Testament*. Grand Rapids: Baker, 2010.

Nanos, Mark D. *The Mystery of Romans: The Jewish Context of Paul's Letter*. Minneapolis: Fortress, 1996.

———. "To the Churches within the Synagogues of Rome." In *Reading Paul's Letter to the Romans*, edited by Jerry L. Sumney, 11–28. Atlanta: SBL, 2012.

Neusner, Jacob, et al., eds. *The Social World of Formative Christianity and Judaism: Essays in Tribute to Howard Clark Kee*. Philadelphia: Fortress, 1988.

Newman, Carey C. *Paul's Glory-Christology: Tradition and Rhetoric*. NovTSup. Leiden: Brill, 1992.

Noffke, Eric. "Man of Glory or First Sinner?: Adam in the Book of Sirach." *ZAW* 119.4 (2007) 618–24.

O'Collins, Gerald. "The Second Adam." *America* 190 (2004) 10–12.

Oropeza, B. J. "Paul and Theodicy: Intertextual Thoughts on God's Justice and Faithfulness to Israel in Romans 9–11." *NTS* 53 (2007) 57–80.

Ortlund, Dane C. "Inaugurated Glorification: Revisiting Romans 8:30." *JETS* 57.1 (2014) 111–33.

———. "Justified by Faith, Judged According to Works: Another Look at a Pauline Paradox." *JETS* 52.2 (2009) 323–39.

Patte, Daniel, and Cristina Grenholm, eds. *Reading Israel in Romans: Legitimacy and Plausibility of Divergent Interpretations*. Harrisburg, PA: Trinity Press International, 2000.

Pelser, G. M. M. "Could the 'Formulas' Dying and Rising with Christ Be Expressions of Pauline Mysticism?" *Neotestamentica* 32.1 (1998) 115–34.

Petersen, Norman R. *Rediscovering Paul: Philemon and the Sociology of Paul's Narrative World*. Philadelphia: Fortress, 1985.

Peterson, Robert A. *Salvation Applied By the Spirit: Union with Christ*. Wheaton: Crossway, 2015.

Poirier, John C. "Romans 5:13–14 and the Universality of Law." *NovT* 38.4 (1996) 344–58.

Porter, Calvin L. "Romans 1:18–32: Its Role in the Developing Argument." *NTS* 40.2 (1994) 210–28.

Porter, Stanley E. "Allusions and Echoes." In *As It Is Written: Studying Paul's Use of Scripture*, edited by Stanley E. Porter and Christpher D. Stanley, 29–40. Atlanta: SBL, 2008.

———. "The Argument of Romans 5: Can a Rhetorical Question Make a Difference?" *JBL* 110.4 (1991) 655–77.
———. *Paul and His Theology*. Pauline Studies. Leiden: Brill, 2006.
Porter, Stanley E., and Christopher D. Stanley, eds. *As It Is Written: Studying Paul's Use of Scripture*. SBLSS. Atlanta: SBL, 2008.
Postell, Seth D. *Adam as Israel: Genesis 1–3 as the Introduction to the Torah and Tanakh*. Eugene, OR: Pickwick, 2011.
Quesnel, Michel. "La Figure De Moïse En Romains 9–11." *NTS* 49 (2003) 321–35.
Rapinchuk, Mark. "Universal Sin and Salvation in Romans 5:12–21." *JETS* 42 (1999) 427–41.
Ridderbos, Herman N. *Paul: An Outline of His Theology*. Grand Rapids: Eerdmans, 1975.
Röhser, Günter. "Paulus Und Die Herrschaft Der Sünde." *ZNW* 103.1 (2012) 84–110.
Rodriguez, Rafael. *If You Call Yourself a Jew: Reappraising Paul's Letter to the Romans*. Eugene, OR: Cascade, 2014.
Rosner, Brian S. "Paul and the Law: What He Does Not Say." *JSNT* 32 (2010) 405–19.
Sabou, Sorin. "A Note on Romans 6:5: The Representation (Omoiōma) of His Death." *TynB* 55 (2004) 219–29.
Sailhamer, John H. *Introduction to Old Testament Theology: A Canonical Approach*. Grand Rapids: Zondervan, 1995.
———. *The Meaning of the Pentateuch: Revelation, Composition, and Interpretation*. Downers Grove, IL: IVP, 2009.
———. *The Pentateuch as Narrative: A Biblical-Theological Commentary*. Grand Rapids: Zondervan, 1992.
Sanders, E. P. *Paul and Palestinian Judaism: A Comparison of Patterns of Religion*. Philadelphia: Fortress, 1977.
Sarna, Nahum M. *Exodus*. JPS. Philadelphia: Jewish Publication Society, 1991.
Schellenberg, Ryan S. "Does Paul Call Adam a 'Type' of Christ?: An Exegetical Note on Romans 5,14." *ZNW* 105 (2014) 54–63.
Schnelle, Udo. *Apostle Paul: His Life and Theology*. Translated by M. Eugene Boring. Grand Rapids: Baker, 2005.
———. *Theology of the New Testament*. Translated by M. Eugene Boring. Grand Rapids: Baker, 2009.
———. "Transformation Und Partizipation Als Grundgedanken Paulinischer Theologie." *NTS* 47.1 (2001) 58–75.
———, ed. *The Letter to the Romans*. Bibliotheca Ephemeridum Theologicarum Lovaniensium 226. Walpole, MA: Peeters, 2009.
Schreiner, Thomas R. "Did Paul Believe in Justification by Works? Another Look at Romans 2." *BBR* 3 (1993) 131–55.
———. *Paul, Apostle of God's Glory in Christ: A Pauline Theology*. Downers Grove, IL: IVP, 2006.
———. *Romans*. BECNT. Grand Rapids: Baker, 1998.
———. "'Works of Law' in Paul." *NovT* 33 (1991) 217–44.
Schweitzer, Albert. *The Mysticism of Paul the Apostle*. Translated by William Montgomery. Baltimore: The Johns Hopkins University Press, 1998.
Schweizer, Eduard. "Dying and Rising with Christ." *NTS* 14 (1967) 1–14.
Scobie, Charles H. H. *The Ways of Our God: An Approach to Biblical Theology*. Grand Rapids: Eerdmans, 2003.

Scroggs, Robin. *The Last Adam: A Study in Pauline Anthropology*. Philadelphia: Fortress, 1966.
Seifrid, Mark A. *Christ, Our Righteousness: Paul's Theology of Justification*. NSBT. Downers Grove, IL: IVP, 2000.
———. "Romans." In *Commentary on the New Testament Use of the Old Testament*, edited by G. K. Beale and D. A. Carson, 607–94. Grand Rapids: Baker, 2007.
Shaw, David A. "Apocalyptic and Covenant: Perspectives on Paul or Antinomies at War?" *JSNT* 36 (2013) 155–71.
Shemesh, Aharon. "The Scriptural Background of the Penal Code in the Rule of the Community and Damascus Document." *DSD* 15.2 (2008) 191–224.
Skehan, Patrick W., and Alexander A. Di Lella. *The Wisdom of Ben Sira: A New Translation with Notes*. AB. New York: Doubleday, 1987.
Smith, Philip C. "God's New Covenant Faithfulness in Romans." *ResQ* 50 (2008) 235–48.
Snodgrass, Klyne. "Spheres of Influence: A Possible Solution to the Problem of Paul and the Law." *JSNT* 32 (1988) 93–113.
Snyman, A.H. "Style and the Rhetorical Situation of Romans 8:31–39." *NTS* 34 (1988) 218–31.
Soderlund, Sven, and N. T. Wright, eds. *Romans and the People of God: Essays in Honor of Gordon D. Fee on the Occasion of His 65th Birthday*. Grand Rapids: Eerdmans, 1999.
Spitaler, Peter. "An Integrative, Synergistic Reading of Romans 1–3." *BI* 19 (2011) 33–71.
Stanley, Christopher D. *Arguing with Scripture: The Rhetoric of Quotations in the Letters of Paul*. New York: T. & T. Clark, 2004.
———. *Paul and the Language of Scripture: Citation Technique in the Pauline Epistles and Contemporary Literature*. Society for New Testament Studies 69. Cambridge: Cambridge University Press, 1992.
———. "Paul's 'Use' of Scripture: Why the Audience Matters." In *As It Is Written: Studying Paul's Use of Scripture*, edited by Stanley E. Porter and Christopher D. Stanley, 125–55. Atlanta: SBL, 2008.
———. "'Pearls Before Swine'?: Did Paul's Audiences Understand His Biblical Quotations?" *NovT* 41.2 (1999) 124–44.
———, ed. *Paul and Scripture: Extending the Conversation*. Atlanta: SBL, 2012.
Steenburg, Dave. "The Worship of Adam and Christ as the Image of God." *JSNT* (1990) 95–109.
Stenschke, Christoph. "Römer 9–11 als Teil des Römerbriefes." In *Between Gospel and Election*, edited by Florian Wilk and J. Ross Wagner, 197–225. WUNT. Tübingen: Mohr Siebeck, 2010.
Stone, Michael E. *Ancient Judaism: New Visions and Views*. Grand Rapids: Eerdmans, 2011.
Stowers, Stanley K. *A Rereading of Romans: Justice, Jews, and Gentiles*. New Haven: Yale University Press, 1994.
Stuhlmacher, Peter. *Biblische Theologie des Neuen Testaments*. 2 vols. Göttingen: Vandenhoeck & Ruprecht, 1992–1999.
———. *Paul's Letter to the Romans: A Commentary*. Translated by Scott J. Hafemann. Louisville, KY: Westminster John Knox, 1994.
Sumney, Jerry L., ed. *Reading Paul's Letter to the Romans*. Atlanta: SBL, 2012.

Sun, Wendel. "Biblical Theology and Cross-Cultural Theological Education: The Epistle to the Romans as a Model." *Global Missiology* 4.12 (July 2015) 1-14. ojs. globalmissiology.org/index.php/english/article/view/1809.

———. "Difficult Texts: Romans 6:14." *Theology* 120.3 (May-June 2017) 208-10.

———. "Seeking (Exchanged) Glory: The Gentiles of Romans 2." *Journal of Asian Evangelical Theology* 20.2 (Sept. 2016) 45-54.

Tannehill, Robert C. *Dying and Rising with Christ: A Study in Pauline Theology.* BZNW. Berlin: Töpelmann, 1967.

Tanner, J. Paul. "The New Covenant and Paul's Quotations from Hosea in Romans 9:25-26." *BibSac* 162 (2005) 95-110.

Tate, Marvin E. "An Exposition of Psalm 8." *PRS* 28 (2001) 343-59.

Taylor, John W. "From Faith to Faith: Romans 1:17 in the Light of Greek Idiom." *NTS* 50 (2004) 337-48.

Teeter, D. Andrew. "On 'Exegetical Function' in Rewritten Scripture: Inner-Biblical Exegesis and the Abram/Ravens Narrative in *Jubilees*." *HTR* 106.4 (2013) 373-402.

Thate, Michael J., et al., eds. *"In Christ" in Paul: Explorations in Paul's Theology of Union and Participation.* WUNT 2. Tübingen: Mohr Siebeck, 2014.

Thielman, Frank. "The Story of Israel and the Theology of Romans 5-8." In *Pauline Theology.* Vol. 3, *Romans*, edited by David M. Hay and E. Elizabeth Johnson, 169-95. Atlanta: SBL 2002.

Tobin, Thomas H. "What Shall We Say that Abraham Found? The Controversy Behind Romans 4." *HTR* 88 (1995) 437-52.

Tomson, Peter J. "What Did Paul Mean by 'Those Who Know the Law'? (Rom 7:1)." *NTS* 49 (2003) 573-81.

Toolan, Michael J. *Narrative: A Critical Linguistic Approach.* London: Routledge, 1988.

Tooman, William A. "Between Imitation and Interpretation: Reuse of Scripture and Composition in *Hodayot* (1QHa) 11:6-19." *DSD* 18 (2011) 54-73.

———. *Gog of Magog: Reuse of Scripture and Compositional Technique in Ezekiel 38-39.* Tübingen: Mohr Siebeck, 2011.

Tromp, Johannes. "Literary and Exegetical Issues in the Story of Adam's Death and Burial (GLAE 31-42)." In *The Book of Genesis in Jewish and Oriental Christian Interpretation: A Collection of Essays*, edited by Judith Frishman and Lucas van Rompay, 25-41. Lovanii: Peeters, 1997.

———. "The Story of Our Lives: The Qz-Text of the Life of Adam and Eve, the Apostle Paul, and the Jewish-Christian Oral Tradition Concerning Adam and Eve." *NTS* 50.2 (2004) 205-23.

Tsui, Teresa Kuo-Yu. "Reconsidering Pauline Juxtaposition of Indicative and Imperative (Romans 6:1-14) in Light of Pauline Apocalypticism." *CBQ* 75 (2013) 297-314.

Turner, Geoffrey. "The Righteousness of God in Psalms and Romans." *SJT* 63 (2010) 285-301.

Tzoref, Shani. "The Use of Scripture in the Community Rule." In *A Companion to Biblical Interpretation in Early Judaism*, edited by Matthias Henze, 203-34. Grand Rapids: Eerdmans, 2012.

Udoh, Fabian E., ed. *Redefining First-Century Jewish and Christian Identities: Essays in Honor of Ed Parish Sanders.* Notre Dame: University of Notre Dame Press, 2008.

van Ruiten, Jacques. "Biblical Interpretation in the Book of *Jubilees*." In *A Companion to Biblical Interpretation in Ancient Judaism*, edited by Matthias Henze, 121-56. Grand Rapids: Eerdmans, 2012

VanGemeren, Willem A. *Psalms*. Edited by Tremper Longman III and David E. Garland. EBC 5. Rev. ed. Grand Rapids: Zondervan, 2008.

Vanhoozer, Kevin J. "From 'Blessed in Christ' to 'Being in Christ': The State of the Union and the Place of Participation in Paul's Discourse, New Testament Exegesis, and Systematic Theology Today." In *"In Christ" in Paul*, edited by Michael J. Thate et al., 3–33. Tübingen: Mohr Siebeck, 2014.

VanderKam, James C. "Sinai Revisited." In *Biblical Interpretation at Qumran*, edited by Matthias Henze, 44–60. Grand Rapids: Eerdmans, 2005.

van Kooten, George H. *Paul's Anthropology in Context*. Tübingen: Mohr Siebeck, 2008.

Vickers, Brian. "Grammar and Theology in the Interpretation of Rom 5:12." *TJ* 27 (2006) 271–88.

Wagner, J. Ross. "The Christ, Servant of Jew and Gentile: A Fresh Approach to Romans 15:8–9." *JBL* 116.3 (1997) 473–85.

———. *Heralds of the Good News: Isaiah and Paul "in Concert" in the Letter to the Romans*. NovTSup. Leiden: Brill, 2002.

Walker, William O., Jr. "Romans 1:18—2:29: A Non-Pauline Interpolation?" *NTS* 45 (1999) 533–52.

Wallace, Daniel B. *Greek Grammar Beyond the Basics: An Exegetical Syntax of the New Testament*. Grand Rapids: Zondervan, 1996.

Waltke, Bruce K., and Charles Yu. *An Old Testament Theology: An Exegetical, Canonical, and Thematic Approach*. Grand Rapids: Zondervan, 2007.

Ware, James P. "Law, Christ, and Covenant: Paul's Theology of the Law in Romans 3:19–20." *JTS* 62 (2011) 513–40.

Watson, Francis. "Is There a Story in These Texts?" In *Narrative Dynamics in Paul*, edited by Bruce Longenecker, 231–39. Louisville, KY: Westminster John Knox, 2002.

———. *Paul and the Hermeneutics of Faith*. London; New York: T. & T. Clark, 2004.

———. *Paul, Judaism, and the Gentiles: Beyond the New Perspective*. Rev. and exp. ed. Grand Rapids: Eerdmans, 2007.

———. "Scripture in Pauline Theology: How Far Down Does It Go?" *JTI* 2 (2008) 181–92.

———. *Text and Truth: Redefining Biblical Theology*. Grand Rapids: Eerdmans, 1997.

———. *Text, Church and World: Biblical Interpretation in Theological Perspective*. Grand Rapids: Eerdmans, 1994.

Watts, Rikki E. "Consolation or Confrontation: Isaiah 40–55 and the Delay of the New Exodus." *TynB* 41 (1990) 31–59.

———. "Echoes from the Past: Israel's Ancient Traditions and the Destiny of the Nations in Isaiah 40–55." *JSOT* 28 (2004) 481–508.

Wedderburn, A. J. M. *The Reasons for Romans, Studies of the New Testament and Its World*. Edinburgh: T. & T. Clark, 1988.

Wells, Kyle B. *Grace and Agency in Paul and Second Temple Judaism*. NovTSup. Leiden: Brill, 2014.

Wenham, Gordon J. *Genesis 1—15*. WBC. Waco, TX: Word, 1987.

Westerholm, Stephen. *Perspectives Old and New on Paul: The "Lutheran" Paul and His Critics*. Grand Rapids: Eerdmans, 2004.

———. "The Righteousness of the Law and the Righteousness of Faith in Romans." *Interpretation* 58 (2004) 253–64.

White, R. Fowler. "The Last Adam and His Seed: An Exercise in Theological Preemption." *TJ* 6 (1985) 60–73.

Wilckens, Ulrich. *Der Brief an Die Römer*. 3 vols. EKKNT. Zürich: Benziger; Neukirchen-Vluyn: Neukirchener Verlag, 1978–1982.

Wiles, Virginia, et al., eds. *Putting Body and Soul Together: Essays in Honor of Robin Scroggs*. Valley Forge, PA: Trinity, 1997.

Wilk, Florian, and J. Ross Wagner, eds. *Between Gospel and Election*. WUNT. Tübingen: Mohr Siebeck, 2010.

Williams, Sam K. "Again *Pistis Christou*." *CBQ* 49.3 (1987) 431–47.

Windsor, Lionel J. *Paul and the Vocation of Israel: How Paul's Jewish Identity Informs His Apostolic Ministry with Special Reference to Romans*. BZNW. Berlin: Walter de Gruyter, 2014.

Wischmeyer, Oda. "Römer 2.1–24 Als Teil Der Gerichtsrede Des Paulus Gegen Die Menschheit." *NTS* 52 (2006) 356–76.

Wise, Michael, et al. *The Dead Sea Scrolls: A New Translation*. Rev. ed. San Francisco: Harper, 2005.

Witherington, Ben. *Paul's Narrative Thought World: The Tapestry of Tragedy and Triumph*. Louisville, KY: Westminster John Knox, 1994.

Witherington, Ben, and Darlene Hyatt. *Paul's Letter to the Romans: A Socio-Rhetorical Commentary*. Grand Rapids: Eerdmans, 2004.

Woyke, Johannes. "'Einst' Und 'Jetzt' in Röm 1–3?: Zur Bedeutung Von Νυνι Δε in Röm 3,21." *ZNW* 92 (2001) 185–206.

Wright, N. T. *The Climax of the Covenant: Christ and the Law in Pauline Theology*. Minneapolis: Fortress, 1992.

———. "Israel's Scriptures in Paul's Narrative Theology." *Theology* 115 (2012) 323–29.

———. *Justification: God's Plan and Paul's Vision*. Downers Grove, IL: IVP, 2009.

———. "The Law in Romans 2." In *Paul and the Mosaic Law*, edited by James D. G. Dunn, 131–50. Grand Rapids: Eerdmans, 2001.

———. "The Letter to the Romans." In *The New Interpreter's Bible*. Vol. 10, edited by Leander Keck, 393–770. Nashville: Abingdon, 2002.

———. "New Exodus, New Inheritance." In *Romans and the People of God*, edited by Sven Soderlund and N. T. Wright, 26–35. Grand Rapids: Eerdmans, 1999.

———. *The New Testament and the People of God*. London: SPCK, 1993.

———. *Paul and the Faithfulness of God*. COQG. Minneapolis: Fortress, 2013.

———. "Paul and the Patriarch: The Role of Abraham in Romans 4." *JSNT* 35 (2013) 207–41.

———. *Paul: In Fresh Perspective*. Minneapolis: Fortress, 2005.

———. *Pauline Perspectives: Essays on Paul, 1978–2013*. Minneapolis: Fortress, 2013.

———. *The Resurrection of the Son of God*. COQG. London: SPCK, 2003.

———. "Romans 2:17—3:9: A Hidden Clue to the Meaning of Romans." *JSPL* 2 (2012) 1–25.

———. "Romans and the Theology of Paul." In vol. 3 of *Pauline Theology*, edited by David M. Hay and E. Elizabeth Johnson, 30–67. Atlanta: SBL, 2002.

———. "Translating Δικαιοσύνη: A Response." *ExpT* 125 (2014) 487–90.

———. *What Saint Paul Really Said: Was Paul of Tarsus the Real Founder of Christianity?* Grand Rapids: Eerdmans, 1997.

Wu, Jackson. "Paul Writes to the Greek First and Also to the Jew: The Missiological Significance of Understanding Paul's Purpose in Romans." *JETS* 56 (2013) 765–79.

———. *Saving God's Face: A Chinese Contextualization of Salvation through Honor and Shame*. EMS Dissertation Series. Pasadena, CA: William Carey, 2012.

Young, Stephen L. "Paul's Ethnic Discourse on 'Faith': Christ's Faithfulness and Gentile Access to the Judean God in Romans 3:21—5:1." *HTR* 108 (2015) 30–51.

———. "Romans 1:1–5 and Paul's Christological Use of Hab 2:4 in Rom 1:17: An Underutilized Consideration in the Debate." *JSNT* 34 (2012) 277–85.

Zakovitch, Yair. "Inner-Biblical Interpretation." In *A Companion to Biblical Interpretation in Early Judaism*, edited by Matthias Henze, 27–63. Grand Rapids: Eerdmans, 2012.

Index of Ancient Documents

OLD TESTAMENT

Genesis

1–3	41, 42, 43, 49, 50, 51, 52, 53, 55, 73, 224
1:1	44
1:20	48
1:24	48
1:26–28	44
1:27	44, 45
1:28	56, 75, 173, 181
2:17	44, 48, 73, 96, 104, 190
3	42, 46, 47, 48, 49, 53, 54, 59, 64, 70, 73, 82, 88, 91, 95, 96, 97, 100, 103, 181, 230
3:13	91, 94, 104
3:15	104, 141,
5	101, 195
12	73
12:3	75, 147
15	73, 147
15:6	145, 146
17	147
17:5	75
18:18	147
22:18	147

Exodus

4:22–23	101
4:23	195
11:7	169
13:17–22	194
14:4	167
19–20	27
19:6	127
20:17	95
24	27
32	46, 47, 95, 210
33:19	210

Leviticus

16:2	142
19	27

Numbers

14:20–25	96
16–17	27
31:21	188

Deuteronomy

9:4	114, 215, 215, 217
23	27
30:6	128, 129, 131, 216
30:10	119
30:11–14	216
30:12	215, 217
30:14	217
30:15	96, 190
32	101, 195

Job

40:10	61

Psalms

8	56–58, 68, 69, 71, 137
8:5–8	58
8:5	58
8:6	60, 67, 68
21:6	156
30:1–2	138
44:23	202
89:27	200
89:28	103
106:20	44, 46, 50, 55, 112

Isaiah

6:3	198
11:10	227
28:16	79, 215, 216, 218
35:1–2	100, 198
44:3	156
50:7	202
50:8	202
52:3	171
52:5	124, 125, 126, 171
52:6	125
52:7	171
53:10–12	149
53:11	171
53:12	148, 149
54:10	190

Jeremiah

2:11	47, 50
31:31–34	118, 119, 129, 131, 189
31:33	118, 119, 121, 123, 177

Ezekiel

28:12	68
36	80, 118, 126, 127, 129, 155, 167, 182, 189,
36:16–21	126
36:20	126
36:22–23	126
36:25–27	126, 131, 167
36:26	121, 126, 156, 182, 191,
36:27	189
36:28	156
37	175, 189
37:5	189
43:1–5	198

Daniel

7	58

Hosea

1–2	178
11:1	101

Habakkuk

2:4	212

APOCRYPHA

Wisdom of Solomon

2:23–24	52
3:2	28
7:6	28
10:1	53
10:15–21	28
13–14	44, 52
15:1–4	46
19:1–9	28

PSEUDEPIGRAPHA

Jubilees

1:7–18	24
8–9	52
50:5	24

Sirach

44–50	24
49:16	65, 66

1 Enoch

85–90	24

Greek Life of Adam and Eve

19:3	93
20–21	54, 69
20:2	54
21:6	54

4 Ezra

7:11	94

Apocalypse of Abraham

24	94

Luke

3:38	101

Romans

1:1-4	135
1:3-4	109, 123, 161, 165, 166, 202, 208, 227, 234
1:1-6	12
1:1	12
1:2	1, 25, 89
1:4	75, 101, 149, 193
1:5	60, 109, 155, 176, 212, 220
1:6	110, 164, 176, 210
1:7	120, 131
1:11	12
1:14	12
1:17	1, 92, 134, 212, 214
1:18—2:12	111
1:18-32	43-55, 60, 107, 108, 111, 112, 113, 115, 116, 125, 130, 145, 185, 225, 227, 230, 231
1:20	44, 45, 50, 74, 75, 100, 113
1:21-24	61
1:21	59, 100, 122, 125
1:23	44, 45, 46, 47, 48, 50, 54, 55, 59, 60, 99, 125, 197, 210
1:24	48, 92, 122, 226
1:25	44, 48, 54, 208,
1:26-27	44, 48, 52
1:32	44, 49, 92, 113
2:1-11	111, 113
2:1	111, 112, 113, 118
2:4	118
2:5	118, 129, 130, 157
2:6	118, 121
2:7	59, 118, 125, 198
2:10	59, 60, 118, 198
2:13	114
2:14-16	110, 112, 113, 114, 116, 124
2:14-15	60, 107, 114
2:14	116, 122
2:15	115, 118-23, 128, 129, 145, 177, 189, 208, 217, 225
2:16	122, 123, 124
2:17-24	124
2:23	61, 124
2:24	1, 124-27, 129
2:25-29	126, 127, 147, 185, 189
2:25	127
2:26	127, 145, 146, 189
2:27	116, 127
2:28-29	110, 113, 114, 115, 123, 128, 209
2:29	60, 112, 122, 128, 129, 139, 182, 186, 192, 216, 217, 218
3:2	28, 127
3:4	1
3:5	134, 135
3:10	115
3:10-18	116, 117, 134
3:11	60, 117, 118
3:12	117
3:21-26	64, 71, 80, 132-44, 158, 163, 175, 212, 213, 214, 231
3:21	25, 89, 132, 153, 175, 185
3:22	61, 62, 71, 133, 135, 136, 140, 142, 162
3:23	47, 56-71, 79, 81, 85, 92, 99, 107, 132, 134, 137, 138, 141, 142, 156, 160, 163, 167, 197, 230
3:24	138, 139, 141, 160, 171, 176, 197, 199, 211, 214, 220
3:25	80, 148, 188
3:26	143, 145, 154, 162, 213
3:29-30	209
4:1	145
4:2	145, 155
4:5	74, 107, 156
4:9-12	146, 150
4:13	147, 196

Romans (continued)

4:16–18	147
4:17	1, 74, 75, 147, 211
4:20	72, 73, 74, 79, 100, 198
4:21	75
4:24–25	148, 181, 234
4:24	75
4:25	149
5:1–11	78, 81, 153–57, 158, 159, 180, 202
5:1	80, 154, 190, 213
5:2	79, 176, 197, 211, 220
5:5	79, 177, 217
5:6–11	223
5:8	80, 201
5:9	157
5:10	157, 193, 223
5:11	158
5:12–21	40, 64, 67, 71, 77–90, 92, 97, 104, 107, 138, 153, 157, 158–64, 166, 169, 175, 176, 181, 183, 186, 213, 231
5:12–14	159, 160
5:12	62, 63, 81, 83, 85, 183, 184, 191, 210
5:13	87
5:15	176
5:16	184, 185, 186
5:17	171, 173, 176
5:18–21	162
5:18	81, 185
5:19	81, 162, 188
5:20	165, 176, 187
5:21	81, 85, 100, 171, 176
6:1–4	166, 168, 180
6:1–11	157, 164–74, 178, 195, 202, 221
6:2	165, 168, 179, 232
6:3–4	167, 186, 223
6:3	179, 186
6:4	165, 168, 173, 179, 182, 223, 234
6:5–11	167
6:5	149, 157, 164, 179, 199
6:6–7	168–72
6:6	172, 179
6:7	170, 171, 172, 184
6:8	182
6:11	146
6:12–23	174–77, 213
6:12–14	174
6:12	92, 171
6:14	179
6:15–23	176, 177
6:17	177, 218
6:18	184
6:23	177, 223
7:1–6	178, 181, 182
7:1	178, 179
7:4	178, 179, 180, 182, 183
7:5	178, 181
7:6	28, 182
7:7–13	90–98, 177, 181, 210
7:7–8	92
7:7	92
7:8	87
7:9	92, 94
7:10	92
7:11	91, 92, 104, 108, 226
7:12	92
7:13–25	96
7:13	97
7:25	109, 184, 185, 208
8:1	99, 184, 185, 192, 201, 202
8:1–11	183–92, 194, 213
8:2–4	186, 188
8:2	189, 223
8:3	35, 99, 101, 174, 193, 200, 208, 223, 234
8:4	99, 187, 189, 208, 225
8:5–8	190, 193
8:6	184, 190
8:10	149
8:9–11	190, 193, 199, 207, 208
8:11	189, 192, 199
8:12–17	99, 101, 193–96
8:14–17	195, 199, 207
8:14	99, 101, 193
8:16	122, 195, 215
8:17–30	60
8:17	99, 197, 201
8:18	99, 102, 198, 201, 211, 216
8:18–30	196–200
8:19	101
8:19–22	99, 100, 101, 102, 108

8:21	209, 216	11:17	221
8:23–27	199	11:17–24	221
8:27	218	11:21–22	221
8:28–30	99, 108, 219	11:23	222
8:29	102, 193, 199, 225	11:23–24	221
8:30	197, 201	11:26	1
8:31	201	11:33–36	206
8:31–39	200–203, 205, 208	12–16	222–28, 232
8:32	193, 202	12:1	223
8:33–34	202	12:1–2	223
8:36	1	12:3–8	180, 223, 226
8:39	156, 207	12:5	224
9:1	4, 206	12:9—13:7	225
9:1–5	206–9	13:1–7	225
9:4	207–8	13:8–10	225
9:5	208	13:14	92, 223, 225, 226
9:6–29	206, 209–12	14:1—15:13	13, 226
9:13	1	15:1–13	226
9:15	210	15:3	1
9:16	210	15:6	61
9:17–18	220	15:7	227
9:19–22	210	15:8–9	227
9:23	211	15:9	1
9:24	210, 211	15:12	227
9:30—10:21	206, 212–19	15:14–33	13
9:30	212	15:21	1
9:33	1, 215, 216, 218	16:18–20	39, 98, 103–5, 204
10:1	217	16:20	104, 201
10:3	214, 215, 218		
10:4	215	## 1 Corinthians	
10:5–21	212	9:23	222
10:6	212, 214	15:24–28	56
10:6–8	214, 215, 216	15:49	200
10:9	212, 221	15:51–54	225
10:9–10	217		
10:11	212, 215, 216, 218	## 2 Corinthians	
10:14–17	212	3:18	200
10:15	1	4:4	200
11:1	220	5:1–4	225
11:1–36	219–22		
11:2–5	25, 29	## Galatians	
11:2	219	3:26–27	225
11:8	1		
11:11	220	## Colossians	
11:12	220	1:15	200
11:13	205	1:27	199
11:14	220	3:9–10	225
11:15	220, 221		

Colossians (continued)
3:12   225

Ephesians
4:20–24   225
6:10   225

Hebrews
8   119
10   119

DEAD SEA SCROLLS

Damascus Document
3:9–11   24
3:12–21   25
3:20   66, 67

Community Rule
4:23   66, 67

Hodayot
4:15   66

Pseudo-Ezekiel
4Q383–391   27

The Words of Heavenly Lights
1Q504 Frag. 8   68

Index of Names and Subjects

Abraham, 2, 7, 23, 24, 27, 33, 34, 72–76, 100, 127, 136, 144–50, 154, 155, 175, 180, 181, 196, 201, 203, 205, 208, 209, 211, 212, 216, 228, 230, 231, 232
Adam-Christology, 4, 6, 66, 87,
Adams, Edward, 30, 44, 72, 74, 75, 94, 95, 99, 200
adoption, 108, 193, 194, 199, 200, 207,
allusion, 1, 5, 8, 11, 16, 16, 17, 18, 19, 20, 21, 25, 26–29, 32, 34, 36, 38, 39, 40, 41, 42, 43, 44, 45, 46, 48, 49, 50, 51, 53, 54, 55, 56, 58, 61, 63, 64, 66, 67, 69, 70, 71, 72, 74, 77, 78, 79, 80, 81, 82, 83, 84, 85, 90, 91, 92, 93, 95, 97, 98, 99, 100, 101, 102, 103, 104, 106, 107, 108, 110, 111, 112, 113, 115, 116, 119, 120, 121, 123, 124, 126, 128, 129, 132, 134, 135, 137, 141, 142, 147, 148, 149, 152, 153, 155, 158, 159, 164, 172, 177, 181, 182, 183, 189, 196, 197, 199, 202, 204, 210, 217, 220, 230, 231, 232
apocalyptic approach to Pauline theology, 21, 32, 35, 82, 84–85, 89, 234
atonement, 132, 142

baptism, 165, 166, 167, 168, 170, 178, 213, 226, 232
Barclay, John M.G., 30, 47, 147, 164, 176, 177, 191, 209, 210, 211, 221, 224, 226

Beale, G.K., 37, 57, 58, 59, 70, 95, 167, 182, 189, 202
Beker, J. Christiaan, 81, 82
Bird, Michael, 14, 115, 136, 149
blessing, 61, 73, 75, 99, 118, 120, 131, 146, 154, 157, 159, 162, 180, 190, 197, 201, 206, 207, 208, 220, 225,
body of Christ, 5, 178, 179, 180, 223, 224, 225, 226

Campbell, Constantine R., 3, 5, 6, 8, 64, 109, 124, 140, 154, 162, 166, 173, 198, 225, 233
Campbell, Douglas A., 30, 35, 44, 137, 188, 196, 212
church, 2, 31, 34, 37, 55, 98, 137, 159, 177, 178, 191, 195, 202, 211, 219, 224, 225, 227, 232, 234; in Rome, 9–15, 21, 91, 103, 104, 110, 147, 153, 159, 164, 165, 181, 201, 205, 206, 212, 223, 225, 226, 228, 234
circumcision, 60, 107, 110, 114, 127, 128, 129, 130, 131, 134, 145, 146, 147, 192, 216, 218
clothing (metaphor), 223, 225, 226
covenant, 2, 4, 6, 8, 9, 19, 24, 25, 27, 28, 31, 32, 34, 37, 38, 39, 47, 60, 71, 73, 74, 75, 79, 80, 96, 100, 107, 110, 111, 112, 114, 115, 116, 117, 118, 119, 120, 121, 122, 123, 124, 125, 126, 127, 128, 129, 130, 131, 132, 133, 134, 135, 136, 138, 139, 142, 143, 144, 145, 146, 147, 148, 149, 154, 155, 156, 167, 168, 175, 176, 177, 178, 181, 182, 183,

Index of Names and Subjects

covenant *(continued)*
189, 190, 191, 192, 195, 200, 206, 207, 208, 211, 213, 214, 216, 217, 218, 220, 225, 231, 232, 235,
creation, 19, 23, 24, 33, 34, 36, 42, 43, 45, 46, 48, 49, 50, 52, 53, 56, 57, 58, 59, 64, 68, 71, 73, 74, 75, 83, 84, 92, 95, 99, 100, 101, 102, 107, 108, 125, 133, 134, 136, 137, 147, 148, 160, 161, 181, 197, 198, 201, 211, 221, 235
cross, 131, 156

Dead Sea Scrolls, 25, 26, 67, 68, 69
death, 25, 28, 48, 52, 78, 81, 82, 83, 84, 85, 86, 87, 88, 89, 92, 93, 94, 95, 96, 97, 99, 105, 106, 107, 108, 159, 161, 162, 163, 166, 168, 170, 173, 174, 175, 176, 178, 179, 180, 181, 183, 184, 186, 187, 190, 192, 210, 216; of Jesus, see Christ
De Boer, Martinus C., 21, 85, 87
Dunn, James D.G., 4, 11, 13, 42, 44, 45, 49, 64, 66, 67, 71, 79, 90, 94, 95, 96, 100, 103, 109, 112, 115, 116, 120, 121, 127, 133, 136, 140, 141, 143, 150, 155, 160, 161, 166, 169, 173, 176, 179, 180, 182, 185, 187, 190, 191, 192, 193, 195, 199, 200, 201, 202, 205, 207, 208, 210, 215, 216, 218, 219, 222, 225, 227,

eternal life, 60, 61, 78, 81, 118, 125, 162, 163, 164, 177, 190
ethnicity, 47, 61, 82, 145, 147, 165, 182, 208, 209, 218, 232
Eve, 48, 53, 54, 55, 59, 64, 94, 95, 102, 104, 173, 181, 190
exile, 22, 24, 28, 47, 75, 96, 124, 126, 129, 137, 139, 147, 156, 198
exodus, 22, 24, 28, 49, 54, 62, 95, 96, 101, 102, 103, 124, 125, 126, 139, 141, 143, 167, 168, 169, 170, 171, 172, 173, 175, 183, 189, 194, 195, 199, 232

faith/faithfulness, of God, 2, 29, 32, 71, 72, 74, 76, 127, 133, 134, 137, 143, 149, 206, 207, 209, 219, 220, 227, 228, 235; of Jesus, 78, 107, 109, 123, 136, 137, 138, 139, 140, 141, 143, 145, 154, 155, 160, 161, 162, 163, 164, 172, 188, 190, 195, 196, 198, 213, 214, 219, 223; of people, 3, 4, 5, 12, 25, 55, 56, 60, 67, 68, 72, 75, 76, 81, 109, 129, 131. 136, 137, 140, 143, 145, 146, 147, 148, 150, 153, 154, 163, 178, 181, 209, 212, 213, 214, 215, 216, 217, 218, 219, 222, 223, 225, 228, 234, 235
Fee, Gordon D., 66, 103, 130, 131, 191, 198
flesh, 68, 82, 133, 146, 174, 178, 184, 187, 188, 190, 192, 200, 203, 207, 208, 226, 231
Fitzmyer, Joseph A., 10, 49, 50, 60, 61, 79, 81, 90, 91, 112, 115, 136, 140, 156, 200, 205, 208, 209, 216

Garlington, Don B., 82, 103
Gentile, 2, 7, 9, 10, 11, 12, 13, 14, 15, 21, 28, 43, 44, 46, 47, 49, 50, 51, 52, 53, 54, 55, 60, 61, 62, 66, 67, 71, 72, 74, 75, 76, 81, 82, 84, 86, 87, 88, 89, 91, 95, 96, 97, 98, 99, 100, 103, 105, 110, 111, 112, 113, 114, 115, 116, 117, 118, 119, 120, 121, 122, 123, 124, 125, 126, 128, 129, 130, 131, 132, 134, 137, 141, 142, 144, 145, 146, 147, 148, 150, 157, 158, 160, 162, 165, 174, 176, 177, 179, 182, 185, 187, 191, 192, 193, 195, 199, 201, 203, 205, 206, 209, 210, 211, 212, 213, 214, 215, 217, 218, 219, 220, 221, 222, 223, 224, 227, 228, 229, 230, 232, 233
glory, 6, 25, 37, 38, 47, 48, 49, 54, 56, 57, 58, 59, 60, 61, 62, 63, 64, 65, 66, 67, 68, 69, 70, 71, 72, 73, 74, 78, 79, 81, 85, 92, 99, 100, 102, 107, 108, 109, 118, 123, 125, 126, 132, 137, 138, 139, 141, 155, 156, 160, 162, 167, 183, 195, 197, 198, 199, 200, 206, 207, 210, 211, 213, 216, 227, 228, 230, 235

Index of Names and Subjects 263

Gorman, Michael J., 4, 5, 109, 128, 136, 137, 166, 201, 224, 227
Gospel, 1, 3, 7, 12, 14, 15, 21, 25, 31, 32, 34, 35, 36, 42, 44, 65, 76, 85, 89, 91, 120, 123, 124, 126, 133, 135, 139, 142, 161, 165, 171, 175, 199, 205, 206, 207, 210, 212, 217, 218, 219, 220, 221, 224, 227, 234
grace, 67, 79, 80, 87, 88, 97, 104, 107, 109, 110, 132, 138, 155, 159, 160, 161, 162, 163, 165, 171, 175, 176, 177, 191, 220, 221

Hays, Richard B., 15–17, 18, 20, 31–32, 36, 37, 42, 133, 134, 136, 143, 146, 157, 158, 202, 205, 206, 216, 228, 233
honor, 37–38, 56, 57, 58, 60, 61, 63, 64, 65, 67, 79, 80, 107, 113, 115, 118, 122, 123, 124, 125, 126, 130, 138, 139, 141, 149, 156, 167, 196, 215, 216
Holy Spirit, 4, 80, 82, 99, 101, 108, 120, 122, 123, 126, 129, 130, 131, 134, 156, 168, 182, 183, 184, 186, 187, 188, 189, 190, 191, 192, 194, 195, 196, 198, 199, 200, 207, 208, 216, 217, 218, 222, 224, 232, 234, 235
hope, 23, 25, 28, 54, 55, 67, 78, 79, 81, 100, 104, 128, 129, 131, 133, 139, 154, 155, 156, 196, 197, 198, 199, 211, 215, 222, 227

identity, 7, 10, 13, 14, 27, 39, 41, 55, 77, 86, 89, 90, 95, 97, 98, 101, 106, 112, 113, 114, 116, 120, 124, 127, 130, 134, 138, 142, 144, 145, 150, 160, 164, 165, 166, 167, 172, 182, 200, 203, 209, 215, 217, 225, 226, 231, 232
idolatry, 45, 46, 47, 48, 55, 99, 100, 107, 116, 220
image (of God), 45, 46, 47, 49, 52, 56, 57, 58, 59, 68, 94, 101, 102, 103, 107, 108, 117, 199, 200, 219, 225

Jesus Christ, story of, 7, 19, 25, 30, 31, 32, 33, 34, 35, 36, 37, 41, 137, 143, 156, 157, 158, 162, 163, 165, 166, 170, 172, 188, 196, 234; as Messiah, 7, 14, 19, 25, 26, 34, 41, 65, 71, 73, 76, 78, 80, 83, 87, 88, 89, 104, 105, 123, 127, 131, 133, 135, 136, 137, 138, 139, 140, 143, 147, 150, 154, 155, 172, 174, 180, 181, 184, 185, 186, 188, 190, 191, 195, 196, 198, 199, 200, 201, 202, 203, 205, 206, 208, 209, 212, 213, 214, 215, 216, 218, 219, 220, 222, 227, 228, 232, 235; as son of God, 137, 149, 157, 165, 188, 193, 194, 195, 196, 199, 200; death of, 19, 35, 80, 85, 143, 148, 149, 150, 156, 157, 160, 165, 166, 167, 168, 169, 170, 172, 173, 174, 175, 179, 180, 182, 185, 186, 187, 188, 189, 196, 201, 202, 203, 211, 223, 225; resurrection of, 7, 14, 19, 35, 75, 85, 101, 148, 149, 150, 157, 164, 165, 166, 167, 168, 170, 172, 173, 175, 179, 180, 181, 182, 192, 196, 202, 216, 217, 220, 221, 235
Jewett, Robert, 15, 37, 38, 45, 48, 59, 61, 63, 64, 79, 80, 83, 84, 86, 88, 91, 100, 112, 113, 116, 120, 125, 128, 136, 138, 139, 143, 157, 161, 167, 168, 169, 178, 185, 188, 190, 192, 196, 198, 201, 202, 208, 209, 215, 216, 217
judgment, 47, 88, 113, 114, 121, 123, 185, 215,
justification, 2, 3, 4, 5, 9, 37, 72, 74, 107, 121, 132, 138, 139, 140, 141, 143, 145, 146, 148, 149, 150, 153, 154, 155, 156, 160, 161, 162, 163, 171, 172, 176, 181, 183, 186, 188, 213, 218, 234, 235

Käsemann, Ernst, 44, 45, 46, 59, 64, 72, 79, 84, 85, 89, 97, 119, 161, 178, 227 king, kingdom, kingship, 7, 14, 57, 58, 79, 80, 85, 89, 101, 103, 123, 127, 141, 147, 161, 165, 166, 168, 174, 200, 227

Longenecker, Richard N., 1, 9, 10, 11, 12, 13, 14, 38, 57, 72, 205, 206, 226

Macaskill, Grant, 3, 6, 7, 8, 53, 64, 65, 66, 67, 68, 70, 81, 90, 178, 194, 233
marriage, 178, 179, 180, 182
Martyn, J. Louis, 32, 35
mercy, 210, 211, 227
mercy seat, 142
mission, 12, 13, 14, 15, 127, 163, 164, 165, 171, 173, 177, 181, 196, 106, 210, 227, 229, 234
Moo, Douglas J., 62, 64, 79, 90, 109, 111, 112, 115, 121, 133, 134, 136, 140, 148, 149, 157, 169, 170, 172, 197, 207, 208, 214, 226, 227
mysticism, 3

obedience, 12, 23, 48, 54, 60, 67, 88, 99, 104, 109, 116, 117, 118, 122, 123, 127, 143, 145, 160, 162, 163, 177, 188, 189, 212, 216, 217, 218, 226

participation, 4, 5, 13, 42, 58, 64, 67, 85, 137, 140, 141, 150, 165, 170, 173, 179, 181, 182, 188, 192, 193, 195, 196, 213, 214, 219, 235
Passover, 143, 169
peace, 60, 61, 80, 118, 154, 155, 157, 190
Porter, Stanley E., 17, 63, 64
promise, 1, 2, 25, 32, 34, 54, 60, 67, 68, 72, 73, 74, 75, 76, 79, 80, 89, 96, 100, 102, 104, 110, 119, 120, 121, 122, 126, 127, 129, 132, 133, 134, 135, 136, 137, 138, 141, 144, 145, 147, 149, 150, 155, 156, 171, 177, 181, 183, 189, 190, 191, 198, 201, 205, 206, 207, 208, 209, 211, 214, 215, 216, 222, 227, 232

redemption, 3, 42, 55, 60, 62, 64, 80, 98, 99, 100, 102, 107, 108, 109, 113, 124, 130, 131, 132, 139, 140, 141, 142, 144, 155, 158, 171, 172, 176, 198, 199, 214, 216, 231, 232, 235
resurrection, of Jesus, see Jesus Christ; of believers, 75, 149, 166, 167, 168, 182, 189, 192, 196, 199, 220, 221
retelling (of Scripture), 19, 20, 22, 23, 24, 25, 26, 27, 28, 29, 32, 34, 49, 54, 91
Ridderbos, Herman, 78, 84, 130, 144, 172, 196, 200, 224
righteousness, 3, 37, 56, 71, 73, 76, 78, 80, 88, 92, 106, 109, 122, 123, 127, 132, 133, 134, 135, 136, 137, 138, 140, 143, 144, 146, 147, 148, 149, 150, 158, 161, 162, 163, 164, 171, 175, 187, 188, 189, 191, 208, 212, 213, 214, 215, 217, 218, 219, 222, 225, 227, 228

salvation, 3, 4, 7, 8, 28, 42, 60, 70, 74, 79, 84, 86, 87, 89, 102, 106, 109, 124, 132, 141, 157, 159, 170, 201, 207, 211, 213, 217, 218, 219, 220
Sanders, E.P., 3–4, 72
Schnelle, Udo, 170, 192,
Schweitzer, Albert, 3
servant, 6, 36, 37, 149, 171, 172, 202, 227
shame/shameful, 37, 38, 61, 62, 63, 67, 79, 81, 107, 125, 130, 138, 139, 141, 149, 156, 167, 202, 212, 215, 216
slave/slavery, 21, 101, 102, 124, 139, 168, 169, 170, 172, 174, 175, 176, 180, 194, 195,

temple, 6, 24, 52, 65, 70, 79, 80, 155, 190, 191, 192, 208,
theosis, 4, 200
Tooman, William, 15, 17–18, 20

unity, in Adam, 41, 43, 47, 55, 84, 85, 87, 88, 93, 98, 106, 150; in Christ,

2, 4, 7, 12, 13, 14, 39, 47, 55, 82,
84, 88, 93, 97, 98, 106, 141, 142,
144, 150, 157, 158, 159, 160, 163,
164, 165, 173, 177, 181, 186, 196,
199, 206, 207, 210, 212, 219, 223,
224, 225, 226, 227, 229, 234, 235

Watson, Francis, 13, 34–36, 47, 55, 95,
96, 97, 215
work(s) of the Law, 115, 118, 119, 120,
121, 122, 133, 145

worldview, 18, 19, 33, 34, 36, 50, 233
wrath, 43, 44, 48, 54, 55, 99, 108, 112,
113, 114, 115, 123, 125, 131, 154,
157, 210,
Wright, N. T., 7–8, 9, 13, 15, 18–20,
21, 30, 31, 32–34, 36, 37, 49, 64,
72, 79, 80, 84, 90, 93, 95, 97, 98,
101, 102, 104, 112, 116, 126, 127,
133, 136, 138, 139, 146, 163, 165,
166, 174, 181, 188, 191, 194, 202,
205, 212, 215, 220, 224, 233

www.ingramcontent.com/pod-product-compliance
Lightning Source LLC
Chambersburg PA
CBHW071246230426
43668CB00011B/1609